Understanding Drugs and Behaviour

Understanding Drugs and Behaviour

Andrew Parrott

Department of Psychology, University of Wales Swansea, Swansea, UK

Alun Morinan

School of Health & Bioscience, University of East London, London, UK

Mark Moss

Division of Psychology, Northumbria University, Newcastle-upon-Tyne, UK

Andrew Scholey

Division of Psychology, Northumbria University, Newcastle-upon-Tyne, UK

John Wiley & Sons, Ltd

Other Wiley Editorial Offices

John Wiley & Sons Inc., 111 River Street, Hoboken, NJ 07030, USA

Jossey-Bass, 989 Market Street, San Francisco, CA 94103-1741, USA

Wiley-VCH Verlag GmbH, Boschstr. 12, D-69469 Weinheim, Germany

John Wiley & Sons Australia Ltd, 33 Park Road, Milton, Queensland 4064, Australia

John Wiley & Sons (Asia) Pte Ltd, 2 Clementi Loop #02-01, Jin Xing Distripark, Singapore 129809

John Wiley & Sons Canada Ltd, 22 Worcester Road, Etobicoke, Ontario, Canada M9W 1L1

Wiley also publishes its books in a variety of electronic formats. Some content that appears in print may not
be available in electronic books.

Library of Congress Cataloging-in-Publication Data

Understanding drugs and behaviour / Andrew Parrott ... [et al.].
    p. cm.
  Includes bibliographical references and index.
  ISBN 0-470-85059-0 (cloth : alk. paper) – ISBN 0-471-98640-2 (pbk. : alk. paper)
  1. Psychopharmacology.   2. Drugs of abuse.   3. Drugs.   I. Parrott, Andrew.
  RM315.U45 2004
  615′.78 – dc22   2004000221

British Library Cataloguing in Publication Data

A catalogue record for this book is available from the British Library

ISBN 0-470-85059-0 (hbk)
ISBN 0-471-98640-2 (pbk)

Project management by Originator, Gt Yarmouth, Norfolk (typeset in 10/12pt Times and Stone Sans)
Printed and bound in Great Britain by Antony Rowe Ltd, Chippenham, Wiltshire
This book is printed on acid-free paper responsibly manufactured from sustainable forestry
in which at least two trees are planted for each one used for paper production.

For Felicity, Rebecca and Laura
For Mary, Ciarán and Gareth
For Holly Mae
For Lola

Contents

About the authors

Andy Parrott has published over 300 journal articles and conference papers, covering a wide range of psychoactive drugs. The first publications from his PhD at the University of Leeds were concerned with antipsychotic medications. Then, as a postdoctoral researcher with the Human Psychopharmacology Research Unit at Leeds University, he investigated the effects of second-generation antidepressants and benzodiazepines on cognitive performance and car-driving skills. Moving to the Institute of Naval Medicine in Hampshire, he was tasked with determining the practical utility of anti-seasickness medications, such as transdermal scopolamine, in land and sea trials. Further trials investigated the cognitive side effects of nerve agent prophylactics. At the University of East London he established the Recreational Drugs Research Group, which investigated a number of disparate topics: caffeine in shift workers, anabolic steroids in weightlifters, amphetamine and LSD in party goers and nootropics as potential "smart drugs". At Humboldt State University in California, he assessed the everyday functioning of excessive cannabis users. However, his two main research areas are nicotine and MDMA/Ecstasy. In an extensive research programme he has shown how nicotine dependency is psychologically damaging and causes increased psychological distress. The Recreational Drugs Research Group which he founded at the University of East London is, however, most well known for its work with recreational MDMA/Ecstasy users. Their cognitive research papers have been awarded the British Association for Psychopharmacology Organon prize on two occasions. Professor Parrott's work is featured regularly in the media. He sits on the editorial boards of leading psychopharmacology journals, and he has organised a number of international symposia. Recently, he moved to the University of Wales at Swansea. Here, he is continuing with a number of collaborative studies, including a large UK/US prospective study investigating the effects of recreational drug use during pregnancy.

Alun Morinan graduated in Biochemistry from the University of Wales at Aberystwyth and went on to complete an MSc in Pharmacology at the University of London and a PhD in Neuropharmacology at the National University of Ireland in Galway. After postdoctoral research in Pharmacology at Galway and Biochemistry at the Institute of Psychiatry, he was appointed Lecturer in Pharmacology at North East Surrey College of Technology before moving to his current post of Principal Lecturer at the University of East London. His publications have been mainly in the fields of experimental psychopharmacology and neurochemistry covering topics such as alcohol dependence, anxiety, schizophrenia and enzymology.

Mark Moss studied applied chemistry and spent 10 years in industry before returning to university to study Psychology. He completed his PhD in 1999 and was involved in the establishment of the Human Cognitive Neuroscience Unit at Northumbria University. His research portfolio has focused primarily on aspects of cognitive functioning in healthy young volunteers, with journal articles and conference presentations relating to both enhancement through natural interventions and drug-induced impairments. Mark is currently programme leader for the Division of Psychology at Northumbria University.

Andrew Scholey is a Reader in Psychology at the Division of Psychology, Northumbria University, Newcastle-upon-Tyne. He has published hundreds of journal articles and conference papers, covering the cognitive effects of many recreational and medicinal drugs. His PhD and postdoctoral fellowship at the Brain and Behaviour Research Group, Open University, examined the neurochemical substrates of memory formation. He moved to Northumbria University in 1993, where his research has concentrated on the acute and chronic impairing and enhancing effects of various drugs including benzodiazepines, alcohol, caffeine, glucose, oxygen (with Mark Moss) and herbal extracts. In 1999 Andrew established the Human Cognitive Neuroscience Unit, of which he is the director. The work of this unit concentrates on the potential for non-mainstream treatments to enhance cognitive performance. These have ranged from metabolic interventions (notably glucose and oxygen) to low doses of alcohol and even to drinking water (in thirsty individuals) and to chewing gum. Andrew is also the co-director of the Medicinal Plant Research Centre. His present focus of research aims to disentangle the neurocognitive effects of herbal extracts, to attempt to identify relationships between their behavioural effects and their neurochemical properties and to identify safe treatments that may be effective in the treatment of conditions where cognition becomes fragile, including dementia. He is currently involved in trials examining the effects of herbal extracts in Alzheimer's disease. Andrew is also committed to the public dissemination of science which has led to numerous appearances in the print, radio and television media.

Preface

Drugs are a crucial part of modern society. Many are used for recreational purposes, with alcohol, nicotine and caffeine all being legal. However, others are illegal, and they include cannabis, Ecstasy, cocaine and heroin. In the past 50 years a number of medicinal compounds have been developed for schizophrenia, depression and other clinical disorders. They have dramatically improved the well-being of many people diagnosed with these disorders. But what exactly are the effects of these different types of drug? How precisely do they alter behaviour? How is it that such small chemicals can have such dramatic effects on mood and cognition, sensation and awareness, health and well-being? Why are only *some* drugs highly addictive? Our core aim is to provide detailed answers for all these questions.

We hope this book will not only be of interest to students of psychology, behavioural sciences, health sciences and nursing but also to undergraduates of physiology and pharmacology who wish to find out more about the behavioural aspects of drug use. Our aim throughout is to present the material in a reader-friendly fashion. We have taught undergraduates in many different disciplines and have therefore become skilled at explaining this material to students without any formal scientific background. We will describe how psychoactive drugs can alter brain chemistry and, hence, modify behaviour. We offer an accessible route through basic aspects of brain organisation and functioning. Normally, these areas are difficult for many undergraduate students. However, by approaching them through the mechanisms of drug action, we hope to stimulate an active interest in this area.

We have planned every chapter to be self-contained. Each commences with a general overview, before the core material is presented in depth; this is followed by a list of questions that should prove useful for both students and their lecturers. Finally, there are several key articles, followed by a list of further references. Many of the chapters in this book have been tested out on our students. Not only did they report that the chapters were all excellent (in feedback sessions that were obviously not blind!) they also informed us that they particularly liked this reference format. They found it useful when writing essays, preparing projects and, most importantly, when "cramming" for exams.

In terms of its overall structure, we have focused on the main types of drug used in society. Thus, alcohol and nicotine have chapters largely dedicated to them. Similarly, there is a whole chapter on cannabis, while another is shared by LSD and Ecstasy/MDMA. We also cover opiates, such as heroin, and CNS stimulants, such as amphetamine and cocaine. Turning to drugs for clinical disorders, one chapter is dedicated to antipsychotic medications for schizophrenia, while another covers antidepressant drugs. We also look at more novel areas, such as drugs for Alzheimer's disease, as well as nootropics and herbal preparations to improve cognitive functioning. In every chapter we have focused not only on drug effects but also on how these interact with environmental factors. We have also noted how drugs often need to be combined with psychological therapy to achieve the optimal clinical outcome.

One of the benefits of working as a team of four co-authors is that between us we have a great deal of knowledge about all aspects of drugs and behaviour. Thus, every chapter is informed by a high level of research expertise. Indeed, in several fields the authors are leading international research authorities. We believe that drugs are not only very important for society but also very fascinating in their own right. Certainly, they have intrigued us for many years, and we hope to pass on some of this interest and fascination to our readers.

Andy Parrott
Alun Morinan
Mark Moss
Andy Scholey

Universities of Swansea, East London and Northumbria

PART I

Drugs and Their Actions

Chapter 1

Psychoactive drugs: introduction and overview

Overview

Psychoactive drug use is not just a phenomenon of the 20th century; many different types of drug have been used throughout recorded history. In this chapter we will outline the main classes of psychoactive drug. We are able to do this in a single chapter because, despite there being thousands of different drugs, they can be classified in a few main groups (Table 1.1). The crucial role of neurotransmitters will also be described because psychoactive drugs alter mood and behaviour by modifying nerve activity in various ways. Thus, a basic understanding of neurotransmitter actions is vital in order to understand how drugs can affect behaviour. Tolerance and addiction may also develop, when regular drug use causes long-term changes in neurotransmission activity. Next, we will emphasise that all drugs have a range of positive and negative behavioural effects. Positive or desirable effects, such as feelings of pleasure, are the reasons people take drugs. But drugs also cause negative effects, which is why drug taking can cause so many psychosocial problems.

Psychoactive drugs over the ages

Since before the dawn of civilisation, humans have used **drugs**[1] to alter their mood and behaviour. **Opium** poppy (*Papaver somniferum*) seeds have been found by archaeologists in Neolithic burial sites. Some of the earliest writing on clay tablets from Mesopotamia described laws to control the alcohol consumption in local taverns. Many societies have discovered that different species of plant and fungi can induce powerful hallucinations. Native Americans have used the peyote cactus (*Lophophora williamsii*) (containing **mescaline**) to foster spiritual insights during their religious ceremonies. Vikings used the *Amanita muscaria* mushroom for its hallucinogenic and excitatory effects, before raiding and pillaging

[1] Boldface terms are defined in the Glossary.

Table 1.1. Psychoactive drug groups.

Chapter	Drug group	Main properties	Examples
4	CNS stimulants	Increase alertness, intensify moods	Amphetamine, cocaine, caffeine
5–7	Recreational drugs	Various disparate effects	Nicotine, cannabis, LSD, MDMA
8	Opiates	Reduce pain, increase pleasure	Heroin, morphine, codeine
9–10	CNS depressants	Increase drowsiness, relax moods	Alcohol, barbiturates, benzodiazepines
11	Antipsychotics	Reduce hallucinations and delusions	Chlorpromazine, haloperidol, clozapine
12	Antidepressants	Relieve sadness and depression	Imipramine, fluoxetine
13	Nootropics	Slow cognitive decline in dementia	Aricept, tacrine
3, 14	Other drug types	Various disparate effects	Herbal and other medications

in their longboats. In ancient Greece, Homer's epic poem *Odysseus* describes how the hero and his crew were drugged by the sorceress Circe, a skilled "polypharmakos", or drug user, who laced their wine with drugs that stunned their memories and ensnared their minds. The wary Odysseus managed to avert this only because he had taken the precaution of taking an antidote beforehand (Caldwell, 1970; Palfai and Jankiewicz, 1996).

Many drugs are taken for their curative or medicinal effects. In South American silver mines, for many centuries the miners have chewed coca leaves (containing **cocaine**), to aid their physical and mental vigilance working high in the oxygen-poor Andes (Chapter 4). Tea, which contains **caffeine**, was recommended as a general tonic by sages in Ancient China (Chapter 4). In the Indian subcontinent the Indian snake root *Rauwolfia serpentina* was used as a treatment for people suffering manic excitement, or hallucinations and delusions. Its effectiveness at reducing the symptoms of schizophrenia has been scientifically confirmed in the 20th century. Rauwolfia contains **reserpine**, a powerful psychoactive drug that depletes dopamine stores; this is how it leads to calmer and more manageable behaviour. In some ways, reserpine displays properties similar to more modern antipsychotic drugs. However, its broad spectrum of effects in deleting the stores of several neurotransmitters means that it can also cause feelings of severe depression. Thus, reserpine is not used clinically, since modern antipsychotic drugs do not have this unwanted side effect (Chapters 3 and 11).

Psychoactive drug use remained popular throughout the 20th century. Several drugs are legal, and their use has grown during the past 100 years. The advent of machines to produce cigarettes at the beginning of the 20th century led to a marked increase in tobacco consumption. By the end of the second world war, helped by the free distribution of cigarettes to the armed forces, around 70% of the male population in the UK were regular nicotine users. In global terms the world consumption of tobacco is still increasing, despite reductions in a few Western countries where its adverse health effects have been emphasised. Yet, even where marked reductions have occurred, particularly in the USA, Britain and Australia, this decrease in consumption has not been maintained. Recent years have shown a resurgence of cigarette smoking among the young, particularly adolescent females (Chapter 5). Alcohol use also shows no sign of reduction, and at the same time the age of first drinking continues to fall. In the USA many high schools offer formal programmes to help their teenage pupils to quit smoking, or reduce excessive alcohol consumption (Chapters 9 and 10). Another legal drug – caffeine – is consumed by over 90% of the adult population in their daily tea and coffee. Caffeine is also present in the fizzy soft drinks and chocolate bars consumed by children each day (Chapter 4). Many other psychoactive drugs are deemed illegal, yet even the threat of long prison terms does not halt their popularity. Around 50 million Americans have smoked **cannabis** (marijuana), although only 49,999,999 admit to inhaling since former President Bill Clinton admitted to having tried marijuana but without inhaling! (Chapters 7 and 15). The use of **amphetamine**, cocaine and **heroin** has increased in recent decades, while new recreational drugs have also been specifically "designed" for their mood-altering effects (Shulgin, 1986). **Ecstasy** (MDMA, or methylenedioxymethamphetamine) first became popular in the mid-1980s and since then its use has steadily increased, with young people trying it at an increasingly early age (Chapter 6).

One of the most dramatic changes for modern society was the advent of effective psychoactive medicines in the 1950s. The first **antipsychotic** drug **chlorpromazine** was developed in 1950, and since then the management and treatment of schizophrenia has been transformed, with most patients now seen as outpatients and the majority of "mental hospitals" being closed (Chapters 11 and 15). The advent of **antidepressant** drugs in 1957 led to a similar change in the treatment of people suffering from depression (Chapter 12). Thus, we now have a range of drug treatments for two of the most severe psychiatric disorders. It should be emphasised that the advent of these drugs has not been entirely beneficial. Numerous schizophrenics now suffer greatly, because society has failed to provide the support mechanisms. Antipsychotic drugs are only partially effective on their own. To maximise their effectiveness, they need to be complemented by behavioural therapy, or social skills training. This is expensive, and in most Westernised countries this support structure is generally lacking. Another contentious area is the treatment of "hyperactive" young children with CNS (central nervous system) stimulant drugs. The clinical diagnosis of **Attention Deficit Hyperactivity Disorder** (ADHD) is a very recent phenomenon, but since the early 1980s an increasing number of young children have been given this diagnosis. Is it defensible to label continuous fidgeting or poor concentration on school work as clinical symptoms in 5 and 6-year-olds and then administering them with powerful psychoactive drugs, especially when it is the parents and teachers who are "suffering" the most? This issue will be critically examined in Chapter 4. Pharmaceutical companies are now attempting to develop **nootropic** drugs for **Alzheimer's disease** and other disorders associated with ageing (Chapter 13). If effective drugs for the elderly are successfully developed, the impact on society could become even more marked than was the development of antipsychotic and antidepressant drugs in the 1950s. Finally, there have been numerous attempts to produce cognitive enhancers that modulate cell metabolism and brain activity in various ways (Chapter 14).

How many types of psychoactive drug are there?

There are hundreds of different drugs that can affect mood and behaviour, although they can be categorised into a few basic drug types. Table 1.1 outlines the main categories of psychoactive drug. This classification system also reflects their psycho-pharmacological effects. Thus, CNS-stimulant drugs, such as amphetamine and cocaine, generate feelings of alertness and lead to faster behavioural responses; indeed, this is why they are banned in sport (Chapter 4). CNS-depressant drugs generate feelings of sleepiness and impair skilled psychomotor performance; this is why piloting a plane or driving a car are so dangerous under the influence of alcohol, with numerous road deaths being caused each year (Chapter 9). **Opiate** drugs, like heroin and **morphine**, are again similar in their effects, leading to feelings of euphoria and reduced pain, in relation to both physical and mental pain (Chapter 8). Many other drugs are not categorised so readily. Thus, cannabis is unlike many other drugs (Chapter 7), while **LSD** (lysergic acid diethylamide) also has many unique properties (Chapter 6).

The reason some drugs have similar behavioural effects is that they have similar pharmacological effects. Take amphetamine and cocaine as an example. Their origins are quite dissimilar: cocaine is extracted from the leaves of the coca plant (*Erythroxylon coca*), whereas amphetamine is artificially manufactured in the laboratory; amphetamine is an amine, whereas cocaine is an alkaloid. However, they each stimulate the release of the neurotransmitter dopamine and inhibit its inactivation; this explains why their psychoactive effects are so similar, in terms of boosting mood and alertness. In fact, most CNS-stimulant drugs boost dopamine and/or noradrenaline, which is why they have broadly similar behavioural effects (Chapters 3 and 4). Let us now consider another drug group – the opiates. Different drugs in the opiate class all tend to have similar types of effect on other types of neurotransmitters, such as the neuropeptides, which is why they have similar behavioural effects (Chapter 8). In an equivalent fashion, CNS-depressant drugs all seem to affect the **GABA** (γ-aminobutyric acid) receptor – again helping to explain why they all tend to have similar effects on behaviour (Chapter 9).

Drug effects on neurotransmission

Normal behaviour is dependent on a complex system of chemical messages passed between neurons in the brain. Each nerve cell or neuron communicates with the next neuron by means of chemicals called neurotransmitters (e.g., dopamine, noradrenaline, serotonin, acetylcholine, histamine, GABA). Psychoactive drugs exert their effects by increasing or decreasing the activity of these neurotransmitters, this is why a basic understanding of the CNS and neuronal activity is essential for a psychoactive drugs textbook (Chapter 2). Only then will it become clear how drugs can modify neuro-transmission and thus alter behaviour (Chapter 3). Hence, a thorough understanding of these two introductory chapters is necessary before attempting to read the other sections. This knowledge also helps to explain related phenomena like drug addiction (Chapter 10). The very first time a drug is taken it has a different effect on neurotransmission than when it is taken a hundred times later. The first ever cigarette will lead to nausea and sickness, because nicotine stimulates the neurons in the vomiting centres of the brainstem. However, the 100th cigarette no longer induces feelings of nausea, because neuronal tolerance has developed. In a similar way a small amount of alcohol will induce feelings of light-headedness and tipsiness in a novice drinker, whereas a heavy regular drinker would have no perceptible response. Tolerance explains why heavy drinkers need to binge-drink in order to feel drunk (Chapters 9 and 10). Neurons tend to adapt and change following regular drug use and neuronal **tolerance** reflects these adaptive changes in neurotransmitter systems. Neuronal tolerance also helps explain why it can be so easy to become addicted to certain drugs, although many non-pharmacological factors are also important; these will all be described in Chapter 10, where they will illustrate how and why heroin addiction, nicotine dependency and alcoholism have become such enormous problems for society.

Positive and negative drug effects

Psychoactive drugs modify behaviour by altering neurotransmission. However, each neurotransmitter system generally underlies various diverse aspects of behaviour; this means that any one drug will generally have a wide range of behavioural effects. Some of these may be pleasant, but others may be unpleasant. Recreational drugs are taken for their pleasant effects. Alcohol can release social inhibitions and help foster feelings of closeness with other people. The caffeine in tea and coffee can help regular users maintain feelings of alertness. Similarly, psychoactive medicines are taken for specific purposes. Antidepressant drugs can help relieve feelings of profound sadness. Antipsychotic drugs can reduce delusions and hallucinations and can enable those suffering from schizophrenia to lead more normal and contented lives. Every psychoactive drug has *some* positive uses – which is why they are taken (Chapters 4–15).

Yet, these same drugs also produce a range of negative effects. Alcohol can lead to increased aggression and antisocial behaviour, while its disinhibitory effects cause many individuals to commit crimes that they would not have undertaken if they had remained sober. Most antidepressant and antipsychotic drugs generate unpleasant side effects, such as drowsiness and dry mouth. Therefore, the main focus of many pharmaceutical company research programmes is to develop new drugs that are more specific in their effects, so that they relieve the target symptom while causing the fewest side effects (Chapters 11 and 12). Other problems include tolerance and **dependence** (see above and Chapter 10). Cigarette smokers soon develop nicotine dependency and gain no real benefits from their tobacco; they just need nicotine to function normally (Chapter 5). Opiate users similarly develop drug dependency. One reason for these negative effects is drug tolerance. The basic mechanism behind the development of tolerance and dependence are described in Chapters 3 and 10. Therefore, most drugs have a balance of positive and negative effects. Thus, cocaine can make people feel alert, dynamic and sexy ... all pleasant or desirable effects. Yet, it can also make them anxious, aggressive and suspicious and reduce their inhibitions. This combination of behavioural changes can be dangerous: initially, they may want to socialise with their friends but soon argue, leading in extreme cases to their committing murder on the spur of the moment (some examples are given in Chapter 4). There is marked individual variation in the development of drug-related problems; this is best understood in relation to the diathesis stress model, where any behavioural outcome is seen as the result of an interaction between internal factors (e.g., genetic and biochemical predispositions) and environmental events (abuse, poverty, stress, psychoactive drugs). This model is debated more fully in Chapters 6 and 10.

However, every chapter will describe both positive and negative drug effects. One core aim will be to assess their cost–benefit ratios (Chapter 15). Most psychotherapeutic drugs have an advantageous ratio, with the benefits outweighing the unwanted side effects (Chapters 11 and 12). Estimating the cost–benefit ratio for recreational drugs can however be more difficult, since their positive and negative effects are influenced by numerous factors including dosage, frequency of use and duration of use. There is often little correspondence between the legal status of each drug and the amount of harm it causes. Thus, two of the most widely used drugs in society, nicotine and alcohol, have numerous deleterious consequences. In the UK tobacco smoking causes around 350–400 deaths each day, but regular cigarette smokers get no genuine psychological benefits from nicotine dependency (Chapter 5). The regular use of illicit recreational drugs, such as cannabis, opiates and CNS stimulants, are also linked with numerous problems (Chapters 4–10). The notion of cost–benefit ratios will be debated more fully in the final chapter.

Questions

1   Is drug taking just a phenomenon of the 20th century?

2   Explain how you might categorise psychoactive drugs into just a few groups.

3   Provide examples of psychoactive drug use from earlier periods.

4   Why is knowledge about neurotransmission necessary in order to understand psychoactive drug effects?

5   Do all psychoactive drugs have a mixture of good and bad behavioural effects?

If you have just started this book your answers to these questions may be rather brief. Try answering the same questions after you have read the whole book, and compare your answers!

Key references and reading

Caldwell AE (1970). History of psychopharmacology. In: WG Clark and J DelGiudice (eds), *Principles of Psychopharmacology*. Academic Press, New York.
Julien RM (2001). *A Primer of Drug Action* (10th edn). Freeman, New York.
Palfai T and Jankewicz H (1996). *Drugs and Human Behavior*. Wm. C. Brown, Madison, WI.
Parrott AC (1998). Social drugs: Effects upon health. In: M Pitts and K Phillips (eds), *The Psychology of Health*. Routledge, London.

Chapter 2

The brain, neurons and neurotransmission

Overview

The structure and functions of the central nervous system (CNS) and peripheral nervous system (PNS) will be briefly outlined. The most important type of cell in the nervous system is the electrically excitable neuron, with most being found in the cerebral cortex. There are three main types of neuron: sensory afferents which are stimulated by environmental events (light, sound, touch), interneurons which process this information in the CNS and motor efferents which activate muscles or glands – and thus cause behaviour. The conduction of information throughout the nervous system occurs via a combination of electrical and chemical events. Communication within each individual neuron is by means of electrical changes in the cellular membrane. This action potential will be described in detail. Communication between neurons occurs at the synapse and is chemical or molecular in nature. The molecules involved in synaptic transmission are called neurotransmitters, and the ways in which neurons communicate by means of these neurotransmitters will also be covered in some detail. Psychoactive drugs exert their behavioural effects by either reducing or increasing this neurotransmitter activity. Hence, a basic knowledge of neurotransmitters and their actions is essential in order to understand how drugs affect neurotransmission and behaviour.

Structure of the nervous system

Anatomically, the human nervous system may be divided into the central nervous system (CNS) and the peripheral nervous system (PNS). The major subdivision of the central nervous system is into the brain and spinal cord. The peripheral nervous system is divided into the motor or efferent system (efferent = "away from"), and the sensory or afferent (afferent = "toward") nervous systems (Figure 2.1).

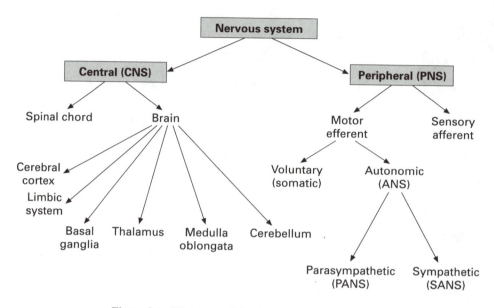

Figure 2.1. Divisions of the human nervous system.

The nerve cells or **neurons** of the sensory afferent nervous system convey information about our internal and external environments. There are five types of sensory **receptors** which provide all sensory information. **Chemoreceptors** respond to chemical stimuli, with the best example being the taste buds on the tongue. **Mechanoreceptors** respond to pressure, with many being in the skin, while others are situated on the hair cells of the inner ear, being stimulated indirectly by sound. **Nociceptors** respond to pain and are located throughout the body, in the skin, intestines and other inner organs. **Photoreceptors** are sited in the retina of the eye, where blue, green and red cones are selectively stimulated by coloured wavelengths, while the rods respond to all visible light waves and, thus, convey black-and-white information. **Thermoreceptors** are sited in the skin and are sensitive to changes in temperature. Most sensory receptors are unimodal, being only activated by one type of stimulus. They behave as transducers, converting one form of energy (light, sound) into an electrical signal that can be conducted along the axon of the neuron.

Each sensory afferent neuron connects with an **interneuron** or accessory neuron. These interneurons are located entirely within the CNS, with the majority occurring in the cerebral cortex. They form numerous interconnections and are the means by which all cognitive information, thoughts and feelings, are processed. It should be emphasised that the main role of this processing of information is inhibitory. The sensory receptors provide the CNS with a massive amount of data. The interneurons process and filter this into a limited amount of useful and important information. Conscious information processing forms just one part of this activity. A great deal of brain activity is concerned with routine processes, which continue without conscious awareness.

At the end of this processing sequence, some of the interneurons connect with motor efferent neurons. These motor efferents leave the CNS and stimulate the peripheral effectors. Most of the effectors are muscles of various types: smooth, cardiac and striated or skeletal muscle. The other effectors comprise all the exocrine glands and some of the endocrine glands.

"Motor" implies movement, and here it means muscular contraction/relaxation. Other effectors stimulate the secretion of a mixture of chemicals from a gland: for instance, saliva from the exocrine salivary glands or catecholamine hormones from the adrenal medulla – which is an endocrine gland. The latter contributes to the so-called "adrenaline rush" and the feeling of "butterflies" in one's stomach. Skeletal muscle contraction is controlled by voluntary (somatic) motor efferents, whereas the cardiac muscles, smooth muscles and glands are regulated by autonomic motor efferents (Figure 2.1). The autonomic nervous system (ANS) can be subdivided according to anatomical (CNS origin and axonal length), biochemical (neurotransmitter type) and physiological (functional) criteria into the parasympathetic and sympathetic branches. Many tissues are innervated by both branches, and this dual innervation means that they can experience opposing physiological effects. For example, stimulation of the parasympathetic vagus nerve decreases the electrical activity of the sinoatrial node (pacemaker), thus slowing the heart rate and resulting in "bradycardia". In contrast, stimulation of the sympathetic cardiac accelerator nerve leads to faster heart rate or "tachycardia". As a general guide to the different physiological effects of the ANS, remember these five words: rest and digestion for the parasympathetic system and fright, fight and flight for the sympathetic system. The parasympathetic nervous system stimulates **anabolism**, the building up of the body's energy stores, and predominates during periods of rest. In contrast, the sympathetic nervous system stimulates **catabolism**, the breaking down of stored chemicals to release energy for physical activity and work, or dealing with threat and danger.

An interneuron together with a sensory afferent and motor efferent form a polysynaptic reflex (Figure 2.2); this comprises the initial stage of information input (sensory afferent), the processing/computing an appropriate response (interneurons) and the execution of a behavioural response (motor efferent). The simplest reflexes in the nervous system are **monosynaptic reflexes**, such as the familiar tendon (knee) jerk, these do not involve an interneuron. The sensory afferent activated by the mechanoreceptor (the tap of the patellar hammer) forms a synapse with the motor efferent in the spinal cord, which then causes the skeletal muscle to contract and the crossed leg to jerk forward. With a synaptic delay of 1 millisecond (ms), the time between input and output increases with the number of **synapses** introduced into the circuit. As an

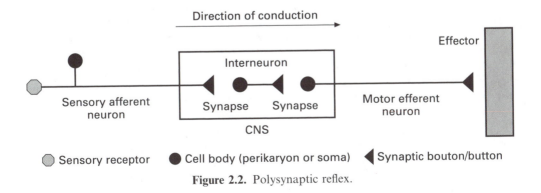

Figure 2.2. Polysynaptic reflex.

example, the knee jerk reflex typically takes around 30 ms (0.03 s) from the onset of the stimulus (tendon tap) to the behavioural response (contraction of the quadriceps muscle). Contrast this with the time it takes to process even the simplest piece of information. In a simple reaction time task you would be required to press a button as quickly as possible when a single, anticipated stimulus appeared on a screen. It usually takes humans upwards of 200 ms (0.2 s) between stimulus and response in this task. During a choice reaction task, when you would be required to respond as quickly as possible while making a decision about a stimulus or stimuli (e.g., whether it was the word "YES" or the word "NO" on the screen), your reaction time would typically increase to above 450 ms. Hence, reaction times increase as a function of the amount of information processing. They have proved very useful in human psychopharmacology, being very sensitive to **drug** effects. CNS-stimulant drugs reduce reaction time, whereas CNS-depressant drugs retard it; this has made reaction time a very useful index for the degree of stimulant or sedative drug action (Hindmarch et al., 1988).

The brain

In terms of understanding how medicinal and recreational psychoactive drugs affect behaviour, knowledge of the basic anatomy of the brain and spinal cord is required. To say the brain is the most complex organ in the human body is an obvious understatement. Some years ago Professor Steven Rose described it as *two fistfuls of pink-grey tissue, wrinkled like a walnut and something of the consistency of porridge, [that] can store more information than all the computers and the libraries of the world can hold.* Despite recent developments in information technology and artificial intelligence, the brain stills remains the greatest challenge for science (Rose, 1976, p. 21). For a more recent popular account of the brain, Greenfield (1998) is worth reading, while Barker et al. (1999) and Bloom et al. (2001) provide more detailed but useful overviews. For those who would like an even more in-depth coverage of neuroscience there are a number of full-colour textbooks (some with an accompanying CD-ROM) to recommend, including Carlson (1999), Kolb and Whishaw (2001), Matthews (2001), Nicholls et al. (2001) and Purves et al. (2001).

The 1.4-kg human brain is enclosed within the skull of the skeleton and protected by a triple layer of connective tissue called the **meninges**. Meningitis, or inflammation of the meninges caused by a virus or bacterium, is medically quite serious and can occasionally prove fatal. The outermost of the three layers, closest to the inside of the skull, is the dura mater, the innermost the pia mater, while the arachnoid membrane lies in-between them. Damage to the blood vessels in the pia mater (e.g., by cerebral trauma) allows blood to leak into the subarachnoid space between this layer and the arachnoid membrane, causing a subarachnoid haemorrhage. The brain is cushioned within the skull by a liquid, the **cerebrospinal fluid**, which circulates through four internal chambers. There are two lateral ventricles and a 3rd cerebral ventricle in the forebrain; these are linked via the cerebral aqueduct to the hindbrain's 4th ventricle. This whole system acts as a general "shock absorber" for the brain and reduces its effective weight by almost 95%. Obstruction of the flow of cerebrospinal fluid, arising either congenitally or from a tumour, results in the medical condition hydrocephalus.

Textbooks on neuroscience often describe the location and function of hundreds of individual brain regions (see references above). However, for current purposes these will be kept to a minimum (Figure 2.1). Anatomically, the brain can be subdivided into the forebrain containing the **telencephalon** and **diencephalon**, the midbrain or **mesencephalon** and the hindbrain (**metencephalon** and **myelencephalon**). The telencephalon includes the left and right cerebral hemispheres encompassed by the **cerebral cortex** (neocortex). Cortex is a translation of the word "bark" and is so-called because its surface, made up of numerous sulci (grooves or invaginations) and gyri (raised areas), is on the outer surface of the brain like the bark of a tree. Each hemisphere is divided into four lobes, named from the front (rostral) to back (caudal) of the brain: frontal, temporal, parietal and occipital.

The left and right hemispheres perform different functions (Greenfield, 1998), but somewhat surprisingly they have not been a focus for much psychopharmacological research; perhaps this will change in the future. The **corpus callosum** is a dense neuronal network that bridges the hemispheres and enables the overall integration of information. Damage to the corpus callosum results in a "split brain" where the left and right hemispheres operate independently. Within the cerebral cortex are discrete regions that integrate and interpret inputs from our environment. The primary somatosensory cortex together with its association area processes information from mechanoreceptors, nociceptors and thermoreceptors. The auditory, gustatory, olfactory and visual cortices and their respective association areas are involved in hearing, taste, olfaction and vision, respectively. The primary motor and premotor cortices, together with several extra-cortical structures, are involved in the central control of voluntary movement. The cerebral cortex together with the limbic system are important in emotional responses, learning and memory. Finally, there are a number of "higher cortical functions" that in terms of their level of complexity and sophistication delineate human beings from other primates; these are language and cognitive processes (cognition), including intelligence, reasoning, decision making, complex problem solving and consciousness.

Deep within the telencephalon are the subcortical **limbic system** and **basal ganglia**; these are a collection of networked structures involved in the regulation of a number of behaviours: moods and emotions, learning and memory (limbic system) and voluntary movement (basal ganglia). The major limbic structures are the **hippocampus** (memory) and **amygdala** (mood). The basal ganglia include the **caudate nucleus** and **putamen** (making up the **corpus striatum**, or neostriatum), **globus pallidus** and in the mesencephalon the **substantia nigra**. The limbic system and the basal ganglia connect "upstream" with the cerebral cortex and "downstream" with the **hypothalamus** (limbic system), **thalamus** (basal ganglia) and ANS – to produce a fully integrated response. The hypothalamus controls the release of hormones from the pituitary gland and indirectly influences the output from the adrenal cortex. This **Hypothalamic–Pituitary–Adrenal** (HPA) axis means that the limbic system interfaces with the endocrine system. Its functioning is important for health and well-being, but many types of drug can adversely influence its actions; this may help explain why so many forms of drug taking result in adverse health consequences.

The **cerebellum** is located in the metencephalon of the hindbrain, and like the basal ganglia it has an important role in the control of voluntary movement. The cerebellum is responsible for the execution of fine-controlled movements and the maintenance of posture and balance. The **medulla oblongata** of the myelencephalon provides the anatomical connection between the two parts of the CNS and contains a number of regions controlling autonomic and voluntary nervous system function; these are often referred to as brainstem reflexes (the brainstem comprising the medulla together with the **pons**) and include the vasomotor centre (blood pressure), cardiac centre, respiratory centre, vomiting centre and cough centre. Complete cessation of these reflexes is referred to as brainstem death and can occur with an overdose of CNS depressants (Chapter 9). Running through the core of the brainstem up into the thalamus is a dense neuronal network called the **Ascending Reticular Activating System** (ARAS). ARAS maintains arousal, and as sedative–hypnotic drugs reduce basic ARAS activity they induce sleepiness. In contrast, antipsychotic drugs, such as chlorpromazine, attenuate the sensory and cortical input into the ARAS; this leaves the person awake but less arousable, either by events in the environment or by their own thoughts and feelings; this is possibly the mechanism by which hallucinations and delusions are reduced (Chapter 11). The thalamus is the brain's higher "relay station" where messages from sensory receptors via afferents to the spinal cord are processed for onward transmission to the cerebral cortex.

The neuron

Neurons were first described by Purkinje in 1839 (whose name is attached to a particular type found in the cerebellum), but much of our understanding of their structure comes through the pioneering work of Ramon y Cajal (cited in Raine, 1976). There are some 100 trillion (100,000,000,000,000) neurons in our nervous system, the vast majority of them located in the cerebral cortex. Each neuron can synapse and thus communicate with between 1,000 to 10,000 other neurons: a single gramme of brain tissue may contain up to 400 billion synapses The neuron comprises a cell body (or **soma**), which contains various subcellular organelles, including nucleus, mitochondria, ribosomes and endoplasmic reticulum. Radiating outward is a profusion of **dendrites** and a longer and thicker **axon** emerging from the soma at the axon hillock (Figure 2.3). Visually, the neuron might be conceptually compared with a rolled-up hedgehog, with the dendrites being the spines. However, in a field of these "hedgehogs", none of them would be visually similar; this is because the sizes and shapes of neurons are extremely variable. Indeed, they are the most polymorphic cells in the body, following no standard shape or size. Neurons may be unipolar (one axon), bipolar (one axon and one dendrite) or multipolar (one axon and many dendrites), and their axons may be of similar length to their dendrites, up to 100 mm in length.

The total human complement of neurons is laid down around birth, and if they die they cannot be replaced – unlike most cells in our body. However, this central dogma of neuroscience has been challenged by the recent finding that neurogenesis can occur in the adult rat hippocampus, and these new cells seem to be required for at least one type of memory (Shors et al., 2001). Whether this will also be the case in

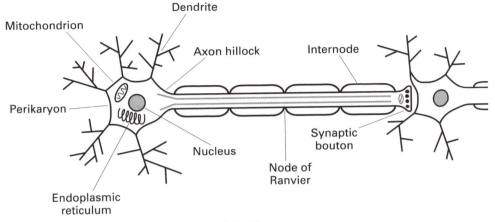

Figure 2.3. The neuron.

humans is currently unknown. What is known is that from a relatively young age, neurons are lost at an apparently alarmingly high rate of 20,000 per day. Fortunately, given the total of 100 trillion, this number is somewhat insignificant. However cerebral trauma (head injury), neurodevelopmental insult *in utero* (some forms of schizophrenia?), senile dementia and some neurotoxic drugs (possibly MDMA, or methylenedioxymethamphetamine), may aggravate age-related neuronal loss and result in faster cognitive decline. If neurons do not increase in number, how then do we learn and remember things? Neurons modify the strength of existing synapses and form new synapses with their neighbours, and this underlies new learning and memory. Neuronal networks are not "rigid", fixed in time and space, but rather demonstrate a degree of plasticity which even in comparatively simple nervous systems is exquisitely complex.

Action potential

Neurons are described as electrically excitable cells, having the ability to generate and propagate an electrical signal (current); this is referred to as the **action potential**, or nerve impulse. Like other cells, the internal compartment of neurons is separated from the outside by a plasma membrane. The unique information-processing capacity of neurons is partly due to the presence of a large electrochemical gradient across the plasma membrane of the neuron arising from the unequal separation of **ions** (charged molecules) on either side of the membrane. Sodium (Na^+) and chloride (Cl^-) ions are found at concentrations 10 times higher in the extracellular fluid outside the cell than inside it in the cytoplasm, while potassium (K^+) ion concentration is 20 times higher in the cytoplasm. However the concentration of calcium ions (Ca^{2+}) is up to 10,000 times higher in the extracellular fluid than in the cytoplasm. The overall difference in ion distribution across the membrane is termed "the electrochemical gradient" (when referring to the difference in charge between the inside and outside of the cell) or concentration gradient (when referring to the difference in ion concentration). The

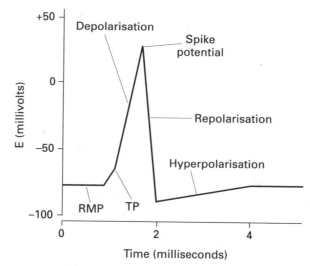

Figure 2.4. The action potential.

difference in electrical charge for the cell at rest is approximately 70 mV (millivolts). The inside of the cell is negatively charged compared with the outside, and this is conventionally denoted as −70 mV, a value referred to as the resting membrane potential (Figure 2.4).

This electrochemical gradient arises from two core properties of the plasma membrane: first, its relative impermeability to all but K^+ ions and, second, the presence of a highly active sodium/potassium pump, which drives any Na^+ ions that have leaked into the cytoplasm back outside the cell, in exchange for those K^+ ions that have left. Each sodium/potassium pump is extremely active, transporting hundreds of ions across the membrane per second. Since there are about a million such pumps on even a small neuron, the movement of these ions against the concentration gradient requires a great deal of energy; this is provided by **adenosine triphosphate** (ATP) (often described as the universal "energy currency" of nature). The hydrolysis (breakdown) of one ATP molecule releases around 31 kilojoules or 7 kilocalories of energy. Around 80% of the neuron's energy production is used to fuel this Na^+/K^+ pump, and since most ATP is synthesised via the aerobic breakdown of **D-glucose** the importance of an adequate supply of this carbohydrate and oxygen is evident. In Chapter 14 the roles of these chemicals are described more fully, since some **cognitive enhancers** may be influencing these basic metabolic processes. The crucial importance of energy is illustrated by the fact that, while the human brain comprises 2% of body weight, it consumes 20% of the body's glucose and receives 20% of its cardiac output. This rate remains constant, day and night, sleeping or studying.

When a neuron is stimulated electrically, either artificially via electrodes or chemically via neurotransmitters or drugs, there is a rapid and transient reversal of the resting membrane potential; this is caused by the opening of normally closed voltage-operated sodium channels in the plasma membrane. The Na^+ ions passively flow down their concentration gradient into the cytoplasm and slowly change the resting membrane potential from −70 mV to the threshold potential of −55 mV. On reaching this threshold there is a rapid depolarisation to about +30 mV, which corresponds with the peak or spike (Figure 2.4); this is caused by positive feedback mechanisms that open more and more channels. However, they are only open for less than 1 ms before they close again. At this time the delayed rectifier voltage-operated potassium channels open, and K^+ ions passively leave; this restores the cell to its resting membrane potential value of around $-70\,mV$, a process termed repolarisation. In fact the normal resting potential value briefly overshoots, so that the cell membrane becomes even more negative or hyperpolarised. Finally, the Na^+/K^+ pump retrieves K^+ ions that have left the cell during repolarisation and pumps out Na^+ ions that have entered during depolarisation, thus restoring the resting potential back to around $-70\,mV$ (Figure 2.4). The whole cycle of a single action potential, from the start of depolarisation to the restoration of the resting membrane potential, is very rapid, lasting less than 3 ms (three-thousandths of a second).

The action potential is not static, but is propagated rapidly along the length of the neuron, from the dendrite that is initially stimulated to the synaptic bouton at the far end of the neuron; this occurs by the spread of positive charges (local currents) from one patch of membrane to the next (Figure 2.3). The action potential velocity ranges from 1 to 120 metres per second, and although quite rapid these ionic currents are still far slower than current flow in an electrical wire. The action potential velocity is increased by the degree of myelination of the neuronal axon. **Myelin** is a lipoprotein that gives the characteristic white colour to axons and, therefore, the white matter of the brain and spinal cord. Myelin serves as a bioelectrical insulation and is laid down in internodes, or sections, with tiny gaps in-between, called the **nodes of Ranvier**. This process is undertaken by neuroglial cells called oligodendrocytes in the CNS or Schwann cells in the PNS. The autoimmune disease **multiple sclerosis** occurs as a result of damage to the myelin sheath and is characterised by progressively worsening visual and motor disturbances. The voltage-operated sodium channels are located at these nodes, so that the current "jumps" along the axon from node to node, thereby increasing the action potential velocity. This saltatory or "skipping/dancing") conduction is fastest in the large-diameter voluntary neurons serving the muscles of our limbs.

The generation of the action potential can be blocked by a number of chemicals, many of which are lethal animal toxins. Tetrodotoxin is a sodium channel blocker from the Japanese puffer fish (*Fugu rubripes*), charybdotoxin is a potassium channel blocker from the scorpion *Leiurus quinquestriatus hebraeus*, while dendrotoxin is also another potassium channel blockers found in the venom of the green mamba (*Dendroaspis angusticeps*). These chemicals block either depolarization or repolarization of the action potential and, thus, result in the cessation of electrical activity in the neuron. However, some channel blockers are reversible, and these short-acting chemicals have clinical applications. Local anaesthetics (e.g., **lignocaine**, or lidocaine) are sodium channel blockers which are used in dentistry to produce analgesia by inhibiting the propagation of the action potential in sensory afferent neurons.

When the action potential reaches the synaptic bouton, depolarisation triggers the opening of voltage-operated calcium channels in the membrane (Figure 2.5). The concentration gradient for Ca^{2+} favours the passive movement of this ion into the neuron. The subsequent rise in cytoplasmic Ca^{2+} ion concentration stimulates the release of **neurotransmitter** into the synaptic cleft, which diffuses across this narrow gap and binds to **receptors** located on the postsynaptic neuronal membrane (Figure 2.5).

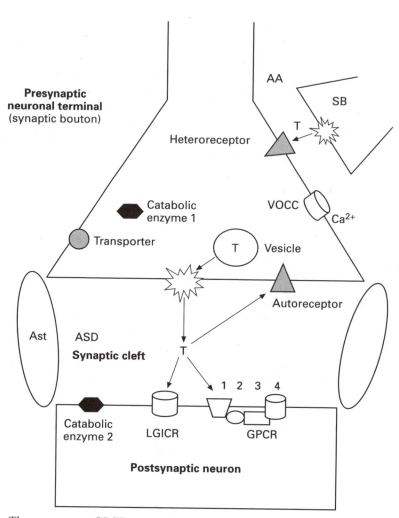

Figure 2.5. The synapse. GPCR = guanine nucleotide-binding protein-coupled receptor, LGICR = ligand-gated ion channel receptor, SB = synaptic bouton, T = neurotransmitter, VOC = voltage-operated ion channel protein, VOCC = voltage-operated calcium channel protein, Ast = astrocyte, AA = axoaxonal synapse, ASD = axosomatic *or* axodendritic synapse. GPCR: 1 = receptor protein, 2 = G-protein, 3 = enzyme, 4 = ion channel protein.

Synapses and neurotransmission

Communication between neurons involves neurotransmitters. Up until the beginning of the last century, synaptic transmission was regarded as probably electrical. It was suggested that the close apposition of two neurons allowed the current to "jump" the synaptic cleft, rather like an electrical spark between two closely positioned wires. There is indeed evidence for electrical synapses in animal species where the synaptic cleft is particularly narrow (2 nm, or nanometres), as well as in the myocardium where the close coupling of cells allows electrical current to flow from one cell to the next,

Table 2.1. Chemical families of neurotransmitters.

Amines

Acetylcholine	Quaternary amine (*or* choline ester)
Dopamine	Monoamine (a catecholamine)
Noradrenaline *or* norepinephrine	Monamine (a catecholamine)
Adrenaline *or* epinephrine	Secondary amine (a catecholamine)
5-Hydroxytryptamine (5-HT) *or* serotonin	Monoamine (an indoleamine)
Histamine	Monoamine (an imidazoleamine)

Amino acids

Glycine (GLY *or* G)	Monocarboxylic inhibitory amino acid
γ-Aminobutyric acid (GABA)	Monocarboxylic inhibitory amino acid
L-Aspartic acid *or* aspartate (ASP *or* D)	Dicarboxylic excitatory amino acid
L-Glutamic acid *or* glutamate (GLU *or* E)	Dicarboxylic excitatory amino acid

Neuropeptides[a]

Thyroliberin (thyrotropin-releasing hormone, TRH)	Tripeptide
Endomorphin 1	Opioid tetrapeptide
Methionine (MET)-enkephalin	Opioid pentapeptide
Cholecystokinin-8S (CCK-8S)	Octapeptide
Vasopressin (Antidiuretic hormone, ADH)	Nonapeptide
Neurokinin A (Substance K)	Tachykinin decapeptide
Substance P	Tachykinin undecapeptide
Neurotensin	Trisdecapeptide
α-Endorphin	Opioid hexadecapeptide
Dynorphin A	Opioid heptadecapeptide

[a] The examples given have between three *tri-* and 17 *heptadeca*-amino acids.

effectively making the heart one giant cell. However, when the synaptic cleft or neuroeffector junction is wider (20–80 nm), chemical transmission takes place.

The definitive experiment to demonstrate the existence of neurotransmitters was published in 1921 by Otto Löwi (cited in Hoffman et al., 1996). He electrically stimulated the vagus nerve of a frog heart *in vitro* (isolated in an organ bath containing Ringer's physiological salt solution). He then collected a chemical he postulated to be released from the nerve ending which slowed down the heart rate. This chemical was then transferred to a second organ bath containing another heart, and in response this second heart slowed down. Thus the chemical in the transferred solution had caused bradycardia, in a way apparently identical to that found when electrically stimulating the vagus nerve directly. Löwi initially named the chemical *vagusstoff*, and 5 years later it was identified as **acetylcholine**, one of the most widely distributed neurotransmitters in the nervous system.

Since then some 100 chemicals have been identified as putative neurotransmitters, and neuroscientists believe there are many more to be discovered (Table 2.1). Broadly speaking the neurotransmitters can be grouped into three major chemical families: the **amines** (first discovered in the 1920s), **amino acids** (1950s) and **neuropeptides** or peptides (1970s). There are also a number of neurotransmitters that do not fit into any of these families, and this "miscellaneous" group includes purines, like adenosine and ATP, and lipids, like **anandamide**, the physiological ligand for cannabinoid receptors. Some of these molecules can have dual functions as both neurotransmitters and hormones: for example, **adrenaline** and **noradrenaline** are not only neurotransmitters but also hormones, released from the adrenal medulla; **histamine** is a local hormone, a mediator of inflammation; thyroliberin stimulates the release of thyroid-stimulating hormone from the anterior pituitary gland; and vasopressin is a hormone released from the posterior pituitary gland. In addition, the amino acids **aspartate**, **glutamate** and **glycine** are found in proteins and neuropeptide transmitters (e.g., aspartate in cholecystokinin-8S, glutamate in neurotensin and glycine in methionine-enkephalin). Up until the discovery of the neuropeptides, scientists believed that a single neuron could only contain one neurotransmitter – Dale's law. However, it became apparent that neuropeptides and amines could co-exist as co-transmitters in the same neuron with the neuropeptide modulating the release of the amine. Here, the neuropeptides are referred to as **neuromodulators**, and in most cells they inhibit the release of an amine: for instance, neurotensin inhibits the release of dopamine from certain forebrain neurons.

Unlike many chemicals in the brain, neurotransmitters are not homogeneously distributed, but concentrated in certain regions. For example, almost two-thirds of the **dopamine** in the brain is found in the bilateral **nigrostriatal** (mesostriatal) **tract** (pathway), where the neuronal cell bodies are located in the substantia nigra and the axons terminate in the corpus striatum. When over 85% of these dopaminergic neurons are lost, the characteristic motor dysfunction of **Parkinson's disease** is seen.

Neurotransmitters are synthesised at the "point of use", with the biosynthetic **enzymes** being located in the synaptic bouton. The enzymes can be identified when looking at neurotransmitter pathways by the fact that they usually end in the suffix "-ase": for example, choline-O-acetyltransferase ("choline acetylase") is necessary for the synthesis of acetylcholine; and tyrosine-3-hydroxylase, dopa decarboxylase and dopamine-β-oxidase are each required for the synthesis of noradrenaline. In contrast, neuropeptides are synthesised in the neuronal cell body and transported the length of the axon to the synaptic bouton. It is important that a neurotransmitter's action is brief – allowing a sharp, clean signal. So, as soon as neurotransmitter is released mechanisms are brought into play that inactivate it and/or clear it from the synaptic cleft. In order to terminate the action of a neurotransmitter, enzymatic and/or non-enzymatic mechanisms of inactivation are required. **Acetylcholinesterase** is an example of a catabolic ("breaking down") enzyme (Figure 2.5, catabolic enzyme 2) and rapidly breaks down acetylcholine into acetic acid and choline. Some 50% of the choline produced in this process can be reused to make more acetylcholine; this follows its uptake into the presynaptic neuron via the high-affinity choline uptake system (choline carrier or transporter). The monoamines, dopamine, 5-HT (serotonin) and noradrenaline are inactivated by a combination of presynaptic reuptake and catabolism. Dopamine has the dopamine **transporter** and serotonin, or 5-HT, also has its own transporters (5-HTT or SERT), as does noradrenaline (NAT or NET). They return their respective neurotransmitters into the synaptic bouton where all three may be broken down into inactive metabolites by monoamine oxidase (**MAO**; Figure 2.5, catabolic enzyme 1). In the case of the catecholamines, an additional enzyme **catechol-O-methyltransferase** (COMT) is also involved. The amino acid **GABA** (γ-aminobutyric acid) is inactivated by a combination of reuptake into the presynaptic neuron and uptake into the **astrocytes** (a type of glial cell) surrounding the synaptic cleft. **Neuropeptides** are inactivated in the synaptic cleft by plasma membrane-bound ectopeptidases. As we will see in Chapters 12 and 13, certain types of drugs act by inhibiting the processes of breakdown and reuptake, thus increasing the neurotransmitter's effects.

Receptors

Neurotransmitters exert their physiological effects through binding to specialised plasma membrane proteins called receptors, so allowing the flow of information from one neuron to another. The binding of neurotransmitters to their **receptors**, is often likened to a key turning a lock. This chemical interaction is high affinity since low concentrations of the neurotransmitter are required and, where the neurotransmitter has isomeric (enantiomeric, or mirror image) forms, it is stereospecific, only one of the forms is active. To illustrate the latter, take the example of noradrenaline, which contains an asymmetric carbon atom (chiral centre) where four different chemical groups or atoms are attached to the β-carbon atom:

A single, asymmetric carbon atom in the noradrenaline molecule means it can exist as two **enantiomers** (stereoisomers), designated L- (*laevo*) and D- (*dextro*), which contain the same chemical groups in a slightly different spatial arrangement. Only the L-noradrenaline binds to the receptor with high affinity or **potency**. Other neurotransmitters with chiral centres are aspartate, glutamate and the neuropeptides. In each case it is the L-enantiomer that is physiologically active. Stereospecific binding, giving rise to different pharmacological activities, can also occur if a drug has one or more chiral centres: for instance, D-amphetamine is more potent than L-amphetamine.

Neurotransmitter receptors can be divided into two superfamilies: class 1 comprises the ligand-gated ion channel (LGICR), or ionotropic, receptors; class 2 comprises the G-protein-coupled (GPCR), or metabotropic, receptors. Both types of receptor are proteins with three distinct regions: (1) extracellular ("outside the cell"), or synaptic, cleft region to which the neurotransmitter binds; (2) a lipophilic ("lipid loving") membrane-spanning region; and (3) the cytoplasmic region (the cytoplasm is the fluid that fills the inside of all cells). Class 1 receptors are complex proteins made up of subunits clustered in a cylindrical formation; the centre comprises an ion channel or pore. One of the most extensively studied of these receptors is a class of **cholinergic receptor** known as the nicotinic acetylcholine receptor (nAChR). The binding of acetylcholine results in a conformational change to the protein's structure, which opens up the ion channels; this allows the passage of Na^+ ions into the cell and K^+ ions out. This inward current of Na^+ causes depolarisation of the muscle membrane and so results in muscular contraction. A broadly similar mechanism occurs in the CNS. Class 1 receptors respond rapidly to neurotransmitter binding (<1 ms) and are therefore ideally suited to the demands of rapid phasic activity, such as skeletal muscle contraction.

Other examples of class 1 receptors include the **GABA$_A$ receptor**, which in addition to its neurotransmitter binding sites has a number of other sites; these include those for **benzodiazepine** drugs that regulate the binding of GABA to its site and thus the opening of the Cl$^-$ ion channel. The resulting influx hyperpolarises the neuron, making it less likely to fire. Thus, GABA is an inhibitory neurotransmitter (Chapter 9). Another class 1 receptor is the glutamate NMDA (N-methyl-D-aspartate) receptor, which principally controls the movement of Ca^{2+} into the neuron. The movement of Na$^+$ and Ca^{2+} ions into the cell results in depolarisation and an increase in postsynaptic neuronal excitability. Thus, glutamate acid is an excitatory neurotransmitter. The amine neurotransmitters can be either excitatory or inhibitory, depending on the type of receptor and their neuroanatomical location: for example, with acetylcholine, nicotinic receptors are excitatory in skeletal muscle, whereas muscarinic receptors are inhibitory in cardiac muscle. Similarly with noradrenaline, the β_1 receptors are excitatory in cardiac muscle, whereas β_2 receptors are inhibitory in bronchial smooth muscle.

It is clear from the foregoing discussion that there are several different receptors for each neurotransmitter. These multiple receptors are designated receptor subtypes. The nomenclature for these different receptor subtypes has developed piecemeal and is very confusing. Many of the names have historical origins, with muscarinic coming from the fungal alkaloid muscarine and nicotinic coming from the tobacco alkaloid **nicotine**. With dopamine, Arabic numerals are used to denote receptor subtypes: D$_1$-like and D$_2$-like. With GABA, Roman letters are used: GABA$_A$ and GABA$_B$. While with noradrenaline, Greek letters are used: α and β. Just to make life even more interesting, each receptor subtype has a number of further subclasses: for example, noradrenaline has β_1, β_2 and β_3 receptors. Serotonin, or 5-HT, currently holds the record, with 14 receptor subtypes.

The vast majority of receptor subtypes are class 2, or GPCRs. Class 2 receptors are sometimes referred to as **metabotropic**. Rather than change the excitability of their cell immediately through the rapid passage of ions, they induce a less immediate and longer lasting metabolic cascade in the cell. Here, when the neurotransmitter binds to its receptor, the conformational change activates a closely coupled **G-protein** which in turn regulates the activity of an intracellular enzyme; this stimulates (or inhibits) the biosynthesis of a second messenger molecule, so-called because the signal (or message) is passed onto it from the "first messenger" system, the neurotransmitter–receptor complex. There are several different types of G-proteins, G standing for guanine nucleotide, including G$_s$, G$_i$ and G$_q$. Table 2.2 summarises the main features of these systems.

Each class 2 receptor follows the general mechanism of receptor binding causing a change in a G-protein which then activates a second messenger system (see Table 2.2). The second messengers then go on to activate specific protein kinases that phosphorylate (add phosphate groups to particular amino acids) ion channel proteins in the plasma membrane, opening up a channel in the centre of these proteins, thus allowing the passage of ions into or out of the cell. It is evident from these events that GPCRs are much slower in response time than the LGICRs; however, this

Table 2.2. Class 2 receptor (GPCR) systems.

G protein	Receptor subtype	Second messenger system
G_s	Noradrenaline β_1 and β_2 Dopamine D_1 and D_5 Histamine H_2 Serotonin 5-HT$_4$	Stimulates adenylate cyclase increasing the concentration of cAMP (cyclic-adenosine-3′,5′-monophosphate)
G_i	Noradrenaline α_2 Muscarinic m_2 Dopamine D_2, D_3, D_4 Serotonin 5-HT$_{1B}$ GABA$_B$ Opioid δ, κ, μ Cannabinoid CB$_1$ and CB$_2$	Inhibits adenylate cyclase decreasing the concentration of cAMP
G_q	Noradrenaline α_1 Muscarinic m_1 and m_3 Histamine H_1 and 5-HT$_{2A}$	Stimulates phosphoinositidase C, increasing the concentration of the lipophilic 1,2-diacylglycerol (DAG) and the water-soluble inositol-1,4,5-trisphosphate (IP$_3$)

cascade of biochemical reactions does enable amplification of the extracellular (neuro-transmitter) signal.

G_i-protein-coupled receptors are often located on the presynaptic plasma membrane where they inhibit neurotransmitter release by reducing the opening of Ca^{2+} channels; like inactivation and breakdown of the neurotransmitter by enzymes, this contributes to the neuron's ability to produce a sharply timed signal. An α_2 receptor located on the presynaptic membrane of a noradrenaline-containing neuron is called an autoreceptor; but, if located on any other type of presynaptic neuronal membrane (e.g., a 5-HT neuron), then it is referred to as a heteroreceptor (Langer, 1997). Autoreceptors are also located on the soma (cell body) and dendrites of the neuron: for example, somatodendritic 5-HT$_{1A}$ receptors reduce the electrical activity of 5-HT neurons.

Finally, perhaps one of the oddest of recent discoveries is that toxic gases, such as **nitric oxide** (NO) and carbon monoxide (CO), can act as dual first/second messengers in the nervous system (Haley, 1998). Our current ideas of how drugs affect the complex events and regulation of synaptic neurotransmission are very simplistic and the real situation is obviously vastly more complicated. Some of these issues will be addressed in more detail in Chapter 14.

Questions

1   Summarise the major divisions of the central and peripheral nervous systems.

2   Describe one neurophysiological or neurobehavioural function for five different brain regions.

3   Describe the components of a multipolar neuron.

4   Using diagrams, explain the different phases of the action potential.

5   Give two examples for each of the following types of neurotransmitter: monoamine, amino acid and neuropeptide.

6   What is the main difference between a first and second messenger?

7   Explain why the electrophysiological responses to class 1 receptors are much more rapid than to class 2 receptors.

Key references and reading

Bloom FE, Nelson CA and Lazerson A (2001). *Brain, Mind and Behavior*. Worth, New York.

Carlson NR (1999). *Foundations of Physiological Psychology*. Allyn & Bacon, Needham Heights, MA.

Greenfield S (1998). *The Human Brain: A Guided Tour*. Phoenix, London.

Hindmarch I, Aufdembrinke A and Ott H (1988). *Psychopharmacology and Reaction Time*. John Wiley & Sons, Chichester, UK.

Langer SZ (1997). 25 years since the discovery of presynaptic receptors: Present knowledge and future perspectives. *Trends in Pharmacological Sciences*, **18**, 95–99.

Matthews GG (2001) *Neurobiology: Molecules, Cells and Systems*. Blackwell, Malden, MA.

Purves D, Augustine GJ, Fitzpatrick D, Katz LC, LaMantia A-S, McNamara JO and Williams SM (2001). *Neuroscience*. Sinauer Associates, Sunderland, MA.

Rose S (1976). *The Conscious Brain*. Penguin, London.

Shors TJ, Miesegaes G, Beylin A, Zhao M, Rydel T and Gould E (2001). Neurogenesis in the adult is involved in the formation of trace memories. *Nature*, **410**, 372–376.

Chapter 3

Principles of drug action

Overview

The first part of this chapter covers pharmacokinetics, or how the body physiologically processes a drug. In pharmacology textbooks the topic of pharmacokinetics is often treated mathematically. However, the approach adopted here is largely descriptive. The pharmacokinetic process can be remembered by the acronym ADME – absorption, distribution, metabolism and elimination. Each of these key stages will be described using practical drug examples. The various routes of drug administration, although not strictly covered by the term pharmacokinetics, will also be described as a prelude to ADME. Drugs can be administered by injection, tablet, snorted or inhaled, with each route displaying particular characteristics. Following initial drug absorption, drugs are distributed to the different body tissues, where they are metabolised into breakdown products and, finally, they are excreted. These four stages can vary considerably, so that while some drugs remain psychoactive for only a short period (e.g., crack cocaine), others have effects lasting weeks or months (e.g., depot injections of some antipsychotic drugs). The second part of this chapter covers pharmacodynamics, or how drugs modify brain activity. The key topic is how each drug interacts with the neuronal receptors, or modifies neurotransmission. There are many different neurotransmitters, and their actions can be enhanced or blocked in numerous different ways. The diversity of altered transmission patterns helps explain the wide range of behavioural changes produced by different drug types. Thus, a basic understanding of pharmacodynamics is essential to understand how each class of drugs exerts its characteristic effects. Finally, drug tolerance, addiction/dependence and the placebo response will be covered at the close of the chapter.

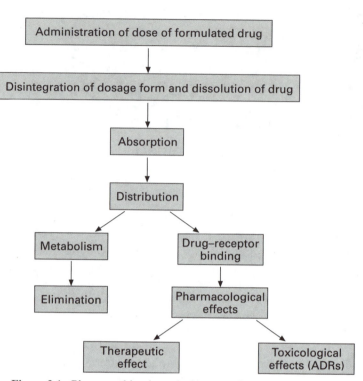

Figure 3.1. Pharmacokinetic and pharmacodynamic processes.

Pharmacokinetics

Pharmacokinetics encompasses four stages in the journey of a **drug** through the body: absorption, distribution, **metabolism** and elimination (Figure 3.1). Drug administration is a prelude to this process; however, in standard textbooks on pharmacology it is not included within the pharmacokinetics section. Thus, the disintegration of a tablet, followed by the release of the drug and its dissolution into the stomach fluids, is referred to as the pharmaceutical phase and is the subject of the branch of pharmacy called pharmaceutics. It is also important to note that not every drug necessarily passes through all four pharmacokinetic stages. The absorption phase may be bypassed and some drugs are eliminated from the body unaltered by metabolism.

Drug administration routes

Topical routes of drug administration are where the drug is applied directly to the site of action. Many medicines are applied directly: for example, **hydrocortisone** can be rubbed into the skin to relieve a local area of inflammation. The anticholinesterase **neostigmine** is dropped directly onto the eye surface to relieve glaucoma, a condition characterised by raised intra-ocular pressure which if untreated can lead to blindness.

Table 3.1. Parenteral routes of drug administration.

Intravenous (IV)	Into a vein. Because the drug enters directly into the circulation, there is no absorption phase; this means that the peak plasma concentration is reached almost immediately. This route is used when a rapid onset of action is required.
Intramuscular (IM)	Into skeletal muscle. This route is used to deliver "depot" antipsychotic drugs like fluphenazine and haloperidol decanoate, which are used in the treatment of schizophrenia.
Subcutaneous (SC)	Into the layer just under the skin; this is most commonly associated with insulin in diabetes mellitus.
Intrathecal (IT)	Into the subarachnoid space between two of the membranes (meninges) separating the spinal cord from the vertebral column. This route is used for drugs that do not penetrate the blood–brain barrier, but which are required for their central action (e.g., antibiotics). Drugs can also be injected spinally (into the epidural space) for local anaesthesia or analgesia.
Intraperitoneal (IP)	Into the peritoneal cavity of the abdomen; this provides a large surface area for absorption and is widely used for administering drugs to laboratory animals. It is very rarely used clinically.

The skin provides a method for administering several types of **psychoactive** drugs. Thus, transdermal nicotine patches contain a reservoir of drug, which is slowly absorbed through the skin and provides a useful aid for smoking cessation (Chapter 5). Transdermal **scopolamine** is also used to prevent the development of sea and air sickness, with the antimuscarinic drug scopolamine reducing cholinergic activity in the vomiting centre of the brain stem (Parrott, 1989). However, in both these cases the drug is absorbed from the skin patch into the general circulation and is therefore actually a systemic route. Topical administration is thus not a route for psychoactive drugs; perhaps you might like to consider why this is so?

Systemic routes result in the drug entering the body and, then, being distributed to any organ and affecting numerous physiological systems. Many drugs are administered by injection, a route often referred to as parenteral since it avoids the gastrointestinal tract. Often, the complete dose, or "bolus", is given rapidly under pressure using a hypodermic syringe. In other cases it is released as a slow controlled infusion via an osmotic pump or gravity "drip" feed. There are several injection routes used in experimental and human pharmacology (Table 3.1). For humans the three main routes are under the skin (subcutaneous injection) into a vein (intravenous injection) and into muscles (intramuscular injection). Some practical examples of each route are given in Table 3.1.

Another of the main systemic routes is oral (Table 3.2). Sometimes raw plant material is chewed in order to release the psychoactive compound into the mouth cavity. Examples include the chewing of coca leaves to extract **cocaine** (Chapter 4) and the tobacco leaf to extract **nicotine** (Chapter 5). The problem with this is that many other plant chemicals remain in the mouth, and many of these are carcinogenic. Tobacco leaf chewing leads to oral cancers of the mouth, lips, jaw and tongue, often

Table 3.2. Non-injection routes of drug administration.

Oral (PO = per os)	By the mouth. Oral administration is the most common route employed for a variety of dosage forms: tablets, capsules, liquids, suspensions. The major site of absorption is the small intestine. Alcohol is absorbed from the stomach.
Sublingual (SL)	In the mouth under the tongue; this allows the tablet or gum to slowly dissolve, so that the released drug can be gradually absorbed across the buccal mucosal membrane. Nicotine gum is administered by this route.
Nasal (NS)	Through the nose. Cocaine is snorted up the nose and then absorbed through blood capillaries in the thin nasal membrane.
Inhalation (IH)	The administration of volatile gases and vapours, followed by drug absorption in the lungs or nasal mucosa. Examples include general anaesthetics like nitrous oxide, nicotine from the tar droplets in tobacco smoke, cannabinoids from cannabis leaf smoke and various opiates from burning opium resin.

only 10 years after commencing the tobacco chewing habit/addiction (compared with a 20–30-year induction period for cancers of the lung in cigarette smokers; Chapter 5). Nicotine gum is thus a healthier method for oral nicotine intake. The gum must however be chewed slowly, since nicotine is only absorbed from the mouth cavity; if nicotine-replete saliva is swallowed, it can cause irritation in the stomach resulting in hiccups (Chapter 5).

Psychoactive drugs are predominantly taken as oral tablets, especially some of the main illicit recreational drugs: **amphetamine**, **Ecstasy/MDMA** (methylenedioxymethamphetamine) and **LSD** (lysergic acid diethylamide; Chapters 4 and 6). Many medicines are also typically given as oral tablets, including **benzodiazepines**, **antipsychotics** and **antidepressants** (Chapters 9, 11 and 12). However, it should be noted that many of these drugs can also be given as liquid preparations, as they are then easier to swallow; they can also be injected. One limitation of the oral route is that it can lead to varying concentrations in the systemic circulation; this is because absorption is influenced by numerous factors: the distance the drug has to travel to the site of absorption, the area of the absorbing surface, its blood supply and various other local factors (see below). A closely related route is nasal, since the mouth and nose form one interlinked cavity. The blood capillaries inside the nose are very close to the surface, which make them a good site for drug absorption. Cocaine is typically administered or "snorted" by the nasal route (Chapter 4).

Another systemic route is smoke inhalation; this is a surprisingly efficient route, with inhaled tobacco smoke generating a bolus or "hit" of nicotine which reaches the brain in only 7–10 seconds (Chapter 5). Smoking is thus used to deliver various illicit drugs, including crack cocaine (Chapter 4), **cannabis** (Chapter 7) and **opiates**, such as raw **opium** and **heroin**, when it is called "chasing the dragon" (Chapter 8). One of the benefits of smoke inhalation is the degree of control it provides to the individual smoker. By controlling the frequency and depth of inhalation, they can self-administer different amounts of drug. In regular tobacco smokers the first inhalation of the day tends to be long and deep, then successive inhalations of the cigarette become lighter and more widely spaced, as the need/desire for further hits of nicotine decreases (Chapter 5). Cannabis smokers often display similar patterns of self-titration, so that when they are replete they stop further smoking and avoid further **cannabinoid** intake (Chapter 7). Inhalation of burning plant material is always very unhealthy, since tobacco, cannabis and opium smoke contain numerous poisonous chemicals and carcinogens. The adverse health consequences of smoke inhalation are covered more fully in Chapter 5. Finally, there are two problems common to every systemic route and thus all forms of psychoactive drug administration: first, it is extremely difficult to retrieve the drug and so treat overdose; and second, because the drug may be distributed throughout the body, there is always the potential for unwanted side effects.

Absorption

Absorption describes the process by which a drug enters the blood circulation. With the exception of some forms of injection, all systemic routes involve an absorption phase. This process can be illustrated with the most common route of administration, oral (PO). Orally administered drugs pass down the oesophagus into the stomach and then the small intestine. The main drug to be absorbed from the stomach is alcohol (Chapter 9). With the majority of other ingestible drugs the major site of absorption is the small intestine. Drugs in the small intestine traverse the mucosa to enter the circulation via the hepatic portal vein, by the process of passive lipid diffusion. The more lipophilic (fat-loving) the drug the more easily it is absorbed. The presence of food delays absorption, which is why drugs are best absorbed "on an empty stomach". The hepatic portal vein enters the liver where drugs may be broken down into inactive metabolites. This initial metabolism is termed the **first-pass effect**, and where it is substantially high only a small proportion of the absorbed drug enters the systemic circulation via the hepatic vein; this is why oral tablets result in lower drug concentrations than other routes.

Drug distribution

In theory, once in the systemic circulation drugs may travel to any organ in the body. However, there are two physicochemical barriers that modify this distribution: the **blood–brain barrier** and the placental barrier. The blood–brain barrier is formed by capillary endothelial cells and astrocytes and ensures that there is no direct contact between blood circulation and brain neurons (Pardridge, 1998). The advantage of the blood–brain barrier is that it excludes many potentially toxic chemicals from the neuron. The disadvantage is that it can block access to some potentially useful therapeutic drugs. However, it is not completely effective, which is just as well because there would be no drugs for treating neurological and psychiatric disorders unless they were given by direct intracerebroventricular injection. The placental barrier excludes drugs from foetal circulation, thereby reducing possible damage to the developing baby. Unfortunately, some drugs can cross this barrier and may have teratogenic effects, giving rise to birth defects. They should not therefore be prescribed during pregnancy. Nobody is sure about the proportion of congenital birth defects resulting from either prescribed or recreational drugs. Rarely is the link so obvious as was the case with the antiemetic thalidomide, prescribed for first-trimester "morning sickness" in the late 1950s. However, congenital problems can certainly arise from some recreational drugs, including physiological dependence in babies born to cocaine users (Chapter 4) and the **fetal alcohol syndrome** in the children of excessive alcohol drinkers (Chapter 9).

In the circulation, drugs may be bound to plasma proteins, such as **albumin**, or they may remain unbound or free. A drug bound to albumin cannot bind to its target **receptor** site; therefore, only the free drug is pharmacologically active. However, the bound drug does provide a reservoir or storage pool. There is a dynamic equilibrium between the bound and free fractions: as the free drug is removed more of the bound drug dissociates from the albumin to become available for receptor binding. Many drugs are highly (>95% of the total concentration in the plasma) albumin-bound, and in some cases it may be necessary to give an initial "loading" dose which would be two to three times higher than the subsequent "maintenance" doses in order to achieve a sufficiently high concentration of active free drug. As the binding sites on albumin are non-selective, there may be competition between different drugs for these sites; this can lead to serious clinical drug interactions. Fatal haemorrhages have occurred when the oral anticoagulant warfarin has been prescribed at the same time as other highly albumin-bound drugs.

In addition to binding to proteins in the blood plasma, some drugs bind to other chemicals in the body. Fat makes up around 15% (males) to 20% (females) of total body weight but, with increasing obesity, these figures are becoming much higher. Highly lipophilic drugs accumulate in **adipose tissue** and are released into the circulation over a long period of time. This property is exploited clinically in the formulation of depot preparations of neuroleptics for the treatment of schizophrenia. With oral antipsychotics, patient non-compliance often hinders effective treatment, since one-third of day patients and up to 65% of outpatients stop taking their tablets within 6 weeks of commencing treatment (Johnson, 1988). In depot preparations the drug is rendered more lipophilic by adding a chain of 10 carbon atoms to the molecule, making a decanoate (e.g., fluphenazine decanoate, haloperidol decanoate); these are administered by intramuscular injections that last up to 4–8 weeks, with the drug being released gradually into the circulation (Chapter 11).

Metabolism or biotransformation

Metabolism converts a lipophilic molecule into a more hydrophilic (water-loving) metabolite that can be excreted in urine by the kidneys. In the majority of cases the drug is detoxified, or made pharmacologically inactive by this metabolic breakdown. However, a few drugs need to be metabolised to become psychoactive: for instance, the sedative–hypnotic **chloral hydrate** is converted to the active metabolite trichloroethanol. In this case the parent molecule is referred to as a prodrug. With many drugs, both the parent compound and its metabolites are psychoactive. An example of this is the tricyclic antidepressant **imipramine** which is metabolised to **desipramine**, with both drugs displaying antidepressant efficacy (Chapter 12). Furthermore, whereas imipramine is non-selective in inhibiting the inactivation of both noradrenaline and 5-HT (serotonin), its metabolite desipramine is highly selective for noradrenaline.

The liver is the major organ of drug metabolism, and the **enzymes** principally responsible for drug metabolism are located in the hepatocytes, bound to the membrane of the smooth endoplasmic reticulum. These enzymes are unusual in two respects: first, they are non-selective, since a single enzyme may metabolise hundreds of different drug substrates; and second, their activity is inducible. Enzyme induction means that activity can be stimulated by particular chemicals of which the classic example is the **anti-convulsant, phenobarbitone**. As a result of treatment with phenobarbitone, there is an increase in activity of these enzymes which may lead to a decrease in the therapeutic efficacy of any other drug taken at the same time. One potentially dangerous interaction between phenobarbitone and warfarin comes through an acceleration in the rate of warfarin metabolism, leading to an increased risk of blood clotting. Another problematic drug is alcohol, since regular drinkers have quite different liver characteristics to non-drinkers. The adverse consequences of enzymatic induction in alcohol drinkers are described more fully in Chapters 9 and 10.

Cytochrome P-450 is the collective name given to a group of over 230 structurally and functionally related enzyme proteins (**isoenzymes**), which are central to the metabolism of thousands of different drugs (Lewis, 1996). The three subfamilies CYP3A (44%), CYP2D (30%) and CYP2C (16%) account for the metabolism of almost 90% of drugs. Hepatic drug metabolism usually takes place in two stages: the first phase is oxidation which involves cytochrome P-450 and the second phase comprises the addition of a chemical group to the metabolites from the first phase. In addition to cytochrome P-450, some other enzymes account for the metabolism of other drugs: for instance, alcohol dehydrogenase metabolises alcohol and xanthine oxidase metabolises caffeine (Chapters 4 and 9).

A number of individuals show idiosyncratic responses to drugs at doses that would be well tolerated by the majority of the population. Such responses may be due to hypersensitivity (e.g., penicillin allergy) or altered metabolism. A pharmaco-genetic disorder is an inborn error of drug metabolism and is only manifested when the individual takes particular drugs. Five polymorphisms (variations in the nucleotide or base sequence of DNA coding for a particular protein) in **CYP2D6** may account for differences in the metabolism of some 25% of all drugs, including many **psychotropics** (Marshall, 1997). Poor/slow and extensive/fast metabolizers may show adverse reactions (Bondy and Zill, 2001). Several drugs inhibit these enzymes, and this can result in beneficial or adverse effects. The selective serotonin reuptake inhibitor **fluoxetine** used in depression (Chapter 12) inhibits numerous reactions catalysed by CYP2D6, and this may give rise to clinically significant interactions with other drugs (Lane et al., 1995), including MDMA (Chapter 6). **Disulfiram** inhibits aldehyde dehydrogenase, and this property is used clinically in the aversion therapy to prevent relapse in former alcoholics (Chapter 10). Irreversible monoamine oxidase (**MAO**) inhibitors inhibit the breakdown of dietary amines, especially tyramine, and this has resulted in fatal cerebrovascular haemorrhage (Chapter 12). Finally, it should be noted that any decline in liver function as a result of age or pathology (e.g., hepatic cirrhosis) will slow metabolic breakdown. Thus, elderly patients typically need lower doses of many psychoactive medications.

Table 3.3. Plasma half-lives.

Drug name	Drug family	Half-life (hours)	Active metabolite
Heroin	Opiate	0.03	Morphine
Morphine	Opiate	3	
Imipramine	TAD[a]	6–20	Desipramine
Fluoxetine	SSRI[b]	96–144	Norfluoxetine
Venlafaxine	SNRI[c]	5	
Lithium	Antimanic	20	
Haloperidol	Antipsychotic	20	
Clozapine	Antipsychotic	10–16	
Diazepam	Benzodiazepine	100	Nordiazepam
Temazepam	Benzodiazepine	6–10	
Phenobarbitone	Barbiturate	80–120	
Tacrine	Nootropic	3–4	

[a] TAD = tricyclic antidepressant.
[b] SSRI = selective serotonin reuptake inhibitor.
[c] SNRI = serotonin–noradrenaline reuptake inhibitor.
Data from Grahame-Smith and Aronson (1992) and Kaplan and Sadock (1996).

Elimination

The kidney is the principal organ of elimination, with drugs leaving the body mainly in the urine by renal excretion. Drugs can also be eliminated in faeces via the large intestine or in sweat, saliva and expired air. The appearance of unmetabolised ethanol in the breath of alcohol drinkers is the basis of the breathalyser. Saliva samples can also be used for drug testing. Unmetabolised drugs can also be secreted in breast milk in doses that may harm the baby and, thus, many drugs are contra-indicated during lactation.

The half-life $(t_{1/2})$ is the time required for the concentration of a drug to reach half its peak plasma concentration and provides a guide to the duration of action of the drug and the dosing interval required to maintain optimal therapeutic concentrations. The value of $t_{1/2}$ is related to a number of the pharmacokinetic factors mentioned above: binding to plasma proteins, accumulation in adipose tissue, metabolism and rate of elimination. In addition, normal age-related and pathological changes may significantly modify $t_{1/2}$, and many drugs (e.g., the selective serotonin reuptake inhibitors, fluoxetine and sertraline) have active metabolites that contribute to their long lasting pharmacological effects. The plasma half-lives of a number of clinical psychotropic drugs, ranging from 2 minutes to 6 days, is shown in Table 3.3.

Pharmacodynamics

The ultimate psychopharmacological effects of a drug result form a sequence of physicochemical interactions between the drug, a relatively small molecule and a macromolecule; the latter is usually a protein or glycoprotein termed a receptor. Thus, the drug is seen as a "foreign" molecule, whereas the receptor is a physiological or endogenous molecule. Here, the term "receptor" is used in a comparatively narrow sense to apply specifically to the plasma membrane-bound proteins found in neurons, muscle cells and endocrine/exocrine glands, which interact with the **neurotransmitters**. In addition to brain-synaptic neurotransmitter receptors, other macromolecular targets for psychotropic drugs comprise catabolic enzymes (e.g., monoamine oxidase), voltage-operated **ion channel** proteins (e.g., sodium) and transporter (carrier) proteins (e.g., dopamine transporter).

Drugs and neurotransmission

Psychoactive drugs can influence neurotransmission at its five different stages (Chapter 2). First, they may modify the **biosynthesis** of a neurotransmitter. Second, they can increase or decrease their storage within the presynaptic neuron. Third, they may stimulate or inhibit neurotransmitter release from the synaptic bouton. Fourth, they may affect the binding of the neurotransmitters to its receptor. Finally, they can retard the neurotransmitter's inactivation. Some examples of each of these stages will be given below, but it should be noted that many drugs affect several of these processes.

L-dopa is effective in the treatment of **Parkinson's disease**, a disorder characterised by low levels of dopamine, since L-dopa is metabolised into dopamine. However, this biosynthesis normally occurs in both the peripheral nervous system (PNS) and the central nervous system CNS. The related drug **carbidopa** inhibits aromatic L-amino acid decarboxylase only in the periphery, since it does not cross the blood–brain barrier. So, when carbidopa is given with L-dopa, it reduces the biosynthesis of L-dopa to dopamine in the periphery and, thus, increases the bioavailability of L-dopa for the dopaminergic neurons in the brain. Hence, carbidopa increases the clinical efficacy of L-dopa for Parkinsonian patients.

Reserpine inhibits the synaptic vesicular storage of the monoamines: dopamine, serotonin and noradrenaline. As a result they leak out into the cytoplasm where they are inactivated by monoamine oxidase; this causes their long-lasting depletion. The resulting low levels of dopamine underlie the antipsychotic actions of reserpine (Chapter 11), whereas the reduced noradrenaline levels underlie its antihypertensive actions. Finally, the resulting low levels of serotonin and noradrenaline mean that reserpine also induces depression. These severe side effects mean that reserpine is no longer used clinically as a treatment for schizophrenia (Chapter 11).

D-amphetamine stimulates the release of monoamines independently of the electrical activity of the neuron. This release leads to an increased concentration of monoamines in the synaptic cleft and, thus, an increase in receptor stimulation. Drugs, such as amphetamine, that do not bind to receptors, but increase the availability of the neurotransmitter by stimulating its release or inhibiting its inactivation, are called indirect agonists.

Agonist drugs can also bind directly to the **postsynaptic receptor**, so mimicking the physiological effect of the neurotransmitter: for example, **morphine** and heroin bind to the brain's opiate receptors and, thus, directly stimulate feelings of pleasure and pain relief (Chapter 8; see also Snyder, 1996). **Antagonists** also bind directly to the receptor, but they block or inhibit the actions of the neurotransmitter. **Naloxone** is an opiate antagonist that blocks the receptors and, therefore, does not cause any of the subjective feelings induced by the opiate receptor agonists. It is used clinically in the treatment of opiate addiction (Chapter 8). Another example of an antagonist is the antipsychotic drug **chlorpromazine** which binds to postsynaptic dopamine **D_2-like receptors** and leads to reduced dopaminergic activity; this results in a mixture of desirable effects, such as lessened hallucinations/delusions, together with undesirable side effects, such as psychomotor problems. Blockade of these dopamine receptors is thought to be a key mechanism of action for most antipsychotic drugs (Chapter 11).

Drugs can also bind to **presynaptic receptors** controlling the release of the neurotransmitter. An agonist at the inhibitory α_2-noradrenaline receptor will mimic the effect of noradrenaline in activating the negative feedback loop, so reducing the release of this neurotransmitter. The α_2-agonist **lofexidine** has been used successfully to control the noradrenergic hyperactivity seen during alcohol **detoxification** (Brunning et al., 1986). In contrast, an α_2-antagonist will block access of noradrenaline to the receptor and, thus, override the inhibitory feedback mechanism, resulting in an increased release of noradrenaline. The antidepressants, **mianserin** and **mirtazepine**, are both α_2-antagonists that raise the concentration of noradrenaline in the synaptic cleft, an observation consistent with the monoamine theory of depression (Chapter 12).

Many neurotransmitters are inactivated by a combination of enzymic and non-enzymic methods. The monoamines – dopamine, noradrenaline and serotonin (5-HT) – are actively transported back from the synaptic cleft into the cytoplasm of the presynaptic neuron. This process utilises specialised proteins called **transporters**, or **carriers**. The monoamine binds to the transporter and is then "carried" across the plasma membrane; it is thus transported back into the cellular cytoplasm. A number of psychotropic drugs selectively or non-selectively inhibit this reuptake process. They compete with the monoamines for the available binding sites on the transporter, so slowing the removal of the neurotransmitter from the synaptic cleft. The overall result is prolonged stimulation of the receptor. The tricyclic antidepressant imipramine inhibits the transport of both noradrenaline and 5-HT. While the selective noradrenaline reuptake inhibitor **reboxetine** and the selective serotonin reuptake inhibitor fluoxetine block the noradrenaline transporter (NAT) and serotonin transporter (SERT), respectively. Cocaine non-selectively blocks both the NAT and dopamine transporter (DAT); whereas the smoking cessation facilitator and antidepressant **bupropion** is a more selective DAT inhibitor.

Inside the cytoplasm of the presynaptic neuron the monoamines are exposed to the mitochondrial outer membrane-bound enzyme monoamine oxidase (MAO). MAO breaks the monoamines down into inactive metabolites before they are taken up into the vesicles. However, if MAO is inhibited, then the monoamines enter the vesicles and are available for release. MAO inhibitors, such as **moclobemide**, have been used in the treatment of depression, since they increase the availability of noradrenaline and serotonin. **Selegiline** is used for Parkinson's disease, since it raises dopamine levels.

Finally, some neurotransmitters, like acetylcholine, are inactivated solely by a catabolic enzyme. **Acetylcholinesterase** rapidly breaks down the neurotransmitter to acetate and choline, and the choline is then actively transported into the presynaptic neuron by the choline carrier protein. Inhibitors of this enzyme, called **anticholines-terases** or cholinesterase inhibitors, prolong the duration of action of acetylcholine and are used in "acetylcholine-deficient disorders": for example, **rivastigmine** in Alzheimer's disease (Chapter 13).

Tolerance and dependence

Tolerance is defined as the need for an increasing dose of a drug to achieve the same psychopharmacological effect. There are various underlying causes of tolerance: **pharmacodynamic** tolerance reflects the changes in receptor activity which accompany repeated drug use. Pharmacokinetic tolerance reflects changes in liver enzymes, most typically hepatic enzyme induction. Some drugs do not display tolerance (e.g., LSD; Chapter 6), while with many others its rate of development can be highly variable (e.g., cocaine; Chapter 4). Tolerance also depends on the dose administered, the regularity of dosing, the individual and, most importantly, the reasons for which the drug is being used (see cocaine in Chapter 4 and opiates in Chapter 8). **Pharmacokinetic** tolerance results in the reduced bioavailability of the drug and, usually, involves changes in drug metabolism; this is often caused by the enzymatic induction of cytochrome P-450 in the liver. The most potent liver enzyme inducers are long-acting barbiturates, such as phenobarbitone; these accelerate the metabolism of a large number of other drugs in addition to themselves. If the drug is detoxified, then more will have to be taken to achieve the desired effect. Pharmacokinetic tolerance is also very important with **alcohol**, since its regular use leads to the induction of cytochrome P-450.

Pharmacodynamic tolerance is a result of changes at the cellular level, resulting from adaptation to the presence of the drug. Such changes may involve desensitisation or down-regulation of the neurotransmitter receptors, which may result from prolonged stimulation by the drug. Uncoupling of the receptor protein from its second messenger system can occur rapidly and, over a longer time period, there tends to be a decrease in the number of receptors; this reflects their removal from the plasma membrane and can occur either through internalisation when they move into the cytoplasm or by enzymic degradation.

Other drugs may produce tolerance by prolonged stimulation of release and subsequent exhaustion of vesicular stores of the neurotransmitter, so that supply cannot match demand, or through the activation of a negative feedback mechanism they may decrease the synthesis and release of a neurotransmitter or hormone. Pharmacogenomics, an offshoot of the human genome project, has suggested that inter-individual variation in beneficial and adverse drug responses may be related to subtle variants in **gene** coding for neurotransmitter receptors and transporters (Marshall, 1997; Bondy and Zill, 2001). By analysing such differences it might then be possible to introduce "designer" drugs for each individual rather than the current practice of the "same drug for all". Genetic variants may also predispose individuals to a particular disease, so giving rise to a complex interaction between pharmacological and pathophysiological factors in predicting treatment outcomes. Tolerance to one drug may produce **cross-tolerance** to another in the same family. Thus, tolerance to amphetamine can result in a degree of cross-tolerance to other CNS stimulants, such as cocaine (Chapter 4). Opiates also show a marked degree of cross-tolerance to each other (Chapter 8).

Abrupt withdrawal from many drugs can precipitate an abstinence syndrome; this is characterised by a spectrum of symptoms opposite to those shown when taking the drug: for instance, with **sedative–hypnotics**, such as alcohol, benzodiazepines and barbiturates, withdrawal typically results in feelings of panic or anxiety, disturbed sleep and strong cravings for the drug (Chapter 9). An abstinence syndrome is indicative of a drug's ability to produce physical **dependence** where the body's physiological systems only function normally in the presence of the drug. Alcohol, barbiturates, benzodiazepines, nicotine, amphetamine, cocaine and the opiates can all produce a strong physical dependence syndrome (Chapters 4–10). Some drugs are said to produce psychological dependence where the abstinence symptoms are less strong and less physical. Thus, cannabis users do not report many physical symptoms of abstinence, but state that they miss the drug's positive feelings (Chapter 7). MDMA is not generally seen as a drug of dependence, although some regular Ecstasy users state that they find it difficult to enjoy themselves on a Saturday night without the drug (Chapter 6).

One difficulty with the notions of physical and psychological dependence is that they perpetuate the Cartesian mind–body dualism, in suggesting that psychological feelings are independent of physical phenomena. If this were so, then they could occur in the absence of any neurotransmission activity. The supposed distinction between physical and psychological is qualitatively similar to that made between hard and soft drugs or between legal and illicit drugs. In all three examples the implicit suggestion is that the second of these pairs is safer in terms of individual health and the overall well-being of society. This notion is disproved by the massive number of deaths caused by tobacco smoking and alcohol drinking (Chapters 5, 9 and 10). The judgemental term "drug abuse" is also best avoided and may be replaced with the less emotive term "drug misuse". However, the word "addiction" went through a period when it was replaced with the (then) less judgemental word "dependence". However, as with many problematic areas, subsequent changes in word interpretation/usage have evolved rapidly, so that in recent years "drug dependency" has gained similar emotional overtones to "drug addiction"; this emphasises that all scientific concepts are best considered in a value-free way. As Goldstein (1994, p. 2) noted: "The objection to [such] phrases is not a matter of mere semantics; incorrect use of language shapes and reinforces incorrect ways of thinking."

Placebo response

The word **placebo** is Latin for "I shall please", and placebo treatments (and responses) are a feature of clinical trials of new drugs and laboratory psychopharmacological research (Stevenson, 1998). At their simplest, two groups of volunteers are randomly assigned to either the control (placebo) or test (drug) group. However, as complete randomisation could result in one group having a majority of a particular gender, age and ethnic group and severity of illness, stratified randomisation (stratification), where these independent variables are equally balanced between the two groups, may be used. To eliminate bias, the best trials are double-blind where neither the volunteers nor the staff involved in assessing the responses are aware of the treatment received or given. Coded placebo and drug treatments are identical in presentation – size, colour and formulation – the only difference being that the placebo tablet, capsule or lozenge contains a pharmacologically inert chemical. By using a crossover design the power of a single clinical trial can be increased, as it enables both between and within-subject comparisons. Here, group *A* starts on placebo and group *B* on the drug. The two groups continue with these treatments for the period of time necessary for an agreed outcome. Placebo and drug administration is then stopped and, after a relatively short time to allow for complete elimination of the drug and any active metabolite(s), group *A* is given the drug and group *B* the placebo.

In both clinical and experimental human psychopharmacology, the placebo effect can be highly significant: for example, meta-analysis (a systematic statistical review of studies on the same drug or drug family) of antidepressant clinical trials revealed a beneficial effect of placebo in between one-quarter and one-third of patients and to active drugs in one-half to three-quarters of patients (Bauer et al., 2002). Placebos are also reported to give adverse drug reactions, or side effects, most frequently headaches, difficulty in concentration, nausea and dry mouth (Grahame-Smith and Aronson, 1992). There are a number of reasons for the placebo response. Set or expectancy that the treatment will be having an effect is one obvious reason. The high status of the administrator, either as a physician or scientist, is another factor. It has also been demonstrated that several tablets are better than one, coloured pills are better than white and injections are better than pills. However, very small white tablets can induce a very strong placebo effect, presumably because the contents are seen as inherently very powerful. Another factor is the implicit desire and need for a positive outcome; this may help explain the widespread use of many herbal medicine remedies and food supplements, although many of them do also contain psychoactive ingredients. This last point emphasises that even with psychoactive substances (opiates, CNS stimulants, antipsychotics), part of the drug response will always contain a psychological component. Indeed, this can help explain the wide variety of individual responses to a psychoactive drug. Finally, it is not just psychological phenomena that are susceptible to the placebo response; one of the strongest placebo responses comes with seasickness prophylactics, where a placebo can prevent up to 80% of motion-induced vomiting (Reason and Brand, 1975).

With recreational drugs the physical and social environment can also contribute to the response. An individual is more likely to have a pleasant experience in the company of their friends, whether the drug is legal (alcohol) or illicit (cannabis); this means that those members of the social group who are not taking any drug will also generally have a good time at a club, tavern or pub. Indeed, there were few differences in the self-rated levels of happiness of MDMA users and non-users while out clubbing on a Saturday night (Parrott and Lasky, 1998). Thus, a positive social atmosphere can lead to very pleasant feelings, which may be largely independent of the drug status. The main difference will then be in the attribution of positive feelings, either to the social situation *or* to the drug (Parrott, 2001). In relation to this, a secure non-threatening environment is essential when taking illegal drugs. Furthermore, the paraphernalia associated with drug administration – cigarettes, pipes and syringes – can all contribute to the positive sense of expectancy. Thus, conditioning phenomena are often important aspects of the drug experience. Some opiate users can become high simply by injecting themselves with *what they know* is water; these "needle freaks" have learnt to associate injections with pleasure (Chapter 8).

In many clinical trials a positive control of a clinically established drug is often used for comparison purposes: for example, a novel **selective serotonin reuptake inhibitor (SSRI)**, may be compared with a more established tricyclic antidepressant, such as imipramine. The aim is to see whether the new SSRI is more efficacious or has fewer adverse side effects than the more established tricyclic (Chapter 12). In many such comparisons the new and older treatments are equally efficacious at relieving depression, but the newer drugs display fewer side effects; this means that they are better tolerated by patients, so that they are more willing to continue taking the tablets. The high rates of compliance also mean that, in overall terms, newer drugs with fewer side effects tend to be more efficacious.

Questions

1   Compare the advantages and disadvantages of the different routes for drug administration.

2   What factors influence the bioavailability of a drug following its oral administration?

3   Why is cytochrome P-450 important for an understanding of psychoactive drugs?

4   What are the principal routes for the elimination of drugs from the body?

5   Describe the roles and functions of the blood–brain and placental barriers.

6   Outline how psychoactive drugs can modify the five stages of synaptic neuro-transmission.

7   Through what mechanisms do pharmacokinetic (metabolic) and pharmaco-dynamic (cellular) tolerance arise?

8   Describe the placebo effect.

Key references and reading

Goldstein A (1994). *Addiction from Biology to Drug Policy*. W.H. Freeman, New York.

Grahame-Smith DG and Aronson JK (1992). *Oxford Textbook of Clinical Pharmacology and Drug Therapy*. Oxford University Press, Oxford, UK.

Kaplan HJ and Sadock BJ (1996). *Pocket Handbook of Psychiatric Drug Treatment*. Williams and Wilkins, Baltimore.

Liska K (2000). *Drugs and the Human Body: With Implications for Society*. Prentice Hall, Englewood Cliffs, NJ.

Snyder SH (1996). *Drugs and the Brain*. W.H. Freeman, New York.

PART II

Non-medical Use of Psychoactive Drugs

Chapter 4

CNS stimulants: amphetamine, cocaine and caffeine

Overview

Stimulant drugs, such as amphetamine and cocaine, can increase alertness. Cocaine is a plant extract, whereas amphetamine is a laboratory product; but, both lead to increased dopamine and noradrenaline activity. By boosting neurotransmitter activity an acute dose of amphetamine or cocaine will heighten alertness and intensify moods. On drug withdrawal these positive moods are replaced by negative moods and lethargy, during the period of neurochemical recovery. Nevertheless, positive feelings can be reinstated by taking the drug again, which is why they can be so addictive. Their addiction potential is greatest for drug administration routes that cause a rapid release of neurotransmitter, followed by rapid neurochemical depletion, as with crack cocaine. Tolerance can develop readily, when increased dosage levels are needed to produce the same subjective effects. Regular stimulant users often develop psychobiological problems. Regular periods of dopamine overactivity can generate feelings of suspiciousness and paranoia, so that excessive amphetamine/cocaine users can be indistinguishable from paranoid schizophrenics. They also suffer numerous health problems and a reduced life expectancy. The high-addiction potential of CNS-stimulant drugs restricts their medical use. Nevertheless, amphetamines are clinically used for narcolepsy (sudden sleep onset during the day), and ADHD in young children. The upsurge in stimulant drug use among young children raises serious ethical concerns. Stimulant drugs have also been used as slimming agents, endurance aids for the armed forces, to boost athletic performance and for depression and neurasthenia. Several other stimulant drugs will be briefly discussed, including the atypical stimulant caffeine. It is consumed by 90% of the population in tea, coffee, chocolate, fizzy drinks and many over-the-counter medicines (e.g., analgesics). Regular caffeine users display a brief withdrawal syndrome; it is unclear whether caffeine generates real alertness gains or just allows normal alertness levels to be maintained.

Cocaine and its uses

The coca plant (*Erythroxylon coca*) grows in the mountains of Colombia and Bolivia. It was cultivated by the Incas in Peru who stated that it was a gift from the Sun God. Coca leaves were consumed during religious ceremonies and while working in gold and silver mines. Peruvian miners still use them to facilitate this strenuous work in the oxygen-depleted air of the Andes Mountains. The chewing of coca leaves was imitated by the Spanish conquistadors in the 16th century, just as they mimicked tobacco smoking (Chapter 5). They also attempted to import these coca leaves into Europe, but after lengthy sea trips little psychoactivity remained. In the Victorian era the alkaloid cocaine was extracted from the coca leaf, and this led to a range of preparations using coca extract as the active ingredient. One of the most popular beverages was Vin Mariani, a mixture of fortified wine and cocaine which became popular among the rich and famous. One regular user was the American President William McKinley. Another advocate and user was Pope Leo XIII who issued a gold medal to its originator Monsieur Mariani, citing him as a general benefactor for humanity (Palfai and Jankiewicz, 1997; Snyder, 1996). Many other cocaine beverages were marketed around this time, including Coca-Cola. At that time it contained extracts from the coca nut (containing **caffeine**), and cola leaf (containing **cocaine**) to form a tonic beverage. Later variants used soda water instead of still water, and it was marketed as an "intellectual beverage and temperance drink" (since it had no alcohol), in the soda fountains of American **drug** stores.

Sigmund Freud tried cocaine and extolled its effects in his glowing treatise on cocaine: *Ueber Coca*. He urged his fiancée and other friends to use it, including Fleischl-Marxow who was attempting to overcome morphine addiction, which he had developed after being prescribed morphine for a painful limb amputation. But Fleischl-Marxow soon increased his self-dosing and rapidly become addicted; he is probably the first documented case of cocaine **psychosis** (see below); this made Freud realise that the drug was problematical, and he ceased using it himself – although with difficulty. It was during this late Victorian period that the perils of cocaine dependence became increasingly apparent, so that governments restricted its availability. In 1906 the Coca-Cola company was required to remove the cocaine from the coca leaves (substituting more caffeine), although *treated* coca leaves are still used in the drink today. During the next 70 years, cocaine was used by various subcultural groups, but its popularity only increased again in the 1980s; this was due to several factors: reduced prices, higher purity and the success of government programmes to restrict amphetamine supplies. Cocaine production and its distribution was controlled by powerful international drug cartels. It soon became the major export commodity for several South American countries, including Colombia, Bolivia and Peru. Cocaine was termed the "yuppie" drug of the 1980s, when its use was linked to the expensive, fast life styles of film stars, supermodels and inner-city finance dealers. In 1990, 11% of the population in the USA reported having used it at least once. During the 2000s its use has become even more widespread, particular among the young; it is now strongly associated with all night clubbing and dancing.

Amphetamine and its uses

The plant ma huang (*Ephedra vulgaris*) was used as a herbal remedy in China for many centuries. In 1924 its active ingredient **ephedrine** was isolated and shown to be effective as a treatment for asthma, since it facilitates breathing by dilating the bronchioles in the lungs. In the USA, fears arose about the supplies of *Ephedra* from China running out, so pharmaceutical companies attempted to find a replacement; this led to the redis-covery of **amphetamine**, which had been synthesised many years earlier although its practical uses had not been recognised. Soon it was being used for a range of clinical problems, and in the 1930s the American Medical Association recommended am-phetamine for narcolepsy, asthma, depression and as a tonic, or "pick-me-up". It was available without prescription, and informed opinion stated that it was probably not addictive; this paved the way for its military use during World War II, when it was given to British, German, American, Japanese and other armed forces. It was routinely supplied to special operations groups who worked behind enemy lines for extended periods and was also used more widely. Seashore and Ivy (1953) reported a series of British trials into amphetamine, methamphetamine, caffeine and **placebo**. Various military scenarios were assessed: driving army trucks for 22 hours with only brief rest breaks; night-time truck driving under blackout conditions; all-night marches across a desert followed immediately by guard duty. Reaction time and other psycho-motor task performance was also assessed in the field, in order to measure whether vigilance was being maintained. Some benefits were found, although many assessment measures were not significantly improved by the active drugs. Stimulant drugs were also widely used in Japan, especially toward the end of the war, in an attempt to maintain the dwindling military capacity. After the war many civilian workers were addicted to amphetamines. This problem was tackled successfully by the Japanese government, by severely restricting the manufacture and commercial distribution of all stimulant drugs.

In post-war America, amphetamines were used by students cramming for exams and long-distance lorry drivers crossing the continent on extended runs. They were also used as slimming agents and general tonics, or pick-me-ups. During the 1950s many Americans were taking **barbiturates** at night as sleeping pills and then amphetamines in the morning to counteract the residual barbiturate-induced sedation. This problem was widespread. McKenzie (1965) described his experiences as the new medical officer at an American Air Force base. The pilots were flying B-52 bombers loaded with nuclear payloads on circumpolar routes near to the USSR (Russia). In order to provide continuous "coverage" the pilots flew extended periods around the clock. Often, they were required to sleep in the afternoon, take off late in the evening and then fly all night. McKenzie found that 70% of the base aircrew were being prescribed barbiturate sleeping pills to get to sleep and 64% were prescribed central nervous system (CNS) stimulants to make them more alert before flying. The problem was resolved in a few weeks by withdrawing all drugs and arranging for the flying schedules to be re-organized. Finally, stimulants have been closely associated with the music and dance scene, and this association has continued during the past few decades, when other amphetamine derivatives, such as MDMA (methyldioxymethamphetamine), or **Ecstasy**, have also been widely used (Chapter 6).

Administration and neurochemistry

Amphetamine is generally administered as oral capsules (Chapter 3). This route results in a gradual increase in drug concentration, which peaks in around an hour and maintains effective drug levels for 8–12 hours. Of all the administration routes it is the safest and is always used when amphetamines are given medically (see below). Amphetamine can also be injected, when it results in an immediate "hit" or "rush" (Table 4.1). This far more dangerous route is only used by recreational drug users who have developed tolerance to oral doses; the many problems associated with amphetamine injecting are outlined below. When Peruvians chew coca leaves the slow oral absorption results in a steady supply of cocaine into the circulation. This rather inefficient route produces comparatively low concentrations of cocaine and is thus associated with few drug-related problems. In contrast, when recreational users sniff, or snort, cocaine (hydrochloride), the thin capillaries in the nasal cavity readily absorb this small chemical into the blood circulation, producing the rapid hit or rush. Cocaine can also be injected, although this dangerous route causes the same types of problems as intravenous amphetamine. It can also be smoked in its crystalline, or freebase, form

Table 4.1. Stimulant drugs: clinical uses and recreational abuses.

Amphetamine	Clinically used for narcolepsy (sudden day-time onset sleep) and Attention Deficit Hyperactivity Disorder (ADHD); formerly used as a short-term slimming agent, as an antidepressant and to boost athletic performance; recreational use widespread; tolerance develops readily; highly addictive; regular users suffer many health problems and a reduced life expectancy; amphetamine psychosis may develop, with similar symptoms to acute paranoid schizophrenia.
Cocaine	Clinically used as a local anaesthetic during eye surgery; recreational use widespread; tolerance develops readily; highly addictive, especially crack cocaine; severe potential problems similar to amphetamine; users often become suspicious and paranoid, displaying antisocial and troublesome behaviour patterns.
MDMA (Ecstasy)	No clinical uses, although it has been used for psychotherapy; recreational use widespread; acute hyperthermic problems; midweek depression during neurochemical depletion; long-term problems include neurotoxicity, memory/cognitive deficits and a range of psychiatric problems.
Phenmetrazine	Clinically used for short-term appetite suppression; in the longer term its supposed benefits for weight control are very doubtful; recreational use is rare, with weaker CNS effects than amphetamine, but it is still addictive.
Strychnine	No clinical uses since it is lethal at low doses; present as an impurity in some recreational drugs produced in illicit laboratories; its presence as a low-dose impurity of LSD tablets may generate alertness.
Caffeine	No clinical uses; the most widely used social psychoactive drug in the world; few health problems at low and moderate doses; high doses can cause nervousness and disrupt sleep.

as **crack cocaine**; this produces an even stronger hit than snorting. The nasal route produces a hit within 3 minutes, whereas smoking crack produces a bolus of cocaine which reaches the brain 5–10 seconds later. The strength and immediacy of these effects, coupled with the rapid but equally severe rebound effects, makes crack cocaine one of the most addictive of all drugs, a dubious distinction it shares with inhaled/smoked methamphetamine or "ice".

In neurochemical terms, amphetamine and cocaine boost monoamine activity. Amphetamine has a threefold mode of action: first, it causes dopamine and noradrenaline to leak into the synaptic cleft; second, it boosts the amount of transmitter released during an **action potential**; and third, it inhibits the reuptake of neurotransmitter back into presynaptic vesicles. These three modes all result in more neurotransmitter being available at the **synapse**, thus generating an increase in postsynaptic stimulation. Cocaine exerts a similar overall effect, but mainly by reuptake inhibition. The main neurotransmitters affected are **dopamine** and **noradrenaline**, although serotonin is boosted to a lesser extent. These modes of action are outlined in Chapter 3, and the neurochemical rationale for drug tolerance is covered more fully in Chapter 10. The main differences between amphetamine and cocaine are their administration routes (summarised above) and the more rapid onset and shorter duration of action for cocaine.

Psychological effects in novice drug users

The initial effects of a small dose of amphetamine or cocaine are often very positive; these include feelings of alertness, increased energy, feelings of being powerful and a range of other positive mood states. The drug user often feels more confident and lively and perceives the world as more interesting and pleasurable. These positive moods are caused by stimulation of the **median forebrain bundle**, a tract of dopaminergic nerve fibres in the core of the brain, which underlies reward and pleasure (Pinel, 1998). Amphetamine and cocaine boost activity in these dopaminergic nerve tracts and, hence, increase the strength and intensity of these primary reward activities. Amphetamine and cocaine also boost activity in the **Ascending Reticular Activating System** (ARAS), the brainstem area that underlies alertness and arousal (Chapter 2). This boost in activity leads to greater mental vigilance and physical endurance. Thus, events and activity are perceived as more pleasurable, while thoughts and mood states become more intense.

However, the psychological effects are not always positive or pleasant, since negative feelings can also be enhanced; this can occur after low or moderate doses, particularly when the person is in a poor frame of mind before taking it, although negative moods seem to be most problematical following high doses. The combination of strong feelings of irritability, suspiciousness, power and/or invincibility may result in extremely dangerous behaviour. Thus, cocaine and amphetamine are both associated with acts of violence. Angrist (1987) described a number of drug-related murders, often of an apparently motiveless nature. Licata et al. (1993) similarly showed that cocaine could lead to increased violence not only in the street but also in laboratory-controlled trials. Amphetamine and cocaine can also induce stereotypy, or repetitive movements, in laboratory rats, and similar behaviour is also displayed by human recreational users, with motor tics and repetitive movements after high doses. Similar changes also occur with the amphetamine derivative MDMA (Chapter 6). CNS stimulants also have strong sympathomimetic effects. The increased heart rate and blood pressure can lead to an increased chance of cardiac arrest or cerebrovascular stroke, although most cardiac problems occur in regular users due to repeated drug-induced stress on the heart and circulatory system (see below).

Regular stimulant use: tolerance and related problems

Repeated drug use can lead to **tolerance**, where the same dose of drug has diminishing physiological and psychological effects. The various ways in which drug tolerance can develop are explained in Chapters 3 and 10. Regular stimulant users need to increase their dosage if they wish to generate the same strength of effect. For instance, a novice amphetamine user may start with a single oral dose of 5 or 10 mg and may stick to that dosage if they take it only rarely, but, once they start using it more regularly, their friends and more experienced peers may suggest taking several tablets together. Several months later they may be using 50 mg each time, but tolerance will still occur to this higher dose. Eventually, they may need to increase their daily consumption to 1,000 mg or more, but this can be very costly. They may graduate to the more effective but far more dangerous route of intravenous injection; this generates a rapid upsurge in drug and a more powerful rush, but further tolerance will still develop. The heavily dependent user may now binge, by taking the drug continuously for days without sleep or respite – until eventually crashing. Alternatively, in order to obtain the increasingly elusive rush, they may mix stimulants with other types of psychoactive drug.

Another problem is **cross-tolerance**, where tolerance to one drug affects any other drug with a similar neurochemical profile. Regular dosing with amphetamine leads to the reduced density of dopamine and noradrenaline postsynaptic **receptors** (down-regulation; Chapter 3), which is the neurochemical basis for drug tolerance; but, this means that any other drug that affects dopamine or noradrenaline will also be affected. Thus, a regular amphetamine user will display tolerance to cocaine, even though they have never taken it before! Cross-tolerance has important practical implications for recreational stimulant users. If they have developed tolerance to one drug, it will not be particularly effective to try other drugs within the same class. This is another reason many stimulant users, including users of MDMA, or Ecstasy, become polydrug users (Chapter 6). They mix and combine drugs in order to achieve the increasingly elusive hit. There are numerous types of drug combination not only with other stimulants, such as MDMA, but also with opiates and other CNS depressants (Chapters 5–9).

Health consequences of stimulant abuse

Acute health problems are those that directly follow drug ingestion, whereas chronic problems develop after repeated use. Stimulants, such as amphetamine or cocaine, can affect a wide range of physiological functions. All drugs within this class are sympatho-mimetic – they boost or mimic the sympathetic nervous system; this is the part of autonomic nervous system concerned with preparing the body for action (Chapter 2). Sympathetic nervous system stimulation will lead to increased heart rate, faster breathing, increased body temperature and a redistribution of the blood from the gut toward the muscles, in order to prepare the body for fight or flight (Pinel, 1998). By boosting sympathetic nervous system activity, stimulant drugs facilitate physical activity and alertness, which is why their use is strongly associated with all night clubbing and dancing. However, this increase in sympathetic nervous system activity also heightens the tendency toward physical aggression. Another function affected is sexual behaviour, and a minority of users use stimulants primarily for enhanced sexual performance (Angrist, 1987), although others state that quality of the experience is not increased. The acute boost in sympathetic activity induced by cocaine or amphetamine can have fatal consequences. Death can occur because of cerebral haemorrhage (bleeding within the brain), convulsion or cardiac arrest. Most fatalities occur in those using high doses, following the development of neuronal tolerance. Overdosing can also occur with illicit drug supplies that are less adulterated and thus purer.

However, the majority of health problems are caused by chronic, or repeated, drug use. Once the stimulant abuser has progressed to injecting, their whole life tends to be dominated by drug taking. Similar problems characterise those who smoke crack cocaine or ice amphetamine. Their two main concerns are obtaining drug supplies and using the drugs. They often have few other interests. The most extreme examples of this are seen in the crack houses of American inner cities, where people will do anything for the drug, with thieving, prostitution and murder all commonplace (Maisto et al., 1998). The general health of regular stimulant users tends to be poor, since they fail to eat regularly, lose weight and are more susceptible to diseases. Drug-abusing parents often fail to care for their children, while drug injectors are susceptible to the usual problems associated with syringe sharing: hepatitis, **HIV** (human immunodeficiency virus) and **AIDS** (acquired immunity deficiency syndrome). Snorting cocaine leads to a thinning of the septum (the dividing wall between the nostrils) in the nose. It becomes increasingly tender and then develop holes or lesions. In former times, drug squad police officers used to pinch the nose of a suspected cocaine user to test their initial hunch – but this is no longer seen as acceptable practice! The small chemical size of cocaine and amphe-tamine allow them to readily cross the placenta, so that pregnant drug-users have an increased incidence of spontaneous abortion, fetal death and birth complications. Live babies of cocaine-using mothers tend to be underweight and can show signs of acute drug withdrawal. They sometimes demonstrate neurological deficits, are more at risk from sudden infant death syndrome (**SIDS**), or cot death, and often demonstrate learning disabilities during childhood. However, these problems almost certainly reflect a combination of adverse factors: multiple drug use, poverty, poor nutrition and inadequate pre/postnatal care.

Drug-related problems are not restricted to socially disadvantaged groups. Stimulant drugs can be expensive, and their use is often associated with the affluent young and upwardly mobile. Cocaine use, cocaine dependence and cocaine-related deaths are regularly reported among Hollywood film stars, supermodels, sports person-alities and financial dealers. Across all social groups, there is also an association with the personality dimension of sensation seeking, with stimulant drug users reporting a desire for fast action, risk taking and immediate gratification; but, while the immediate drug effects are often seductively exciting, their regular use makes people increasingly suspicious and untrustworthy. Some users become small-time dealers in order to fund their own drug taking. However, former networks of friends now become networks of fellow abusers and petty dealers, with everyone trying to rip each other off. The regular stimulant users themselves often state that they are not pleasant drugs to be involved with. In overall terms they are probably the most pernicious drugs of abuse. The hippie guru and beat poet Allen Ginsburg, an eloquent advocate for cannabis and **LSD** (lysergic acid diethylamide), was strongly against the use of speed (amphetamine) and other stimulant drugs: "Speed is antisocial, paranoid making, its a drag, bad for your body, generally speaking, in the long run uncreative and it is a plague on the whole dope industry" (Ginsberg speaking in 1965; cited in Palfai and Jankiewicz, 1997).

The treatment for drug **dependence** is covered in detail elsewhere (Chapter 10), but the general principles apply to stimulants. Abstinence is initially very unpleasant, but it is not the main problem. Although the drug cravings can be severe, they are not life-threatening and subside fairly soon as long as abstinence is maintained. Various substitute medications (antidepressants, etc.) have been investigated as potential aids during the immediate withdrawal period, but placebo-controlled trials show that they provide little real assistance (Grilly, 2001). The main problem is how to prevent **relapse**, as it is with every other form of drug addiction. The former addict's network of friends and acquaintances are often involved with the same illicit drugs, which provide a core for their lifestyle. Furthermore, many regular users become small-time dealers, so that their financial income becomes dependent on drugs. As with alcohol dependence and opiate addiction, a fundamental change in lifestyle and friendship networks is necessary to prevent relapse. Some examples of how this may be facilitated are outlined in later sections on alcohol and opiate addiction (Chapter 10).

Clinical uses

When amphetamine was first introduced it was seen as potentially useful for a range of clinical disorders. Amphetamine inhalers were used to relieve the symptoms of asthma for many years, until bronchodilator drugs without CNS activity were developed. Newer drugs, such as salbutamol, can widen the bronchioles to facilitate breathing without modifying alertness. Amphetamine was used as an **antidepressant** in the 1930s, before modern antidepressants were developed (Chapter 12). Stimulant drugs can certainly improve mood states in the short term: Sigmund Freud used cocaine to relieve his depression. But these effects tend to wane as tolerance develops, so that they lose their effectiveness in the longer term. Amphetamine was also recommended as a general tonic, or pick-me-up, particularly for "neurasthenia", an outmoded clinical term that encompassed a range of problems including lassitude, nervousness and lethargy. Cocaine used to be used as a local anaesthetic and is still used during eye surgery. Novocaine, or procaine, was developed from cocaine and is now widely used during dental surgery. An injection of novocaine blocks the peripheral pain messages from the tooth to the brainstem, so that pain perception does not occur (Chapter 2).

Stimulant drugs are banned by the International Olympics Committee (IOC) and all other major sports organisations; this is because they can improve athletic performance, sometimes quite dramatically. When highly trained college athletes were given matching capsules of either 14 mg amphetamine or placebo in double-blind trials, many of them recorded their "personal bests" (fastest performance ever) under the stimulant drug. Significant improvements were found across a range of sports, including sprinting, long-distance running, swimming events and some field sports (Smith and Beecher, 1959; details in Parrott, 1987). Stimulant drugs also reduce appetite and feelings of hunger and have therefore been used in the past as slimming agents. Several amphetamine derivatives are currently used for this purpose; this topic is covered in the next section, "Other stimulant drugs". The main clinical disorder for which amphetamine is currently prescribed is **narcolepsy**; this is a rare disorder where the person falls asleep suddenly during the day-time, with little warning. The fast electroencephalograph (EEG) brainwaves needed for alertness (alpha and beta) rapidly change to the slower brainwaves indicative of sleep (theta) in a few seconds. This disabling disorder limits the range of potential occupations for narcolepsy sufferers; thus, they cannot drive or use dangerous machinery. However, by boosting the arousal system, amphetamine can reduce the incidence of narcoleptic episodes (Soldatos et al., 1979).

The other main area where stimulant drugs are prescribed is **Attention Deficit Hyperactivity Disorder** (ADHD). An increasing number of young children are being diagnosed with ADHD: they display short attention spans, find it difficult to sit still, often sleep for short periods and are seen as disruptive at school. Several stimulant drugs have been shown to be clinically useful in ADHD, including amphetamine, **methylphenidate** (Ritalin) and pemoline. Placebo-controlled trials have shown that they improve attention span and allow children to undertake their school work more effectively (Brown and Cooke, 1994). Most drugs and behaviour textbooks describe these effects as paradoxical ... how can a stimulant drug reduce hyperactivity, when it should be expected to increase it? However, it is not paradoxical if ADHD children are conceptualised as cortically underaroused. This explanatory model is closely related to the relationship between cortical arousal and the personality dimension of extraversion in adults (Eysenck, 1983). Extraverts are seen as cortically underaroused: they seek out environmental stimulation in order to boost their understimulated cerebral cortex. Introverts are naturally aroused, which is why they prefer quieter and less exciting activities. Children with ADHD can be seen as chronically underaroused, so their constant search for stimulation and excitement can be seen as natural – even if very exhausting for their carers. Administration of stimulant drugs will however boost their cortical arousal and, thus, reduce their need for environmental stimulation. By boosting the reticular-activating system, a given amount of external stimulation or internal cognitive ideas will have a greater alerting effect, so that their need for general stimulation is reduced.

There are however problems with the concept of ADHD as a clinical disorder. In the USA the number of child prescriptions for methylphenidate rose by 500% in the mid-1990s (Maisto et al., 1998), while an even more dramatic rise in prescriptions from a near-zero baseline has occurred during this period in the UK. Although profitable for the pharmaceutical industry, the reasons for this dramatic increase in clinical diagnoses need to be uncovered. Possible sources include artificial food additives, junk foods or otherwise poor diets. Another is less appropriate modes of play, including computer games, watching television or reading books, rather than physically tiring psychosocial sports like football. However, perhaps the main cause is our altered expectations about appropriate child behaviour. Until recently, high spirits, a preference for running about rather than sitting still, fidgeting, arguing and fighting have been seen as annoying but normal behaviours for 5-year-old children – particularly boys, who comprise the majority of ADHD diagnoses. Now, these same behaviours are seen as "disruptive", and those children who display them are often diagnosed with a *clinical disorder*! This has also been linked to the pressure for school achievement at an increasingly younger age. More of the school curriculum is being dedicated to narrow, convergent skills, such as writing, mathematics and reading or computer terminal work; this has led to a reduction in the time available for physical exercise, non-directed play and other creative activities. Another problem may be that many parents are in full-time employment and intolerant of the childish demands of their children. All these questions raise the issue of whether it is ethically correct to administer powerful psychoactive drugs to young children, particularly when the behaviours being "treated" are not causing suffering to the children themselves, but are primarily a problem for their parents and teachers.

Other stimulant drugs

There are a large number of drugs with stimulant properties. During the 1980s the amphetamine derivatives MDMA, or Ecstasy, became popular as a recreational drug. It not only displays some similarities to the parent compound but also has a number of unique aspects (Chapter 6). Several amphetamine derivatives have weak effects on alertness but comparatively stronger appetite suppression effects. Several are marketed as slimming aids including **phenmetrazine**, although in the UK these drugs are only available on private prescription. They reduce feelings of hunger in the short term and are thus well received by the clients, at least for the first few weeks. However, they do not have longer term benefits for weight control. The attempt to achieve permanent weight loss through **anorectic** drugs is always problematical, for the same reason that any short-term dieting is ineffective. Maintenance of a healthy weight depends on the permanent adoption of an appropriate dietary intake, coupled with lifestyle improvements that include increased exercise. The use of stimulant anorectics for weight control is also inadvisable because of their addiction potential. Thus, amphetamine was originally marketed as an appetite suppressant, but it had to be withdrawn because of its abuse. Phenmetrazine was introduced as a slimming aid in the 1950s. In Sweden the government successfully curtailed the illicit supplies of amphetamine, but many amphetamine abusers switched to phenmetrazine. Thus, the original Swedish amphetamine abuse problem evolved into a new problem with phenmetrazine abuse. Another appetite suppressant is **fenfluramine**, which, although an amphetamine derivative, has a different neurochemical profile and comparatively weak mood and cognitive effects.

Strychnine is a convulsant, used commercially as a rat poison. However, at low doses it can act as a CNS stimulant. Small amounts of strychnine are sometimes present in LSD tablets produced in illicit laboratories. It has been suggested that the degree to which an LSD tablet is alerting may reflect its strychnine content (Chapter 6). **Khat**

(*Catha edulis*), or Qat, leaves are grown in Ethiopia and other counties on the Horn of Africa. When chewed the active ingredient **cathinone** (norpseudoephedrine) is released, with effects broadly similar to those of amphetamine; so, it is also very addictive. Khat leaves are legally imported into many Western European ports, and during the 1990s their use spread from the original immigrant users to the wider population. There are numerous other drugs with stimulant properties. Indeed, the list of stimulants banned by the IOC covers several pages. Details of some of these other drugs may be found in standard drugs and behaviour textbooks (Grilly, 2001; Julien, 2001; Maisto et al., 1998). Finally, **nicotine** is often categorized as a CNS stimulant, although its very different neurochemical actions and unique psychopharmacological profile make it quite distinct from the true stimulants: for instance, regular cigarette smokers do *not* display higher levels of daily alertness than non-smokers, but do suffer from reduced alertness when nicotine-deprived (Chapter 5).

Caffeine

Caffeine is the most widely taken drug in the world, with an estimated 90% of adults using it. In numerous societies it is consumed in tea, coffee and chocolate. Tea was originally taken as a herbal remedy in China millennia ago, and from there its use spread worldwide. An average cup of tea may contain around 50–70 mg caffeine, depending on the variety of tea, duration of brewing, size of cup and other factors, so that a moderate tea drinker may consume 300–400 mg caffeine each day. Coffee is sometimes stated to have originated in Ethiopia, whence it was introduced into Western Europe via Arabia; however, its origins probably reach back to Neolithic times. Like tea it has now become a worldwide beverage. A large cup of strong, freshly brewed coffee can have up to 170 mg caffeine, whereas instant coffee has far less; even "decaffeinated" coffee contains a small residue of caffeine (Table 4.2). Other dietary sources of caffeine include chocolate and fizzy beverages. Thus, children and adolescents are frequent consumers of caffeine. Another source of caffeine is over-the-counter medicines. Cold relief preparations, headache pills and general pick-me-ups, such as Lucozade, contain caffeine, sometimes in quite large amounts (Parrott, 1998a). These palliatives may help prevent the development of caffeine withdrawal symptoms in

Table 4.2. Dietary sources of caffeine.

Dietary source	Average caffeine content (mg per cup)
Coffee: freshly brewed	70–180
Coffee: instant	50–100
Coffee: decaffeinated	2–4
Tea: strong brew	40–90
Tea: weak brew or green tea	20–40
Chocolate: hot drink	5–20
Chocolate: confectionary bar	5–25
Fizzy beverage (Coca-Cola, others)	20–50
Over-the-counter medicines	5–100

regular tea/coffee drinkers who reduce their normal tea/coffee intake during illness. Many other species of plant contain caffeine or other xanthine derivatives, such as theophylline; these include mate and cola from Africa and yoco from South America, which are all used to make local beverages.

Caffeine does not directly alter catecholamine activity and is therefore neurochemically very different from amphetamine and cocaine. It exerts its psychoactive effects by blocking adenosine receptors (Snyder et al., 1981). **Adenosine** is a neurotransmitter of the purine family and has inhibitory effects in both the central and peripheral nervous systems (Chapter 2). By blocking adenosine receptors, caffeine reduces its inhibitory influences, so that the overall effect is slightly excitatory. However, as with many other psychoactive drugs, neuronal tolerance can occur. The regular use of caffeine blocks the adenosine receptors and the number of postsynaptic receptors is increased (note: the adenosine receptor system is up-regulated). However, when the regular coffee/tea drinker goes without caffeine the high density of adenosine receptors means that the overall level of inhibitory activity is increased. Thus, without caffeine they now feel tired and lethargic; this raises the conundrum of many psychoactive drugs. Does the caffeine-adapted organism gain positive advantages from their drug use, or do they need a regular intake of caffeine just to prevent the unpleasant abstinence symptoms from developing (James, 1994)? This question is debated below.

Caffeine is lipid-soluble and, thus, easily absorbed from the gut. However, it takes 30–60 minutes for peak plasma concentrations to occur and around an hour for psychoactive effects to be detected in placebo-controlled trials. The feelings of alertness when drinking the first cup of tea or coffee in the morning are thus an example of conditioned anticipation, rather than a pharmacological effect. Various factors contribute to this. Before and after waking, the circadian biorhythm is already on an upward curve, with alertness and body temperature increasing naturally irrespective of other factors (Smith, 1992). Thus, waking is already accompanied by a gradual increase in alertness. There are also conditioned factors that allow beverage consumption to be positively associated with increased alertness. Then, throughout the day caffeine intake follows a typical routine, with tea and coffee breaks at set times. These are often periods for rest and sociability, so that, although they allow caffeine levels to be restored, the positive resultant feelings reflect a combination of psychosocial factors, real psychoactive effects and conditioned drug effects. This pattern holds true for the other psychosocial drugs, most typically tobacco smoking (Chapter 5).

Regular tea/coffee drinkers report a range of psychobiological effects, which can be categorized into two groups: cortical arousal and emotional arousal. An acute dose of caffeine in an overnight-deprived regular tea/coffee drinker will generate EEG brainwaves indicative of increased arousal, coupled with feelings of greater alertness. This increase in arousal is also evident in event-related potentials, which is a psychophysiological index of information processing (Ruijter et al., 2000). Therefore, regular users generally demonstrate faster responses and greater vigilance after drinking caffeinated beverages, in comparison with decaffeinated drinks (Brice and Smith, 2001); hence, the widespread use of caffeine when attention needs to be maintained at work and during endurance tasks, such as long-distance driving. Caffeine also boosts emotional arousal, and this is exemplified in feelings of nervousness, tension, jitteriness and irritability. Some very high coffee users develop a disorder termed **caffeinism**. Their daily intake of caffeine between 600 and 1,500 mg/day can increase nervousness to such an extent that they may be diagnosed as suffering from anxiety neurosis. However, once their caffeine intake is reduced, their nervous symptoms rapidly subside. Caffeine can also interfere with sleep, since it reduces the amount of EEG slow-wave sleep and increases nocturnal awakenings. While most caffeine research has focused on moderate to heavy users, many take caffeine less frequently (50–150 mg/day) and around 10% of the adult population avoid caffeine. In controlled trials, the latter tend to respond adversely to caffeine, reporting unpleasant feelings of tension, even at quite small doses.

When excessive caffeine users are deprived of their usual supplies, they generally display a withdrawal syndrome. The core symptoms are tiredness, or lethargy, which may even result in falling asleep during the day. Another withdrawal symptom is headache, while individual drinkers also report a range of more idiosyncratic feelings. The caffeine withdrawal syndrome typically starts within 12–24 hours of abstinence and may be pronounced for a couple of days in regular users, although most symptoms dissipate within a few days. It is only recently that the caffeine withdrawal syndrome has been researched adequately, and it has been shown that mood and cognitive performance can deteriorate during this period (James, 1994; Rogers et al., 1995); this has given rise to a debate over whether caffeine provides true psychobiological gains or whether the positive changes only reflect the reversal of abstinence effects. Some researchers have suggested that caffeine leads to true psychobiological gains and that caffeine increases alertness and improves sustained attention ability (Lieberman et al., 1987; Brice and Smith, 2001). Others have suggested that the supposedly positive effects only represent the reversal of abstinence effects (James, 1994; Rogers et al., 1995). There is supporting evidence for both explanatory models; it may be that the issue can only be resolved by long-term prospective studies, such as those undertaken with regular cigarette smokers (Chapter 5).

Questions

1   Summarize the acute neurochemical and behavioural effects of acute doses of amphetamine and cocaine.

2   In psychobiological terms what happens when a stimulant drug is taken repeatedly?

3   Which factors influence the addiction potential for cocaine and amphetamine?

4   Why was the hippie poet Allen Ginsburg against the use of stimulant drugs?

5   Describe the historical and contemporary clinical uses for stimulant drugs.

6   You are employed as a school psychologist and a 5-year-old pupil has just been diagnosed with ADHD. The parent and teacher have asked for your expert advice. What advice would you give them *and* the child?

7   Describe the use of caffeine and its psychobiological effects.

Key references and reading

Brice C and Smith A (2001). The effects of caffeine on simulated driving, subjective alertness and sustained attention. *Human Psychopharmacology*, **16**, 523–531.

Gupta BS and Gupta U (1999). *Caffeine and Behaviour: Current Views and Research Trends.* CRC Press, London.

James JE (1994). Does caffeine enhance or merely restore degraded psychomotor performance? *Neuropsychobiology*, **30**, 124–125.

King GR and Ellinwood EH (1992) Amphetamines and other stimulants. In: JH Lowinson and P Ruiz (eds), *Substance Abuse: A Comprehensive Textbook* (pp. 247–266). Williams & Wilkins, Baltimore.

Snyder SH (1996). Stimulants. *Drugs and the Brain* (pp. 121–149). Freeman & Co., New York.

Chapter 5

Nicotine and cigarette smoking

Overview

Cigarette smoking causes around 130,000 deaths each year in the UK, yet worldwide the proportion of adults who smoke tobacco continues to increase. Deaths are caused by tar and carbon monoxide in the inhaled smoke. Tar-induced deaths include lung cancer, throat cancer, jaw cancer, pneumonia and emphysema. Carbon monoxide reduces the oxygen-carrying capacity of the blood, causing circulatory problems in the heart and other organs. Therefore, numerous deaths occur through heart attack and numerous limb amputations are required because of peripheral tissue death and gangrene. Other smoke-induced problems include premature skin wrinkling, erectile dysfunction and sexual impotence. Despite this, numerous children commence smoking between the ages of 11 and 15, with female adolescents the main target group for tobacco advertisers. Tobacco smoke generates a "hit" of nicotine in the brain 7–10 seconds after inhalation. Nicotine affects the nicotinic acetylcholine neurons in complex ways, with regular smoking displaying a number of cholinergic adaptations. For many years it was believed that nicotine relieved stress and boosted alertness. However, it is now recognised that nicotine dependence causes stress. Thus, the feelings of contentment and relief on smoke inhalation only represent the reversal of unpleasant abstinence effects. Regular smokers feel tense and irritable without nicotine, and cigarette smoke reverses these abstinence effects for a brief period. The repeated experience of tension in-between cigarettes causes tobacco smokers to suffer from increased levels of daily stress and depression; this explains why adolescents who take up smoking become more stressed and depressed and why quitting smoking leads to enduring mood improvements. However, stopping smoking can be difficult, although successful cessation packages have been devised. They often employ nicotine substitute devices, such as gum, transdermal patches or nicotine inhalers. Cigarette smokers who manage to quit soon experience marked health improvements: better lung functioning, improved cardiac output and reduced rates of cancer.

Tobacco smoking

Leaves of the tobacco plant (*Nicotiana tabacum*) were smoked by the indigenous peoples of North and South America, before the arrival of the Spanish conquistadors in the 16th century. Christopher Columbus wrote in his log that he had met: "men and women who carried fire in their hands, and who smoked to keep off the tiredness." This is the earliest known description of a psychological function underlying tobacco smoking, but notice its ambiguity. Thus, it may be that the smoker benefits from greater alertness or that they just feel tired without **nicotine**. The empirical evidence for these contrasting explanations will be examined later. These early descriptions also emphasised how smoking was easy to imitate, yet difficult to stop. When the invading soldiers were reprimanded for copying the native habit and "drinking smoke", they replied that it was not in their power to refrain (Mangan and Golding, 1984; Parrott, 1998a). Smoking soon became fashionable in many European cities. Many initiates saw it as clever and amusing, whereas others described it as disgusting. King James I of Britain in his *Counterblaste to Tobacco* described smoking as: "A custome lothsome to the Nose, hermful to the Braine, dangerous to the Lungs, and of the blacke stinking fume therof, neerest resembing the horrible Stigian smoke of the pit that is bottom-lesse." Nevertheless, governments soon realised that it could provide a valuable source of revenue, explaining why they are often loath to take effective action against it. Pipe smoking, cigars and chewing tobacco were the main forms of consumption until the end of the 19th century, but the development of commercial cigarette machines allowed cigarette smoking to gain its preponderance in the 20th century.

The peak period of cigarette consumption in the UK was during the Second World War, when 70% of adult males were smokers. A proportion stopped smoking at the end of the war when cigarettes were no longer given out free – the armed forces had been provided with cigarettes as part of their rations. Other smokers quit when its adverse health effects became more widely known during the 1960s, with the UK and US governments funding public education campaigns. By the 1990s around 30% of adult British males were smokers. At the beginning of the 20th century few females used tobacco, and it was a social taboo for women to be seen smoking in public. With female emancipation the proportion of female smokers increased, so that by the mid-1990s, there were similar numbers of male and female smokers. If current trends continue, female smokers will outnumber males during the 21st century; indeed, this is already occurring among the youngest age groups. Female adolescents between the ages of 11 and 15 are now the main target group for cigarette-advertising campaigns. This gender imbalance is heightened by the less successful cessation rates in females.

Adult rates of cigarette consumption have reduced in a few countries, such as the USA, the UK, Australia and New Zealand, where anti-smoking health campaigns have been most prominent. However, in many other Western countries, smoking is still accepted as the norm, even in otherwise enlightened Scandinavian societies, such as Denmark. Throughout most of the Third World the proportion of adults who smoke is still increasing, from the current estimated rate of 47% of adult males and 12% of adult females. In China and many other developing countries the rates of cigarette smoking are particularly high, with local tobacco products very cheap and the more expensive American brands seen as status symbols.

Adverse health effects

When organic plant matter is burnt the resulting smoke contains numerous chemicals, including many that are poisonous and/or cancerous. Over 400 chemicals have been measured in unadulterated tobacco smoke; yet tobacco companies add chemicals, such as ammonia, to intensify the nicotine hit. Some of the chemical components of tobacco smoke are listed in Mangan and Golding (1984). In health terms the two constituents of most concern are **carbon monoxide** (CO) and tar: a generic term for the heavy organic chemicals (such as nitrosamines) which form the visible smoke mist. Around 4% of this smoke comprises carbon monoxide (CO), which is readily taken up by the haemoglobin in the red corpuscles of the blood. Haemoglobin normally combines with oxygen in the air to form oxyhaemoglobin, which is then transported by the circulation to all tissues throughout the body. The oxygen is then released, where it is utilised in basic cell metabolism. Without oxygen, cells are unable to undertake these fundamental energy-dependent processes and eventually die. Unfortunately, haemoglobin binds with carbon monoxide far more readily than with oxygen, so that eventually 15% of the haemoglobin of a heavy smoker is bound to carbon monoxide; this leads to oxygen deficiency in peripheral tissues, gradually causing cell death in those regions served by the smallest blood vessels. Therefore, tobacco smokers develop premature skin ageing and wrinkling – one of the health messages that most influences the attitudes of adolescent females. In males the blood supply to the penis is reduced, eventually causing erectile dysfunction and sexual impotence – information that is far more influential with adolescent males! These peripheral circulation problems also lead to arteriosclerosis in the lower limbs, causing leg pains, tissue death and gangrene, which then necessitates limb amputation; this can be prevented if the smoker immediately stops smoking, since the blood supply rapidly improves. However, if they continue smoking a series of amputations may then be necessary: first, the toes and feet; then, the leg below the knee; and, finally, the leg above the knee. Around 500 limb amputations are undertaken in the UK each year for this reason. There is an infamous photograph of a smoker who has had both legs amputated and both arms surgically removed because of smoking-induced circulatory problems, but who still continues to smoke! The photo reveals him sitting in his chair, leaning toward a lit cigarette, held by an ingenious wire contraption fixed around his neck.

The heart is covered by an elaborate network of microcapillaries that supply it with the large amounts of oxygen it needs. Tobacco smoking reduces this crucial supply of oxygen. Thus, the single highest cause of death in tobacco smokers is cardiac arrest or heart attack, while numerous other cardiac disorders occur in smokers. Doll and Peto (1976) reported the following incidence rates for heart disease in their classic study of British doctors. In the under-45 age group there were 7 per 100,000 of non-smokers, 41 per 100,000 of light smokers (1–14 cigarettes/day) and 104 per 100,000 of heavy smokers (+25 cigarettes/day). Similar trends were apparent in older age groups, although the actual incidence rates were higher in every group, because of the numerous factors that cause heart disease in middle and old age. Smoking exacerbates all circulatory disorders. Diabetes mellitus leads to circulatory problems, so that heart disease is considerably higher in diabetics than non-diabetics. Tobacco exacerbates these circulatory deficits, so that diabetic smokers suffer from even higher rates of cardiac disorder and death. Circulatory impairments can also affect brain functioning, so that cigarette smokers suffer from increased rates of cerebrovascular stroke. Carbon monoxide crosses the placenta, so that the fetus suffers from oxygen deficits in its developing tissues. Thus, pregnant smokers give birth to more stillborn babies, live births are generally underweight and the incidence of postnatal complications is increased. The placenta of smoking females tends to be larger than normal, possibly as an adaptive mechanism to provide the developing fetus with oxygen.

Tar is the other main component of tobacco smoke which makes it so lethal. Tar comprises the mist of heavy organic chemicals that form the visible smoke cloud. On inhalation, much of this tar settles on the respiratory tract as a sticky residue. One practical demonstration of this is to ask a smoker to inhale though a handkerchief – a clear ring of black tar will be visible. Then, ask them to exhale through a different part of the handkerchief. Far less tar will now be visible, indicating the amount of tar that has been retained in the lungs. These tar droplets are necessary to deliver **nicotine** into the lungs. Nicotine can only be absorbed once it has settled onto the lung surface as minute tar droplets; this explains why the correlation between tar and nicotine delivery for any brand of cigarette is always very high ($r = +0.90$). Tar sticks to every part of the airways: lungs, upper bronchioles, tongue, gum, lips and throat. Many of the constituents of tar are carcinogenic, particularly the nitrosamines (Mangan and Golding, 1984). Cancers of all regions of the respiratory tract are thus markedly increased in tobacco users, although the region mostly affected will depend on the exact mode of tobacco administration. Cigarette smokers inhale smoke deep into their lungs and tend to develop lung cancers. Doll and Peto (1976) found that moderate smokers (15–24 cigarettes/day) had *10* times the lung cancer rate compared with non-smokers, whereas heavy smokers (+25 cigarettes/day) had *22* times the lung cancer rate for non-smokers.

Pipe and cigar smokers retain the smoke in the mouth (for better nicotine absorption from alkaline pipe/cigar smoke) and, thus, develop cancers in the mouth cavity and upper bronchioles. Oral tobacco chewers also tend to develop cancers of the gums, lips and jaw. Tobacco chewing is particularly prevalent in the southern states of the USA, with around 12 million regular tobacco chewers, but is also common in such countries as Sweden. The wad of soggy tobacco tends to be held in one part of the cheek, and this is replaced when the nicotine supply is depleted. Day after day, the cancerous tars from the soggy tobacco are concentrated in one small region of the mouth, and this is where cancers often develop. Furthermore, whereas lung cancers take 20–30 years to commence, mouth cancers can develop after only 8–10 years of tobacco chewing. Thus, many 20-year-old tobacco chewers develop cancers of the tongue, gum or jaw, which are difficult to treat medically. Surgical removal of the affected jaw region may be effective, although it is often unsuccessful.

Tobacco companies promote low-tar cigarettes, which are used by many smokers in the mistaken belief that they are less unhealthy. However, these cigarettes use the same tobacco leaves, the only difference being that low-tar cigarettes have numerous small air holes in front of the filter, so that the smoker inhales smoke diluted by air. Ultra low-tar cigarettes contain even more air holes, so that the tobacco smoke is further diluted. Smokers compensate for this diluted smoke in several conscious and unconscious ways. Many smokers partially cover the air holes with their fingers, so that the inhaled smoke contains a higher proportion of tar and nicotine than that stated on the cigarette packet. They also inhale more deeply and retain the smoke in their lungs

Table 5.1. Adverse medical effects of tobacco smoking, and health benefits of smoking cessation.

Tar	The nitrosamines and many other organic chemicals in tobacco smoke cause various forms of cancer: cigarette smoking causes cancers of the lung and upper respiratory tract; pipe and cigar smoking cause cancers in the mouth and upper respiratory tract; tobacco chewing causes cancers of the gums, lips and jaw, particularly where the wad of soggy tobacco rests between the gums and tongue. (Note: cancers *outside* the respiratory tract are similar in smokers and non-smokers; thus, smokers are not simply less healthy.)
Carbon monoxide	This combines with haemoglobin in the blood, reducing its oxygen carrying capacity; this leads to oxygen deficiency in all cells supplied by narrow blood capillaries: toes and feet resulting in cell death, gangrene and limb amputation (Reynaud's syndrome); legs resulting in arteriosclerosis, leg pains and limb amputation (Reynaud's syndrome); skin resulting in skin wrinkling and premature ageing; penis resulting in reduced blood supply, erectile dysfunction and premature impotence; heart resulting in many different forms of cardiac disorder, arteriosclerosis, heart attack, exacerbation of cardiac problems caused by other factors (hypertension, diabetes) and reduced success for cardiac surgery; fetus resulting in more prenatal, perinatal and postnatal problems, more stillbirths, birth difficulties and underweight live births.
Nicotine	Few direct health effects; chronic increase in heart rate may exacerbate cardiac hypertension; highly addictive, causing increased stress and depression (see text).
Passive smoking	Non-smokers who breathe air polluted by tobacco smoke can develop the same disorders as smokers: lung cancer, pulmonary diseases, asthmatic attacks, increased rates of pneumonia and bronchitis in children, more debilitating coughs and colds, children spend more time off-school and infant cot deaths (SIDS).
Health benefits of cessation	Lung function improves almost immediately, with aerobic tasks becoming easier; oxygen supply to all tissues improves rapidly, with reduced leg pains and better cardiac functioning; the incidence of heart attack is reduced by 50% within 1 year; respiratory cancers reduce more gradually, with lung cancer rates returning nearer to those of non-smokers within 15 years; and significantly reduced stress 3–6 months after quitting.

Based on Parrott (1998a).

for longer. The time between inhalations is also reduced, so that each cigarette is now smoked more intensively. Finally, more cigarettes are smoked each day, which is why these brands are promoted so heavily by the tobacco industry. These forms of behavioural compensation are generally effective at maintaining desired nicotine levels; but, this means that the smoker continues to inhale similar amounts of tar and carbon monoxide. Thus, there are few health gains for regular smokers who move to low-tar brands. The main effect is an increase the number of cigarettes purchased and smoked each day (Table 5.1).

Passive smoking

When a non-smoker breathes in air polluted by tobacco smoke, nicotine enters their blood circulation, carbon monoxide combines with haemoglobin and the cancerous tars settle on their lungs and respiratory tract. It has been estimated that when a non-smoker works in a smoky office for eight hours, it is equivalent to actively smoking 1–2 cigarettes. In enclosed atmospheres, such as cars with closed windows, submarines or aircraft cabins, the cumulative effects are even more marked; this explains why passive smokers often develop the same tobacco-related diseases as active smokers. One of the first studies to empirically demonstrate this was undertaken in Japan, where cigarette smoking was predominantly a male activity. Hirayama (1981) investigated the incidence of lung cancers in non-smoking females and found a doubled cancer rate in those women whose husbands smoked tobacco. Numerous further studies have confirmed the adverse health effects of passive smoking (NIH, 1993). Passive smoking causes lung cancer, respiratory coughs, reduced lung capacity, middle ear infection, pneumonia and bronchitis. Around 3,000 lung cancers in non-smokers are caused by environmental tobacco smoke each year in the USA (NIH, 1993), which extrapolates to around 1,000 lung cancer deaths/year in British non-smokers (Parrott, 1998a). These findings necessitate a re-examination of the health data for the non-smokers in Doll and Peto (1976). They found very low rates of lung cancers in non-smoking doctors, but many of these were caused by passive smoking; thus, the adverse health effects of smoking are even worse than originally described. Asthma is also exacerbated by passive smoking, with many children having asthmatic attacks induced by passive smoking (NIH, 1993). Research from New Zealand and many other countries has found that passive smoking is a major cause of cot death in children below the age of one (sudden infant death syndrome, or **SIDS**, in the USA). Parents are now routinely advised never to smoke anywhere near their young children, and when this advice is followed it leads to a significant decrease in these deaths.

Nicotine absorption and smoking behaviours

Smoking is a rather odd behaviour. Why should anyone willingly inhale noxious smoke that irritates the lungs and induces coughing? The answer is that smoke inhalation is an extremely rapid and efficient route for drug delivery (Chapter 3). The lungs are designed to readily absorb oxygen, but the fine network of surface blood capillaries allows them to take up other small chemicals also present in the air. Earlier it was noted that nicotine is present on the tar droplets of tobacco smoke. When this smoke settles on the lungs some of this nicotine is absorbed. Thus, smoke inhalation generates a bolus, or hit, of nicotine, which reaches the brain 7–10 seconds later. Smoking is effective for the self-administration of many psychoactive drugs: cannabis (Chapter 7), opiates (Chapter 8) and some central nervous system (CNS) stimulants (Chapter 4). The tobacco in a single cigarette contains 50–60 mg of nicotine. If this were extracted and injected, then it would be sufficient to kill any individual through cardiac and respiratory failure (Leonard, 1997). However, most of the nicotine in the leaves is combusted, so that only 0.5–2.0 mg is present in the inhaled smoke and around 0.1–0.4 mg nicotine is then absorbed by the lungs.

Smokers titrate their nicotine administration in subtle but habitual ways. The initial inhalation of the first cigarette of the day is generally quite deep, with the smoke being retained deep in the lungs for several seconds; this provides a substantial bolus of nicotine, which helps to reverse the state of overnight nicotine depletion; this is why most smokers state that the first cigarette of the day is the most satisfying. Successive draws tend to be shallower and more widely spaced, as the smoker self-titrates increasingly smaller amounts of nicotine. When two cigarettes are smoked in quick succession, inhalations on the second cigarette tend to be shallower and more widely spaced; it may even be extinguished before it is finished. But when a regular smoker experiences a prolonged period without smoking (2–3 hours), their inhalations on the next cigarette again tend to be quite deep, as they self-administer more substantial amounts of nicotine to reverse the temporary abstinence effects. Therefore, there is a direct linear relationship between the inter-cigarette interval and the degree of satisfaction provided by each cigarette (Fant et al., 1995). When cigarettes are smoked in quick succession they have little measurable effect and are being smoked to forestall abstinence symptoms from developing; this also occurs in smokers who are about to enter prolonged no-smoking situations, when they preload with nicotine beforehand.

Pharmacological effects of nicotine

Nicotine binds to nicotinic **acetylcholine receptors**, which are widely distributed throughout the peripheral nervous system (PNS) and the CNS. In the PNS, nicotine affects both the parasympathetic and sympathetic nervous systems (Chapter 2). However, sympathomimetic changes predominate, although why this occurs is not clear. In regular smokers, nicotine increases resting heart rate by 10–30 beats per minute (b.p.m.) with the first cigarette of the day. Over a day of unrestrained smoking, the resting heart rate of a regular smoker is around 10 b.p.m. higher than that of non-smokers. One of the few adverse health effects of nicotine itself is therefore an exacerbation of hypertension and cardiac distress (Table 4.1).

In the CNS, the effects of nicotine on acetylcholine receptors are extremely complex. Despite the large amount of pharmacological research, no clear or simple explanatory model for its neurochemical effects has emerged. Zevin et al. (1998, p. 44) have described some of the complexities of nicotine **pharmacokinetics** and **pharmacodynamics**: "There is a multitude of different subtypes of neuronal nicotine receptors. Different nicotinic receptors are found in different brain regions and have different agonist-binding affinities and different electrophysiological responses to stimulation (Karlin, 1993; McGehee and Role, 1995); this may explain the diversity of effects of nicotine in the body." The effects of nicotine on the many different nicotinic ACh receptor systems can change and alter in complex ways. The initial effects of nicotine are to open **ion channels** and, thus, activate the neuron. However, its continued presence then leads to a deactivated or desensitised state when the ionic channels close. The dose response effects of nicotine are also complex, with low and high doses producing opposite effects. The regular use of nicotine also leads to an increased number of nicotinic receptors, a phenomenon not predicted with a receptor agonist, since receptor down-regulation generally occurs. Finally, nicotine receptor activation results in the release of many other neurotransmitters including dopamine, noradrenaline, glutamate and serotonin, in addition to acetylcholine (Zevin et al., 1998; Karlin, 1993; McGehee and Role, 1995). These complexities make nicotine one of the most confusing of all psychoactive drugs to model in neurobehavioural terms. In most undergraduate drugs and behaviour textbooks, nicotine is only covered briefly and rarely are its complexities fully described. Furthermore, it is sometimes categorised as a stimulant, in others as a relaxant, although most describe its psychopharmacological effects as contradictory (Grilly, 2001).

Psychological effects of nicotine

When tobacco smokers are asked why they smoke, they often have difficulty in giving a clear reason. Many smokers state that that they find it satisfying and crave a cigarette if they have not smoked recently, but it is generally unclear what this craving actually means. Various mood states are affected by smoking: stress/relaxation, irritation/pleasure and alertness/concentration. The exact nature of these mood changes is also difficult to summarise. Around 80–90% of smokers state that smoking helps them to cope with stress, but, paradoxically, they fail to demonstrate clear evidence for genuine relaxation: for instance, taking up smoking during adolescence prospectively leads to increased feelings of daily stress (note: the reasons for this conundrum are debated below). Similar problems surround the data on smoking and pleasure. Although many smokers state that cigarettes provide feelings of relief and satisfaction, they report only normal/average self-ratings of pleasure when replete with nicotine and suffer from heightened feelings of anger, irritability and annoyance when deprived of nicotine. Thus, it is difficult to find any empirical evidence for a *genuine* increase in pleasure after smoking.

Another reason given by many smokers is that cigarettes help with work and concentration, especially when having to perform long and boring tasks, such as radar tracking or long-distance driving. There is also an extensive body of empirical data, demonstrating that smokers are better at cognitive tasks when they smoke than when they are not smoking (Wesnes and Parrott, 1992; Heishman et al., 1994). However, closer inspection of these data again raises serious questions about whether this indicates true cognitive gains. In a classic series of studies, Wesnes and Warburton (1983) investigated the effects of different strength cigarettes and different doses of oral nicotine on performance in the rapid visual information processing (RVIP) task, a sensitive measure of cognitive vigilance. The standard procedure involved assessing overnight nicotine-deprived smokers (+12 hours' abstinence), in order to obtain baseline values. Then, they were given cigarettes of different strengths to smoke (low or high nicotine), while in other studies they were administered nicotine or **placebo** oral tablets. Mid to high nicotine conditions led to better vigilance performance than low, zero or high nicotine conditions. Furthermore, significant performance improvements could be demonstrated after just two inhalations from the first cigarette of the day

(Revell, 1988). These studies were interpreted as showing that nicotine was a **cognitive enhancer**, boosting alertness through an increase in cholinergic activity (Parrott and Winder, 1989; Revell, 1988; Wesnes and Warburton, 1983; Wesnes and Parrott, 1992).

One methodological weakness with the above studies was the absence of a non-smoking control group; this is crucial since, without control data, it is unclear whether smokers' performance is impaired during abstinence and restored by smoking or normal during abstinence and boosted by nicotine/smoking. When non-smoking controls are used the cognitive performance of the active smokers is generally similar to that of the non-smokers. Ashton et al. (1972) tested smokers and non-smokers on a driving simulator and showed that the overall performance levels for the two groups were very similar, although, when physically smoking, the performance of the smokers was significantly more variable, suggesting that looking for and picking up the cigarette may have interfered with attention toward the simulator. Subsequent studies have generally confirmed that non-deprived smokers generally show similar cognitive task performance to non-smokers; although a few have found better performance in smokers and a few have found better cognitive performance in non-smokers (for reviews see Heishman et al., 1994 and Wesnes and Parrott, 1992). Overall, therefore, there is very little empirical evidence to suggest that smokers benefit from cognitive gains; this was confirmed by Herbert et al. (2001), who found that, when non-deprived smokers had a cigarette, RVIP task performance remained completely unchanged. This suggests that the earlier findings of vigilance task gains, when overnight nicotine-deprived smokers were given nicotine/cigarettes, may reflect the reversal of abstinence effects (Revell, 1988; Wesnes and Warburton, 1983). Thus, an understanding of nicotine abstinence seems to be crucial for an explanation of these mood and cognitive effects.

Nicotine abstinence

When regular smokers are deprived of nicotine they typically report a range of negative feelings: irritability, tenseness, anxiety, depression and poor concentration (Hughes et al., 1990). Furthermore, when assessed on object performance tasks, their ability level is typically below that of either non-smokers or non-deprived smokers: on laboratory vigilance tasks, deprived smokers miss more targets; on reaction time tasks, their responses tend to be slower and more variable; and on memory tasks, they often forget more information (Heishman et al., 1994; Wesnes and Parrott, 1992). These psychobiological impairments mean that temporarily deprived smokers suffer from a range of everyday problems, so that, when regular smokers agreed to abstain from cigarettes for a day, in the evening they reported having experienced more hassles, less uplifts and more cognitive failures (Figure 5.1). Their day without nicotine also led to a range of mood deficits, with significantly greater stress, less pleasure and lower arousal/alertness (Parrott and Kaye, 1999). The non-deprived smokers were similar to non-smokers, confirming that nicotine does not provide smokers with any psycho-logical advantages (Parrott and Garnham, 1998; Parrott and Kaye, 1999; Figure 5.1).

This raises the question of how rapidly these abstinence effects take to develop. In one study, deprived smokers were found to be worse than continuing smokers after 2–4

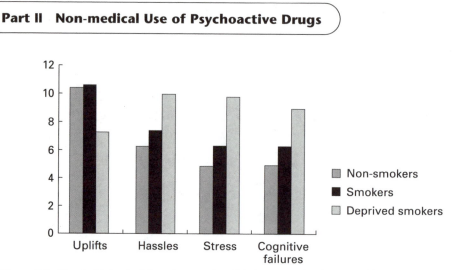

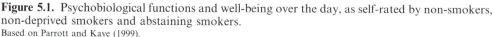

Figure 5.1. Psychobiological functions and well-being over the day, as self-rated by non-smokers, non-deprived smokers and abstaining smokers.
Based on Parrott and Kaye (1999).

hours of abstinence, with higher irritability and depression, worse feelings of concentration and poorer cognitive task performance (Parrott et al., 1996). However, significant mood and cognitive deficits have also been demonstrated after just 1 hour of abstinence (Parrott et al., 2000). This timescale agrees with everyday patterns of cigarette use, since moderate to heavy smokers tend to light up a new cigarette every 30–60 minutes. In a naturalistic study of 105 smokers, self-rated mood states were recorded before and after every cigarette over a day of normal smoking (Parrott, 1994). Most smokers reported fluctuating mood states over the day, with below-average moods before lighting up, followed by normal/average moods immediately after each cigarette. The most heavily dependent smokers experienced the strongest mood vacillations over the day (Figure 5.2). They reported the highest stress and lowest alertness in-between cigarettes, followed by the greatest amount of mood normalisation, with each cigarette restoring their moods to average/normal values (Parrott, 1994, 2003).

Nicotine dependence: a direct cause of psychological distress

Therefore, smokers feel normal when replete with nicotine, but suffer from unpleasant abstinence symptoms when deprived of nicotine (Parrott, 1994, 1999, 2003; Parrott et al., 1996; Parrott and Garnham, 1998); this is why the strongest satisfaction ratings are given to cigarettes smoked after an extended period without nicotine (Fant et al., 1995). However, the repetitive experience of abstinence symptoms in-between cigarettes causes smokers to suffer from increased distress over the day. Nicotine **dependence** is therefore a direct psychobiological cause of stress; this explains why youngsters who take up smoking report increasing stress and depression in later years. Johnson et al. (2000) assessed several hundred Americans over on two occasions six years apart. Smoking when aged 16 led to an increase in generalised anxiety when 22 years old, whereas high

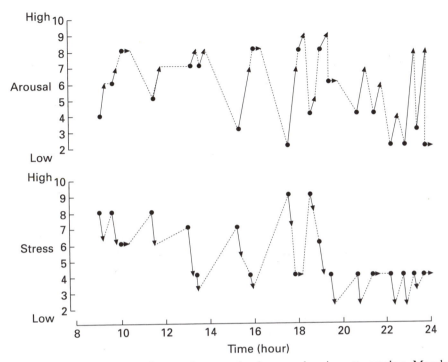

Figure 5.2. Feelings of stress and arousal over a day in a regular cigarette smoker. Moods were self-rated immediately prior to each cigarette, then again immediately afterward. Thus, each arrow represents the mood effects of one cigarette. Dotted lines show the mood changes in-between cigarettes.
Reproduced from Parrott (1994).

anxiety at 16 did *not* lead to an increased incidence of later smoking. Smoking led to increased stress, whereas stress did not lead to smoking. McGhee et al. (2000) monitored the mental health, behavioural problems and drug use of 900 New Zealand youngsters aged 15, 18 and 21. Those adolescents who were regular smokers at 18 reported a significant increase in anxiety and depression 3 years later. Similar increases have been shown for panic attacks (Breslau et al., 1998), and depression (Wu and Anthony, 1999; Breslau et al., 1998; Goodman and Capitman, 2000). Some of these prospective studies also found that the most disadvantaged youngsters were at greatest risk from becoming smokers. However, cigarette smoking never led to psychobiological gains; instead, the reverse occurred, with the uptake of smoking leading to an increased incidence of stress, depression or panic attack in later years.

This also explains why quitting smoking leads to psychobiological gains. Several prospective studies have found that when adults quit smoking they report significantly lower levels of stress 6 months later (Cohen and Lichtenstein, 1990; Parrott, 1995). Self-rated feelings of depression also reduce in smokers who manage to successfully quit (Hughes, 1992). The data are thus clear and consistent: nicotine dependence causes increased stress (Parrott, 1999), greater depression and other psychobiological problems (Parrott, 2003).

Heavy nicotine use versus light/occasional smoking

Around 80–85% of cigarette users are nicotine-dependent, following a fairly standard pattern of smoking. Their cigarettes are spaced over the day, often in close conjunction with routine situations: meals and work breaks. They represent the classic nicotine-dependent smoker, the main focus for discussion so far (Figure 5.2). However, there are other patterns of tobacco/nicotine use ranging from very heavy to very light. The most intense nicotine use is shown by the shamans or spiritual leaders in some South American tribes. They smoke chillums (thick pipes) full of tobacco, inhaling amounts of nicotine that would be lethal for any untrained initiate; this generates a trance-like state involving intense visions, which are intrinsic to their religious rituals. Each shaman is trained for this intense smoking from an early age, since they need to build up tolerance to the large amounts of nicotine involved. The other members of the tribe never use tobacco, so that when the first cigarette-smoking Western anthropologists were seen, they were treated with great reverence. Among Western smokers, the highest rates of nicotine consumption are found with chain smokers, when each new cigarette is lit from the stub of the previous one. Chain smokers may consume 60–80 cigarettes every day, with more or less continuous nicotine inhalation during the waking hours. Brown (1973) found that these very heavy smokers had electroencephalographs (EEGs) indicative of heightened arousal. Continuous nicotine intake can therefore increase arousal, but only when there are few periods of abstinence, since arousal would then start to decline.

At the opposite end of the spectrum there are light, or occasional, smokers whom Shiffman (1989) described as "chippers". They may go for several days without a cigarette, but then smoke intensively in social situations, such as parties. They are generally influenced by the social group and setting, smoking heavily when with other smokers but content not to smoke with non-smokers. Occasionally, they may smoke on their own. Around 10–15% of adult smokers fit this pattern, although it is more characteristic of young novice smokers. One explanatory model suggests that this represents the early stages of nicotine dependence, with occasional smokers gradually moving toward higher rates of tobacco consumption as they develop stronger nicotine dependence. However, that does not explain why a minority of smokers continue to maintain occasional use for many years. One intriguing finding by Shiffman (1989) was that chippers report few mood changes when smoking and do not experience mood decrements during abstinence. Thus, it may be the lack of abstinence symptoms, accompanied by the absence of mood normalisation when smoking, which explains how a few individuals maintain occasional patterns of drug use.

Occasional smokers display many of the non-pharmacological factors that accompany cigarette use. Thus, they often state that they feel and look attractive when smoking. This factor has reduced in importance in a few societies (the USA, the UK, Australia, New Zealand), but in most countries cigarettes are still associated with maturity and affluence, particularly among adolescents. Tobacco advertising is important for maintaining this belief. The sensory, cognitive and psychomotor components of smoking can also be pleasurable: spending money, breaking open the new packet, lighting up and the sensorimotor manipulations of fingers and lips. Hollywood films are also important, with smoking generally portrayed as sexy and pleasurable, rather than addictive and problematical. Indeed, the film industry often accepts tobacco company sponsorship for product placement. Smokers are thus bombarded by positive advertising images for smoking, which is why funding for accurate health information is so important. Russell et al. (1974) developed the smoking motivation questionnaire to measure the different factors associated with tobacco; several primary factors emerged, which factorised into two broad groups of pharmacological and non-pharmacological factors. The pharmacological factors included: dependence and addiction, automatic or unconscious smoking, the relief of anger and stress and the maintenance of alertness. The non-pharmacological factors comprised: psychological image (looking good) and sensorimotor aspects (having something to do with your hands). These non-pharmacological aspects typify the motives reported by occasional smokers, while dependent smokers score heavily on the pharmacological/dependence factors.

Smoking initiation

Most adult smokers had their first cigarette between the ages of 10 and 15. So, if a youngster can avoid experimentation before the age of 16, they are unlikely to become a smoker (USA Department of Health, 1994). One of the main influences on childhood smoking is the peer, or conformity, group, with slightly older siblings being particularly influential. Younger children imitate their older sisters/brothers and then become key figures of influence among their own age group. Peer pressure is often important, when group members are expected to conform and experiment with the new forbidden activity. However, peer selection is also important, with many children changing group allegiances. Those group members who do not wish to conform gravitate toward other subgroups whose views are consistent with their own (Ferguson et al., 1995). Those factors that increase rates of smoking uptake include parental smoking, low socio-economic status, poor self-image and exposure to cigarette advertising. Factors that contribute toward low smoking rates include higher tobacco taxes, enforcement of laws to reduce under-age purchase and school-based anti-smoking programmes. The most successful school-based packages are comprehensive and well-constructed, student-centred rather than lecture-based and are given regularly as part of a systematic programme. However, even the most effective programmes lose their influence once they have ended (USA Department of Health, 1994). Finally, future programmes should include data on the adverse psychological effects of nicotine dependence. Many youngsters believe that smoking can help relieve stress. They need to be find out why this belief is incorrect and work out how smoking actually increases stress and depression.

Smoking cessation

Around half of American and British adults who used to smoke have now stopped. Furthermore, 80–85% of current smokers state that they would like to quit and wish they had never started. However, quitting can be difficult, with many smokers relapsing after a short period. Various commercial stop smoking packages are available and generally claim high rates of success, but their optimistic calculations are often quite misleading. They are often based on short-term data (stopping for a few weeks), abstinence is indicated by self-reports (notoriously inaccurate) and misleading calculations are used to generate the impressively high success rates (e.g., exclusion of any participant who fails to complete the programme). To estimate genuine cessation, far tougher criteria need to be employed: inclusion of everyone who commences the package, abstinence for 6–12 months and regular biochemical confirmation of non-smoking via plasma **cotinine** or expired breath carbon monoxide measurements. Viswesvaran and Schmidt (1992) undertook a meta-analysis of 633 published studies that met these criteria, involving around 70,000 participants. The control subjects reported an annual quit rate of around 6%, but this improved slightly to 7% in those who had been advised by their physician to quit. More detailed cessation packages involving information on the adverse health effects coupled with basic counselling led to 17% cessation rates. But the most impressive rates were found in multi-component programmes; here, abstinence rates of 30–40% were achieved when nicotine substitution was combined with social skills training.

The reason these packages were most successful was that they tackled both aspects of cigarette use: pharmacological and non-pharmacological. Nicotine substitution can help relieve abstinence symptoms, and social skills training can help the individual to relearn how to live without continually reaching for a cigarette. Several controlled nicotine delivery systems are available: nicotine gum, transdermal patches and nicotine inhalers. By delivering controlled amounts of nicotine, they can help relieve nicotine withdrawal symptoms. In double-blind, placebo-controlled trials, they have each been shown to significantly improve quit rates, generally doubling the success achieved under placebo (Viswesvaran and Schmidt, 1992). However, on their own, nicotine substitution devices are still only marginally successful: for instance, the nicotine patch leads to a 10% annual quit rate, compared with the placebo patch with around 5% success (Stapleton et al., 1995). Smokers need advice and assistance to enable them to handle the numerous social pressures for relapsing: the skill of saying "no" when desperately wanting to say "yes"; the recognition and avoidance of high **relapse** situations, especially those where they used to smoke; the support gained when quitting with a friend (note: if the partner remains a smoker, relapse rates are extremely high). Most smokers also need to develop far more knowledge about the adverse health effects. Passively listening to a lecture often has limited impact; it is much more useful to actively investigate the topic, possibly as a group project. Knowledge acquisition is most effective when it is an active process, resulting in more elaborate and robust cognitive structures, which have thus far been found to be useful when faced with the temptation to relapse.

Many smokers recognise that the first few days of quitting will be very difficult and, indeed, many return to smoking within a short period. However, many abstain for months or years, but still relapse again. The American Surgeon General (1990) noted that 15% of former smokers still return to smoking after abstaining for two or more years. Therefore, quitting smokers need to be informed about the dangers of relapse. There are various situations where susceptibility to relapse is greatest, particularly periods of increased stress, such as bereavement or divorce; the same is true of any situation involving **alcohol**, since it reduces inhibitions and heightens misbeliefs, such as

"I can handle just one cigarette". Nicotine and alcohol also have opposing psycho-biological profiles, with alcohol reducing arousal and nicotine partially reversing this. Thus, around 90% of heavy drinkers/alcoholics are heavy smokers. When quitting smokers do relapse how should they respond to this setback? Many smokers believe that it proves their nicotine addiction, they are failures and might just as well carry on smoking. Marlatt (1996) has termed this the abstinence violation effect and counsels those who relapse on how to learn from the experience. They should examine why they relapsed and how they might handle high-risk situations more effectively in the future. Most importantly, it does *not* mean that they have to take up smoking again. Since they were successful for a period, they can be successful again. The evidence confirms that most former smokers have a few relapse periods before they stop permanently.

Nicotine: a powerful drug of addiction

Nicotine is certainly one of the most powerful drugs of addiction. Sigmund Freud used **cocaine** and nicotine and, although he managed to stop using cocaine, he was unable to stop smoking. He developed cancer of the jaw, which gradually killed him over a long and painful period. Despite numerous attempts at quitting and various surgical inter-ventions on his cancerous jaw, he remained a smoker until his death. Opiate users often state that withdrawing from heroin was easier that quitting smoking; group data on cessation rates generally confirms this. In relation to initial drug uptake, many who experiment with cocaine or **amphetamine** do not develop stimulant dependence, while moderate non-dependent alcohol use is the norm. In contrast, most youngsters who occasionally smoke during early adolescence become regular smokers. McNeill et al. (1987) studied the smoking behaviour pattern of young adolescent female smokers at school and found that many had attempted to quit smoking but failed, with nicotine dependence already evident in some 13–15-year olds.

One crucial difference between nicotine and other addictive drugs is the psycho-biological state of the individual when on drugs. Opiate users, stimulant abusers, cannabis smokers and alcohol drinkers become abnormal when replete with drug. Thus, they describe themselves as being "stoned", "high" or "spaced out" (Chapters 5–9). In contrast, tobacco smokers are *almost* normal when replete with nicotine, so that in psychobiological terms active smokers are similar to non-smokers (Figures 5.1 and 5.2); this is why the motives for cigarette craving can be so difficult to describe. How can a heavy smoker explain their overpowering need for a cigarette – when it is taken just to feel normal? The continual use of nicotine/tobacco to maintain normal feelings also becomes strongly conditioned over time. A heavy smoker inhales tobacco smoke 70,000 times each year, with each inhalation generating another nicotine hit, which is why it can become such a difficult habit to quit. Cigarettes are also associated with pleasurable personal activities and social events: after meals, during tea/coffee breaks, visits to taverns and public drinking houses, social functions and celebrations and after sex. The close association with this vast array of everyday activities, coupled with the need for nicotine to remain feeling normal, helps explain why nicotine is so strongly addictive. Indeed, it would be difficult to design a more powerful drug of addiction.

Questions

1   The World Heath Organisation has stated that cigarette smoking is the single most preventable cause of death in the world. Explain why breathing in tobacco smoke is so lethal.

2   Why is it dangerous for non-smoking adults and children to breathe in air polluted by cigarette smoke?

3   Oscar Wilde stated in 1891 that: "A cigarette is the perfect type of a perfect pleasure. It is exquisite, and it leaves one unsatisfied." Has modern psychopharmacological research confirmed this description?

4   Many smokers believe that nicotine/cigarettes help them to cope with stress, but are they correct in this belief?

5   Grilly (2001) noted that: "Despite the numerous studies on tobacco use, it is still not clear what is so reinforcing about the practice." Do you agree or can you outline an explanatory model?

6   Why do adolescents who take up smoking soon report increased levels of daily stress and depression?

7   What practical advice would you give someone who wanted to quit smoking?

8   Design a health promotion package that explained the psychological processes underlying tobacco smoking and the psychological gains that follow cessation.

Key references and reading

Goodman E and Capitman J. (2000). Depressive symptoms and cigarette smoking among teens. *Pediatrics*, **196**, 748–755.

Parrott AC (1998a). Social drugs: effects upon health. In: M Pitts and K Phillips (eds), *The Psychology of Health* (2nd edn). Routledge, London.

Parrott AC (1998b). Nesbitt's Paradox resolved? Stress and arousal modulation during cigarette smoking. *Addiction*, **93**, 27–39.

Parrott AC (1999). Does cigarette smoking cause stress? *American Psychologist*, **54**, 817–820.

Parrott AC (2003). Cigarette derived nicotine is not a medicine. *World Journal of Biological Psychiatry*, **4**, 49–55.

Shiffman S (1989). Tobacco "chippers": Individual differences in tobacco dependence. *Psychopharmacology*, **97**, 539–547.

Chapter 6

LSD and Ecstasy/MDMA

Overview

This chapter covers two widely used recreational drugs, LSD and MDMA (Ecstasy), while other illicit drugs with diverse pharmacological profiles will also be outlined. LSD is the archetypal psychedelic drug that causes profound changes in perception and understanding, through a complex pattern of effects on serotonin neurotransmission. Colours become more intense, shapes change in weird ways, thoughts and cognitions are altered, with dramatic insights during "good trips" but intense fear and paranoia during "bad trips". The effects of LSD are unpredictable, reflecting the exacerbation of internal cognitive/emotional factors and external environmental stimuli. A small minority of users may develop psychotic breakdown, especially those individuals with a predisposition. The diathesis stress model for psychiatric breakdown and how psychoactive drugs such as LSD can be readily integrated into this model will be outlined. Ecstasy, or MDMA, is a synthetic amphetamine derivative that boosts serotonin and several other monoamine neurotransmitters. The acute effects can be extremely pleasant, with strong feelings of elation and empathy toward other people. However, lethargy, midweek depression and other psychobiological deficits develop during the period of neurochemical depletion afterward. Hyperthermia (heat exhaustion) can often develop in the hot and crowded conditions at dances and raves. High doses of MDMA causes the loss of serotonin's distal axon terminals in laboratory animals, and there is an increasing body of evidence for similar neurotoxic damage in humans. Thus, regular Ecstasy users often suffer from poor memories and complain of other serotonergic disorders including depression, impulsivity, phobic anxiety, reduced appetite and sleep disorder. Finally, there are many other types of drug that induce profound experiential changes including ketamine and phencyclidine. Their recreational use, neurochemical actions and behavioural effects will be outlined.

Lysergic acid diethylamide (LSD)

Lysergic acid diethylamide (LSD) is the most powerful psychoactive **drug** yet discovered, since a minuscule dose produces profound changes in perception and understanding. Several other drugs have similar effects, including **mescaline** from the Peyote cactus (*Lophophora williamsii*) and psilocybin from magic mushrooms ((Pilocybe spp.). Their effects are qualitatively similar to LSD but far weaker and only evident after larger doses. These types of drugs are generally termed "psychedelic", or mind-expanding, although several other labels have also been applied, including **hallucinogens** and psychotomimetics (see Table 6.3 on p. 82). The psychoactive effects of LSD were discovered by chance. In the 1930s the pharmaceutical company Sandoz was researching medicinal uses for ergot derivatives. Ergot is present in the *Claviceps* fungus that sometimes grows on rye wheat. In the Middle Ages, if bread was baked with rye containing this fungus, it could induce cerebral convulsions, cause abortions in pregnant women and damage the peripheral blood circulation leading to gangrene. In medieval times it was used by midwives to induce labour.

Sandoz was intending to develop a range of synthetic ergot derivatives and, indeed, some proved useful as medications during labour, others relieved migraine and **hydergine** was found to improve cerebral blood flow (Chapter 14). The common nucleus for all these ergot derivatives was lysergic acid. The 25th batch was labeled "lyserg saure diethylamid-25", or LSD-25, but has become more widely known as lysergic acid diethylamide (direct translation from the German). It is now generally termed LSD. It was found to be ineffective in standard laboratory animal tests; but, when working on it one afternoon, the research scientist Albert Hofmann did not feel his normal self and went home to recover. After an eventful cycle ride home that was accompanied by some interesting changes in visual perception, he lay down in an attempt to recover but perceived: "An uninterrupted stream of fantastic pictures, extraordinary shapes with intense kaleidoscopic play of colors" (Sandoz Company Memorandum from 1943, cited in Hofmann, 1980; also Maisto et al., 1999; Snyder, 1996).

Like all good researchers Hofmann believed in empirical replication. So, 3 days later, he self-administered a controlled dose of LSD-25 to see if it *was* the drug that had induced the strange sensory experiences. He reasoned that it must be very powerful, since his previous accidental ingestion could only have involved a very small amount. So, he only took 0.25 mg, which although minuscule by normal standards is still far higher than that now known to be necessary (normal range: 0.025–0.10 mg). The resulting experiences were indeed extremely powerful, with many unpleasant and frightening aspects; indeed, it was the first documented bad trip. The perceptual distortions were far more powerful than the milder changes he had experienced earlier; pieces of furniture were seen to change into fantastic figures with grotesque faces and threatening forms. As these perceptual experiences became even stronger and uncontrollable, he asked his next door neighbour to bring him some milk (the standard antidote to poisoning), but he perceived her as a malevolent witch with a wicked face like a mask. As the trip developed and deepened, he felt that his selfhood, or ego, was disintegrating, that he was losing his mind and that his body was being invaded by a demon. He entered another world and another place. However, once the peak of this experience had subsided, during the gradual "comedown" period, he was more able to appreciate these novel and unique sensory experiences and thoughts. This time course is typical of many LSD trips, and it is often during the comedown period that the profound perceptual and cognitive changes can be most savoured. The overall duration of Hofmann's second trip was 14 hours ... confirmation of the very large dose taken, since LSD trips generally last around 8–12 hours (Hofmann, 1980; Maisto et al., 1999; Snyder, 1996).

Fellow research scientists at Sandoz tried LSD in smaller amounts and confirmed its powerful effects. The company attempted to find therapeutic uses for LSD, and it was given to various patient groups in the 1950s in an attempt to see if "widening the ego" might facilitate psychotherapy; but, although some psychiatric patients found the LSD experience illuminating and helpful, many others found it frightening and unpleasant. The heyday of LSD was during the 1960s. The Californian psychologist Timothy Leary became involved in some LSD research and started to advocate its wider use in order to foster enlightenment in everyone: "turn on – tune in – drop out". Cannabis and LSD soon became integral to the youth culture and pop music of the 1960s, as exemplified in the Beatles' film *Yellow Submarine*, the Sergeant Pepper track *Lucy in the Sky with Diamonds*, acid rock groups like the Grateful Dead and numerous psychedelic record sleeves. The Haight Ashbury district of San Francisco became the epicentre for youth counterculture worldwide; but, while many found temporary enlightenment, others had less pleasant experiences (see below). The proportion of young people trying LSD declined in the 1970s, but increased again during the 1980s and has continued right up to the present day in parallel with the rising use of other recreational drugs.

Pharmacological and psychological effects of LSD

The pharmacological basis for LSD's powerful psychoactive effects are only partially understood. Many psychedelic drugs (LSD, psilocybin, etc.) are indolealkylamines – the same chemical groups as the neurotransmitter serotonin, but only some of them alter serotonin activity. However, LSD, psilocybin and many other psychedelics do bind to **serotonin** receptors, and there is a positive correlation between the degree of **receptor** binding and the strength of their psychedelic effects (Glennon, 1996). The exact nature of these neurochemical changes is unclear, since in some situations they seem to act as agonists (boosting serotonin activity), while in others they act more as antagonists (blocking activity; Chapter 3). The untypical psychedelic drug mescaline is not an indolealkylamine and affects noradrenaline rather than serotonin activity (Abraham et al., 1996). The two main brain areas affected by psychedelic drugs are the (noradrenergic) **locus coeruleus** and the (serotonergic) **raphe nuclei**. These nuclei are sited in the reticular activating area of the brain stem and have important functions in relation to the processing of stimulus input. When the locus coeruleus is electrically stimulated via a microelectrode, a laboratory animal will display hyperalertness to the environment. It will stare at stimuli in a state of apparent panic, suddenly jump at any new sound or be startled by a puff of air. All psychedelic drugs boost locus coeruleus activity, whereas similar drugs that are not psychedelic tend not to display this property. The main neurotransmitter for the locus coeruleus is noradrenaline, and mescaline has a direct agonist effect on locus coeruleus activity. The effects of LSD and many other psychedelic drugs is more indirect. Their primary action is on the raphe nuclei, which is mainly comprised of serotonergic cell bodies. LSD is thought to boost serotonergic activity in the raphe nuclei, which then leads indirectly to a boost in locus coeruleus activity (Snyder, 1996); this is only one of several possible explanatory models. But, whatever the mechanism, it is almost certainly complex and indirect.

The initial effects of LSD are to boost stimulus reception. In the early stages of an LSD trip, colours become more intense, shapes alter and change and distances are more difficult to gauge, with near objects becoming more distant and vice versa; this can make crossing a road or driving a car very difficult and dangerous. Drugs and behaviour textbooks often repeat the story that people walk in front of cars believing they can stop them or jump from buildings in the belief that they can fly. While this may occur on rare occasions, most of these accidents and fatalities are probably a result of impaired distance perception (e.g., stepping in front of a moving car because it *seems* a long way off), rather than a belief in immortality. These intensifications of visual perception probably reflect stimulation of the locus coeruleus (see above). Another rarer experience is **synaesthesia**, when information from different sense modalities becomes integrated together. Colours and shapes may change and evolve in parallel with the prevailing music and individual dust particles may bounce on the floor in parallel with the beat of the music or rhythm of the dancers. In rare instances, sounds may be perceived as colours. However, the raphe nuclei and locus coeruleus do not only intensify *external* environmental input. The reticular activating system also receives information from higher brain regions via internal feedback loops. As the LSD trip intensifies, colours and shapes can take on a life of their own and change in ever more spontaneous ways. Cognitive processes, thoughts and ideas are also boosted and may be perceived as particularly important or insightful. One common but unpleasant effect is **paranoia** – when ideas of reference are boosted; this may be similar to the "cognitive overload" that underlies some aspects of schizophrenia (see below). Positive thoughts may also be boosted. New cognitive fusions may occur, just as environmental input may be combined in new and exciting ways (similarly to synaesthesia). New thoughts, ideas and realizations are characteristic of the LSD experience. People report that they have met god or developed unique and profound understandings about the meaning of existence. They may write down these powerful insights on a scrap of paper – only to find them unintelligible the next morning.

The psychological effects of LSD can be very difficult to predict. Some people describe fascinating mind-opening experiences, whereas others have a frightening and unpleasant time. Even those who have taken it many times occasionally have bad trips. The nature of the experience often seems to depend on the state of mind when the drug is taken, since LSD boosts and intensifies the prevailing stimulation. Hippie folklore in the 1960s recommended that LSD should only be taken when in a good frame of mind and in a supportive and non-threatening environment. Friends with a personal experience of psychedelic experiences were deemed helpful, particularly when taking LSD for the first time. They could provide personal reassurance and talk people through a "bad" period; This was the rationale behind the drop-in centres that originated in the Haight Ashbury district of San Francisco during the 1960s. They were staffed by volunteers with personal experience of drugs and provided assistance for those suffering bad trips. Similar facilities are now provided at many pop festivals and raves. The basic principles remain unchanged, although some volunteers have psychopharmacological expertise or medical training. An alternative approach for the relief of bad trips is pharmaceutical, the administration of drugs that counteract the LSD-induced overstimulation. Two drug types are generally used: **antipsychotics**, such as chlorpromazine (Chapter 11), and anxiolytic **benzodiazepines**, such as diazepam (Chapter 9). The effects of chlorpromazine are opposite to those of LSD, since chlorpromazine reduces activity in the raphe nuclei and makes stimulus and cognitive input *less* arousing. However, those treated with chlorpromazine sometimes state that the resulting lack of motivation or interest is more unpleasant than a bad LSD trip.

Adverse drug reactions and the diathesis stress model

Some further personal descriptions of LSD trips are contained in Snyder (1996) and Maisto et al. (1999). Psilocybin's effects are outlined in Julien (2001), while the personal experience of mescaline was described by Huxley (1954). Aldous Huxley advocated the use of mind-expanding drugs for personal enlightenment and took his final psychedelic trip when on his deathbed. However, not everyone benefits from these powerful drugs, and the LSD experience can at times be frightening and disorienting. The unpleasant aspects of Hofmann's LSD trip were briefly noted earlier. At the peak he felt he was losing his mind, but these negative experiences were replaced by more pleasant and controllable feelings once the peak of the trip had passed. However, not everyone recovers so readily, and some individuals develop a full psychotic breakdown after taking LSD (Boutros and Bowers, 1996); this can occur after a single LSD experience, but more often after repeated usage. The incidence rates for psychiatric disorder induced by LSD are difficult to estimate, given the absence of baseline data on non-problematical LSD usage and standardized psychiatric casualty data. However, in hospital trials where LSD has been given in a controlled setting as an "aid" for psychotherapy, around 1–4% of patients develop psychotic breakdowns following the LSD experience (Abraham and Aldridge, 1993); this raises the question of whether such breakdowns *only* occur in those predisposed to **psychotic disorder**. Many such casualties do indeed have a previous psychiatric diagnosis, but some studies have shown that breakdowns also occur in individuals without a previous psychiatric diagnosis (Abraham and Aldridge, 1993; Boutros and Bowers, 1996).

Explanatory models for schizophrenia emphasize the interaction between internal genetic or biochemical predispositions, with external environmental stressors. According to this **diathesis stress model** (Davison and Neale, 1998), various types of schizophrenia can develop when an individual with a psychobiological disposition to schizophrenia (e.g., genetic, biochemical, acquired viral) is subjected to the appropriate cocktail of environmental stressors (family stresses, odd communication patterns, other stressful overstimulation). There are several ways in which psychedelic drugs, such as LSD, might exacerbate these problems and, hence, exacerbate a psychotic breakdown: for instance, LSD makes all stimulus events and internal cognitive thoughts more arousing and, hence, potentially stressful. It is also well established that schizophrenics are prone to cognitive overstimulation and poor at handling stress (Davison and Neale, 1998). The other main problem is that LSD may increase uncertainty/confusion and question the subtle internal cognitive models of the world, particularly where these models of the psychosocial world are inherently weak. Hence, it is not surprising that LSD can precipitate a psychotic breakdown in predisposed individuals. Furthermore, this will be increased following large and/or frequent doses of LSD. It should also be noted that much of the psychiatric breakdown data was collected when LSD and **cannabis** were the two main illicit recreational drugs (Chapters 7 and 11). The picture in recent years has become far more complex, with the advent of a wide range of powerful psychedelics, stimulants and other drugs that may exacerbate psychotic breakdown (see the following sections). Finally, many reports have suggested that psychiatric breakdowns *only* reflect the exacerbation of an existing predisposition, with the implicit message that it is the predisposition that is the crucial factor. It should be emphasized that these individuals would still be functioning adequately if they had not taken the drug; thus, drug use is the crucial factor. Furthermore, psychotic and other mental health breakdowns often develop in the absence of any documented predisposing factors (Soar et al., 2001; see below). Thus, all these psychoactive drugs can cause problems in apparently "normal" individuals.

MDMA, or Ecstasy

MDMA (3,4-methylenedioxymethamphetamine) was originally patented in 1912, but remained on the laboratory shelves until re-synthesised by Alexander Shulgin in the early 1970s. Shulgin was a research chemist at the Dow Chemical Company, employed to develop structural variants of mescaline. Among the new drugs he developed was DOM (dimethoxymethylamphetamine; see Table 6.1 on p. 79), but he also developed a number of other synthetic amphetamine derivatives including MDMA (3,4-methylenedioxymethamphetamine), MDA (3,4-methylenedioxyamphetamine) and MDE (3,4-methylenedioxyethylamphetamine). He tried increasing doses of MDMA on himself, noted that 75 mg or more had very pleasant effects and, so, recommended it to his friends. Soon it was being manufactured in illicit laboratories and, so, became one of many psychoactive drugs available in San Francisco during the 1970s. At that time MDA was more widely used than MDMA, but early in the 1980s MDMA became more popular. Around that time the original street names "Mellow" and "Empathy" gradually evolved into "Ecstasy" and "XTC" (Parrott, 2004). It remained fairly obscure until 1985 when the American Drug Enforcement Agency scheduled it as a Class 1 illicit drug, deciding that it had no clinical/medical uses (Parrott, 2001); this was challenged in the courts, and the resulting dispute was featured in popular magazine articles. Similar reports appeared in the European press, warning about this new and dangerous drug. But these articles, coupled with the more exciting street name of Ecstasy, only helped to fuel interest. Demand for these "new" designer drugs increased dramatically, and during the late 1980s it was widely used at weekend raves in out-of-town venues. Following police action against these popular events the use of Ecstasy moved to inner-city dance clubs. During the 1990s it was widely used in most Westernised societies, with around half-a-million Ecstasy tablets being taken each weekend in the UK (Saunders, 1995; Schifano, 2000) and 13% of British university students have taken it (Webb et al., 1996). In America, Ecstasy has become second in popularity to cannabis as an illicit recreational drug (Pope et al., 2001a, b).

Pharmacological and psychological effects of MDMA

MDMA affects several neurotransmitter systems and has thus been termed "neuro-chemically messy". Its main effect is as an indirect 5-HT (hydroxytryptamine, or serotonin) agonist, since an acute dose releases up to 80% of serotonin into the synaptic cleft (Green et al., 2004). However, it also displays weaker agonist actions on various other monoamine neurotransmitter systems including **dopamine, noradrenaline, histamine** and **acetylcholine** (Green et al., 2004). Serotonin is involved in various psychological functions: feeling states, such as happiness and sadness; cognitive functions, such as executive planning and memory for new information; and basic psychobiological functions, such as sleeping and sex. The boost in serotonin turnover induced by MDMA tends to generate feelings of contentment, elation, liveliness and intense emotional closeness to others. The resulting non-judgemental atmosphere at many raves and clubs allows people to enjoy themselves without their normal concerns and inhibitions (Cohen, 1998). Rhythmical and repetitive movements such as dancing, become more pleasurable. Sexual performance can be affected in a number of ways, with reports of sexual/emotional enhancement, difficulty in maintaining an erection and/or delayed ejaculation often leading to enhanced pleasure (Parrott, 2001); these effects can also be produced by selective serotonin reuptake inhibitors, such as **fluoxetine** (Chapter 12).

Although many of the immediate effects of MDMA are generally very positive, it displays a number of less desirable effects. It is a powerful sympathomimetic and allows physical exertion to be maintained for prolonged periods. But, it also impairs temperature control in the hypothalamus, so that in the hot and crowded conditions at raves many dancers become overheated or hyperthermic (Dafters, 1994). Experienced ravers/dancers learn to alternate their periods of exertion, with rest periods in the chill-out room, in order to forestall hyperthermia from developing too much. However, this increase in body temperature is an important contributory factor in causing serotonergic neurotoxicity (Malberg and Seiden, 1998; Parrott, 2001). In extreme cases the hyperthermia can become disabling, with professional medical treatment being required: hence, the many MDMA casualties treated each weekend in the accident and emergency of city hospitals. Most Ecstasy users are aware of the dangers of over-exertion and maintain regular fluid intake in order to counteract *dancing-induced* fluid loss. However, if too much fluid is taken the electrolytes in the blood circulation can be diluted to dangerous levels, with the resulting **hyponatraemia** proving fatal, as in the tragic case of Leah Betts. Thus, while some Ecstasy users die from hyperthermia, others die from the excessive fluids taken to counteract heat exhaustion.

Although few Ecstasy users die from taking MDMA, the majority experience psychobiological problems in the days afterward; these occur during the period of serotonergic depletion that follows the drug-induced boost in neurotransmitter activity and include feelings of lethargy, irritability and depression. Curran and Travill (1997) reported clinically borderline levels of depression in the midweek period that followed an Ecstasy trip; these midweek blues were also found in a study of East London clubbers: "I had the occasional midweek depression, and occasionally found myself crying for no reason" (Parrott and Lasky, 1998). This midweek depression is seen by many regular users as an occupational hazard of taking MDMA. In the above study Parrott and Lasky compared Ecstasy users with similar aged non-users before and after they had self-administered their chosen recreational drugs on Saturday night. Their self-rated moods were broadly similar, with the non-Ecstasy users just as happy and energetic as the Ecstasy/MDMA users. Thus, many of the "positive" moods associated with Ecstasy partially reflect the expectations of going out clubbing with friends. The main difference between groups was the significantly worse midweek moods in the recovering Ecstasy users (Parrott and Lasky, 1998).

MDMA/Ecstasy and neurotoxicity

One of the main concerns about MDMA is the laboratory animal data demonstrating that it is neurotoxic. In rats and monkeys, brain levels of serotonin are reduced by repeated doses of MDMA, a finding replicated in numerous studies (e.g., Steele et al., 1994), while there is also evidence for dopaminergic nerve damage (Ricaurte et al., 2002). The main effect is destruction of serotonin nerve axons in the cerebral cortex and other higher brain areas. The cell bodies in the dorsal raphe nucleus of the brainstem are spared, whereas the prolonged axon terminals and distal projections are destroyed, leading to reduced serotonin activity in the higher brain regions. Thus, there is concern over whether higher brain functions, such as information storage and retrieval, complex stimulus analysis and decision taking, might be impaired. Many other brain regions are also affected, including the **hypothalamus** and **suprachiasmatic nucleus**, areas that subserve temperature regulation, feeding behaviour and biological rhythms.

The data from laboratory animals administered MDMA raises the possibility that recreational Ecstasy may also be neurotoxic for humans. It is not possible to investigate this hypothesis directly (see below), but there is a great deal of evidence for serotonergic damage in recreational Ecstasy users. Drug-free, regular MDMA users demonstrate reduced serotonin neural activity in the cerebral cortex in PET (positron emission tomography) scans, reduced levels of cerebrospinal 5-HIAA, or hydroxyindoleacetic acid (the main serotonin metabolite) and other indices of reduced serotonin activity (McCann et al., 2000; Reneman et al., 2001). Regular Ecstasy users display significant deficits in a number of psychobiological functions subserved by serotonin. The most thoroughly studied area is memory, and significant deficits in abstinent Ecstasy users have been found on a wide range of episodic and working memory tasks (Fox et al., 2002; Rodgers et al., 2001; Verkes et al., 2001; see Table 6.1). Deficits have also been found in some measures of cognitive planning and higher executive processing, although many basic cognitive functions remain unimpaired.

Halpern et al. (2004) described some intriguing findings from a study of young ravers in Salt Lake City, where the prevailing religious beliefs have led to very low rates

Table 6.1. Memory and learning tasks where drug-free recreational Ecstasy users have displayed significant performance deficits.

Memory task	Example reference source
Auditory prose passage: immediate and delayed recall	Zakzanis and Young (2001)
Calev matched word recall and recognition task	Fox et al. (2001)
Cambridge neuropsychological battery (CANTAB): spatial working memory	Fox et al. (2002)
Cognitive Drug Research (CDR) battery: immediate and delayed word recall	Parrott et al. (1998)
Corsi block memory span	Verkes et al. (2001)
Figure recognition: simultaneous and serial	Verkes et al. (2001)
Prospective Memory Questionnaire (PMQ): self-rated deficits	Heffernan et al. (2001)
Rey Auditory Verbal Learning (RAVLT): English edition	Fox et al. (2001b)
Rey Auditory Verbal Learning (RAVLT): Dutch edition	Reneman et al. (2000)
Rey Auditory Verbal Learning (RAVLT): German edition	Gouzoulis-Meyfrank et al. (2000)
Rey–Osterreich Complex Figure: delayed visual recall	Bolla et al. (1998)
Rivermead paragraph memory: immediate and delayed recall	Morgan (1999)
Spatial recall (windows-in-houses task): brief delay	Fox et al. (2001)
Supraspan auditory word list: brief delay, written recall	Parrott and Lasky (1998)
Verbal paired associates: delayed recall	Rodgers (2000)
Visuospatial memory (VIG): complex shape learning	Gouzoulis-Meyfrank et al. (2000)
Visual paired associates: delayed recall	Rodgers (2000)
Wechsler Memory Scale (WMS): total spatial span	Halpern et al. (2004)
Wechsler memory (WAIS): immediate and delayed paragraph recall	Krystal et al. (1992)
Word recognition: simultaneous and serial	Verkes et al. (2001)
Working memory: information-processing accuracy	Wareing et al. (2000)
Working memory: serial subtraction	Curran and Travill (1997)
Working memory: serial add and subtract	McCann et al. (1999)

Note: a single reference is provided for each task. On many tasks significant deficits have also been reported by other groups. Many of the above studies also found deficits in additional memory measures.
Reproduced from Parrott (2001).

of tobacco, alcohol, cannabis or other illicit drug consumption. However, many of these ravers did use MDMA and, while moderate users were not cognitively impaired, high users (60–450 lifetime occasions) displayed significant deficits on many of the cognitive test measures, particularly those associated with processing speed, memory and impulsivity (Table 6.1). These deficits remained even after controlling for a range of potential confounding factors. However, cognition and memory are not the only areas of psychobiological deficit. Regular Ecstasy/MDMA users have been reported to experience sleep impairments, eating disorders, reduced sexual functioning, phobic anxiety, depression, heightened impulsivity, aggressiveness and a range of occupational, health and financial problems (McCann et al., 2000; Parrott, 2000; Schifano et al., 1998; Schifano, 2000; Topp et al., 1999). Many recreational users are fully aware of these problems. In a World Wide Web (WWW) study of 283 unpaid volunteers (Parrott et al., 2002), around 73% of the excessive Ecstasy users stated that they had experienced

Table 6.2. Novice, moderate, and heavy recreational Ecstasy/MDMA drug users (1–9, 10–99 and +100 lifetime occasions). Percentage of each group reporting problems when drug-free, which they attribute to the use of Ecstasy.

	Novice	Moderate	Heavy	χ^2
Ecstasy/MDMA user group				
Ecstasy usage (occasions)	1–9	10–99	+100	
Sample size (N)	109	136	37	
Mood and cognitive problems attributed to Ecstasy use				
Depression	33%	54%	65%	16.23 ***
Mood fluctuation	38%	70%	80%	31.21 ***
Impulsivity	18%	26%	32%	3.79 NS
Anxiety	32%	40%	60%	9.37 **
Poor concentration	32%	62%	70%	29.80 ***
Memory problems	19%	52%	73%	42.74 ***
Physiological and medical problems attributed to Ecstasy use				
Weight loss	10%	37%	48%	28.99 ***
Infections	5%	9%	35%	24.94 ***
Tremors/Twitches	14%	20%	38%	9.95 **
Poor sleep	37%	41%	52%	2.15 NS
Sexual problems	7%	11%	22%	3.94 NS

$2 \times 3 \chi^2$ analyses ($df = 2$; two-tailed)) were performed on the yes/no responses from the three groups.
*** $= P < 0.001$.
** $= P < 0.01$.
NS = Non-significant.
Reproduced from Parrott et al. (2002).

memory problems that they attributed to the use of Ecstasy, while many other problems were also reported (Table 6.2).

Methodological difficulties in recreational drug research

The optimum design for a psychopharmacology study would involve the random allocation of volunteer subjects to each drug condition. After collecting drug-free baseline data, each naive volunteer would be randomly allocated to either a **placebo** or an active drug, then regularly assessed over time (Chapter 3). This powerful experimental design is used when investigating many new medications (Chapters 11–14), but it is obviously less appropriate for social/recreational drug research. Thus, if one wished to investigate whether the regular use of Ecstasy was neurotoxic in humans, then it would not be acceptable to administer one randomly selected group of volunteers placebo tablets for 6 months, while the others were given MDMA tablets each week, followed by routinely assessing changes in the integrity of the serotonergic system, memory ability and feelings of depression over time. It is not just with MDMA that this randomised design cannot be followed. It would not be ethical for opiates, cocaine, cannabis or even legal drugs, such as alcohol and nicotine, to be repeatedly administered to normal volunteers in long-term prospective studies. Instead, a range of alternative approaches need to be followed.

The standard approach is to compare drug users with non-users as controls; but, there are many problems with this design. The main one is that groups are self-selected and may differ in important characteristics related to the decision to use illicit drugs. It is often possible to measure or match groups on some of these factors: age, gender and socioeconomic background can all be measured fairly easily; and intellectual ability could be estimated by measures of school attainment or verbal comprehension tasks. Although, both these measures may be affected by drug use. Similarly, a variety of personality questionnaires might be administered. However, even if the different groups were matched on a range of factors, it could be that they still differed a priori on some important but unassessed attributes. Another problem is lack of control over drug administration. The standard approach is to ask subjects to recall which drugs they have taken; but, this raises the question of how accurate these estimates might be – particularly with heavy users. There is also the question of drug strength and purity, since illicit drug supplies can sometimes be quite variable (Parrott, 2004).

However, there are several ways in which the influence of these disparate factors could be investigated. For instance, it is often possible to statistically control for the influence of other psychoactive drugs, by multiple regression or partial correlation. Where this has been done the cognitive/memory deficits displayed by Ecstasy users still remain (Verkes et al., 2001). The use of other psychoactive drugs may add to the cognitive problems of Ecstasy users. Rodgers et al. (2001) found that cannabis use was significantly associated with everyday memory problems, whereas MDMA was significantly linked with prospective memory deficits (e.g., remembering an appointment with a friend). Thus, those who use both cannabis and Ecstasy suffered from both types of memory deficit! The study by Halpern et al. (2004) of relatively "pure" MDMA users confirms the crucial role of MDMA in inducing cognitive problems.

The purity and strength of Ecstasy samples can also be measured biochemically. Schifano (2000) analysed 5,000 Italian Ecstasy tablets and found that 90% contained MDMA, while the remaining 10% largely comprised other ring-substituted amphetamine derivatives, such as MDA (impurities were not generally noted). While current evidence suggests a profile of specific cognitive deficits in regular MDMA users, a number of important questions remain, nevertheless. How much MDMA needs to be taken before problems develop? The answer would seem to be not a lot (Halpern et al., 2004). Is there evidence for neural recovery once drug taking has stopped? Morgan et al. (2002) suggested that psychobiological problems recovered whereas selective memory deficits remained. Another core topic is the contributory role of high temperature. Animal studies have shown that neuronal toxicity is heightened when rats are allowed to become hyperthermic; this raises the question of whether neurotoxicity also develops most in those recreational Ecstasy users who become overheated (McCann et al., 2000; Parrott, 2000, 2002; Ricaurte et al., 2000).

Other mind-altering recreational drugs

There are many other types of drug that can disrupt normal cognitive processes and, hence, may be termed mind-expanding (Table 6.3). Some of these drugs have quite unpredictable effects. Their use is generally sporadic, but occasionally they become popular among experienced drug users, who are searching for ever more extreme experiences. **Phencyclidine** (PCP) and **ketamine** are dissociative anaesthetics that make the person feel dissociated from their environment and unlike their normal selves. Their effects can be quite strange and bizarre. PCP and ketamine users may become immobile, take up strange postures, appear drunk and unresponsive or stare blankly. Some users report "near-death" experiences or enter the "K-hole" of bright light which supposedly leads to another world. These drugs tend to have powerful physiological consequences and, although most users try to avoid becoming unconscious, high doses can lead to coma or death. The combination of environmental dissociation with profound anaesthesia can also be dangerous. Some ketamine users have accidentally set themselves alight, not perceived any pain and failed to take meaningful action, such as trying to extinguish the flames.

Table 6.3. Psychedelic and other recreational drugs: selected examples.

Psychedelic drugs	
LSD	Synthetic, with profound effects on perception and cognition at very low doses.
Psilocybin	Present in many species of "magic" mushroom that are eaten raw; some toxic mushroom species are visually similar to the psychedelic varieties; effects are very variable, depending on the exact species and drug concentration.
Mescaline	Present in the Peyote cactus; legal use by some Native American groups in religious mystical ceremonies.
DOM	Weaker than LSD but with more prolonged effects and a higher incidence of bad trips; sometimes termed "STP" (serenity–tranquillity–peace); a synthetic amphetamine derivative, which could alternatively be included in the next grouping.
Synthetic amphetamine derivatives	
MDMA, or Ecstasy	Positive feelings of elation, euphoria and closeness to others; replaced by depression and lethargy in the days afterward; regular use is neurotoxic in laboratory animals; extensive but indirect evidence for similar serotonin nerve damage in human recreational users.
MDA or "Adam"	Similar effects to MDMA.
MDA, or MDEA, or "Eve"	Similar effects to MDMA and MDA.
Other drug types	
Phencyclidine (PCP), or "angel dust"	A dissociative anaesthetic.
Ketamine	Another dissociative anaesthetic with similar effects to PCP.
Scopolamine doses	An anticholinergic that induces mental clouding or "twilight sleep" at high doses.

The dissociative effects of ketamine generally last only an hour, although PCP is generally longer lasting. Recovery from small doses can be quite rapid, although, after higher doses, mental confusion and memory lapses combined with odd and bizarre behaviours may be evident for days afterward. Psychotic behaviours lasting weeks or months are not unusual, particularly after high or repeated doses. These drugs are said to generate the highest rates of subsequent psychotic behaviour of any of the "recreational" hallucinogens (Julien, 2001; Maisto et al., 1999). In neurochemical terms these two drugs have a similar basic structure and both bind to the N-methyl-D-aspartate (NMDA) glutamate receptor complex. By binding to this largely postsynaptic receptor complex, PCP and ketamine prevent the ionic channels from opening and, so, block neurotransmission. Since glutamate is the main excitatory system in the brain (Chapter 3), this causes the wide spectrum of analgesic, amnesic, psychedelic and psychomotor actions.

Scopolamine, or hyoscine, is an antagonist at the muscarinic acetylcholine receptor. It blocks ACh receptor sites and, so, reduces cholinergic neural activity (Chapter 2). In small doses it cannot only be used to prevent motion sickness but also to reduce memory and impair sustained attention (Parrott, 1986, 1989). At moderate doses it generates drowsiness and marked amnesia. At high doses it leads to mental confusion and a cloudy state of dreamy awareness called "twilight sleep". There is marked variation in responsiveness to scopolamine, which means that mental confusion can develop at low doses in susceptible individuals. Scopolamine and the other cholinergic antagonists are rarely used for recreational purposes. However, in medieval times, plants with **anticholinergic** ingredients were taken for a variety of interesting purposes. Small amounts of the atropine-containing deadly nightshade (*Atropa belladonna*, or beautiful woman) were used by medieval beauties as a cosmetic aid, since it dilates the pupil and, thus, signifies sexual arousal (Julien, 2001; Maisto et al., 1999). **Atropine** is used by the armed forces as a prophylactic against nerve agent poisoning, since it helps to prevent the massive cholinergic overstimulation that results from a nerve agent attack. At high doses, atropine can prove lethal, and deadly nightshade has been employed by criminal poisoners over the centuries. Other plants with anticholinergic ingredients include jimson weed (*Datura stramonium*, or thorn apple, or devil's apple) and the mandrake (*Mandragora officinarum*) root mentioned in John Donne's poem *Go Catch A Falling Star*. High doses of these plants can lead to delirium and the perception of flying – a useful trait for aspirant witches.

Questions

1   Describe the acute neurochemical and experiential effects of LSD.

2   Explain why hippies in the 1960s believed that LSD should only be taken when in a good frame of mind and in a supportive environment.

3   Why might LSD be particularly inadvisable in an individual with a predisposition to psychotic breakdown?

4   Describe the psychobiological consequences of a single dose of MDMA, or Ecstasy.

5   Outline the long-term neuropsychological consequences of regular MDMA/ Ecstasy use in humans.

6   It has been suggested that MDMA and cannabis are "soft" drugs without many adverse effects. Do you agree ? (Note: this question also applies to Chapter 7.)

7   Debate the methodological problems involved in undertaking research into illicit recreational drugs.

8   Compare the neurochemical and behavioural effects of ketamine, phencyclidine and scopolamine.

Key references and reading

Abraham HD, Aldridge AM and Gogia P (1996). The psychopharmacology of hallucinogens. *Neuropsychopharmacology*, **14**, 285–298.

Cohen RS (1998). *The Love Drug: Marching to the Beat of Ecstasy*. Haworth Medical Press, New York.

Glennon RA (1996). Classic hallucinogens. In: CR Schuster and MJ Kuhar (eds), *Pharmacological Aspects of Drug Dependence: Towards an Integrated Neurobehavioral Approach*. Springer-Verlag, Berlin.

Green AR, Mechan AO, Elliott JM, O'Shea E and Colado MI (2004). The pharmacology and clinical pharmacology of 3,4-methylenedioxymethamphetamine (MDMA, "ecstasy"). *Pharmacological Reviews* (in press).

Parrott AC (2001). Human psychopharmacology of Ecstasy/MDMA: A review of fifteen years of empirical research. *Human Psychopharmacology*, **16**, 557–577.

Parrott AC, Buchanan T, Scholey AB, Heffernan T, Ling J and Rodgers J (2002). Ecstasy/ MDMA attributed problems reported by novice, moderate, and heavy users. *Human Psychopharmacology*, **17**, 309–312.

Saunders N (1995). *Ecstasy and the Dance Culture*. Neal's Yard Desktop Publishing, London.

Chapter 7

Cannabis

Overview

Cannabis has been used for thousands of years in cultural and religious ceremonies and as a "treatment" for various medical ailments. For centuries beliefs about cannabis were based on personal anecdotes and reflected sociocultural wisdom. Then, in the 20th century during the "golden age" of empirical pharmacology, the main focus was on the development of new disorder-specific compounds; this led to cannabinoids being ignored as possible therapeutic agents. Cannabis was then widely used for recreational purposes and, despite government edicts describing it as dangerous and addictive, it has remained the most popular of the illicit recreational drugs. Furthermore, although legal restrictions have been relaxed in some countries, other governments have seen it as a "gateway drug" that leads to harder, more damaging compounds. The active ingredients of smoked or ingested cannabis are several cannabinoids including tetrahydrocannabinol; these bind to the cannabinoid receptor and increase hyperpolarisation, inhibiting neuronal activity in a dose-dependent manner. Cannabis's behavioural effects are therefore primarily sedative, with emotional relaxation, euphoria, distorted time perception, psychomotor slowing and impaired memory. Some regular users also display sensitisation rather than tolerance, needing less drug to achieve the same subjective effect. In Westernised societies many recreational users develop intensive patterns of use, when drug taking predominates over other more useful activities, although the exact nature of this amotivational syndrome has been extensively debated. However, in other societies (India, Jamaica), cannabis is used to facilitate physically tiring work, such as cane cutting. Chronic users display a range of cognitive/memory impairments, although it is unclear whether these deficits are restricted to the periods of cannabis intoxication or endure following drug cessation. Regular cannabis use can also exacerbate schizophrenic breakdowns in predisposed individuals. However, their analgesic and muscular-relaxant properties may make cannabinoids medically useful for several disorders including multiple sclerosis, glaucoma and the relief of nausea/pain during chemotherapy.

Cannabis

Cannabis sativa is the specific name for the marijuana plant that grows wild in many parts of the world. The plant is unique in producing the psychoactive chemicals known as cannabinoids, the most important being tetrahydrocannabinol (tetrahydro-6,6,9-trimethyl-3-pentyl-6H-dibenzo[b,d]pyran-1-ol), or **THC**. Within the plant the THC content is greatest in the flowering buds, with much less in the leaves, stems and seeds, successively. Different subspecies of the plant contain different quantities of THC, and selective breeding has led to the production of varieties with very high concentrations (6–20% of dried preparation). Marijuana (grass) is prepared by drying the flowering buds and upper leaves of the plant. Hashish (solid) is produced by sifting the mature cannabis tops through a series of fine sieves until a resinous powder remains. This powder is compressed and heated to allow the resins to melt, binding the remaining vegetable matter into a block.

Historical use

The earliest documented reference to cannabis was 2737 BC in China in the world's first pharmacopoeia *Shen Nung's Pen Ts'ao* where it is described as a "superior herb". Chinese doctors prescribed it extensively as a medication for rheumatism, malaria, bowel disorders, "female weakness" and, curiously, considering the (now) well established subjective and cognitive effects, absent-mindedness. Mixing with wine reportedly produced a potent anaesthetic. However, its use as a recreational **drug** was not condoned in China, and it was called the liberator of sin (Bloomquist, 1971). Over the centuries use of the plant gradually spread around the globe. The people of India had a much different attitude toward using the plant than did the Chinese. Hinduism is and has been for millennia the major religion if India, where cannabis use has long been associated with religious activities. The perception-altering effects of smoked cannabis have been used in Hinduism to enhance concentration on prayer by inducing a removal from the normal world and its distractions. Aside from religious uses, variations of **cannabis** were used to treat dysentery, sunstroke, indigestion, reduced appetite, speech impediments and to bring "alertness to the body and gaiety to the mind", as noted in the *Sustra*, a book compiled sometime before 1000 BC. Around the time of the life of Christ the renowned physician Galen extolled the recreational uses of cannabis and recommended its use in curing gas pains, earaches and other ailments. In medieval Islam, cannabis consumption was chiefly connected to religious and mystic events and, although there were no social sanctions regarding its use, warnings were made that overconsumption could lead to "madness".

In America, George Washington was a hemp farmer, although it seems that there was little knowledge of the intoxicating properties of the plant until Mexican immigrants later introduced social consumption of the plant. By the 19th century, cannabis use had spread from the Middle East to the artists and writers of Europe, most notably by "Le Club des Haschischins" (The Club of Hashish Eaters) in Paris, and as a result popular fiction also raised the profile of cannabis use thanks to the writings of some of the members of the club: *The Count of Monte Cristo* by Dumas and *Artificial Paradise* by Baudelaire. Medical use of cannabis in Western culture became increasingly widespread after Napoleon's invasion of Egypt, and physicians, such as O'Shaughnessy and Aubert-Roche, began to call attention to the drug's uses in treating rheumatism and increasing appetite (Abel, 1980). Queen Victoria's menstrual cramps were reputedly treated with cannabis. At the same time, cannabis was being widely promoted in the USA as a medicine and a euphoriant. Cannabis eventually became sufficiently well known to enter legend: for example, the Hashishiyya religious cult reputedly murdered political enemies of Hasan-Ibn-Sabbah, an Eastern warlord who allegedly used cannabis to coerce them into committing the violent acts. Although numerous sociologists and socio-psychiatrists have refuted the historical truthfulness of this story, it was, coincidentally, one of the "concrete" examples used by the Commissioner of the Federal Bureau of Narcotics in his 1937 efforts to put a prohibition on marijuana in America (Bloomquist, 1971).

Recreational use in the 20th and 21st centuries

Cannabis use for recreational purposes first became prevalent in the USA in the 1920s and, due to the strong anti-drugs sentiment at the time, was removed from the pharmacopoeia, classed as a narcotic and made illegal. However, its use did not decline – President Kennedy used cannabis for pain relief and in later years President Clinton also admitted to cannabis smoking, although apparently without inhaling (Chapters 1 and 15). There was a dramatic increase in the recreational use of cannabis by the young in Western society during the 1960s and 1970s, with the advent of the hippie culture and consumption being believed mainly by adolescents to bring about a relaxed state. The popularity of cannabis as a social intoxicant remains the case today despite its legal status. In the UK a survey carried out for the Department of Health (2001) indicated that 12% of 11 to 16-year-olds and 28% of 15 to 16-year-olds had used cannabis. A further survey by Miller and Plant (2002) identified that 7.6% of 15 to 16-year-olds reported being heavy users (40 or more occasions). By comparison, in 1995 in America 42% of high school students reported having tried cannabis, with 5% using it on a daily basis. Under the Clinton administration 1,450,751 people were arrested for cannabis offences (86% for possession only). In the UK the number of arrests for possession of cannabis rose from 11,493 in 1986 to 24,386 in 1995 (*The Guardian*, 1998). However, this figure is set to fall in the 21st century as the legal status of cannabis is revised and the attitude of the police softens. British police and customs seized over 30,000 kilos in 1990; this rose to 45,000 kilos in 1995, with a street value of several million pounds. However, it is estimated that this represents less than 10% of the amount consumed. Cannabis is by far the most widely cultivated, trafficked and abused illicit drug. Half of all drug seizures worldwide are cannabis seizures. The geographical spread of these seizures is also global, covering practically every country of the world (United Nations Office for Drug Control and Crime Prevention, 1991).

How does THC get to the brain?

Cannabis is usually smoked in a joint, which is approximately the size of a cigarette, and tobacco may be included to assist burning and/or to reduce **potency**. Smokers tend to inhale the smoke deeply and hold it in the lungs for long periods in order to maximise absorption of the active compounds. Cannabis can be eaten. However, the amount of drug required to produce **psychoactive** effects is approximately 2–3 times more than when it is smoked; this is because the lungs are more efficient at transporting the airborne THC to the blood (bioavailability β of ∼20%) than the gastrointestinal tract is at absorbing the fat-soluble THC across its membrane (bioavailability β of ∼6%). Furthermore, when ingested orally some of the THC is degraded in the stomach and more is metabolised by the liver before it reaches the brain. When smoked the effects are rapid in onset with THC entering the circulation almost immediately and reaching peak concentrations (between 20 and 45% of total THC content) within 10 minutes. When taken orally the time to peak is around 1–3 hours and duration is prolonged due to continued slow absorption from the gut (Chapter 3). As a consequence, smoking provides greater control: it is quicker and easier to self-titrate to the individual's required level of psychoactive sensation when smoking compared with when the drug is eaten (Hall et al., 1994).

Interestingly, however, the peak in blood concentration does not always represent the period when users report experiencing the greatest high; this is unusual when compared with other drugs, and the answer appears to lie in the body's metabolism of THC. Some of the breakdown products of the cannabinoids (e.g., 11-hydroxy-Δ-9-THC) are also psychoactive. As a consequence these breakdown products and THC may act together to produce the greatest effect some 20 to 30 minutes after smoking, when serum THC levels have started to decline (Figure 7.1).

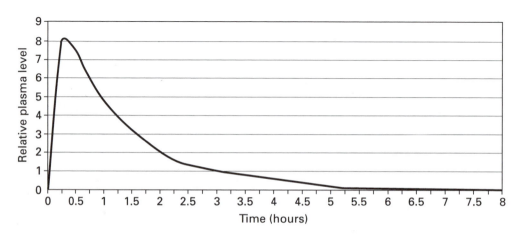

Figure 7.1. Time course of the effects of a single dose of cannabis (smoked).

Neuropharmacology

There are over 400 constituent compounds in marijuana. More than 60 of these are pharmacologically active cannabinoids, of which 4 are the most important. The most psychoactive is delta-9-tetrahydrocannabinol (Δ-9-THC). The other three important natural cannabinoids are Δ-8-THC, cannabinol and cannabidiol (Kumar et al., 2001). In addition, some of the metabolites of THC, such as 11-hydroxy-Δ-9-THC, are also psychoactive. As a consequence and contrary to many other drugs, the metabolism of THC in the liver does not decrease intoxication, rather it prolongs it.

Until fairly recently it was thought that cannabis affected neuronal membrane fluidity, an action shared with alcohol. Research in the 1980s and 1990s then demonstrated that specific **cannabinoid** receptors, named CB_1 and CB_2 existed (Pertwee, 1997a). Subsequently, a further lesser **receptor** has also been identified. These high-affinity, stereoselective, saturable binding sites for cannabinoids in the brain are most densely concentrated in the **hippocampus**, **cerebellum**, **cerebral cortex** and **basal ganglia** (Herkenham et al., 1991), and this distribution is reflected in the biobehavioural effects of cannabis. These binding sites possess all the characteristics of a typical neurotransmitter receptor site. Cannabinoid receptors are coupled to the same G protein as are dopaminergic and opioid receptors; this may indicate a common mechanism underlying the reinforcing properties of cannabis, opiates, cocaine and amphetamine (Self and Stein, 1992). When present at the cannabinoid receptor, THC acts by inhibiting the activity of **adenyl cyclase**, an **enzyme** that stimulates the secondary messenger, cyclic adenosine mono phosphate (**cyclic AMP**), to alter the excitability of the neuron. The higher the concentration of THC the greater the enzyme is inhibited and, consequently, the greater the psychoactive effects. In addition the receptors are also able to block calcium channels and, so, reduce calcium movement into cells and at the same time open potassium channels leading to neuronal hyperpolarisation (Hirst et al., 1998; Pertwee, 1997a, b, 1998). There are also reports that there are effects of cannabinoids that may not be mediated through cannabinoid receptors; these may lead to several different biochemical pathways being affected (Pertwee, 1990).

The cellular actions of cannabinoids clearly support the proposal that the cannabinoid receptor is inhibitory and, consequently, reduces the firing rate of target neurons. However, this is not wholly confirmed by electrophysiological measurements, which suggest that cannabinoid compounds can stimulate neurons in the hippocampus. This apparent discrepancy may be due to the ability of cannabinoids to inhibit the release of an inhibitory substance in the hippocampus and, thus, produce a net excitation.

Half-life and measurement of THC

A two-phase model best describes the half-life of THC. Within the first phase (α), levels of THC fall to 5–10% of initial levels within 1 hour; this is because the drug has been metabolised by the liver and removed from the plasma into lipid tissue. Research has indicated that the elimination phase (β) depends on the experience of the user. Occasional users have a plasma elimination half-life of 56 hours, compared with chronic users of 28 hours. However, because cannabinoids accumulate in fat the tissue half-life is about 7 days and complete elimination may take up to 30 days. As a result, it is easy to test if someone has used cannabis in the last month, but more difficult to establish if the person was intoxicated at the time of testing. Cannabis use can be identified through tests of urine, blood, sweat, saliva and even hair. The most widely used forensic urine test actually measures a metabolite, 9-carboxy-THC which is not psychoactive. As such it does not provide information on how much of the drug was taken, when it was taken or the effects of administration on physiology and behaviour. For these reasons it is much more difficult to charge persons with such offences as driving while under the influence of cannabis. Suspects would simply claim that the residual compounds reflected a period of intoxication some days earlier. Such a claim would be difficult to refute.

Endogenous compounds

The human brain possesses about 100 times as many cannabinoid receptors as it does opioid receptors, and they are more densely distributed than any other G-protein-coupled receptor (Feldman et al., 1997); this is because the brain manufactures at least two compounds with properties similar to THC. The most important are **anandamide** and 2-arachidonylglycerol (2-AG), which bind to the cannabinoid synaptic receptors (Devane et al., 1992; Mechoulam et al., 1998; Pertwee, 1999). Whether these compounds are true **neurotransmitters**, or neuromodulators, is not entirely clear at this time. Anandamide produces similar effects to Δ-9-THC but is less potent and has a shorter half-life. 2-AG is present at 170 times higher levels than anandamide in the brain and has been found to act in the hippocampus, where it disrupts long-term potentiation (increased strength of cell communication), a process involved in memory formation. It is suggested that THC acts like 2-AG in the hippocampus, modulating the formation of short-term memories and producing a form of physiological forgetting. Anandamide does not appear to be present in the hippocampus, but research has indicated that it may produce the **analgesic**, hypothermic and locomotor effects ascribed to cannabinoids (Fride and Machoulam, 1993; Smith et al., 1994). It has been suggested that there is a division of labour between the two endogenous cannabinoids, with each serving different functions in different brain areas. Research is still ongoing in an attempt to find further endogenous cannabinoids and identify further the pathways that they may be involved in.

Once THC is bound to presynaptic and postsynaptic receptor sites, a way to stop its action is required. Otherwise, stimulation could continue indefinitely and a perpetual "high" could be maintained from just a few puffs of marijuana. Research has shown that the endogenous cannabinoid anandamide is deactivated by being removed from receptors and transported into the cell, where it is broken down by an enzyme into non-active components. This process is believed to be the same for THC.

Functional neuroanatomy for cannabinoid action

Cannabinoids have been found to modulate a variety of neurotransmitter systems; these include a reduction of cholinergic activity in the hippocampus (Miller and Branconnier, 1983) and an increase in **norepinephrine** activity in animal models (Pertwee, 1990). However, there has been little research that has attempted to localise the behavioural effects of cannabinoids to particular brain regions. Consequently, we do not yet know exactly how the occupation of cannabinoid receptors by the constituents of marijuana lead to the complex behavioural effects observed. However, with a knowledge of the anatomical locations of the cannabinoid receptors, it is possible to speculate. Cannabinoids are able to enhance **dopamine** release in the **nucleus accumbens** (Chen et al., 1990a, b), an action shared with other rewarding or addictive drugs. However, the neurons that link the ventral tegmental area (VTA) to the nucleus acumbens do not possess cannabinoid receptors themselves. It is thought that cannabinoids impinge on other systems that then regulate dopamine neurons in the mesolimbic system. One component of such control may be through the striatonigral system, which has high densities of cannabinoid receptors. This indirect stimulation of the nucleus acumbens may also be related to the low addictive potential of cannabis compared with such highly addictive drugs as heroin and cocaine.

This system is important for integrating sensory information from the cerebral cortex. Thus, the striatonigral cells that express cannabinoid receptors may be involved in the control of the dopamine cells in the substantia nigra, a region known to be involved in the control of voluntary movement. Whether these neurons are responsible for the sedation and hyper-reflexia behavioural effects observed is still not known, but seems plausible. Interestingly, work by Herkenham et al. (1991) also demonstrated that there are very few cannabinoid receptors found in the ventral pallidum, the part of the striatonigral system that is believed to control **limbic** activity and euphoria. Again, these findings support the low reinforcing properties of cannabis.

Cannabinoid receptors are expressed throughout the cerebral cortex and the hippocampus, and a subpopulation of these cells appear to show an unusually high level of activity. It is possible that cells in these areas modulate the sensory effects of cannabis, particularly the effects on perception, task performance and memory. In addition, the **anticonvulsant** properties of cannabis are believed to be mediated here. Parts of the **hypothalamus** show high levels of receptor sites for cannabinoids; this may be related to hypothermia effects. High levels in the cerebellum may be related to mediating the property of cannabinoids that produces the reduction in ataxic (muscle co-ordination) symptoms in certain disorders (Herkenham et al., 1991).

Psychoactive and behavioural effects

The first recorded studies into the effects of cannabis were carried out by the French physician Moreau in the early 19th century, who was interested in the relationship between the state of cannabis intoxication and the characteristics of mental illness. Moreau and his students recorded their subjective experiences after consuming varying quantities of hashish. The reports of perceptual distortions, personality changes and hallucinations at very high doses were drawn together in a book entitled *Hashish and Mental Alienation.*

The rise in social and recreational use of cannabis in the 20th century coincided with the decline of medicinal applications and the development of legal restrictions on the possession and use of the plant. As a consequence the psychoactive and physiological effects and side effects of marijuana have been somewhat shrouded in myth and mystery, rather than the subject of close scientific scrutiny. During the 1920s and 1930s the media and popular press (particularly in the USA) were filled with outlandish accounts of debauchery, violence and the criminal propensities of anyone who smoked cannabis even just once. In keeping with this attitude, early official research was often flawed in terms of design and the nature of its conclusions. Cannabis users who were studied were commonly polydrug users and addicts, although this was often not made explicit, the consequences of cannabis use described being largely inaccurate or at least exaggerated. A large amount of the early research into the effects of cannabis employed participants smoking the drug, but this produced problems related to puff volume, puff rate and length of time the breath is held. Recent years have seen marked improvements in the quality of psychopharmacological research and our knowledge about cannabis has correspondingly improved. The employment of controlled smoking regimes and the administration of active compounds separately – either orally, intravenously or through patches – has led to more replicable results.

Subjective effects

The experiential effects of smoking cannabis are usually "lighter" than many other recreational psychoactive substances. These effects include sensations of **euphoria** and exhilaration, perceptual alterations, time distortion and increased hunger and thirst. The subjective effects can be broadly grouped into positive, neutral/negative and more strongly negative categories (Table 7.1), with many of the strongly negative effects being a consequence of high doses.

The ability to produce a subjective high is probably the most important single action sustaining the widespread and often chronic recreational use of cannabis. Surveys have demonstrated that pleasure and relaxation are the main reasons given

Table 7.1. Subjective consequences of cannabis administration.

Positive	Neutral/Negative	Strongly negative
Mood lift	Increased appetite	Nausea
Relaxation	Mental slowness	Respiratory problems
Creative thinking	Physical tiredness	Racing heart
Heightened sensations	Mouth dryness	Anxiety
Pleasant body feelings	Losing train of thought	Agitation
Pain relief		Headaches
Reduced nausea		Paranoia

by users for taking cannabis (Webb et al., 1998; Chait and Zacny, 1992). The euphoriant effect varies considerably with respect to dose, mode of administration, expectation, environment and personality of the taker. When small doses are taken in social settings the main effects are somewhat similar to those of social doses of alcohol – euphoria, talkativeness and laughter. A greater high can be induced by as little as 2.5 mg of THC in a joint, depending on the taker's previous experience; this is characterised by feelings of intoxication and detachment, combined with decreased anxiety, alertness, depression and tension, in addition to perceptual changes (Ashton, 1999). The intensity of the high is dose-dependent, being increased by higher doses. **Dysphoric** reactions to cannabis are not uncommon in naive takers. These reactions typically include anxiety, panic, **paranoia**, restlessness and a sense of loss of control. Vomiting may occur, especially if cannabis is taken when intoxicated with alcohol. Flashbacks to unpleasant previous cannabis experiences when there has been no further exposure to the drug have been reported, and it has been suggested that these may be psychological reactions similar to that of post-traumatic stress disorder (Ashton, 1999).

Tolerance, addiction and dependence

Laboratory studies indicate that chronic tolerance can often develop with the effects on mood, intraocular pressure (see below) and psychomotor impairment. This tolerance is largely pharmacodynamic and occurs at the level of the cannabinoid receptor. Animal studies have shown that chronic administration produced a global downgrade in the activity of cannabinoid receptors. Furthermore, decreases in noradrenalin and increases in dopamine have been reported, indicating that cannabinoids can produce adaptation in several central nervous system (CNS) pathways. Despite this evidence for cannabinoid **dependence**, there is little evidence for problematic withdrawal symptoms. Abrupt discontinuation after chronic heavy use has been reported to result in a withdrawal syndrome characterised by insomnia, irritable mood, nausea and drug cravings (Miller and Gold, 1989; Jacobs and Fehr, 1987). However, these withdrawal symptoms are usually described as mild and non-specific, although the increasing strength of marijuana has led to the emergence of more severe withdrawal syndrome, particularly in adolescents (Duffy and Millin, 1996). In pharmacological terms, animal models have indicated that withdrawal can interfere with the **serotonin** system, which may be responsible for the mood changes outlined here. Furthermore, cannabinoids may interact with the endogenous opioid system to partially enhance dopamine levels in the reward circuit of the CNS, and, so, increase its addictive potential (Miller and Gold, 1993).

Given the low incidence of severe withdrawal symptoms and the modest effects on the mesolimbic dopamine (reward) system, most investigators have found that cannabis has a low **abuse** or addiction potential. However, it has been argued that if cannabis is a non-addictive substance, why is its use so widespread and why are there so many long-term and heavy users? Finally, contrary to the evidence that cannabis can produce chronic **tolerance**, some regular users report that they require less drug to achieve the same high, or sensitisation (Chapter 3). Three possible explanations may account for this. First, chronic users may focus on the effects that they wish to achieve. Second, the fat-soluble nature of THC and its metabolites means that they are stored in fatty tissues and released back into the plasma gradually. Consequently, chronic users may have higher basal levels of blood-borne cannabinoids than casual users. Third and perhaps most importantly, the livers of people who smoke marijuana regularly for a long time become more efficient at metabolising THC, so that it can be removed from the body. By doing this the liver converts THC into a metabolite that also makes the user "high"; this may be why long-term marijuana smokers get high more easily from a small amount of marijuana than those who do not regularly smoke (Lemberger et al., 1971; Kupfer et al., 1973).

Acute cognitive effects

The effects of cannabis on thought processes are characterised initially by a feeling of increased speed of thinking. Higher doses can lead to thoughts becoming out of control and becoming fragmented, so leading to mental confusion. Impairment of short-term memory is demonstrable even after small doses in experienced cannabis users (Gold, 1992), although memory for simple "real world" information does not seem impaired (Block and Wittenborn, 1986). Cannabis-induced decrements in performance have been demonstrated on a number of verbal and spatial recall tasks, and it is thought that these are produced by a failure to filter out irrelevant material during consolidation (Solowij, 1998; Golding, 1992). The influence of cannabis on perception, motor co-ordination and general levels of arousal combine to impair psychomotor task performance. Reaction time is generally unimpaired at very low "social" doses, but become significantly impaired after two or three joints (30–80 mg THC). This impairment becomes even more pronounced when multiple or integrated responses are required to the environment, as in complex tracking or divided attention tasks (Golding, 1992; Heishman et al., 1997).

Performance on even more complex tasks, such as motoring or aircraft flight simulation, can be significantly impaired by as little as 20 mg THC (Barnet et al., 1985). Dual-control motoring was assessed on both a closed artificial driving course and in the actual streets of Vancouver (Klonoff, 1974). The closed course driving included slalom manoeuvring, reversing, risk judgement and emergency braking. The open street driving involved starting, stopping, lane changing, careless driving and overcautious driving. Under low doses of cannabis, between 33 and 42% of drivers showed a significant degree of driving impairment, and this figure increased to 55–63% under the higher dose (Klonoff, 1974). Several further research groups have demonstrated significant impairments in real world motoring and artificial driving simulation (Parrott, 1987). Analysis of performance on a range of subtasks that make up the simulation exercises indicates that the impairments observed may be due to decreased co-ordination, short-term memory and perception and judgement of time and distance. Furthermore, these impairments are often still present 8 hours after smoking cannabis and have been demonstrated at lower levels 24 hours later (Robb and O'Hanlon, 1993). The level of risk taking has been found to be reduced in some (but not all) studies on these kinds of tasks. Hart et al. (2001) reported that acute marijuana smoking produced minimal effects on complex cognitive task performance in experienced marijuana users.

Prior cannabis use may reduce the adverse cognitive effects of new cannabis exposure, cognitive tolerance may develop in some heavy users or their off-cannabis performance may be impaired by years of regular usage (Cohen and Rickles, 1974). Polydrug usage is another contributory factor, with the psychobiological decrements being potentiated by **alcohol** (Chait and Pierri, 1992) and many other psychoactive drugs (Parrott et al., 2001; Chapters 4–10). The prior drug experience of participants and their regular drug usage patterns are certainly important confounding factors in this and other areas of recreational drug research (Chapter 6).

Chronic cognitive effects

The long-term use of cannabis does not produce the severe impairments of cognitive functioning seen with chronic heavy alcohol use (Chapters 9 and 10). The possibility that chronic heavy cannabis use may lead to a degree of long-term or permanent cognitive impairment has been investigated, but resulted in mixed findings. A number of studies have indicated that heavy users exhibit temporary deficits for hours or days after stopping cannabis use (Pope et al., 1995; Pope and Yurgelun-Todd, 1996; Struve et al., 1999), perhaps due to withdrawal effects or to a residue of cannabinoids lingering in the brain. Rodgers (2000) reported no impairments on a number of computerised reaction time, visual memory, attention and concentration tasks, although a number of verbal memory measures were significantly impaired. Pope et al. (2001a, b) reported detectable cognitive deficits up to 7 days after heavy cannabis use. These deficits were reversible and related to recent cannabis exposure, rather than irreversible and related to cumulative lifetime use.

In contrast, performance on a complex selective attention task was compared between a group of ex-heavy users with mean abstinence of 2 years versus continuing users and controls (Solowij, 1995). The results showed impairments in the continuing cannabis users compared with controls, and, although the ex-users showed partial improvement compared with current users, they remained significantly impaired compared with the controls. The degree of impairment was also related to lifetime duration of cannabis use, and there was no concomitant improvement with increasing length of abstinence; this allowed the authors to conclude that the regular use of cannabis could adversely affect cognitive functioning in the longer term. In a further study, Solowij et al. (2002) reported significant decrements in performance on tests of memory and attention for chronic heavy users, but not short-term users, compared with controls. Unfortunately, the researchers did not exclude users who may have had pre-existing mental disorders or those who were taking medications that may have affected their performance (Pope, 2002). Furthermore, Pope (2002) identified that early onset users (<17 years) performed worse than late onset users on a range of cognitive performance measures, most notably verbal measures. However, the authors note that their results do not exclude the possibility of pre-existing differences between groups or the influence of an "alternative" lifestyle away from mainstream education, rather than the direct effects of cannabis use on the brain. Such confounds may have influenced their findings. Finally, in a study of cognitive decline in persons under 65 years of age, Lyketsos et al. (1999) found no significant differences between heavy users, light users and non-users of cannabis in terms of degree of decline. In conclusion, the long-term cognitive consequences of regular cannabis use remains an area of uncertainty.

Motoring and manual work

The British Government released a road safety report on cannabis and driving in 1999. The report indicated that although laboratory-based cognitive performance tasks revealed clear impairments following cannabis administration, such effects were not as pronounced on tasks with more ecological validity, such as real and simulated motoring; this was considered to be a result of compensatory effort being applied, and is somewhat at odds with the evidence presented above (Klonoff, 1974; Parrott, 1987). Accident risk is difficult to assess based on actual incidents due to the confounding effect of alcohol, which is nearly always present in both fatal and non-fatal road accidents where cannabis is found. The report identifies that research into the area has been impeded by methodological, legal and ethical problems, and, as a consequence, reliable conclusions cannot be drawn at this time. Sexton et al. (2000) produced a report for the government based on "typical" experienced users' performances on a driving simulator. The results showed that participants drove at significantly slower speed when under the influence of both high and low doses, but that no differences were found between braking reaction times or hazard perception times. However, because of the considerable variability in their results the researchers concluded that driving under the influence of cannabis should not be considered safe. Ferguson and Horwood (2001) examined the possible linkages between cannabis use and traffic accidents in a cohort of 18 to 21-year-olds in New Zealand. They concluded that although cannabis was associated with increased risks of traffic accidents among this cohort, these risks more likely reflected the characteristics of the young people who used cannabis rather than the effect of cannabis on driver performance.

In a psycho-sociological study of sugar cane cutters in Jamaica, Comitas (1975) compared groups of labourers who used "ganja", the local name for cannabis, with other labourer groups who did not use it. The cane cutting yields over the harvesting season were very similar, although the groups did differ in their work patterns. The ganja users started the day by lighting up and smoking as a social group before working, then each individual claimed a patch of cane to clear with their machetes. Interviews revealed that work motivation and social bonding were felt to be improved by ganja: "I don't interrupt nobody ... I feel good about everybody." Indeed, many of the farm owners provided free supplies of ganja to the groups that they hired (see Parrott, 1987).

This finding was predated by the three-volume report of the Indian Hemp Commission from 1898, when Queen Victoria's government concluded that the smoking of cannabis, or hemp, did not impair the work rates of farm labourers in the Indian subcontinent. However, it should be emphasised that these reports were concerned with "old-fashioned" natural cannabis, whose THC content was around 1–2%; this was the type used by hippies in the 1960s. But, during the 1970s selective plant breeding and hydroponic plant cultures led to increased THC values of around

8%. Since then the THC content of some cannabis supplies has exceeded 13%; this is probably the major factor in the increased rates of cannabis-related problems during the past few decades (Chapter 15). Reports of cannabis-induced paranoia were comparatively infrequent during the 1960s; but, with higher THC contents, feelings of cannabis-induced paranoia are now far more commonplace, as are other adverse psychiatric sequelae (see below).

Physiological and health consequences

A considerable number of early studies from the late 1960s and early 1970s purported to demonstrate that marijuana or cannabis led to the development of brain damage. Post-mortem examinations indicated that the cerebral cortex had atrophied, producing enlarged ventricles; this was trumpeted by the anti-drug lobby as justification from a health point of view of the legal stance on cannabis. However, it was later found that the brains examined in these studies were rarely from people who were only users of marijuana. Indeed, many had head injuries, suffered from epilepsy or possessed a history of polydrug use. The conclusions reached by this early research were widely discredited, as a consequence.

In terms of acute drug effects, inexperienced smokers display a reduction in cerebral blood flow (CBF) following acute exposure to cannabis, whereas experienced smokers display increases in CBF after smoking a single joint. It has been hypothesised that this may be a result of alterations of cannabinoid receptors secondary to chronic exposure (Loeber and Yurgelun-Todd, 1999). Physiologically, cannabis smoking typically produces **tachycardia**, or increased heart rate, but little change in blood pressure. Other common physical reactions are reddening of the conjunctiva (red-eye) and feelings of hunger. The most common adverse psychiatric effect of taking cannabis is anxiety; however, large doses can cause acute toxic psychosis. Symptoms include delirium with confusion, prostration, disorientation, derealisation and auditory and visual hallucinations (Chopra and Smith 1974). Acute paranoid states, mania and hypomania with persecutory and religious delusions and **schizophreniform psychosis** may also occur. These reactions are generally fairly uncommon and are typically dose-related (Hall and Solowij, 1998). They are usually self-limiting over a few days, but schizophreniform psychosis in addition to depression and depersonalization can last for weeks. However, these are often but not always associated with a family history of **psychosis**.

In relation to chronic drug effects, various neuroimaging studies have demonstrated that abstinence from cannabis leads to decreased regional cerebral blood flow in chronic users and that subsequent acute administration increases cerebral blood flow to levels above those of controls (Loeber and Yurgelun-Todd, 1999). Studies examining structural brain changes as a consequence of cannabis use have been few and far between and those that have been done have often complicated by the inclusion of polydrug users as participants. Computerised axial tomography (CAT) imaging has provided no evidence of brain atrophy in heavy cannabis users compared with controls (Co et al., 1977; Kuehnle et al., 1977). The best current method for assessing structural brain changes is high-resolution magnetic resonance imaging

(MRI), but this has not been reported for participants who solely use cannabis on a regular chronic basis. A number of electroencephalogram (EEG) studies have found no differences between controls and chronic cannabis users for either awake or sleeping EEG patterns (Rodin et al., 1970; Stefanis et al., 1977).

It has been suggested that chronic cannabis use can produce an amotivational syndrome, characterised by apathy, loss of motivation and interest and decreased productivity (McGlothlin and West, 1968; Kolansky and Moore, 1972). However, even if this controversial syndrome does exist and many argue that there is still insufficient evidence (Duncan, 1987; Rao, 2001; McKim, 2003), it may be a cause rather than an effect (Feldman et al., 1997). The diathesis stress model predicts that those individuals with the greatest propensity toward low motivation would be most likely to become even more apathetic and amotivated following regular cannabis use (Chapter 6), although this hypothesis does not seem to have been empirically assessed in cannabis users. However, the link between cannabis use and psychotic breakdown has been widely supported and, more recently, a positive association between cannabis use and depression has also been demonstrated (Rey et al., 2002; Bovasso, 2001). It has been reported that a proportion of long-term heavy cannabis users develop paranoid ideation, delusions and hallucinations; these appear to increase with duration of use and to continue after cessation of cannabis use. As a consequence, it has been suggested that chronic cannabis use may cause **schizophrenia**. The debate over whether cannabis can actually cause schizophrenia in patients who would not otherwise develop it is complex and heated. Perhaps the best evidence comes from the longitudinal study of 50,000 Swedish conscripts (Andreasson et al., 1987; Zammit et al., 2002); this indicated that marijuana use during adolescence was prospectively associated with an increased risk of developing schizophrenia, in a dose-dependent manner. However, others have argued that, while cannabis is a risk factor, it may not be a direct cause of the condition (Turner and Tsuang, 1990). Interestingly, those individuals with psychotic disorder who use cannabis moderately do not exhibit greater cognitive impairment than those who do not use substances (Pencer and Addington, 2003).

Cannabis smoke contains similar unhealthy chemicals to tobacco smoke. Thus, cannabis smokers subject their airways and lungs to a range of bronchial poisons and irritants, carcinogenic initiators and promoters, along with noxious carbon monoxide (Chapter 5). Due to the absence of a filter and the increased depth and duration of inhalation, smoking a cannabis joint leads to a threefold greater increase in the amount of tar inhaled and retention in the respiratory tract of one-third more tar than when smoking a cigarette. Therefore, chronic cannabis smoking is not surprisingly associated with bronchitis, emphysema and squamous metaplasia (transformation of the surfaces of the lungs into a scaly skin). The National Institute on Drug Abuse in its 1990 report found that marijuana smoke and that of tobacco affected the lungs in different ways. Tobacco smoke predominantly caused degeneration of the peripheral airways and alveolar regions of the lung, while marijuana smoke affected mainly the large pathways. Because these two drugs affect different parts of the pulmonary system, their damaging effects can be additive (see Chapter 5 for a detailed description of the adverse health effects of smoke inhalation).

There is some evidence from animal studies that cannabis can lead to reduced sperm production and impaired ovulation (Bloch, 1983). Furthermore, it has been reported that prenatal exposure to cannabis leads to significant impairment of executive functioning, as measured by visual analysis and hypothesis-testing tasks in the developing child. However, it does not appear to lead to the impairment of global intelligence, as has been demonstrated for prenatal exposure to cigarette smoke (Fried, 1993). A limited amount of research has investigated possible immunological effects and has produced conflicting evidence. A small number of studies showing adverse effects have not been replicated. However, Cabral and Pettit (1998) argued that cumulative reports indicating that THC alters resistance to infection both *in vitro* and in a variety of experimental animals support the hypothesis that a similar effect occurs in humans. Currently, there is no evidence that cannabis is associated with premature mortality, although the research is as yet in its early stages (Hall and Solowij, 1998). Finally, in comparison with other drugs, cannabis is extremely non-toxic, with no known cases of lethal overdose in humans. The LD_{50} in rats is the equivalent of eating more than their body weight, which would be the same as a human smoking 7 kilos of THC in one session! The reason that cannabis is so safe is the very low densities of receptors in the cardiovascular and respiratory control centres of the **medulla oblongata** (Herkenham et al., 1991), so that these vital functions remain unaffected even after consciousness is lost.

Medicinal uses

Considerable controversy exists regarding the possible medicinal uses of cannabis. As noted earlier, historically cannabis was widely used for many therapeutic purposes, but only in the latter part of the 20th century have scientific trials into its medicinal efficacy commenced. As recently as 1994, the US Court of Appeals ruled that marijuana should remain as a schedule I drug, defined as having high addiction potential and no medical uses. The US Department of Justice Drug Enforcement Administration similarly stated on its website in January 2002: "There are over 10,000 scientific studies that prove marijuana is a harmful addictive drug. There is not one reliable study that demonstrates that marijuana has any medical value." This is despite the growing evidence to the contrary (see below). In recent years the main research focus, particularly in Europe, has been into possible therapeutic uses for cannabinoids.

Multiple sclerosis is one of the oldest disorders where it has been claimed that cannabis provides symptomatic relief. It is somewhat paradoxical that cannabinoids are reported to be of therapeutic value in a neurological disorder associated with motor spasticity, ataxia and muscle weakness, because similar symptoms can be caused by cannabis itself. Early studies indicated no benefits from administering cannabis, despite anecdotal evidence to the contrary. However, much of this early research was poorly designed, often looking at only single cases with minimal blinding and rarely employing objective measures of improvement. However, more recent studies have described how oral THC can relieve symptoms in both single and double-blind **placebo**-controlled trials (Petro, 1980; Martyn et al., 1995; Consroe et al., 1996; Maurer et al., 1990). In a letter to the journal *Nature*, Baker et al. (2000) described how an animal model of multiple sclerosis: "provided evidence for the rational assessment of cannabinoid derivatives in the control of spasticity and tremor in multiple sclerosis." Other studies have similarly shown that cannabinoids can help to relieve night leg pain, ataxia (inco-ordination caused by dysfunctional sensory nerve feedback), anxiety, constipation and paresthesia (abnormal sensations in the body, including tingling, pins and needles, skin crawling and partial numbness; Robson, 2001). A multi-centre, double-blind study involving 600 multiple sclerosis patients across the UK revealed significant improvements on subjective but not objective measures following cannabis ingestion (Zajicek et al., 2003). However, the design of the study, types of cannabis interventions, mode of administration and outcome measures do rather invite criticism, nonetheless (Metz and Page, 2003).

Cannabinoids are also useful for the treatment of acute pain and chronic pain, when used either on their own or in combination with other drugs. Cannabinoids have been found to possess analgesic, anti-inflammatory and **muscle-relaxant** properties (Pertwee, 1995). Their analgesic effects appear to be mediated by non-opioid mechanisms and are not reversed by the opioid antagonist naloxone (Segal, 1986). Sites of analgesic cannabinoid action have recently been identified in the brain, spinal cord and periphery, with the latter two providing attractive targets for divorcing the analgesic and psychoactive effects of cannabinoids (Rice, 2001). However, although there are many anecdotal reports of relief from bone and joint pain, cancer pain, menstrual cramps and labour, there have been relatively few controlled clinical trials in humans. Significant improvements have been reported with THC in the treatment of cancer pain (Noyes et al., 1975a, b), postoperative pain (Jain et al., 1981) and phantom limb pain (Dunn and Davies, 1974). In contrast, no effects were found for healthy subjects undergoing wisdom tooth extraction (Raft et al., 1977) nor in patients suffering from neuropathic pain (Lindstrom et al., 1987). The efficacy of THC appears to be comparable with that of **codeine**, and its most likely role in the future would be as an adjunct to other analgesics.

The reduction of nausea in patients taking anti-cancer drug therapy is probably the most widely researched area for cannabis therapy. A number of these studies have shown that oral administration of isolated cannabinoids produce significant improvements, particularly for those patients who have failed to respond to standard anti-nausea treatments during chemotherapy (see Tortorice and O'Connell, 1990 for a comprehensive review). Patients and oncologists have subjectively reported that smoked marijuana is as safe (in this patient group) and effective as isolated oral cannabinoids, but more systematic research trials are required.

The relief of **glaucoma** by smoking cannabis is widely recognised by the public, and the consistent effects of the drug in reducing intraocular pressure (IOP) have been well documented. Several studies have shown that smoked or orally administered cannabis and intravenous infusions of THC can decrease IOP, although only two double-blind trials have been reported (Merritt et al., 1980). However, tolerance to the effects on IOP soon develops (Kumar et al., 2001). This finding, coupled with the problem that many of the elderly patients who are diagnosed with glaucoma are more prone to the adverse effects of anxiety, palpitations and confusion, means that the place of cannabinoids in the treatment of this condition still remains to be established.

Cannabinoids have been shown to dilate bronchioles in healthy subjects following acute administration (Hollister, 1986); this led to the suggested possible use by asthma sufferers. However, the lipophilic nature of cannabinoids meant that aerosol inhalers were not very effective. Smoking of the whole plant and oral THC preparations have been shown to have significant effects for at least 2 hours (Tashkin et al., 1976).

Smoking is not a recommended treatment for asthma, however, due to the irritant and carcinogenic nature of cannabis smoke.

Cannabinoids appear to have a very complex interaction with seizure activity, exerting both anticonvulsant and proconvulsant effects. Anecdotal testimonies abound (Grinspoon and Bakalar, 1993), but there has been very little controlled human research. In single-case studies both use and withdrawal of marijuana have been linked to the resumption of seizures (Keeler and Reifler, 1967; Consroe et al., 1975). In a randomised placebo-controlled blind study, patients who responded poorly to standard treatments experienced improved seizure control in response to cannabidiol administration. Cannabidiol does not interact with cannabinoid receptors, and animal studies indicate that it has different anticonvulsant effects to other cannabinoids (Cunha et al., 1980). As such it may prove to have useful therapeutic properties.

Studies have looked at the treatment of appetite loss during cancer and AIDS treatment, with some beneficial effects reported for isolated cannabinoids (Beal et al., 1995). Migraine has been historically linked to marijuana therapy, but no well-designed studies have investigated this. Withdrawing drug addicts and alcoholics have also reported that the use of cannabis can help to reduce the symptoms of withdrawal (Chesher and Jackson, 1985). The euphoric and sedative nature of cannabis has also led to the suggestion that it may be used in cases of depression, anxiety and insomnia. Many of these studies have reported promising findings (Regelson et al., 1976; Carlini and Cunha, 1981; Ilaria et al., 1981). However, human psychopharmacology is notorious for reporting beneficial findings in short-term studies, lasting just a few weeks or months: for instance, amphetamine was described as a useful antidepressant during the 1930s. However, these acute beneficial effects are often not replicated when the drugs are used for more extended periods. This general pattern of acute benefits and chronic deficits may well be replicated with cannabis.

Synthetic cannabinoids

Drug companies have been keen to isolate and synthesise cannabinoid **analogues** with therapeutic effects. Initially, many of these synthesised products were shown to possess little medical efficacy, suggesting that cannabis and cannabinoids probably had only minimal therapeutic value. However, more recent developments have produced at least one synthetic cannabinoid (HU-211) that has potentially beneficial properties (Mechoulam, 2000). HU-211 appears to have neuroprotective characteristics, such that, following exposure to a deadly nerve gas, rats treated with the compound exhibited 87% less brain lesion volume than controls. The general benefits of such a compound to humankind in general, as opposed to the military, are of course debatable. It may also be that it is the combination of psychoactive compounds in cannabis which are important for efficacy. To isolate the single best or most active combination from over 60 pharmacologically active cannabinoids would be a challenge, to say the least. Standardised preparations derived from the whole cannabis plant may provide more effective treatments in the short and possibly long term (Williamson and Evans, 2000). The first cannabis-derived medicinal products are expected to be launched before the end of 2003. In contrast, more recent developments based on analogues of endogenous cannabinoids appear to show greater efficacy than analogues of those from the cannabis plant (Cravatt et al., 2001). It may be the case that increasing the levels of these compounds, which are already present in the brain, may produce clinical benefits.

Questions

1   Describe how cannabis has been used throughout history.

2   Describe the neurochemical and behavioural effects of cannabis.

3   Why does cannabis appear to be less addictive than either heroin or cocaine?

4   Summarise the potential medicinal uses for cannabinoids.

5   Outline the long-term consequences of cannabis on physical and mental health.

6   Describe how cannabis affects cognition both in the short term and long term.

7   How does cannabis affect driving ability, and why is it difficult to detect whether someone is driving while intoxicated?

Key references and reading

Ashton CH (1999). Adverse effects of cannabis and cannabinoids. *British Journal of Anaesthesia*, **83**, 637–649.

Chait LD and Pierri J (1992). Effect of smoked marijuana on human performance: A critical review. In: A Murphy and J Bartke (eds), *Marijuana/Cannabinoids: Neurobiology and Neurophysiology*. CRC Press, New York.

Gold MS (1992). Marihuana and hashish. In: G Winger, FG Hoffmann and JH Woods (eds), *A Handbook of Drug and Alcohol Abuse. The Biological Aspects* (pp. 117–131). Oxford University Press, Oxford, UK.

Golding JF (1992). Cannabis. In: A Smith and D Jones (eds), *Handbook of Human Performance: Health and Performance* (Vol. 2, p. 175). Academic Press, New York.

Gurley RJ, Aranow R and Katz M (1998). Medicinal marijuana: A comprehensive review. *Journal of Psychoactive Drugs*, **30**, 137–147.

Pertwee RG (1990). The central neuropharmacology of psychotropic cannabinoids. In: DJK Balfour (ed.), *Psychotropic Drugs of Abuse* (pp. 355–429). Pergamon Press, Elmsford, New York.

Pertwee RG (1997b). Cannabis and cannabinoids: Pharmacology and rationale for clinical use. *Pharmacology and Science*, **3**, 539-545.

Solowij N (1998). *Cannabis and Cognitive Functioning*. Cambridge University Press, Cambridge, UK.

Chapter 8

Heroin and opiates

Overview

For many centuries men and women have valued the medicinal qualities of opiate narcotics. Sir William Osler noted that, "The desire to take medicine is, perhaps, the greatest feature which distinguishes man from animals" (Cushing, 1925); this reflects the, profound euphoric and analgesic properties of opiates. But while some commentators have seen opiates in a positive light, labelling them as "God's own medicine", others have focused more on the personal and social distress they cause, describing them as "The scourge of society". Thus, while they are most powerful weapons in the clinician's armoury for pain control, they are also one of the most problematic of all illicit drugs, with many users turning to crime to pay for these highly addictive substances. The opium poppy is the source of natural opium and is readily cultivated throughout the world. Opium contains more than a dozen alkaloids, of which the most important are codeine and morphine. Heroin, or diacetylmorphine, is a structural variant of morphine with three times its potency. Opiates can be ingested orally, by smoking or by injection. The body and brain possess numerous opiate receptor sites, where the body and brain's own endogenous opiate chemicals or endorphins function. Research into the neuropharmacology of these natural endorphin systems and artificial opiate administration has provided extensive information about the structural anatomy and circuitry of reward and addiction pathways in the brain. Over time the medical uses of opiates have not changed. However, the development of synthetic compounds, analogues, agonists and antagonists has allowed for more flexibility in clinical use and increased our ability to pharmacologically treat addiction.

Opiates

Opiates are narcotic **analgesics** (from the Greek *narcotikos* meaning "benumbing" and *analgesia* meaning painlessness), and they remain the most powerful painkillers known to medicine. Natural opiates (i.e., opium and codeine) come from the **opium** poppy (*Papaver somniferum*) which grows wild throughout the world. A few days after the flower petals fall a few incisions are made in the seed pod. The "milk" exudes and a day later when gummy and brown it is scraped off and left to dry in a shaded area, while darkening and hardening. Within this opium there are more than a dozen alkaloids, but only a few are of medical or recreational importance. The prototype is **morphine**, a powerful narcotic analgesic that is also highly addictive. The other opiates possess differing degrees of analgesic and addictive properties. In order to obtain morphine the harvested opium is mixed with lime in boiling water, when the organic waste sinks to the bottom and morphine can be drawn off the top; this is then reheated, after the addition of ammonia, filtered and boiled down to form a brown paste called the morphine base. To produce **heroin** the morphine base must be further boiled, after the addition of acetic anhydride, to form diacetylmorphine; this is then purified with chloroform and water and then precipitated out with sodium carbonate. The resulting heroin may then be purified further.

Research into the properties of opiates has provided more insights into the processes that make up psychopharmacological actions than any other class of **drug**; this is because opiates bind to **receptor** sites that are affected by **endorphins** – the brain's indigenous opiates. These endorphins are implicated in pain thresholds, "natural" highs and our capacity for addiction to opiates.

Historical usage

Archaeological evidence and fossilised poppy seeds suggest that Neanderthal man may have used the opium poppy over 30,000 years ago. Less controversially, the use of opiates can be reliably traced back approximately 6,000 years, with the opium poppy being actively cultivated in lower Mesopotamia in 3400 BC, when the Sumerians referred to it as *Hul Gil* or the "joy plant". Poppy harvesting for their euphoric effects was successively passed on to the Assyrians, Babylonians and Egyptians. The latter flourished from the rich trade in opium across the Mediterranean Sea into Greece and Southern Europe. Medicinally, opiates have been employed as a treatment for just about every human physical and psychological disorder at some time in history. Opium was readily available for self-medication at the time of Hippocrates, the father of medicine, who acknowledged its usefulness as a narcotic and styptic (the ability to stop bleeding) in the treatment of disease, but dismissed its magical attributes. However, Galen viewed opium as a panacea and comprehensively listed its medical indications, noting how opium, "... resists poison and venomous bites, cures chronic headache, vertigo, deafness, epilepsy, apoplexy, dimness of sight, loss of voice, asthma, coughs of all kinds, spitting of blood, tightness of breath, colic, the lilac poison, jaundice, hardness of the spleen stone, urinary complaints, fever, dropsies, leprosies, the trouble to which women are subject, melancholy and all pestilences."

As use became more widespread, opium developed into a valuable commodity and worldwide trade grew. Although opium smoking is firmly affixed by folklorists to

"Chinamen" it was many centuries before the Chinese developed their taste for the drug, after Arab traders brought in new supplies during the 7th or 8th century AD. Subsequently, it was chiefly used as a medicine; until the 17th century, that is, when warming globs in a candle flame and inhaling the fumes became popular. In an attempt to counteract the rising tide of opium misuse, the emperor of China passed a decree in 1729 ordering all imports of the substance to cease. This decree had little impact, as Great Britain – under the guise of the East India Company – stepped up trade and began smuggling opium into China through Indian merchants. A House of Commons committee of enquiry was set up in 1830 to scrutinise the affairs of the East India Company, but the government of the day decided not to reject the £2m annual revenue from the opium business. Governments today have similar dilemmas over the taxation funds generated by tobacco and alcohol (Chapters 5, 9 and 10). It is also ironic that many of the countries exploited by the British "legal" trade in opium centuries ago are now under international pressure to stop the current "illegal" trade in the reverse direction.

The recreational use of opium in Europe was not widespread in the early 19th century. It was confined chiefly to artists and writers who often used their intoxicated experiences as inspiration, as exemplified by De Quincey's *Confessions of an English Opium Eater*. In 1806, Frederick Sertürner isolated the primary active ingredient in opium and named it "morphine" after the Greek god of dreams, Morphius. **Codeine** was similarly identified in 1832. The identification of these two compounds, along with the invention of the hypodermic syringe, greatly improved the treatment of pain, but also increased the incidence of addiction. During the 19th century, opiates were widely used for pain relief for war wounds. Because opiates were widely available without prescription, many soldiers were able to maintain their addiction at home, so that opium dependence became known as "the soldier's disease". Around 100 years ago opium poppies were still cultivated in the Cambridgeshire fens in the UK in order to provide oblivion for the working man and his family. Tales abound of children being sent to "fetch a penn'orth of opium" for their parents. The lack of qualified physicians during this time led to the widespread production of opiate-based tonics and elixirs, such as **laudanum**, a popular concoction of opium, wine and spices; these were inexpensive, socially acceptable and effective at relieving aches, pains, nervousness, diarrhoea and coughing. Unfortunately, they were also highly addictive, so that concerns grew about the increasing numbers of addicts. Many overdoses were due to adulterated and uncertain strength supplies. With pressure from the brewing lobby, opiates became controlled drugs needing a physician's prescription. Similar restrictions on opiate availability continue worldwide today. It has also been argued that the general attitudes against opiates may make some patients with chronic pain suffer longer and unnecessarily as a result (McQuay, 2001).

Recent recreational use

The most common illicitly used opiate in modern times is heroin (known on the street as "smack", "H", "skag" or "junk"). In a survey of British schoolchildren aged 15 and 16 in 1999, 3.4% of boys and 3.7% of girls reported having tried heroin, though large

Table 8.1. Users presenting to drug misuse services for the first time in the UK.

	6-month period ending:					
	September 1993	September 1998	March 1999	September 1999	March 2000	September 2000
Total number of users	16,810	28,599	28,499	30,545	31,815	33,093
Main drug						
Heroin	7,720	16,081	16,772	17,936	20,112	21,234
Methadone	3,035	3,088	3,029	2,893	2,898	3,258
Other opiates	547	633	544	591	601	647

regional variations were also found (Plant and Miller, 2000). Furthermore, the number of users presenting themselves to drug misuse clinics in the UK has risen dramatically over the last 10 years (Table 8.1). During the 6-month period ending September 2000 the number of users reported as presenting to drug misuse agencies increased by 4% from the previous 6-month period (to 33,093). Around half of those presenting were in their twenties and around one in seven were aged under 20. Nearly three times as many men as women presented to drug misuse services, and clearly the most commonly used main drug was heroin (used by 64%), followed by **methadone** (10%), **cannabis** (9%), **cocaine** (6%) and **amphetamines** (4%). Interestingly, drug use is less prevalent among ethnic minorities in the UK compared with whites; however, the number of users in ethnic minorities is slowly increasing.

In the US 1999 National Household Survey on Drug Abuse (Feldmann and Rouse, 1999) an estimated 2.4 million American people were estimated to have used heroin at some time in their lives. There were 208,000 current heroin users, an increase of 68,000 since 1993, of whom 80% were under 26 years of age. Furthermore, the high-quality heroin available nowadays (41% purity compared with 10% some 10 years ago) can easily be snorted or smoked, and this may be attracting new users. Certainly, the proportion of injecting heroin users has fallen from 54% in 1991 to 25% in 1998. Worryingly, recent years have witnessed an increase in the use of heroin within drug cocktails: for example, heroin is sometimes smoked with crack cocaine. This combination delivers a more intensely rewarding experience than either drug alone. These speedballs are extremely addictive, ruinously expensive and potentially more fatal than either drug in isolation. Celebrities such as River Phoenix and John Belushi were victims of such cocktails.

A report from the Turning Point Drug and Alcohol Centre in Sydney in 2000 (Kinsey, 2000) indicated that heroin users were injecting more often and using larger hits than 3 years previously. Addicts used heroin almost every day on average in the previous 6 months of that year, compared with 105 days in the corresponding 6 months in 1997, according to the report. In addition, heroin was reported to be increasingly available in larger deals and considerably purer than a decade before. These facts, combined with an increase in overdoses, both fatal and non-fatal, indicated users were injecting more of the (stronger) drug each time they "shot up".

An estimated 6 tons of heroin produced in Colombia alone was sold on the streets of America in 1998; this is around half of that available in the USA. The traditional manufacturing base of South-East Asia now only supplies about 10% of the heroin reaching the USA, compared with 90% of that reaching Europe. During the reign of the ultra-religious Taliban regime in Afghanistan, heroin production was cut by an estimated 95%. However, since the country's "liberation", cultivation of the poppy has soared once more and total production in 2002 is projected to be around 80% of that prior to successful restrictions being enforced.

There is a strong link between heroin use and crime. Research in the UK has investigated how problem users finance their heroin habit (Home Office Report, 1998). There is considerable overlap between heroin and other illicit drugs, such as crack cocaine; however, it has been estimated that dependent heroin users need between one-third of a gram to 1 gram a day. Most addicts do not work and have to rely on stealing and "fencing" stolen property to obtain money; this means that a considerable proportion of these street crimes may be drug-driven, although it is notoriously difficult to obtain reliable estimates. However, the UK has been described as having the most rampant heroin problem in the Western world, with 270,000 users in 2001, the largest number of seizures of heroin in Europe and more heroin-related crime than in the USA (Wilkinson, 2001). However, similar types of drug-related crime are reported in every country where heroin has taken hold.

Chemical structures and psychoactive potency

Opiates have a distinctive chemical structure. Although morphine was first isolated from opium in the 1800s, its chemical structure was not identified until 1925. An important event for pharmacologists was the discovery that minor changes in molecular structure of morphine produced great changes in terms of drug **potency**. Codeine is identical to morphine save for the removal of one carbon and two hydrogen atoms. However, it is a much less potent painkiller and possesses negligible hypnotic qualities, but is still a potent cough suppressant. In 1874 a minor chemical modification of the morphine molecule produced **diacetylmorphine**, or **heroin**. At the time this new drug was hailed as a more potent yet non-addictive substitute for morphine. However, it is now well established that the effects of heroin and morphine are identical because heroin is converted to morphine in the brain. Heroin is much faster acting than morphine because its modified chemical structure makes it more fat-soluble and as such is easier to transport across the membranes of the brain (Chapter 3). A number of synthetic opiates have been developed in an attempt to produce the desired analgesia without the addictive side effects, but with limited success. Methadone was developed during the Second World War in response to shortages of morphine in Germany and has subsequently been employed as a treatment for heroin addiction. Unfortunately, methadone itself is both psychoactive and addictive. However, it is still used therapeutically, mainly because it cannot be injected intravenously, removes the need to obtain street drugs and the dose can be carefully controlled. In general, all synthetic, semi-synthetic and natural opiates possess similar chemical structures that are linked to their potency (Table 8.2).

Table 8.2. Structurally similar opiate compounds and their relative potencies.

Drug	Onset (min)	Peak (min)	Duration (hr)	Half-life (hr)	Typical oral dose (mg)	Origin	Strength
Morphine	20	60	7	2–3	60	Natural	High
Codeine	25	60	4	3–4	200	Natural	Medium
Meperidine	15	45	3	3–4	300	Synthetic	Strong
Methodone	15	120	5	22–24	20	Synthetic	Strong
Heroin	15	60	4	2–3	n/a	Natural	Strong

Administration

As with many psychoactive drugs, there are several possible administration routes (Chapter 3). The oldest route for opiate administration is oral. Various cakes and tonics have been traditionally used, but tablets represent the majority of clinical treatments. However, **bioavailability** is low through this route and, consequently, more of the drug is required to produce the desired effect. Powdered heroin can also be snorted and absorbed through the nasal membranes. This route is not very efficient, but is common in first-time users. Smoking opium is widespread and used to be the most common route of administration for hundreds of years, particularly in China. It also became popular among US soldiers during the Vietnam War. A minority took their opium addiction home with them, although surprisingly large numbers of former soldiers found that they did not need opiates on returning back home from war. As with other psychoactive drugs, smoking and injection produce the quickest rush and high. Indeed, morphine is available as a liquid, while heroin and other water-soluble opiates can all be injected. Heroin abusers may inject six or more times a day, depending on their past experience and chronic tolerance to the drug. This tolerance is rapidly lost after a few days, a factor that causes the deaths of many former addicts who relapse. They take their old high-dose level; but, since they are now no longer tolerant to this amount, they overdose through respiratory failure.

As for half-life and metabolism, there is little difference between the various opiates in terms of speed of onset and duration of effect. However, the process of the **first-pass effect** means that the amount of drug that is "active" varies, depending on the route of administration; this is because drugs administered orally are delivered from the gut via the portal vein to the liver where a proportion of the drug is metabolised and, consequently, less is available to the body for therapeutic effect (Chapter 3). By comparison, intravenous injection delivers the drug to the heart and brain without depletion; this explains why higher doses are required for oral versus intravenous morphine and why therapeutic changes are often best achieved by altering the route of administration or formulation (e.g., slow-release capsules), rather than by just increasing the dose (McQuay, 2001). Once absorbed, opiates are widely distributed throughout the body, including the central nervous system (CNS) where they exert their psychoactive effects. However, surprisingly the drug does not seem to concentrate in the brain; this is because it does not cross the **blood–brain barrier** as easily as less complex chemicals, such as **alcohol** (Chapter 2). Opiates are metabolised by the liver and, for the large part, are excreted in urine. The half-life of most opiates is fairly short, around 3 hours. The one major exception to this is methadone with a $t_{1/2}$ of about 24 hours.

Endogenous opiate compounds

If opiates are such addictive and potentially lethal compounds, why does the body respond to them? As with the cannabinoids (Chapter 7), it has been discovered that the body and brain possess numerous opiate-specific receptor sites. As many as nine receptor subtypes have been identified, with three of them being the most important: μ (mu), κ (kappa) and δ (delta). The finding that the distribution of opiate receptors did not parallel the distribution of any known **neurotransmitter** prompted the search for and identification of a number of endogenous compounds specific to these receptors. These enkephalins and endorphins are manufactured within the brain and other body systems (especially the gut and intestines) and form the body's natural response to pain. They appear to be produced in "bulk" chains of amino acids called "polypeptides", with each active neurotransmitter being composed of around five amino acid molecules. These active neurotransmitters are subsequently cleaved from the larger polypeptides at times of demand: for example, it has been demonstrated that the plasma levels of these active compounds rise during childbirth, traumatic incidents and vigorous physical exercise.

In neuropharmacological terms the general effects of opiates on neuronal functioning include the reduction of membrane excitability with subsequent slowing of cell firing and a general inhibition of neurotransmitter release. The cellular mechanisms producing these effects have been extensively researched. Opiates affect the transport of ions into and out of nerve cells. Specifically, increases are seen for potassium (K^+) channel conductance and decreases for calcium (Ca^{2+}) channel conductance throughout the CNS. These effects induce hyperpolarisation and effectively shorten the duration of **action potentials**, resulting in a reduction in neurotransmitter release; this may generate the analgesic effects (DiChiara and North, 1992). In addition, opiates inhibit **adenyl cyclase** activity, which affects the rate of synthesis of endogenous opiate peptides. Importantly, heroin disinhibits **GABA** (γ-aminobutyric acid) interneurons, which in turn results in activation of the mesolimbic **dopamine** system (Koob, 1992a; Wise, 1996; Schultz et al., 1997). Such effects may be important in terms of drug tolerance and dependence.

In terms of effects on neurotransmitter release, there are at least three subtypes of opiate receptor that seem to have different specific effects. However, the overall consequences of opiate administration are best described in terms of their major influences on neural chemistry. Noradrenaline, dopamine, serotonin and acetylcholine release are all affected by both administered opiates and endogenous opiate peptides. Illes (1989) demonstrated that both endogenous and administered opiates inhibited the release of noradrenaline. Opiate receptors can in contrast increase mesolimbic dopamine release in two ways: first, by altering the rate of dopaminergic cell firing and, second, by acting locally within terminal areas; these combined effects lead to increased dopamine activity in the **nucleus accumbens** and associated systems, producing euphoria and stimulating the reward pathways. Furthermore, opiates appear to affect a range of different neurotransmitter systems and neuromodulators throughout the brain; however, large regional variations exist (Mulder and Schoffelmeer, 1993).

An important neurobiological model of opiate addiction dissociates the neural systems that mediate positive reinforcement from those that mediate negative reinforcement (Wise and Bozarth, 1987); this proposes that the locus coeruleus and periacqueductal grey matter in the brainstem are implicated in opiate withdrawal or negative reinforcement (Legradi et al., 1996). Whereas the ventral tegmental area (VTA) and its target regions, which include the ventral striatum as well as the limbic cingulate and prefrontal cortex, are central to positive reinforcement aspects of addiction (Kim et al., 1986; Wise and Bozarth, 1987; Schulteis and Koob, 1994; DiChiara, 1995; Altman et al., 1996; Masterman and Cummings, 1997). Sell et al. (1999) employed functional magnetic resonance imaging (fMRI) and positron emission tomography (PET) in order to study opiate addict levels of brain activation in response to heroin and heroin-related visual cues. Their results indicated that both sets of stimuli produced increased activation in the periacqueductal and VTA areas implicated in reward-related behaviour as outlined above.

Subjective effects

Within seconds of injection, inhalation or snorting, heroin crosses the blood–brain barrier and is converted into morphine, binding to opiate receptors. For small to moderate doses (5–10 mg) the main subjective effects are drowsiness, a reduction in stimulus sensitivity and reduced anxiety and inhibition; muscles are relaxed, pain relieved and respiration is depressed. In addition, the skin may become flushed, the mouth dry and a "heavy" feeling experienced in the extremities, concentration is difficult and a dreamy sleep often ensues. The intense feelings of pleasure or "high" are a function of how much drug has been administered; this does not usually occur for small doses. Importantly, the "rush" or "kick" referred to by addicts is confined to intravenous administration, or mainlining, and is not experienced by those who smoke, snort or take opiates orally. However, because such users can be equally as dependent as intravenous users, this suggests that the "rush" is not the key to opiate addiction.

First-time users generally experience nausea and possibly vomiting as a result of stimulation of neurons in the medulla, although tolerance is soon established to these unpleasant effects. Indeed, the feelings of pleasure are so intense that the vomiting is not remembered as unpleasant! It is interesting to note that, although intense feelings of euphoria are consistently associated with opiate administration, "well-adjusted" individuals who are pain-free may experience restlessness and anxiety as a consequence of a single dose. The elation occurs most often in persons who are depressed or anxious (Feldman et al., 1997). Furthermore, the analgesia produced by opiates is not at the expense of mental clarity as compared with other agents, such as nitrous oxide. As a consequence, even high doses are not closely associated to slurred speech, confusion or severe motor inco-ordination. Chronic users may then be able to hide their habit for periods of years as they will not exhibit the classic signs of intoxication.

Psychological and physiological effects

Acute physiological responses to opiate administration occur rapidly and include constricted pupils, decreased pulse rate, reduced body temperature, slowed respiration rate and impaired reflexes. In addition, there is a marked slowing of the digestive system through an altering of the tonus and motility of the stomach and intestines, allowing for greater water absorption. This last effect is not subject to tolerance, and constipation is a common side effect even for chronic users. Indeed, some report that this is the worst side effect of opiate use.

In cognitive terms the endogenous opiates modulate memory formation and learning associations. Thus, opiate agonists have been shown to disrupt these processes and antagonists to enhance them. This influence is believed to be mediated via a number of other neurotransmitters including acetylcholine and norepinephrine. Ornstein et al. (2000) compared two groups, whose primary drug of abuse was either amphetamine or heroin, with a group of non-user controls. The study consisted of a neuropsychological test battery that included both conventional and computerised tests, many of which have previously been shown to be sensitive to cortical damage (including selective lesions of the temporal or frontal lobes), basal ganglia disease and to neuropsychiatric disorder. Both groups were found to be impaired in some tests of spatial working memory. However, the heroin group were also deficient in the "index of strategic performance". The heroin group failed to show significant improvement between two blocks of a sequence generation task after training and exhibited more perseverative behaviour on this task. Both groups were profoundly but equivalently impaired on a test of pattern recognition memory sensitive to temporal lobe dysfunction. The authors propose that these results indicate that chronic drug use may lead to distinct patterns of cognitive impairment that may be associated with dysfunction of different components of cortico-striatal circuitry.

Medical uses

Although the first recorded use of opium was for the relief of dysentery and diarrhoea, the main use of opiate analgesics, such as morphine, is for the treatment of pain. The most common route of administration is oral, although they can be given by intravenous, subcutaneous or intramuscular injection. Importantly, opiates are not only effective at relieving pain but also reduce the psychological "suffering" component of chronic pain. Patients in the later stages of cancer and other related terminal diseases are prescribed opiates in order to alleviate such suffering. When under the influence of these drugs, patients are aware that the pain exists, but it no longer affects them. There is an assumption that all types of pain respond equally well to all opiates. However, this assumption may be wrong, and differences in receptor selectivity between opiates could then be exploited to manage different types of pain (note, however, that currently there is no clinical evidence for such differential efficacy). In any case the medical availability of different opiates often reflects socio-political influences (McQuay, 2001).

It should be noted that not all pain is opiate-sensitive. Common causes of opiate-insensitive pain are nerve compression and nerve destruction. The insensitivity is also relative in most cases, with the dose response curve being shifted to the right. However, the opiate dose required for analgesia may then provoke intolerable or unmanageable adverse events. Interestingly, the clinical use of opiates demonstrates a difference between clinical pharmacology and laboratory pharmacology. When opiates are administered to someone suffering from pain, their effects are different from those when they are given to someone not in pain. Specifically, the presence of pain seems to block the respiratory depression observed in healthy volunteers. As a consequence, the most appropriate dosage should reflect the individual's pain control needs (McQuay, 2001). Also, in a clinical setting and among the terminally ill the simultaneous use of cocaine, methylphenidate or amphetamines with heroin or morphine can augment the opiate's analgesic and **anxiolytic** effect while allowing its dosage to be lowered. The risks of respiratory depression are also diminished.

Codeine is still used as a cough suppressant, although synthetic derivatives (e.g., dextromethorphan) are also effective without the sedating and possible addictive properties. Diarrhoea is also successfully treated with opiates; this has been particularly effective in avoiding the deaths of large numbers of children in Third World countries at times of disease epidemics. Finally, the adverse side effects of medical treatment with opiates are a common consequence of multiple dosing (Moulin et al., 1996); these commonly include nausea, dizziness and constipation, although the extent of these symptoms does vary between drugs (Houde, 1989), while the nausea and dizziness commonly abate quite quickly.

Chronic usage

The long-term use of opiates is not invariably linked to physical decline. Medical physicians, nurses and other health personnel have ready access to high-quality supplies of opiates, and a small minority become addicted to them during their periods of initial medical training. Some maintain regular albeit secret patterns of use for many years afterward, when they manage to continue undertaking their normal everyday employment duties without noticeable problems. However, for the large majority of regular opiate users, their family and employment responsibilities come to be ignored. Thus, their regular opiate use becomes linked with financial and social decline. The long-term health costs can also be quite dramatic, as the following scenario describes; although this is from a government-sponsored report, it does certainly dwell on the most negative aspects:

To be a confirmed drug addict is to be one of the walking dead. ... The teeth have rotted out, the appetite is lost, and the stomach and intestines don't function properly. The gall bladder becomes inflamed; eyes and skin turn a bilious yellow; in some cases membranes of the nose turn a flaming red; the partition separating the nostrils is eaten away – breathing is difficult. Oxygen in the blood decreases; bronchitis and tuberculosis develop. Good traits of character disappear and bad ones emerge. Sex organs become affected. Veins collapse and livid purplish scars remain. Boils and abscesses plague the skin; gnawing pain racks the body. Nerves snap; vicious twitching develops. Imaginary and fantastic fears blight the mind and sometimes complete insanity results. Often times, too, death comes much too early in life. ... Such is the torment of being a drug addict; such is the plague of being one of the walking dead ...

THE SUPREME COURT OF THE UNITED STATES (1962)

Regular opiate use is associated with a wide range of medical and psycho-biological deficits. Systolic and diastolic blood pressure are invariably reduced, whereas the cardiac effects are more complex, with resting heart rate often increased compared with controls. Sexual interest is often lost and males may become impotent. Autopsy research indicates that between 5 and 10% of intravenous heroin addicts might have pallidal infarcts, either as the sole lesion or combined with other manifestations of **hypoxic** or **ischaemic** brain injury; the resultant brain damage can lead to severe mental disturbances in those affected. Many intravenous opiate users also develop collapsed veins as a result of repeated injecting. This situation leads the user to progressively move to unused veins, generally beginning with the arms, down to the wrists, then the ankles and feet. In severe cases the users resort to searching for deep veins in the groin or injecting sensitive areas in the genitals.

Children of parents with opiate dependence

The effects of parental opiate addiction on the well-being of their children has long been a topic of concern. Hence, the antenatal effects of parental drug use and the overall poor outcomes for these children have been widely studied. Most antenatal harm caused is believed to be indirect, through the ill health of the mother and/or poor antenatal care. In order to meet the high cost of maintaining a heroin habit the pregnant addict often indulges in robbery, forgery, drug sales or prostitution. Since most of her day is taken up by either obtaining drugs or being overcome by drugs, she spends most of her time unable to function in the usual activities of daily living.

However, there are smaller risks of direct harm caused by heroin. Morphine, the major metabolite of heroin, readily crosses the placenta (Blinick et al., 1969) and can cause placental insufficiency, intrauterine death and abortion. Pregnancies rarely go to full term if the addict does not receive prenatal care, although there has not been an increased incidence of congenital malformations in human infants of heroin addicts (Finnegan, 1979). Furthermore, the premature infant weighs less than is normal for the gestation period and there is an increase in later developmental abnormalities usually manifest as growth retardation (Connaughton et al., 1977; Kaltenbach and Finnigan, 1997). Because heroin crosses the placental barrier, babies can be born addicted to heroin, as a consequence of their regular doses in the womb. Withdrawal symptoms develop within several hours, and, although withdrawal is not considered dangerous in the adult addict, it may be life-threatening to the infant, especially if her nutritional state is poor as a result of inadequate prenatal care. However, perhaps the most serious risk for the newborn infant of a heroin addict is the possibility of being born **HIV-positive** – as a consequence of the mother being infected.

Children of opiate addicts have been shown to have poorer social, educational and health status and to be at higher risk of abuse than their peers (Keen et al., 2000). However, given the high rates of psychiatric comorbidity (in particular, depression) in opiate-dependent patients (Brooner et al., 1997; Khantzian and Treece, 1985), it may be that some of the increased risk in children stems from this greater parental depression. Nunes et al. (1998) reported higher incidence of conduct disorder and global and social impairment for children of addicts with major depression compared to addicts without depression and controls, but not compared with children of depressed patients without substance use disorders.

Addiction and dependence

The concept of opiates being addictive is centuries old. Dr Samuel Crimpe in his *Inquiry in the Nature and Properties of Opium* of 1793 stressed the main features of addiction and the possibilities of withdrawal, though interestingly without signs of moral condemnation. Heroin use does not automatically equal addiction, with a small minority being able to manage non-dependent and occasional patterns of use. Indeed, in this regard, opiates are similar to other highly addictive drugs, such as nicotine, where a minority of users follow intermittent patterns of use (Chapter 5). However, all drug use commences with this pattern of only occasional usage, with every opiate addict believing that he or she would always be able to control the drug, rather than vice versa (Tyler, 1995). For a personal description of heroin addiction, William Burroughs' extraordinary novel *Junky* is recommended. In it he states that heroin is: "The ultimate merchandise. No sales talk necessary. The client will crawl through a sewer and beg to buy."

Chronic tolerance to opiates – the need for a higher dose to achieve the same pharmacological effect – is a remarkable phenomenon. Generally, it develops within only a few days of use and, amazingly, there may be little observable impairment in the intoxicated addict. Tolerance develops to the euphoric, analgesic and nausea effects, but not to the pupil dilatory and constipation effects. Chronic addicts report negligible pleasurable effects even from high drug doses, and administration occurs to some extent at least, to avoid the effects of **withdrawal**. Such withdrawal effects are the consequence of physical dependence due to large-scale reductions in the production of endogenous opiates and the rebound reduction in dopamine release, once administration of the drug ceases. The symptoms are similar to a severe bout of 'flu (i.e., weakness, irritability, hypersensitivity, sweating, shivering, muscle pain and runny nose). Maximum withdrawal symptoms include jerky muscle spasms (hence the term "kicking the habit") and occur between 48 and 72 hours after the last administration. Although very unpleasant, withdrawal is not life-threatening. As noted earlier, the rapid development of tolerance and its equally rapid loss following drug withdrawal is an important factor in many opiate-related deaths.

Opiates are clearly addictive, creating strong needs and cravings in the individual, as a result of the interaction with the mesolimbic dopamine system. Such dependence can lead to lifelong opiate use. This situation can be complicated by the fact that opiates are relatively non-toxic to body organs, so addicts can continue using them without causing physical damage. Methadone, which is usually prescribed in a non-injectable form, can thus be used by addicts for the rest of their lives. However, methadone is a controversial treatment for heroin dependence, since its long half-life means that the withdrawal syndrome is very long and difficult. Thus, methadone is paradoxically even more addictive than heroin. So, the former heroin addict has simply replaced an illegally obtained addiction with a legally prescribed one. Furthermore, around 90% of methadone-treated addicts continue to use illicit opiates for the resulting "hits". Naltrexone, an opiate antagonist, is also used as a treatment for heroin dependence, but it is not well received by addicts. Non-compliance with methadone is very common, although the sustained release form of naltrexone has been demonstrated to improve treatment outcome (Comer, 2002). Interestingly, the same compound has little impact on nicotine addiction as measured by smoking abstinence, indicating a different neurochemical basis for the two addictions.

The difference in opiate pharmacology between people with and without pain also applies to addiction. The drug-seeking behaviour synonymous with drug addiction does not occur in patients given opiates for pain relief in childbirth, operations or heart attacks (Porter and Jick, 1980). Clearly, drug addicts are not in pain, and it has consequently been argued that medical use of opiates does not produce addicts (McQuay, 2001).

Toxicity

In comparison with many psychoactive drugs and contrary to their reputation, pure opiate use causes relatively few adverse clinical consequences. One exception is the synthetic opiate pethidine, which has a toxic metabolite norpethidine (Szeto et al., 1977). Norpethidine produces tremor, twitching, agitation and convulsions, and these adverse effects increase with multiple dosing. However, opiates are certainly not safe. As well as their high addictive potential, their potential for overdose is far greater than that for most other psychoactive drugs. Opiates reduce neuronal activation in the brainstem areas that monitor the levels of blood carbon dioxide. Thus, fatal overdoses result from respiratory depression. In 1995, heroin or morphine was noted on 357 British death certificates. By 1999 this figure had risen to 754. The number of heroin-related incidents recorded in hospital emergency rooms in the USA is outlined in Figure 8.1; this indicates a steady increase year on year. The opiate antagonist **naloxone** has no agonist properties and a short duration of action. It is widely used to reverse potentially fatal respiratory depression following opiate overdose.

Even though methadone treatment reduces the high mortality of intravenous addicts to about 30% of controls, a number of patients and non-patients still overdose on methadone itself (Vormefelde and Poser, 2000), although the availability of methadone itself does not appear to be linked to increases in drug-related deaths (Oliver, 2002).

Finally, intravenous drug administration and the sharing of needles and syringes is common among opiate addicts; this creates a serious risk of cross-infection. Many studies have shown a high incidence of HIV and hepatitis B and C among heroin addicts. This risk is somewhat reduced in medically controlled narcotic prescription

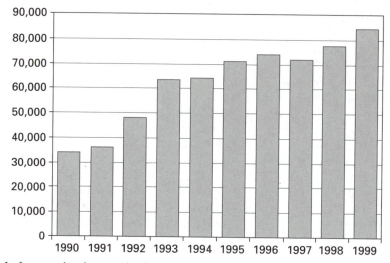

Figure 8.1. Increased opiate use in the USA, leading to more emergency medical treatments.

programmes, due probably to the less risky behaviour of their patients (Steffen et al., 2001).

Questions

1   How similar are natural and synthetic opiates in terms of structure and effects?

2   Outline the reasons for the high addiction potential of heroin.

3   Summarise the short-term and long-term health consequences of opiate use.

4   How can a single does of heroin be fatal in some instances, whereas many users continue using it for years?

5   What areas of the brain are stimulated by opiates, and how is neurotransmission affected?

6   Opiates have been available for 4,000 years or more – describe the changing pattern of use and misuse throughout history.

7   Does the medicinal value of opiates outweigh their propensity for abuse?

Key references and reading

Brick J and Erickson CK (1999). *Drugs of the Brain and Behaviour: The Pharmacology of Abuse and Dependence*. Howarth Medical Press, New York.

Feldman RS, Meyer JS and Quenzer LF (1997). *Principles of Neuropsychopharmacology* (Chapter 12). Sinauer Associates, Sunderland, MA.

Goldstein A (1991). Heroin addiction: Neurology, pharmacology, and policy. *Journal of Psychoactive Drugs*, **23**, 123–133.

Koob GF (1992a). Neural mechanisms of drug reinforcement. *Annals of the New York Academy of Sciences*, **654**, 171–191.

Wise RA (1996). Neurobiology of addiction. *Current Opinions in Neurobiology*, **6**, 243–251.

Chapter 9

CNS depressants: alcohol, barbiturates and benzodiazepines

Overview

Central nervous system depressants display an inhibitory effect on brain activity. Many diverse types of drug have sedative properties including bromides, alkaloids, nitrous oxide (or "laughing gas") and opiates. Here, the focus will be on the three major classes of CNS depressant: alcohol, barbiturates and benzodiazepines. These CNS depressants all display anxiolytic properties, since they reduce feelings of anxiety and induce feelings of relaxation. Alcohol has been used throughout recorded history for its relaxant properties, but it was joined by barbiturates in the 19th century and benzodiazepines in the latter half of the 20th century; these were introduced as anti-anxiety medications and as sedative–hypnotics to aid sleep. Due to the development of chronic tolerance these drugs all lose their efficacy with repeated use. Thus, their regular use can lead to dosage escalation, unpleasant withdrawal symptoms and drug dependence. Therefore, alcohol, benzodiazepines and barbiturates all display a high addiction potential. The common neurochemical mechanism of action is via GABA, the most abundant inhibitory neurotransmitter in the mammalian brain. The GABA system is involved in tonic inhibition throughout the CNS. By activating this system, GABA-ergic drugs further inhibit neural activity and, thus, induce general CNS depression. Their use causes psychomotor accidents in a dose-dependent manner, with even small doses impairing the ability of pilots to fly aircraft and motorists to drive cars. The disinhibitory effects of these CNS depressants also mean that they are associated with antisocial acts including physical and verbal aggression and numerous types of crime. They also display amnesic or anti-memory properties, in addition to their relaxant and sedative–hypnotic effects. Thus, benzodiazepines are thus implicated in date rape, although the most widely used drug for this purpose remains alcohol.

Alcohol

Alcohol refers to beverages containing ethyl alcohol, or ethanol, and is formed naturally as a by-product of the fermentation of yeast. Alcohol has probably been consumed by humans as a recreational **drug** for at least 10,000 years, and there is evidence of a brewery existing as long ago as 3000 BC (Chapter 1). It is one of the most widely consumed psychoactive drugs within the Western world. Most adults in the UK consume it, and 1 in 13 regularly drink more than the recommended weekly levels; these are set at 21 units/week for males and 14 units/week for females, with 1 unit comprising 8 grams of pure alcohol, equating to half a pint of beer, a single measure of spirits or a glass of wine. Among 16 to 24-year-olds, 37% of males and 23% of females consume double the recommended safe level of alcohol (ONS, 2000). Alcohol use increases in parallel with the use of psychoactive substances, such as **MDMA/ Ecstasy**, **amphetamine** and **cannabis**. Hence, young illicit polydrug users report the most intensive patterns of alcohol misuse (Parrott et al., 2001; see also Chapter 6 of this book).

Alcoholic beverages contain varying levels of ethanol, typically ranging from 3 to 5% in beers, 11 to 14% in wines and 40 to 50% in spirits, such as whisky and vodka. The term "proof" is derived from a time when rum was given to sailors in the British navy – if rum mixed with gunpowder could be ignited it was considered proof of a high enough alcohol content. The term corresponds to roughly double the percentage of ethanol; so, a 40% spirit would be described as 80% proof. Although alcohol can be administered via a number of routes including injection and inhalation (and there have even been reports of alcohol enemas!), by far the most popular manner of administration is via drinking. When an alcoholic drink is consumed it passes directly into the stomach, where an initial 10% is absorbed and the remaining 90% is absorbed directly from the upper intestine into the blood stream (Chapter 3).

Ethanol is infinitely soluble in water and, being slightly charged, it readily forms an equilibrium throughout the water-rich areas of the body including heart, kidneys, liver and nervous system. Therefore, those tissues that are dense in cells and have a good blood supply, such as the brain, receive alcohol more rapidly. Conversely, those structures that contain relatively little water, such as bone and fat, take longer to reach equilibrium and generally contain less alcohol. The higher proportion of body fat in females, coupled with their lighter average body weight, means that they need roughly 60–70% of the alcohol intake of an average male to achieve the same blood alcohol concentration (BAC). One benefit for females is that they spend less on alcohol, whereas the main drawback is the ease of reaching excessive BACs.

The problems of alcohol dependence and alcoholism are dealt with in Chapter 10. Suffice it to say here that problem drinkers risk numerous psychological problems, such as anxiety and depression, and may experience physical withdrawal symptoms. There are also numerous medical problems related to heavy, chronic alcohol consumption; these include increased risk of coronary heart disease, liver cirrhosis, impotence and infertility, cancer and stroke (Chapter 10). It is estimated that alcohol plays a part in up to 33,000 deaths per year in the UK (DoH, 2001). Within the last year 1 in 4 adults will have experienced loss of memory following an alcoholic binge, injured themselves or another or failed to carry out some task, including turning up for work the next morning (ONS, 2001).

GABA (γ-aminobutyric acid)

The **GABA$_A$ receptor** is sometimes referred to as the GABA-A-benzodiazepine chloride ionophore complex. It is so-called because it contains binding sites not only for GABA itself but also for alcohol, benzodiazepines, barbiturates, picrotoxin and neurosteroids. Figure 9.1 depicts the GABA$_A$ receptor. A chloride channel lies at the centre of the receptor complex. When the receptor is activated this chloride channel opens, causing negatively charged chloride ions (Cl$^-$) to enter the postsynaptic cell; this makes the neurons less responsive to stimulation, by making the membrane potential more negative, or hyperpolarised (Chapter 2). The widespread distribution of GABA receptors suggests that the brain is generally in a state of inhibition. Indeed, if this inhibition is removed, in some way neurons start firing in an unregulated, uncontrollable manner and seizures and convulsions can follow. Hence, many anti-anxiety drugs including benzodiazepines, barbiturates and alcohol have **anticonvulsant** properties (Harvey, 1985). Conversely, when regular users attempt to come off these drugs the probability of withdrawal-induced seizures is increased (Chapter 10).

As shown in Figure 9.1 the GABA$_A$ receptor has binding sites for various substances including GABA itself. The various ligands (agents that bind to receptors) have different effects on chloride influx; these are depicted in Figure 9.1 and their anxiety-modulating properties are summarised in Table 9.1.

Alcohol neurochemistry and metabolism

In the brain the major effect of alcohol is as a central nervous system (CNS) depressant. Alcohol suppresses both inhibitory and excitatory signals (IPSPs and EPSPs, or inhibitory and excitatory postsynaptic potentials, respectively; see Chapter 2). Like other GABA drugs it disrupts the links between the **Ascending Reticular Activating System (ARAS)** and the cortex which normally integrate higher cortical function. Therefore, higher doses of alcohol (e.g., a BAC approaching 0.1%, or 0.1 mg ethanol

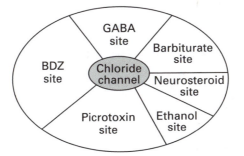

Figure 9.1. The GABA$_A$ receptor.

Table 9.1. Effects of GABA-ergic agents on the GABA$_A$ receptor and anxiety.

Site of action	Ligand	Effect on anxiety
GABA site	GABA (endogenous neurotransmitter)	↓
	Bicuculline (antagonist)	↑
BDZ site	BDZs (agonists)	↓
	β-carbolines (inverse agonists)	↑
Picrotoxin site	Pentylenetetrazol	↑
Ethanol site	Alcohol	↓
Neurosteroid site	Neurosteroids (agonists)	↓
Barbiturate site	Barbiturates (agonists)	↓

per 100 ml blood – see below) disrupt thought processes, self-restraint, speech and movement. The main neuronal effect of alcohol is to disrupt the cellular membrane; this decreases sodium and calcium **ion** influx, depresses glutamate-linked channels and increases nicotinic acetylcholine and serotonin receptor binding (Samson and Harris, 1992).

The notion that alcohol has little neurotransmitter or regional specificity was first suggested by Schmiedeberg in the 1800s; this led to the widespread view that alcohol had a general impairing effect on all cognitive processes and behaviours. This perspective was supported by the discovery that the main neurotransmitter target site for alcohol is the GABA$_A$ receptor, which carries an ethanol-binding site (Figure 9.1). When alcohol binds to this receptor it causes an increase in the influx of chloride ions and a consequent decrease in the firing rate of postsynaptic cells. Since GABA is a ubiquitous inhibitory neurotransmitter, this supported the notion of a generalised, non-specific behavioural impairment. However, alcohol also has somewhat less profound effects on dopamine, opioids, noradrenaline, acetylcholine, glutamate and serotonin systems, although the balance of its effects does change with chronic as opposed to acute consumption. Furthermore, there is increasing evidence that at physiologically realistic doses alcohol differentially affects different neurotransmitter systems in a regional and receptor-specific manner (see White et al., 2000 for one view on this issue). These developments have been paralleled by studies showing more selective effects of alcohol on behaviour.

The rate of alcohol absorption depends on a number of characteristics including the type of beverage, the rate of drinking and the environment of the stomach, so that a drinker with a full stomach will absorb alcohol less rapidly than an individual who has not eaten recently. Hence, alcohol can have greater effects when "drinking on an empty stomach". Other factors can modulate the pharmacokinetics of alcohol, including the concentration and volume of drink. Interestingly, the type of drink also makes a difference, with spirits being absorbed more rapidly than beers; this effect is maintained even if the drinks are diluted to the same volume. Gender also modulates the rate of absorption, primarily due to differences in body mass, fat and water distribution. On average, females contain about 40 litres of water while men are generally bigger and more dilute, containing on average about 60 litres (see earlier). Gender variation may also reflect differences in activity levels of the degrading **enzyme** alcohol dehydrogenase, which exists in the stomach at much higher levels in males than

Table 9.2. Typical effects associated with rising blood alcohol levels.

BAC (mg/100 ml)	Psychological effects
10–20	Detectable increase in feelings of well-being and warmth.
30–40	Light-headedness; feelings of happiness; slight exhilaration, feeling more animated; detectable impairment to some psychomotor skills.
50–60	Noticeable changes in emotion; lowered inhibition; impaired judgement; lack of co-ordination.
70–90	Slowed reaction time; lack of muscle co-ordination; numbness in extremities and face; 0.08% is the UK legal drink-driving limit.
100	Evident impairement to motor and psychomotor function including slurred speech and problems with movement; legal drink-driving limit in most US states.
150	Definite impairment to movement, balance and reaction times; judgement and perception severely compromised.
200	Sensory and motor capabilities severely affected; problems staying awake; difficulty in focusing ("double vision"); problems standing/walking without assistance.
300	Confused; lack of comprehension; possibility of passing out.
400	Anaesthetic effects may be evident; loss of consciousness; skin is clammy.
500	Depression of circulatory and respiratory processes; human LD_{50}.

females. A history of alcohol consumption can also modulate the rate of absorption and the level of subjective impairment associated with alcohol intoxication; so, a naive drinker will feel the effects of alcohol more profoundly than an experienced drinker – an effect that is due to alcohol tolerance (Table 9.2).

The half-life ($t_{1/2}$) of alcohol is around 1–3 hours and is determined by the rate of absorption and metabolism. Around 90% of absorbed alcohol is metabolised in the liver by the enzyme alcohol dehydrogenase, while the remaining 10% is lost through perspiration, urination and exhalation. Thus, breath and urine tests can give a reasonably accurate indication of the level of alcohol in the body, although blood tests are still far more reliable. An average sized adult metabolises about 6–8 grams (approximately 1 UK unit) of alcohol per hour. Although smaller amounts are cleared less quickly, larger amounts are not, so that the maximum amount of alcohol that can be metabolised is between 150 and 200 grams a day.

BAC is an index of the level of alcohol in the blood, usually expressed as the weight of alcohol in mg per volume blood (typically, mg per 100 ml). When the rate of absorption is faster than the rate of elimination the BAC increases. In laboratory experiments a target BAC can be achieved by administering a diluted vodka drink, since commercial vodka is a relatively pure form of alcohol in water. Administering 40% vodka at around 2 ml per kg body weight produces a peak BAC of around 80 mg/100 ml (0.08%, the threshold of the UK drink-driving limit) within an hour. Such a dose reliably produces impairments in psychomotor and cognitive performance.

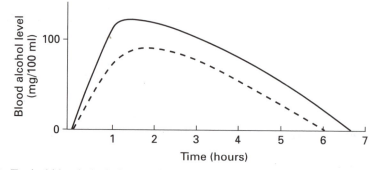

Figure 9.2. Typical blood alcohol curve for an individual drinking 0.5–1 g alcohol per kg in half an hour without prior food (solid line) and following a meal (broken line).

When alcohol is consumed over a relatively short period of time (i.e., as a single dose or several doses over a period of 5–30 minutes) the BAC increases fairly rapidly, peaks and, then, declines relatively more slowly. The rise and fall in BAC are referred to as the ascending and descending limb of the blood alcohol curve (confusingly sometimes also abbreviated to "BAC", though not in this chapter). Following the rapid consumption of a single, reasonably large dose of alcohol (the equivalent of a couple of double vodkas), the rising limb of the blood alcohol curve is relatively steep, whereas the descending limb is more shallow and roughly linear (Figure 9.2). The behavioural effects of alcohol closely mirror the blood alcohol curve, so that the level of impairment associated with alcohol intoxication rises and falls with the ascending and descending limbs. However, impairment is greater during the ascending limb; the reasons for this are not known, but may include the fact that physiological changes are more rapid and, therefore, less readily adapted to or that acute tolerance occurs.

Psychological and physiological effects of alcohol

Despite the well-documented impairing effects of alcohol on cognitive function, intriguingly there is one important exception. Low levels of alcohol can actually improve function on memory tasks: that is, a low dose of alcohol (around 0.5–1 ml per kg producing rising BACs of between 20 and 30 mg/100 ml) administered immediately following exposure to target material appears to improve subsequent recall of that material. The reasons for this are unclear, but may involve protection from interference by material competing for memory resources or the stimulating effects that help the material to be coded better (Scholey and Fowles, 2002). It may be relevant that, during the early rising phase of the blood alcohol curve, alcohol produces typical stimulant effects (including heart rate acceleration).

Apart from this paradoxical exception, it is clear that at higher doses alcohol intoxication is associated with impaired performance across a range of tasks involving psychomotor, attentional and memory processing. At moderate to high doses, alcohol impairs the formation of new memories and disrupts working memory. However, established memory is left relatively unimpaired, suggesting that there may be a stronger effect on encoding than retrieval. Additionally, recall is more severely impaired than recognition: for example, free recall is reliably impaired by administration of 0.66 g/kg ethanol, while recognition is impaired only by higher doses of 0.8 g/kg and above. There is also some evidence that incidental memory is spared by alcohol intoxication; this is also the case for benzodiazepines (see later in this chapter). Duka et al. (2000) found no effect of 0.8 g/kg ethanol on implicit memory, although intoxicated participants had reduced awareness of implicitly retrieved items. In the same study, cued recall was unaffected by alcohol, although the drug did decrease recall of high-association word pairs. The authors also reported that recall benefited from the same drug state. In other words, when volunteers were in the same drug state when recalling items as when learning the items (either **placebo** or alcohol) they recalled more words than when in a different state during the two experimental phases. This situation is familiar to anyone who forgets what they have done when drunk the night before, but may recall their behaviour when they next have a drink.

One influential explanation of the effects of ethanol is alcohol myopia, which is described as "a state of short-sightedness in which superficially understood, immediate aspects of experience have a disproportionate influence on behavior and emotion, a state in which we can see the tree, albeit more dimly, but miss the forest altogether" (Steele and Josephs, 1990). Thus, when drunk at a college social event a student might encounter a lecturer they don't like and feel compelled to tell them so. Whereas when sober the longer term consequences – embarrassment, the prospect of disciplinary proceedings, etc. – might prevent the student from doing so. However, when intoxicated the student can only see the short-term immediate goal of "getting it off their chest". More importantly, there is some evidence that individuals may indulge in riskier sexual practices (e.g., having unprotected sex) when intoxicated. In terms of alcohol myopia this would be explained by the immediate gains of passion and pleasure outweighing the potential long-term risks of sexually transmitted disease and pregnancy. It is easy to see how alcohol myopia can account for a number of problem behaviours associated with excess drinking including increased aggression, crime, impulsivity and accidents. Around 1 in 6 emergency hospital admissions in the UK are due to people who are drunk, and this rises to 8 out of 10 at peak times (HEA, 1998).

Most studies have concluded that alcohol leads to more error-prone behaviour on psychomotor and cognitive tasks. Under the influence of ethanol, greater errors in performance are linked with an increase in the speed of performance, this trade-off of functioning being known as the speed–accuracy trade-off (SATO). Tiplady et al. (2001) argued that the characteristic effect of ethanol on SATO is unlike that of other CNS depressants. Specifically, administration of benzodiazepine resulted in a dose-dependent slowing of responses with a negligible effect on errors. Conversely, ethanol, although causing a similar degree of slowing, was associated with a large increase in error rate. Shifts in the SATO curve are depicted in Figure 9.3.

This coupling of impaired accuracy with increased speed of responding has serious implications for behaviours. In particular, the matter has serious real life implications in the light of the increased risk of road traffic accidents due to alcohol intoxication. Driving skills become adversely affected at BACs well below the 80 mg/100 ml legal limit for driving in the UK. Epidemiological data suggest that this BAC is associated with a doubling of the risk of a fatal crash, while at twice the legal limit the risk increases 10 to 20-fold (Figure 9.4). Koelega's (1995) review of alcohol and

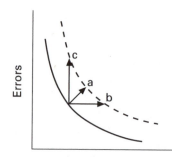

Figure 9.3. The speed–accuracy trade-off (SATO) curve on performance of tasks with elements of both reaction time and accuracy. The black line shows that performance tends to be either slow and accurate or fast and error-prone. The dotted line depicts an impairement in performance as a shift in SATO; this can be observed as a "cost" in either (a) both speed and accuracy, (b) predominantly speed or (c) predominantly accuracy.

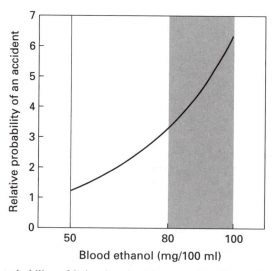

Figure 9.4. Relative probability of being involved in a road traffic accident with rising levels of alcohol. The shaded area indicates typical legal drink-driving limits in Westernised countries (80 mg/100 ml in the UK and some states of the USA, whereas 100 mg/100 ml is still the most prevalent legal level elsewhere in the USA).

vigilance performance found the predominant effects of alcohol are on attention and information processing and, specifically, the ability to divide attention between competing sets of visual stimuli. Indeed, there appears to be a real link between alcohol-related crashes on curves and divided attention (Johnson, 1982).

The relationship between alcohol levels and impairment is further complicated by drinkers' expectancies about the level of impairment produced by alcohol. One study found that, as well as the rate of alcohol absorption, drinkers who expected more impairment from alcohol were worse on a psychomotor task than those who expected relatively less impairment, but had the same weight and history of drinking

(Fillmore and Vogel-Sprott, 1998). Additionally, the effects of alcohol are dependent on situational and dispositional cues. As MacAndrew and Edgerton (1969) put it, "The same man, in the same bar, drinking approximately the same amount of alcohol may on three nights running be, say, surly and belligerent on the first evening, the spirit of amiability on the second and morose and withdrawn on the third." As well as these direct effects of alcohol intoxication, as outlined previously there are numerous health problems related to heavy drinking; these will be covered in more detail in Chapter 10.

Barbiturates

Although **barbiturates** are now mainly of historical interest, it is worth noting that before their development the physician had few choices in the treatment of anxiety or sleep promotion. The alternatives were alcohol, opium, choral hydrate and bromide. Despite displaying comparatively low efficacy, they were associated with many adverse side effects. When their medicinal use was superseded by the development of barbiturates in the mid-Victorian era, the newer drugs soon became the treatment of choice for insomnia and anxiety, and they remained so for over a century. The first barbiturate, barbituric acid, was synthesised in 1846 by Adolph von Baeyer (founder of the Bayer chemical firm). It is thought the name "barbiturate" derives from the fact that the compound was first synthesised on St Barbara's Day. The related compound barbital was the first barbiturate to have demonstrable hypnotic (sleep-inducing) properties. It was given the name Veronal, probably because one of the partnership who first synthesised it was in Verona when he first heard of the compound's existence. Barbital became a popular sedative and anxiolytic; however, it penetrates the brain relatively slowly and has a long half-life, meaning that it produces extended drowsiness over a period of more than a day. Barbital was then superseded by barbiturates with shorter effective half-lives, including amobarbital (Amytal), pentobarbital (Nembutal) and secobarbital (Seconal).

Barbiturates are capable of directly opening the $GABA_A$ receptor Cl^- channel in the absence of endogenous neurotransmitters. They exert an effect called "electrical membrane stabilisation" (Haefely, 1977), which refers to their ability to render resting potentials unresponsive to physiological or electrical stimulation. Hence, they "fix" the membrane at its resting potential, which remains unchanged. This effect is thought to occur via antagonism of sodium ion (Na^+) channels and is presumably what gives the drugs their sedative/anaesthetic properties. At low doses, barbiturates have euphoric/stimulant effects that are replaced at higher doses by the classic hypnotic, anaesthetic, anticonvulsant and anxiolytic effects. These seemingly contradictory effects appear to be due to barbiturate-associated changes in the equilibrium of activity in areas of the ARAS. Low doses result in euphoria due to binding in the medullary region (which normally suppresses cortical activity). Higher sedative doses have more of an effect in the pontine region, which is involved in activating the cortex. Barbiturates cause respiratory slowing, and their use is often linked to deliberate suicides and accidental deaths; this was particularly the case in those who had taken barbiturates together with alcohol for sleep induction. In contrast, benzodiazepines do not cause respiratory slowing and are far less dangerous in overdose; this was one of the main reasons benzodiazepines replaced barbiturates as the anxiolytic "drugs of choice" during the 1960s. However, further reasons for their greater safely are outlined below.

Benzodiazepines

The first **benzodiazepine** (BDZ) to be synthesised was Ro-5-0690; this was soon renamed chlorodiazepoxide, or Librium. It was discovered by accident in 1957: although Ro-5-0690 had been synthesised sometime earlier, it remained untested until a research chemist chanced upon it when tidying up the laboratory. They decided to investigate its psychoactive profile and found that it displayed sedative, anticonvulsant and muscle-relaxant properties; this was followed by the rapid development of many more benzodiazepines throughout the 1960s and 1970s. By the mid-1980s there were 17 commercially available BDZs including oxazepam, nitrazepam, flurazepam, chlorazepate, lorazepam, clobazam and diazepam (Valium). In the early 1970s Valium and Librium accounted for approximately half of all psychoactive drug prescriptions in the USA and it was estimated that over 500 million people had taken a benzodiazepine.

Benzodiazepines have a half-life ($t_{1/2}$) of between 1 and 100 hours, depending on the compound. Unlike barbiturates and alcohol they do not directly influence Cl^- influx at the $GABA_A$ receptor, rather they increase the receptor's affinity for GABA (Figure 9.5). So, their effect is limited by the amount of the neurotransmitter available in the local microenvironment, thereby minimising the possibility of overdose. Benzodiazepines are only effective when GABA-ergic neurons are active and, as there are no receptors outside the central nervous system, this adds further to the relative safety of the drugs. As well as the classic benzodiazepines which act as GABA agonists, there exist several antagonists of the benzodiazepine-binding site, including flumazenil which has little effect on anxiety in normal individuals. There are also inverse agonists, such as the β-carbolines, which can be profoundly anxiogenic – causing acute feelings of fear and panic in human volunteers (Gentil et al., 1990). These inverse agonists uncouple receptors from the chloride channel, decrease Cl^- influx and, thus, make cells more excitable.

The most widely researched properties of benzodiazepines are their ability to reduce anxiety and convulsions through the above mechanisms. Clinically, the avail-

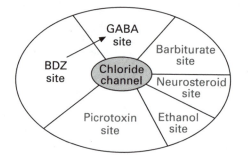

Figure 9.5. Binding of the BDZ site causes the GABA receptor site to be more responsive to GABA itself.

Table 9.3. Classification of anxiety disorders according to the criteria of ICD-10 and DSM-IV.

Neurotic, stress and somatoform disorders (ICD-10, World Health Organisation)	Anxiety disorders (DSM-IV, American Psychiatric Association)
Panic disorder	Panic disorder without agoraphobia
Agoraphobia with panic disorder	Panic disorder with agoraphobia
Agoraphobia without panic disorder	Agoraphobia
Specific phobia	Specific phobia
Social phobia	Social phobia (also called social anxiety disorder)
Generalised anxiety disorder	Generalised anxiety disorder
Mild anxiety and depression disorder	
Obsessive compulsive disorder	Obsessive compulsive disorder
Acute stress disorder	Acute stress disorder
Post-traumatic stress disorder (PTSD)	Post-traumatic stress disorder (PTSD)
Adjustment disorder	

ability of effective anxiolytic drugs is extremely important. In the Western world, diagnoses of anxiety disorders comprise around 5–10% of psychiatrically diagnosed diseases, and these outnumber all other diagnoses. It should be noted that anxiety can be either a state or a trait and can vary enormously in duration and the extent to which they are precipitated by life events. Table 9.3 summarises two major diagnostic criteria for anxiety disorders (**ICD-10** and **DSM-IV**) and gives some insight into the spectrum of pathological states and behaviour that fall into this category.

Benzodiazepines can also impair aspects of mood and cognition. Paradoxical responses of increased anxiety can occur when individuals with low levels of trait anxiety are administered benzodiazepines. In Parrott and Kentridge's (1982) study, high trait anxiety subjects demonstrated the expected decrease in feelings of anxiety. Consolidation of most types of memory seem to be susceptible to benzodiazepine impairment, whereas recall is generally spared. Interestingly, benzodiazepines appear to have little or no effect on tasks testing implicit memory. One exception to this rule may be lorazepam, which has been found to disrupt both explicit and implicit memory in at least five studies. However, by separately examining the effects of the drug on memory itself from reported familiarity with memory items, Bishop and Curran (1995) were able to dissociate lorazepam's effects on "knowing" rather than from remembering *per se*.

Midazolam is often used to induce a state of "conscious sedation" in clinical settings, particularly with dental phobics. The patient is sedated, undergoes the dental procedure and, then, is brought out of sedation by an injection of the BDZ antagonist flumazenil, which has the opposite effects to midazolam on the benzodiazepine receptor. The use of these two opposing drugs in this practical setting offers a useful illustration of their effects on sedation, anxiety, cognitive functioning and mood. On a computerised cognitive assessment battery, midazolam produced clear impairments in reaction time and both recognition memory and recall; this was coupled with decreased feelings of alertness and increased calmness (Thompson et al., 1999). In a second study, patients were assessed while on midazolam and then given the reversal agent flumazenil or a placebo. Their cognitive functioning was then assessed hourly over the next 6 hours. The results suggest that flumazenil reversed midazolam's impairing effects only for certain measures at specific time points and that the patients' reaction times remained impaired despite the administration of flumazenil (Girdler et al., 2002). These results are interesting because the patients seemed to be clinically unimpaired despite these clear cognitive deficits.

The mnemonic effects of benzodiazepine-binding site agonists, which include the BDZs themselves, include disruption of working memory. On the other hand, benzo-diazepine antagonists, such as flumazenil, may enhance performance on such tasks in animals (Herzog et al., 1996). Flumazenil is widely reported to have no intrinsic properties in humans: that is, the drug was believed to have no psychological/cognitive effects when taken at clinical doses in the absence of a benzodiazepine. However, Neave et al. (2000) found a cognition-impairing effect of flumazenil in healthy volunteers. In particular, compared with a placebo group, there was a dose-specific impairment of memory accuracy and a profound slowing of reaction times on attentional tasks for all three doses assessed. Flumazenil was also associated with reduced self-rated alertness. The reason that a drug with opposite pharmacological properties should have similar mood effects to benzodiazepines and cognition-impairing effects is unclear, but may be due to a shifting of GABA activity away from an optimal level. It should also be noted that benzodiazepines do also interact with dopamine, noradrenaline, acetylcholine and serotonin.

The wealth of research into benzodiazepine receptor effects begs the question of whether or not there exist endogenous benzodiazepine-like substances, or endozepines. Several candidates have been isolated over the last decade, but their precise role in normal brain function and in anxiety is not known. One class of natural modulators of the $GABA_A$ receptor complex is the neurosteroids, which bind to a receptor site on the receptor (Figure 9.1). It has been postulated that fluctuating levels of sex hormones may play a part in regulating anxiety states, especially across the menstrual cycle, during pregnancy and postnatally in mothers (Wilson, 1996).

Questions

1   With the aid of diagrams, describe the effects of alcohol, barbiturates and benzo-diazepines on the $GABA_A$ receptor.

2   Describe the many factors which can affect alcohol absorption.

3   Summarise the cognitive and behavioural effects of alcohol intoxication.

4   How might drugs with CNS depressant properties aid in the treatment of anxiety disorders?

5   Compare the neurochemical and behavioural effects of benzodiazepines and barbiturates.

Key references and reading

Argyropoulous SV, Sandford JJ and Nutt DJ (2000). The psychobiology of anxiolytic drugs. Part 2: Pharmacological treatments of anxiety. *Pharmacology and Therapeutics*, **88**, 213–227.

Curran HV and Hildebrandt M (1999). Dissociative effects of alcohol on recollective experience. *Consciousness and Cognition*, **8**, 497–509.

Sandford, JJ, Argyropoulos SV and Nutt DJ (2000). The psychobiology of anxiolytic drugs. Part 1: Basic neurobiology. *Pharmacology and Therapeutics*, **88**, 197–212.

Steele CM and Josephs RA (1990). Alcohol myopia: Its prized and dangerous effects. *American Psychologist*, **45**, 921–933.

Chapter 10

Alcoholism and drug dependence

Overview

Archaeologists digging in Mesopotamia have found ancient Sumerian clay tablets that describe laws to control drinking. Thus, the earliest written records have noted mankind's propensity not only for taking alcohol but also the problems it can cause. Despite these problems many individuals find abstention difficult. Drug use can readily become repetitive and addictive, when it comes to predominate over all other daily activities. Then, it can seriously reduce the individual's happiness and damage their social functioning. Drug dependence involves a complex mixture of behavioural, psychological and biological components that often combine to produce extremely self-destructive scenarios. The condition can become so chronic that, even after apparently successful treatment, relapse is very common. This chapter will critically examine the concepts of drug misuse, drug dependence and addiction. It will show how these phenomena are independent of legal status. Two of the most problematic drugs are alcohol and nicotine, although many illicit drugs also have a high addiction potential. The first half of the chapter will cover the most thoroughly investigated drug in this field – alcohol. It will compare light, moderate and heavy drinking and describe the dose-related health, psychological and neurological problems it can cause. In the UK, 3 million people have serious alcohol-related problems. Alcoholism and its definition will be debated, along with some possible causes. Adolescent alcohol use and the problems of binge drinking will then be described. The second part of the chapter will review different explanatory models for drug dependence. It will critically examine the role of the mesolimbic dopaminergic reward pathway for both normal pleasurable activities and for addictive behaviours. The key concepts surrounding dependence will also be debated, followed by an outline of the different therapeutic approaches for treating drug addiction.

Alcohol misuse and alcoholism

Alcohol – safe or dangerous?

The general public underestimates the dangers of alcohol. Government policies highlight the adverse health effects of tobacco smoking (Chapter 5), the media focus more on deaths from illegal **drugs** (Chapters 4–8), whereas alcohol drinking, even heavy consumption at special occasions, is seen as normal and socially acceptable; this may help to explain its increasing usage not only by adults but also by young children. The UK Institute for Alcohol Studies has stated the average consumption of **alcohol**, the amount of heavy drinking and the extent of alcohol-related harm have all been increasing in recent years. Furthermore, this increase has been greater in women than in men. ONS (2001) suggested that there were 2,500,000 men and 615,000 women in Great Britain who were alcohol-dependent. In the UK, approximately 10,000 people attend alcohol agencies everyday, with 93% of these seeking help for their own alcohol-related problem. Of these, 66% are men and 34% women, with an average age of 41 years. The 1998 survey by Alcohol Concern identified that alcohol abuse cost British firms £3bn/year in days off work and accidents. The financial costs are not limited to business, since more than 65% of those attending alcohol dependence agencies are on sickness or unemployment benefit: there are also the immeasurable costs of family breakdown and divorce, the suffering of other family members, the psychological and physical damage to the alcoholic themself and the health service costs for treatment and **detoxification**. In overall terms the adverse effects of alcohol drinking far outweigh those from every illicit drug combined.

Moderate drinking, problem drinking and alcoholism

There is no simple binary distinction between alcohol use and misuse. Instead, it should be seen as a continuum along which individuals can be placed, according to the amount they drink, how intoxicated they become and how their social functioning is impaired. Moderate drinking may be defined as drinking that does not generally cause *marked* problems for the drinker, their family or for society. In terms of personal safety, British Department of Health guidelines state that for men 4 units per day or two pints of beer and for women 3 units per day represent no significant risks to health. Some research has demonstrated certain benefits from moderate drinking: reduced stress and anxiety, increased conviviality and improved mood have all been reliably reported (Baum-Baicker 1985). However, these may be reflections of expectancy and the social environment, as many people relax and enjoy themselves with non-alcoholic beverages. In the elderly, moderate alcohol consumption has been associated with stimulated appetite and regular bowel function; while in all age groups it has been associated with reduced risk of coronary heart disease (Dufour et al., 1992). However, it should be emphasised that even moderate drinking is not problem-free. Psychomotor functions, alertness and memory are all adversely affected by quite small amounts of alcohol (Chapter 9). Cortical disinhibition along with its numerous social costs is also induced at low doses. Hepatic **enzyme** induction also commences with low doses of alcohol (Chapter 3).

Problem drinking represents the ill-defined middle ground between socially acceptable levels of alcohol intake and alcohol dependence. It can be subdivided into two subcategories: binge drinking and regular heavy drinking. Binge drinking describes a situation where an individual may not touch alcohol for days or even weeks at a time; however, when they do drink they drink very large amounts – often until they are sick and/or lose consciousness (Murgraff et al., 1998). Regular heavy drinking describes the situation where an individual drinks most days or every day of the week and regularly drinks well above the recommended safe limits. Although these drinkers may get drunk only rarely, this pattern of regular drinking can have serious long-term consequences. Regular drinking can damage internal organs even if it does not lead to drunkenness and, in addition to liver damage, heart disease and strokes, individuals will be more prone to high blood pressure, cancers and serious stomach problems.

Alcoholism, also known as alcohol **dependence**, is an altogether more serious condition. It is a chronic disorder with genetic, psychosocial and environmental factors influencing its development and outcome. As a clinical disorder it is often progressive and fatal. The condition is recognised as involving four core symptoms: first, craving, or the overwhelming urge and need to drink; second, loss of control, or not being able to stop once drinking has begun; third, physical dependence, which is indicted by various withdrawal symptoms, such as nausea, sweating, anxiety and shakiness (**delirium tremens** after more prolonged periods of cessation); and, four, chronic **tolerance**, or the need for greater amounts of alcohol to get "high". Why some individuals develop alcoholism whereas others manage to maintain moderate or problem levels of drinking for many years is not very clear. However, a number of factors appear to be implicated in the development and manifestation of severe alcohol dependence (see below).

A number of diagnostic tools for alcoholism have been developed, with the most well known being the American Psychiatric Association's (APA, 2000) *Diagnostic Statistical Manual* (**DSM-IV**). The diagnostic criteria are summarised below.

DSM-IV alcohol abuse (1 or more criteria for over 1 year):

A   Role impairment (e.g., failed work or home obligations).
B   Hazardous use (e.g., driving while intoxicated).
C   Legal problems related to alcohol use.
D   Social or interpersonal problems due to alcohol.

DSM-IV alcohol dependence (3 criteria for over 1 year):

A   Tolerance (increased drinking to achieve same effect).
B   Alcohol withdrawal signs or symptoms.
C   Drinking more than intended.
D   Unsuccessful attempts to cut down on use.
E   Excessive time related to alcohol (obtaining, hangover).
F   Impaired social or work activities due to alcohol.
G   Use despite physical or psychological consequences.

DSM-IV has only limited usefulness for family doctors, given the time needed for evaluation (Pingitore and Sansone, 1998). The Michigan Alcoholism Screening Test (MAST) is far briefer (Selzer, 1971) and has thus become the standard assessment device. It consists of 24 binary items requiring a yes/no response and is designed to provide a rapid screening for lifetime alcohol-related problems and alcoholism. A score of 5 or more indicates alcoholism, while a score of 4 is borderline. It should also be emphasised that identifying alcoholics can be a difficult challenge, especially when most have no desire to be identified as alcohol-dependent. Doctors are often unwilling to question alcohol use and, even if they do, patients will typically hide the truth. Most commonly, it is the concerns of families and employers that lead to a diagnosis of alcoholism.

Given the obvious disadvantages of self-report assessment for alcoholism, a number of laboratory-based methods have also been developed. These biochemical markers can be especially useful when treating patients who are unconscious on arrival at hospital or as part of occupational drug-testing programmes. Biochemical tests can also help clinicians overcome the biggest barrier to caring for alcoholics – denial that there is a problem. Mean corpuscular volume has been used as a screening tool for alcoholism, but it lacks specificity. The enzyme gamma glutamyl transferase provides an index of liver damage and, hence, may indicate alcohol misuse, although liver damage can be caused by numerous factors (Elliott, 2000). A second enzyme, beta-hexosaminidase, can be assayed from urine and has been found to be significantly raised in alcoholics (Taracha et al., 1999), although again it is raised in some other clinical disorders. Measurement of the carbohydrate-deficient form of transferrin (CDT) is a newer test that may prove useful.

Genetic aspects of alcoholism

Several studies in the 1970s demonstrated clear cross-generation patterns of alcohol abuse in families (Cotton, 1979). However, they did not clearly identify whether a child inherits genes that create an underlying predisposition for alcoholism or learns to become an alcoholic from their parents in the home environment. Most probably, it reflects a combination of both. Further progress into genetic vulnerability has involved twin studies. A large-scale study involving 169 pairs of same sex twins (of whom one of each pair had sought treatment for alcoholism) revealed a greater concordance of alcohol dependence in identical twins than in fraternal twins (Pickens et al., 1991); this would imply that a genetic factor might be important in the development of alcohol dependence. Adoption studies have further added to the evidence in support of such a link (Searles, 1988). One genetic marker of interest is for the **dopamine** D2 **receptor**, which is present more often in alcoholics than non-alcoholics. This receptor has been linked to the neurochemical basis of reward, reinforcement and motivation and may modulate the severity of alcoholism (Karp, 1992). The general conclusion from the ever-increasing wealth of research into alcoholism is that "inheritance" is extremely complex. Individuals may inherit personality traits that make them vulnerable to alcoholism or genes that directly affect the way the body metabolises alcohol or both. The situation is further complicated by the likelihood that alcoholism is almost certainly a heterogeneous condition.

Neuropharmacology of alcoholism

It has been suggested for many years that there may be something about the actual structure and function of the brains of alcoholics that leads them to become alcoholics. However, until the latter part of the last century this possibility could not be tested due to the lack of knowledge and microanalytical techniques. Subsequent research has identified that the midbrain dopamine system is a major system involved in establishing and maintaining drug abuse (see below). Specifically, the dopaminergic projections from the **ventral tegmental area** (VTA) to the **nucleus accumbens** have been shown to be involved in the reinforcing effects of alcohol as well as other psychoactive drugs (Cunningham and Dworkin, 1999). More recently, several other neurotransmitter systems have also been implicated in alcohol addiction, and a picture of neuropharmacological vulnerability to alcohol abuse is gradually developing. Opioid receptors have been shown to possess increased density in certain **limbic** areas, and their relative densities can predict some aspects of alcohol consumption in rats (Town et al., 2000). Alcohol exerts many effects on **GABA** (γ-aminobutyric acid) receptor-mediated systems by altering chloride flux into neurons (Chapter 9), and it has been demonstrated that certain selectively bred mice are more sensitive to these effects and are equally more sensitive to the sedative effects of alcohol. The neuronal nicotinic **acetylcholine** receptor is structurally very similar to the GABA receptor, and it may not therefore be surprising that it appears to be a potential target site for ethanol. Interestingly, this system is generally much more sensitive to low levels of alcohol than the systems previously considered here (Narahashi et al., 1999) and may be responsible for some of the early sensations following alcohol consumption. It is possible that down-regulation of this sensitivity exists in the brain of alcohol abusers, leading them to drink more to experience such effects. Continuing research is progressively shedding light on this aspect of alcoholism aetiology; in particular, the employment of rodents that have been genetically modified to possess specific variations in neurotransmitter densities and sensitivities.

Adolescent alcohol use and alcoholism

Alcohol is the most frequently used drug by teenagers, and alcohol use disorders pose major problems for adolescents and society, in general. Alcohol is consumed more frequently than all other illicit drugs combined and is the drug most strongly associated with injury or death from motor crashes, suicides and murders (the three leading causes of teenage deaths) and unplanned pregnancies. Compared with adult drinking, adolescent drinking typically involves infrequent but high-quantity drinking sessions in a social context with their peers (Deas et al., 2000; Murgraff et al., 1998). In addition, adolescents are less likely to report symptoms associated with chronic alcohol abuse, and identify different reasons for their drinking behaviour than are adults (Langenbucher et al., 2000; Chung et al., 2002). Researchers have attempted to identify the risk factors that may lead to the onset of adolescent drinking and alcoholism. Psychiatric problems, psychological maladjustment and personality constellations characterised by interpersonal difficulty, impulsivity and emotional liability have been linked to increased likelihood of alcohol and substance abuse. However, an even stronger predictor was the number of first and second-order relatives who suffered from alcoholism. Most of these risk factors appear to be independent of gender, although females are more likely to have coexisting affective disorders, while for males it is conduct disorder (Brady et al., 1993).

Social consequences of alcohol misuse

It is difficult to measure the exact extent of the social problems caused by alcohol abuse and dependence. Statistics drawn from criminal offences, absenteeism and family breakdown represent only a small percentage of the day-to-day unhappiness and distress caused by intoxication and other alcohol-related problems. Many of the social problems caused by alcohol arise from intoxication in inappropriate settings or reflect the breakdown of relationships as a consequence of chronic alcohol misuse. Domestic discord and even violent abuse is common among those who are alcohol-dependent, and child neglect and abuse, including sexual abuse, are frequently reported by children reared in families where alcoholism exists. Alcohol misuse also causes a range of problems in the workplace: for example, inefficiency, impaired work perform-ance, accidents and absenteeism – at considerable cost to both industry and society. With regard to crime, certain offences, such as drunkenness, drunk and disorderly and drink-driving, are by their very nature alcohol-related. However, alcohol has also been identified as a factor in a variety of other crimes including criminal damage, theft, burglary, robbery and sexual and violent offences. Some individuals with severe drinking problems lose their social and financial support and drift into vagrancy and homelessness. The "skid row" problem drinker in fact constitutes only a tiny minority of those with alcohol problems. However, they form the highly visible stereotype of the alcoholic which can be extremely misleading.

Psychological consequences of alcohol misuse

Prolonged, excessive drinking is associated with a number of psychological and psy-chiatric problems. In some cases it is difficult to determine which came first, though in many instances psychological distress is considerably reduced by abstention. There is a close and causative link between alcohol misuse and heightened depression. The biological changes induced in the brain by drinking mimic many of the changes evident in depressive mood disorders. It is also clear that the life of the problem drinker with anxieties about behaviour and possibly failing work performance all contribute to feelings of depression. In some patients, alcohol misuse may be a symptom of an underlying depressive illness; these patients often have a family history of affective disorders. Between 15 and 25% of all suicides in England and Wales may be associated with alcohol misuse and almost 40% of men and 8% of women who attempt suicide are chronic problem drinkers.

Many individuals use alcohol as a short-term means for coping with social and other anxieties, but this can paradoxically lead to harmful drinking and far greater problems. Patients with phobic anxiety are particularly at risk for developing alcohol problems. In addition, the symptoms of alcohol withdrawal may mimic those of an anxiety state; the dependent drinker may complain of feeling anxious and restless in the morning and these feelings are relieved by drinking. Alcohol problems may be associated with, or else may precipitate, psychotic illnesses, such as **schizophrenia**. In such circumstances the prognosis is often less good than it is for either condition alone and management requires careful collaboration between specialist services. Alcoholic hallucinations are relatively uncommon and usually auditory, occurring in clear consciousness. The hallucinations can occur either during a period of heavy drinking or following withdrawal or a sudden reduction in alcohol intake. They may take the form of non-specific noises or voices, often derogatory in nature, which may be described as coming from inside or from outside the head. Morbid jealousy refers to a state where the person, generally male, develops a delusional belief that their partner is being unfaithful. The victim is beset by accusations of infidelity; a search is frequently made for incriminating evidence and the partner may be followed or attempts made to catch them "in the act". Victims may be in real physical danger and on occasions, tragic, sometimes fatal assaults have occurred.

Health consequences of alcohol misuse

Current estimates suggest that there are around 30,000 alcohol-related deaths a year in the UK. The NHS (National Health Service) spends over £164m a year treating alcohol-related conditions, and one in four male hospital beds is occupied by someone with an alcohol-related illness. Alcohol adversely affects numerous aspects of health, even in those who are only moderate drinkers. However, the effects of high volumes over long periods are certainly the most serious and life-threatening. Alcohol passes through the stomach and small intestine and is then absorbed into the blood stream from where it is metabolised by the liver (the "first-pass effect"; Chapters 3 and 9).

Regular alcohol intake leads to three stages of liver damage. First, deposits of fat appear in the liver and, although there may be no apparent symptoms, it is an indication that drinking is excessive and that permanent liver damage is possible. The second time is alcoholic hepatitis, around one-third of people with "fatty liver" will go on to develop this condition although it is not exactly clear why others drinking the same amount do not. Onset may be sudden and dramatic or slow and progressive with symptoms including loss of appetite, vomiting, abdominal pain and jaundice. Abstinence and good diet may lead to a full recovery in mild to moderate cases, but severe cases can be fatal. About one-third of people with alcoholic hepatitis will go on to develop **cirrhosis** – the third and final stage of liver damage. Normally, when the liver is damaged it is able to regenerate itself. In cirrhosis, however, the healing process fails and scar tissue develops, preventing normal functioning. Symptoms include loss of appetite, jaundice, itching, anaemia, vomiting blood, lower back pain and the retention of fluid in the abdomen. There may also be subtle mental changes or even profound confusion, prior to coma. There is no cure for cirrhosis, but those who stop drinking completely have a better chance of survival. Those who continue to drink will die of liver failure or in 10% of cases liver cancer. Cirrhosis is found in 10–30% of heavy drinkers and kills around 3,000 people a year in the UK.

Many other organs are also sensitive to alcohol abuse. The stomach may develop chronic or acute gastritis, and ulcers are prevented from healing. Pancreatitis (inflammation of the pancreas) results in extreme pain, with vomiting often triggered by a bout of heavy drinking. It is a difficult condition to treat and prognosis is not good, with 350 people dying each year in the UK from alcohol-related pancreatitis. Regular alcohol intake can also produce **hypertension** (high blood pressure), which increases the risk of coronary heart diseases and **stroke**. Hypertension is easily treated by simply stopping drinking. Heavy drinking can also contribute to osteoporosis, or thin weak bones. Other consequences include muscular degeneration, skin diseases, sexual dysfunction and cancers of the digestive tract from mouth to rectum.

During pregnancy, alcohol from the mother's bloodstream crosses the placenta and is taken up by the developing baby. The fetus is most sensitive to alcohol during the early stages of pregnancy when the genitals and nervous system are developing. While low birth weight and increased risk of miscarriage are associated with drinking just three units of alcohol a day the babies of alcoholic mothers are likely to suffer a range of defects that are covered by the term **fetal alcohol syndrome** (FAS). Symptoms include growth deficiencies, central nervous system (CNS) defects, lowered IQ and facial malformations. FAS is only found in women who drink more than 56 units per week (approximately 2 bottles of spirits), and between 2 and 25% of women drinking at this level will have babies suffering from the condition to some extent. Of course, many of these women live under poor diet and social conditions, which will contribute to the neurobiological problems of the developing fetus.

Nervous system consequences of alcohol misuse

Severe alcohol abuse damages both the CNS and the peripheral nervous systems (PNS). **Peripheral neuritis** comprises damage to the main nerves of the legs and arms; this affects around 20% of heavy drinkers, with symptoms including weakness, tingling, muscle pains and numbness. It probably results from a shortage of B vitamins, but some degree of recovery is possible following abstinence. More seriously, prolonged heavy drinking is also linked to several types of brain damage. **Wernicke's encephalopathy** is caused by a lack of thiamine, usually as a consequence of poor diet and/or frequent vomiting. Onset of the condition is quite sudden – days or even hours – and requires emergency hospital treatment. However, because the symptoms of confusion, drowsiness, poor balance and double vision, are similar to drunkenness the condition may often go unnoticed. **Korsakoff's syndrome** develops if Wernicke's encephalopathy is not treated. The most significant symptom of Korsakoff's syndrome is profound memory loss. Patients are unable to recall past events from large parts of their lives or form any new memories and often fill out their memory gaps with elaborate fantasies – a process called confabulation. Treatment takes the form of prolonged **thiamine** administration and alcohol abstention, but even then improvement is only seen in about one-third of cases. Alcoholic dementia describes the condition where general intelligence appears to be intact. However, brain scans will detect tissue atrophy, and detailed assessment reveals specific deficits in abstract reasoning, skill learning and visuospatial abilities. These deficits generally improve with abstinence.

The Wernicke–Korsakoff syndrome follows years of chronic alcohol abuse. However, alcoholics who do not develop this condition typically display a range of other cognitive impairments (Grant et al., 1987). Deficits in performance have been recorded for measures of learning, memory, abstract reasoning, visuospatial skills and complex (but not simple) verbal tasks (Kokavec and Crowe, 1999). These impairments may develop gradually and could be specifically related to how much alcohol has been taken and over how long (Tarter, 1995). Chronic alcoholism has been associated with global changes in brain morphology, such as cortico-subcortical atrophy and decreased brain weight. Interestingly though, several structural imaging studies involving alcoholics have failed to reveal any significant correlation between neuropsychological impairment and structural change brought about by alcohol dependence (Netrakom et al., 1999). As many as 85% of alcoholics without Korsakoff's syndrome show evidence of cognitive decline, whereas up to 50% of abstinent alcoholics show no noticeable signs of cognitive impairment; this indicates that a proportion of these cognitive deficits may be reversible.

Numerous positron emission tomography (PET) and single positron emission computerised tomography (SPECT) studies have demonstrated a reduction in cerebral blood flow and glucose metabolism; this is very characteristic of alcoholism and persists even after 4 years of being alcohol-free (Adams et al., 1993; Gansler et al., 2000). Noël et al. (2001) employed SPECT to compare changes in blood flow in the brain during task performance between alcoholics and healthy controls. They noted that the decrements in working memory in alcoholics were highly correlated with reductions in regional cerebral blood flow in the **cerebral cortex**. Furthermore, performance on the "Hayling" inhibition task indicated that alcoholism was related to deficits affecting control processes (the inhibition of a dominant non-relevant response), but not with the processes involved in the production of an automatic response. It is proposed that deficits in such inhibitory control processes may be at least partly responsible for alcohol relapse in the detoxified alcoholic.

Therapeutic approaches for alcoholism

A wide range of treatments and therapies exist, yet traditionally they are based on clinical experience and intuition rather than rigorous validation of their effectiveness (Woody et al., 1991). However, over the last 20 years this situation has changed with clinical trials evaluating how well the different approaches achieve and maintain abstinence. Self-help groups, such as Alcoholics Anonymous (AA), are the most commonly sought source of help for alcohol-related problems. Although AA appears to produce positive outcomes for many of its members, its efficacy has rarely been assessed in randomised clinical trials. One study found that inpatient treatment combined with AA referral was more effective than AA alone (Walsh et al., 1991). In comparison, Ouimette et al. (1997) found that AA programmes were more effective than either cognitive behavioural therapy (CBT) or AA and CBT combined. The beneficial effects of AA may be attributable in part to the replacement of the participant's social network of drinking friends with a new group who can provide motivation and support for maintaining abstinence. Recent treatment approaches have therefore followed a stronger psychosocial pathway.

Motivational enhancement therapy begins with the assumption that the capacity for change lies within the patient. The therapist and patient then work together to design a plan to implement treatment goals. The findings suggest that this may be one of the most cost-effective treatments. Couples therapy is based on evidence that involvement of a non-alcoholic spouse in a treatment programme can improve patient participation rates and increase the likelihood that the patient will alter drinking behaviour after treatment ends. Many persons with alcohol-related problems receive counselling from general practitioners or nursing staff in the context of five or fewer consultations; this is known as brief intervention and generally consists of straight-forward information on the negative consequences of alcohol consumption along with practical advice on strategies to achieve moderation or abstinence. This approach has been shown to successfully reform those who may be at risk of developing alcoholism. However, many alcohol-dependent patients are encouraged to enter specialised treatment with the aim of complete abstinence.

Pharmacological approaches to the treatment of alcoholism toward the end of the 20th century focused on blocking the alcohol–brain interactions that might promote alcoholism. In 1995 the US Food and Drug Administration approved the use of **naltrexone** as an aid in preventing relapse among recovering alcoholics who were simul-taneously undergoing psychosocial therapy. This approval was largely based on two randomised controlled studies that showed decreased alcohol consumption for longer periods in naltrexone-treated patients compared with those who received a **placebo** (Volpicelli et al., 1992; O'Malley et al., 1992). However, as is the case with all diseases, naltrexone is only effective if taken on a regular basis and, like all medications, naltrexone has side effects. One recent study reported a high rate of side effects, which probably explains why, in contrast with most other studies, it failed to find naltrexone effective (Kranzler et al., 2000). **Acamprosate** showed promise in several randomised control European trials, which involved 3,000 alcoholic patients undergoing parallel psychosocial treatment. The combined results showed a doubling of 1-year abstinence rates with the combined drug/therapy, compared with the psychosocial treatment alone (Swift, 1999).

Some medications may be particularly effective for certain types of alcoholics: for example, when **ondansetron** was combined with psychotherapy, alcoholics who had begun drinking heavily before age 25 (i.e., early-onset alcoholics) decreased their alcohol consumption and increased their number of abstinent days, but late-onset alcoholics did not (Johnson et al., 2000). **Sertraline**, in contrast, appears to reduce drinking in late-onset but not early-onset alcoholics (Pettinati et al., 2000). However, fluoxetine (Prozac), a medication related to sertraline, has not been found to be effective in late-onset alcoholism. In conclusion, research supports the concept of using medica-tions as an adjunct to the psychosocial therapy of alcohol abuse and alcoholism. However, additional clinical trials are required to identify those patients most likely to benefit from such an approach, to determine the most appropriate medications for different patient types, to establish optimal dosages and to develop strategies for enhancing patient compliance with medication regimens.

Drug dependence and addiction

Most psychoactive substances can induce dependence to a greater or lesser extent. Alcohol is the most widely studied drug of dependence (see above). Many of the others were covered in earlier chapters: nicotine dependence and tobacco addiction was described in Chapter 4, CNS stimulant use and misuse was covered in Chapter 4 and opiate dependence was described in Chapter 8. In the remainder of this chapter some of the general principles underlying drug dependence, tolerance and withdrawal will be debated.

The earliest theories of drug dependence concluded that it was a disease, and this concept is still occasionally supported (Kantak, 2003). The disease model fits with the observation that only a proportion of people who take drugs become addicted to them. Furthermore, once addiction is conceptualised as a disease, then the cure should be medical treatment rather than moral criticism or criminal punishment. The disease model has therefore positively influenced many of society's attitudes toward drug dependence. However, the disease model has never been formally proposed in scientific terms. Furthermore, such constructs as loss of control and craving are only descriptive of the condition and are not explanatory concepts. As a consequence the disease model has been widely challenged, and later models have concentrated more on such concepts as physical and psychological dependence (Koob and Bloom, 1988). Here, the key explanatory terms, such as withdrawal and tolerance, have far clearer underlying neurochemical mechanisms. Thus, physical dependence is seen to parallel neuronal adaptation to repeated drug exposure, so that the person comes to function normally only in the presence of the drug.

Physical and psychological dependence both suffer from aspects of circularity as explanations. Thus, a person is seen as psychologically dependent when they use a lot of drug and, because they use a lot of drug, they must be psychologically dependent! There are also some inconsistencies in physical dependence, since some highly addictive drugs, most notably cocaine, do not produce a severe withdrawal syndrome. Animal experiments have also demonstrated that dependence is not a requirement for repeated drug administration. **MDMA** (methylenedioxymethamphetamine; Ecstasy) is also taken regularly by many recreational users, but they are not generally seen as either psychologically or physically dependent (Chapter 6). These and related phenomena have led to the positive reinforcement model for drug addiction (Wikler, 1973; Wise, 1988). This model states that drugs are self-administered because of their pleasant or euphoric properties, rather than to avoid withdrawal. Although this model can explain many aspect of non-addictive drug use, it fails to explain how the very damaging consequences of prolonged drug use do not inhibit further administration.

Tolerance and withdrawal

When opiates and many other addictive drugs are used repeatedly, chronic tolerance soon develops. Tolerance is defined as needing a higher dose to achieve the same effect (see Goudie and Emmett-Oglesby, 1989 for a comprehensive review). Thus, with repeated administration of opiates, tolerance develops to their analgesic effects, so that higher doses are needed to achieve effective pain control. Many further examples of chronic tolerance are provided in Chapters 4–9. This decrease in efficacy with repeated drug exposure can be produced by several different mechanisms (Chapter 3). With opiates, tolerance develops at the level of cellular targets: for example, when morphine binds to opiate receptors, it triggers the inhibition of an enzyme that orchestrates several chemicals in the cell to maintain the firing of impulses. After repeated activation of the opiate receptor the enzyme adapts, so that morphine can no longer cause changes in cell firing. Thus, the effect of a given dose of morphine or heroin is diminished. A distinction should also be made between acute tolerance and tachyphylaxis, which is the decrease in sensitivity that develops during single-drug exposure. For a description of how acute tolerance develops over a single session of alcohol drinking see Chapter 9.

Withdrawal symptoms are the psychophysiological changes that accompany drug cessation (see West and Gossop, 1994 for a review). These withdrawal symptoms develop at varying rates, depending on the drug, and are rapidly reversed by read-ministering the drug. For a description of the daily patterns of mood vacillation experienced by **nicotine**-dependent smokers see Chapter 5. Regular smokers report unpleasant abstinence symptoms in-between cigarettes, which are followed by brief periods of normal moods after restoration of nicotine levels (i.e., after smoking the next cigarette; Parrott, 2003). The withdrawal symptoms for most types of psychoactive drugs are somewhat similar, including agitation, depression, anxiety, fatigue, lack of motivation and irritability. These withdrawal symptoms are very mild with some drugs (e.g., caffeine), moderate with others (e.g., nicotine, amphetamine), but can be severe and uncomfortable with others (e.g., opiates; see Chapters 4–9). With excessive alcohol drinkers they can be both severe (delirium tremens) and life-threatening, particularly when sudden alcohol withdrawal leads to an increased incidence of brain seizures.

Causes of drug dependence

All sources of pleasure are potentially addictive: sex, sport (where adrenaline and cortisol levels are higher), gambling (also an adrenaline rush), leisure and rest/ inactivity (where there is also heightened encephalin release) and eating (the feelings of pleasure and contentment at the end of meal). Indeed, all these activities become problematic in some individuals, with compulsive gamblers, jogging/fitness freaks, sex addicts and the increasingly widespread problem of obesity. Psychoactive drugs are similar in that, while some continue to use them occasionally and intermittently, many others become addicted. The core problem is that with some drugs the ratio of addicted to non-addicted individuals is extremely high. Nicotine, opiates and (crack) cocaine display the highest addiction potential. With these particular drugs, the over-whelming majority of initial experimenters become addicted and find quitting very difficult (Chapters 4, 5 and 8).

Initial drug use can be for a variety of reasons: pleasure, curiosity, enhanced performance, sensation seeking, peer pressure, rebellion against parents, coping with trauma, etc. This initial experimentation does not invariably lead to addiction. So, what factors distinguish the most risky scenarios? Several risk factors have been identified. First, drug availability (Musto, 1973), whether this reflects a child taking a cigarette from a parent's packet, helping themselves to whisky from the drinks cupboard or smoking a cannabis joint being passed round at a party. Second, the use of an initial gateway drug can often lead to other illicit substances, with nicotine and alcohol being most strongly linked to later drug use in adolescents (Botvin et al., 2000). Third, social factors, such as unemployment among the young, have also been identified as leading to increased drug consumption (Hammarström, 1994). Most drug addicts have limited social and economic resources and few legitimate "life opportunities" (Harrison, 1992; MacGregor, 2000). The majority are from deprived backgrounds, with inconsistent parenting, poor access to housing and health care, low educational attainment and limited employment prospects – a constellation of risk factors that also predict heavy involvement in crime – and exposure to many forms of social exclusion.

There is also evidence for genetic influence, and the presence of one or more variant genes may be risk factors for problematic drug/alcohol usage (Glantz and Pickens, 1992). Since the primary neurotransmitter of the reward pathway is dopamine (Chapter 3; and see below), genes for dopamine synthesis, degradation, receptors and transporters are reasonable candidates and the dopamine D2 receptor gene is indeed more common among cocaine addicts. Finally, addictive personality has been described and linked to substance abuse (Verheul et al., 1995). A person possessing this trait has a greater tendency to all kinds of compulsive and repetitive behaviours. So, for example, someone who has overcome an addiction to alcohol might find themself addicted to gambling. One problem with this explanation is that regular and repetitive behaviour patterns are characteristic of all core human needs, with regular times for eating, drinking, sleeping and sex, so that most humans display aspects of the addictive personality. Childhood psychopathologies, such as conduct disorder, have also been associated with subsequent substance abuse (Weinberg and Glanz, 1999). Sensation seeking is another factor in drug experimentation (see recreational MDMA/Ecstasy users in Chapter 6). However, sensation seeking is linked to most exciting and legal activities, such as bungee jumping, skydiving and white water rafting (Zuckerman, 1994). These activities provide an adrenaline rush, with illicit stimulant use being just another avenue for creative exploration.

The reward pathway – the physiological route for addiction?

Acute recreational drug use is generally positively reinforcing or rewarding, and the physiological basis for this reward system lies in the brain. When an electrode is placed in the nucleus accumbens the laboratory rat keeps on pressing the lever that delivers more and more of the electrical stimulus, presumably because it "wants" the experience to be repeated (Berridge and Robinson, 1998). This rewarding feeling is called positive reinforcement. The importance of the neurotransmitter dopamine in this positive reward system has been determined in various experiments: first, there is an increased release of dopamine in this reward pathway immediately after the rat receives the stimulation (Fiorino et al., 1993) and, second, if the dopamine release is prevented (either by an anti-dopaminergic drug or by surgically destroying the pathway), the rat ceases pressing the bar. The key structural parts of this dopaminergic reward pathway are the VTA, the nucleus accumbens and the prefrontal cortex. The VTA is connected to both the nucleus accumbens and the prefrontal cortex and sends information to these structures. The neurons of the VTA contain the neurotransmitter dopamine that is released in the nucleus accumbens and prefrontal cortex.

These dopaminergic reward pathways are critical for normal survival, since they provide the pleasure drives for eating, drinking and reproduction. However, this system produces similar sensations of pleasure with alcohol, **cocaine**, **heroin**, nicotine, compulsive gambling, eating and sex: for example, as a result of cocaine's actions in the nucleus accumbens, there are increased impulses leaving the nucleus accumbens to activate the reward system. This pathway can be activated even in the absence of cocaine (i.e., during craving; Self, 1998). With repeated use of cocaine the body relies on this drug to maintain rewarding feelings. The person is no longer able to feel the positive reinforcement or pleasurable feelings of natural rewards (i.e., food, water, sex); the person is only able to feel pleasure from the cocaine. Thus, the user becomes dependent and, when the cocaine is no longer present, anhedonia (inability to feel pleasure) and depression emerge as part of a withdrawal syndrome. To avoid this the user goes back to the cocaine (Chapter 4). Unlike morphine, cocaine addiction (i.e., craving) and dependence (i.e., anhedonia) both involve structures in the reward pathway.

The development of dependence to morphine also involves specific areas of the brain that are separate from the reward pathway: the **thalamus** and the brainstem. Many of the withdrawal symptoms from heroin or morphine are generated when the **opiate** receptors in the thalamus and brainstem are deprived of morphine. So, different parts of the brain are responsible for the addiction and dependence to heroin and opiates, with the reward pathway underlying the addiction and the thalamus and brainstem underlying the dependence (Chapter 8). As a consequence, it is possible to be dependent on morphine, without being addicted to morphine (although, if someone is addicted, then they are most likely to be dependent as well); this is especially true for people being treated chronically with morphine for pain (e.g., associated with terminal cancer). They may be dependent, but they are not compulsive users of the morphine and are not therefore considered as addicted. Finally, people treated with morphine in hospital for pain control after surgery are unlikely to become addicted; although they may feel some of the euphoria because the analgesic and sedating effects predominate. There is no compulsive use and the prescribed use is short-lived.

Psychosocial consequences of drug addiction

Many people view drug abuse and addiction as a moral problem. Some parents, siblings and other members of the community characterise people who take drugs as morally weak or antisocial. They believe that drug abusers and addicts should be able to change their behaviour and stop taking drugs. There is a degree of truth to this commonly held belief, since the majority of addicts do indeed quit on their own without professional help. However, the belief does stereotype those with drug-related problems and stigmatises their families, their communities and the health care professionals who work to help them. Drug abuse is thus far more usefully conceptualised as a public health problem with psychosocial consequences. Evidence suggests that more people commit their first crime after having started taking drugs, with those consuming heroin or crack cocaine displaying the highest rates of criminal behaviour (Saric et al., 2002). Thus, many of the problems that initially lead to drug addiction become worse as a direct consequence of that addiction, with continued drug use further intensifying the problems.

In psychological terms, addiction may become so consuming that it disturbs the addict's perceptions and attitudes and alters their personality; this is not just because addictive drugs interfere with the chemistry of the brain: the experience of addiction as a whole has an effect on a person's thinking and feeling and the behaviours that are related to them. The psychological effects of addiction depend to some degree on the addict's mental health before becoming addicted and the ongoing circumstances of their lives (Friedmann et al., 2003): for instance, if someone is unemployed or homeless, their psychobiological health is likely to suffer more than if they had a supportive family and regular income. Thus, not everyone who becomes addicted displays the same patterns of outcome, since these can vary in both emotional and cognitive aspects (Chapter 8). On an emotional level the addicted person may avoid others, leading to feelings of isolation. They are ashamed of being unable to cope. Taking more drug is the easiest way to avoid dealing with these feelings, but leads to further isolation and social exclusion. Thus, a vicious circle develops which is often self-perpetuating.

Psychoactive drugs that improve mood in the short term, such as CNS stimulants, also tend to produce longer term mood decrements. Thus, the regular use of amphetamine, cocaine, MDMA/Ecstasy and nicotine all lead to heightened mood problems (Chapters 4–6): for instance, an acute dose of MDMA produces acute euphoria, whereas the regular use of MDMA leads to heightened depression (the serotonergic basis for these changes is described in Chapter 6). The regular drug user may often report a general increase in the very feelings they were trying to escape through drug use, as they suffer from increased levels of depression, anxiety, low self-esteem, anger and boredom (Parrott, 2001, 2003; Ziedonis and Kosten, 1991). In terms of cognition, many of the thought processes can be seen as defence mechanisms that act to "protect" addictive behaviours. Thus, many addicts deny the reality of the situation, claiming that the problem is not too bad and that they are not really addicted and could stop if they really wanted to. Often, thoughts become obsessively focused on the drug, and other life concerns are seen as trivial or pointless. Typically, this leads to serious and prolonged suffering by families, friends and colleagues (Velleman et al., 1993). Deception and betrayal of friends and family is commonplace. Some addicts steal from their own children or sell the family's possessions in order to purchase more drug.

Treatment of drug addiction

The common belief that "once an addict – always an addict" does not stand up to close scrutiny. Most of those addicted to various substances eventually change and either break the habit completely or substantially reduce their drug use (Denning, 2002). Typically, this does not involve formal professional help. The addict becomes increasingly bored with their monothematic and destructive lifestyle, and with the help of friends gradually moves on to other interests. With opiate users this process has been called "maturing out", and it is often encountered after 10 years of continuous drug use, when people reach their late 20s or early 30s. However, many find it difficult to quit on their own and turn to professional agencies for help.

There is a wide range of treatment options provided by the social services and/or medical agencies. The most successful approaches are multi-component. They involve a psychosocial element to increase the appropriate life skills and a drug component to handle the immediate problems of drug withdrawal. Counselling and other behavioural therapies are useful components of most treatment programmes (Epstein et al., 2003).

There are many different types of psychosocial counselling: psychotherapy, family therapy, parenting instruction, vocational rehabilitation and so on. In therapy, patients are required to address issues of motivation, build skills to resist drug use, replace drug-using activities with constructive and rewarding non drug-using activities, and improve problem-solving abilities. CBT also facilitates interpersonal relationships and the individual's ability to function in the family and community (Carroll, 1998). Drug use during treatment or "cheating" must be monitored continuously as lapses can often occur, and immediate feedback to those who test positive is an important element of monitoring. Treatment programmes should also provide assessment for HIV/AIDS, hepatitis B and C, tuberculosis and other infectious diseases and counselling to help patients modify or change behaviours that place themselves or others at risk of such infections.

Medications are the other crucial element for treatment programmes and are generally combined with counselling and other behavioural therapies. Nicotine replacement devices, such as nicotine gum, nicotine patches and nicotine nasal sprays, can double the success rates in smoking cessation programmes, but are always most effective when part of a multi-component programme (Chapter 5). **Methadone** can be effective in helping individuals addicted to heroin or other opiates by stabilising their lives and reducing their illicit drug use (Esteban et al., 2003). Naltrexone is also an effective medication for some opiate addicts and some patients with co-occurring alcohol dependence. However, medical detoxification is only the first stage of addiction treatment and by itself does little to change long-term drug use. Indeed, there is little or no evidence that medications can even help treat cocaine dependence (de Lima et al., 2002). While detoxification alone is rarely sufficient to help addicts achieve long-term abstinence, for some individuals it is a strongly indicated precursor to effective drug addiction treatment.

Indeed, of a large number of young adults addicted to various substances, significant numbers will no longer be using them 10 or 20 years later. No single treatment is appropriate for all individuals. Matching treatment settings, interventions and services to each individual's particular problems and needs is important to their ultimate success in returning to productive functioning in society. Unfortunately, this process is also very expensive and preferred treatment options are not always available. As a result, some potential treatment applicants can slip through the net, despite their desire for help. To be effective, treatment must address the individual's drug use and any associated medical, psychological, social, vocational and legal problems. An individual's treatment and services' plan must be assessed continually and modified as necessary to ensure that the plan meets the person's changing needs.

Relapse

Recovery from drug addiction can be a long-term (even lifelong) process and frequently requires multiple episodes of treatment to achieve long-term abstinence and fully restored functioning; this is because there is a high risk of relapse during or after successful treatment episodes (Hunt et al., 1971). In a study of heroin addicts post-treatment, it was found that ~70% used heroin within a short time of leaving treatment. However, much of this use could be best described as lapses rather than relapse, as it did not signify a return to heroin dependence and many of the addicts were abstinent at 6-month follow-up (Gossop et al., 1989). One of the major dangers of lapses and relapse is the risk of overdose. In spite of the fact that regular drug users are aware of the build-up of tolerance to a drug, many ignore the decline of that tolerance following a period of abstinence; this introduces a real risk of overdose whenever relapse occurs, because the same amount of drug is administered as when tolerance had been established. For intravenous opiate users this can be fatal. What causes relapse? One factor that has been identified is the contextual cues from the environment (Crombag and Shaham, 2002), such that returning to a residential area associated with drug taking may lead to drug seeking and relapse despite a successful period of treatment and abstinence. It has been suggested that coping skills provide one of the main means of relapse prevention (Morgenstern and Longabaugh, 2000), such that being able to identify situations of risk and having strategies to avoid them can increase success rates. Coping skills training during treatment and participation in self-help support programmes following treatment may therefore be helpful in maintaining abstinence.

Questions

1   Compare light, moderate and heavy alcohol drinking.

2   Debate how "alcoholism" might be defined.

3   How do genes influence the development of alcohol dependency?

4   What psychobiological and health effects does alcohol have during pregnancy?

5   Summarise the socio-psychological consequences of alcoholism.

6   Describe alternative therapeutic approaches to alcoholism and predict their differing outcomes.

7   Outline how the mesolimbic reward pathway is implicated in addiction.

8   Describe the similarities and differences between alcoholism and other forms of drug dependency.

Key references and reading

Cotton NS (1979). The familial incidence of alcoholism: A review. *Journal of Studies on Alcohol*, **40**, 89–116.

De Lima MS, de Oliveira Soares BG, Reisser AA and Farrell M (2002). Pharmacological treatment of cocaine dependence: A systematic review. *Addiction*, **97**, 931–949.

Gossop M, Green L, Phillips G and Bradley BP (1989). Lapse, relapse and survival among opiate addicts after treatment: A prospective follow-up study. *British Journal of Psychiatry*, **154**, 348–353.

Karp RW (1992). D2 or not D2? *Alcoholism: Clinical and Experimental Research*, **16**, 786–787.

Kokavec A and Crowe SF (1999). A comparison of cognitive performance in binge versus regular chronic alcohol misusers. *Alcohol and Alcoholism*, **34**, 601–608.

Koob GF and Bloom FE (1988). Cellular and molecular mechanisms of drug dependence. *Science*, **242**, 715–723.

Swift RM (1999). Drug therapy for alcohol dependence. *New England Journal of Medicine*, **340**, 1482–1490.

Clinical and Medicinal Use of Drugs

Chapter 11

Antipsychotics for schizophrenia

Overview

Schizophrenia is one of the most complex and disabling of clinical disorders. It should be conceptualised as a broad grouping of related disorders, with many different causes, cognitive–behavioural aspects and outcomes. The core "positive" symptoms include auditory hallucination, delusions and many other strange thoughts and feelings. The "negative" symptoms include poor communication skills and difficulties with social integration. The positive symptoms may be reflections of cortical overarousal, which causes an excessive flow of thoughts and ideas. During the initial acute breakdown there may be difficulties in filtering and modulating sensory stimulation from the physical and social environment. Neuroimaging data have confirmed that schizophrenia displays elements of both a neurodegenerative and neurodevelopmental disorder. Until the mid-1950s the clinical prognosis was poor, with most people being incarcerated in long-stay mental hospitals. This situation changed dramatically with the development of the first antipsychotic drug chlorpromazine. The advent of antipsychotic or neuroleptic drugs benefited countless patients, as they relieved positive symptoms in 60–70% of patients. However, they are generally less effective against negative symptoms, and they also cause many distressing side effects. Drug-taking compliance can therefore be low, although long-term "depot" injections can resolve this problem. In terms of neurochemistry the antipsychotic drugs act as dopamine receptor antagonists. They reduce cortical overarousal and, so, make thoughts and feelings more manageable. Newer atypical drugs, such as clozapine and risperidone, offer some clinical advantages, possibly because of their broader serotonergic actions. The most recent focus is the glutamate NMDA receptor, as its stimulation may alleviate the more negative symptoms of schizophrenia. The original "dopamine overactivity" hypothesis has thus evolved into a more elaborate model involving dopamine, serotonin and glutamate. Finally, the best therapeutic packages for schizophrenia combine antipsychotic drugs for the relief of positive symptoms, with social skills or cognitive–behavioural training to improve the more psychosocial negative symptoms.

Historical aspects and conceptual issues

The origin of the modern concept dates back to 1899 when the German psychiatrist Emil Kraepelin brought a group of related disorders – paranoia, catatonia and hebephrenia – under the umbrella name of dementia praecox (early or precocious madness). This term was soon to be superseded by the name "schizophrenia", which was first coined by the Swiss psychiatrist Eugene Bleuler in 1911. The split or schism was not about the personality, but rather between internal thought processes and external reality. One of the difficulties about the concept of **schizophrenia** is that it is difficult to know exactly what it means. There are many different causative factors for odd and strange thoughts, and these will certainly vary from one individual to another. Thus, with one person diagnosed as schizophrenic the cause may be primarily genetic, with another it may be **anoxia** during birth (with low oxygen leading to localised minimal brain damage), with another it may be a viral infection at a critical stage of brain development, with yet another it could be a different genetic factor, with another it may be a particularly stressful or abusive family environment. Thus, there can be a wide range of internal or biological factors, coupled with an equally wide range of external or environmental stressors.

The **diathesis stress model** states that a disorder or problem reflects the complex interaction between various internal and external factors. This model helps to explain why identical twins with the same genetic loading do not invariably both become schizophrenic (although they often do). It is the particular combination of internal or biological propensities that interact with stressful events which produce a wide range of possible cognitive–behavioural outcomes: good, bad and mixed. This model also helps explain why schizophrenics are particularly prone to stress and need to be protected from cortical and environmental overload (see later). The model also helps explain why schizophrenia is such a diverse and complex grouping of disorders.

Many of the proposed theoretical explanations have focused on one particular type of factor. Thus, biological theories have seen it as a genetic–biochemical disorder, where the contribution from the social environment is seen as comparatively minor. At the other end of the spectrum are the antipsychiatry theories that reached their zenith in the 1960s and 1970s, with Laing (1965) and Szasz (1974). They regarded psychiatry as a means of social control, believing that it was not the individual who had problems, but the wider world of socio-political control. As Laing wrote in 1965:

A little girl of 17 in a mental hospital told me she was terrified because the atom bomb was inside her. That is a delusion. The statesmen of the world who boast and threaten that they have Doomsday weapons are far more dangerous and far more estranged from 'reality' than many of the people on whom the label "psychotic" is fixed.

The core problem with the antipsychiatry approach is its practical limitations. How exactly does it assist the distressed individual who is suffering from the delusion that they have an atomic bomb inside their body? It will be shown later that psychotherapy *without* **drug** treatment is largely ineffective (as Jung and Fried both concluded), whereas psychological therapy *combined* with active drug treatment is the most effective therapeutic approach.

Clinical symptoms

There has never been agreement about the subtypes of schizophrenia. But, if we accept the notion of a spectrum of closely related disorders, how might they be defined? The older psychiatry texts list four subtypes: simple, hebephrenic, catatonic and paranoid (Linford Rees, 1976). More recent texts have generally used the classification proposed by Crow (1980): type I is where positive symptoms predominate, whereas with type II negative symptoms are more characteristic. This model is covered more fully below (Hughes, 1991). Another binary category is the acute period of initial breakdown and the longer term more chronic condition. Many individuals experience an acute psychotic reaction, which is successfully treated and does not lead to any further problems. More typically, there are intermittent periods of breakdown which often coincide with periods of increased external stressors; but, these are followed by periods of improvement and recovery. Caution should be exercised in diagnosing acute schizophrenia in teenagers or young adults; this is because many psychotic reactions are caused by adverse reactions to recreational drugs. Amphetamine, cocaine, Ecstasy/MDMA, LSD, ketamine and cannabis have all been linked to schizophrenic types of abreaction. Then, the outcome can be variable, with some individuals displaying fairly rapid recovery and others finding the drug-precipitated problems to be far more enduring (Chapters 4 and 6).

The following case study illustrates many of the core aspects of this devastating disorder:

After her A levels, Claire decided to go to a London teaching hospital to train as a nurse. To her friends and family she was a bright, popular and healthy girl. No one could have imagined that she would become so ill. It was in her second term that she had her first symptoms. On her curtains, she saw the face of the devil – but only she could see it. She heard people knocking on her door – when there was no one there. She thought that her fellow students were putting drugs in her drinks. Then it became really frightening. One day she was sitting in a park. And suddenly she was in a grave, under the earth. It was dark and she couldn't breathe properly. People were laughing at her and saying: "You're evil, you're dirty, you deserve to die." Only Claire could hear these voices. The feeling of being dirty became overwhelming. Claire had another bad episode late one night and went out walking the streets on her own. When she saw the water in the Thames, she thought that she could jump in to wash herself. In her state of mind it made sense, she could no longer recognise the dangers around her. The next thing she knew, she was struggling against the currents. She was lucky to be rescued alive. Claire was taken to hospital and later diagnosed with schizophrenia.

(FROM AN APPEALS LETTER BY RETHINK, FORMERLY THE UK NATIONAL SCHIZOPHRENIA FELLOWSHIP)

You may have noticed a number of features of the disorder in this case study. However, it is important to note that not all people with schizophrenia show these very symptoms and that there are other symptoms not evident here. However, the case illustrates several archetypal aspects of schizophrenia. First, it is a young person's disease. Second, it has a similar frequency of occurrence in both sexes, unlike many psychiatric

Table 11.1. Clinical symptoms of schizophrenia.

Disorganised thought	Thought insertion, blocking and retrieval; neologisms or the invention of new words and language; disconnected thought processes or the loosening of associations between thoughts; disorganised speech.
Emotional disconnection	Flat affect with minimal changes in mood; inappropriate emotional responses, such as laughter to sad events; unpredictable mood vacillation.
Hallucination	Most commonly, auditory (hearing voices and verbally responding to them); far less common are other forms of sensory hallucination: tactile, visual, olfactory or gustatory.
Paranoia	Delusions of persecution by friends, colleagues, neighbours, the police, strangers, governments or other organisations; delusions of grandeur, the belief that you are a famous person, historical world leader or religious prophet.
Psychomotor dysfunction	Stereotypy, or stereotypical physical behaviours; bizarre repetitive behaviours, such as rocking backward and forward or pacing up and down for long periods of time; catatonia, or rigid immobility for long periods.
Withdrawal	Emotional, physical and social, resulting in a complete indifference or loss of interest in the environment; poverty of speech.
Neurocognitive impairment	Deficits in attention, information processing, memory, problem solving; heightened sensory "gating" and extreme vigilence in paranoid schizophrenia; Poor attention and slowed cognitive processing in other types of "non-paranoid" schizophrenia.

disorders. Third, Claire was in higher education, and many suffering from schizophrenia display normal or above average intelligence. Although, when the illness results in a "downward drift" to the margins of society, the opposite impression can often be given. Fourth, this young woman exhibits two of the most well-known symptoms of the disease: auditory hallucinations, or "hearing voices", and paranoid delusions, the belief that she was being persecuted.

The core symptoms of schizophrenia are listed in Table 11.1. The main "positive" symptoms include disorganised thought, auditory hallucinations and delusional beliefs. Not all delusions are of persecution, the other main type is delusions of grandeur. Many of these positive symptoms are often thought to reflect cortical overarousal, where there is an overloading of cognitive activity: hence, the hearing of loud voices in the head, which tend to intensify under periods of stress, and the extensive and elaborate networks of delusional thoughts, which are often difficult to modulate and control. Sensory information processing may also be heightened. During the acute phase of a schizophrenic breakdown, the world can become exceedingly bright, noisy and over-stimulating. The wallpaper is perceived as too colourful and overpowering or birds twittering in the trees are seen as too noisy, their chatter impinging on thoughts and feelings. Some aspects of psychomotor dysfunction and cognitive impairment also reflect cortical overload, when it is difficult to organise multiple thoughts and actions. Catatonia, or rigid immobility for long periods, although rarely encountered these days, may reflect the most extreme state of cortical overarousal. The catatonic individual is thought to be attempting to reduce their stimulus overload by minimising all sensory and/or motor connections with the outside world. The negative symptoms of schizophrenia include poor interpersonal communication, poverty of speech, emotional disconnection from other people and general social isolation. Some aspects of psychomotor and neurocognitive slowing may reflect this social withdrawal and poverty of action. In Crow's (1980) classification, type I individuals show predominantly positive symptoms, whereas type II individuals display mainly negative symptoms (see earlier).

Schizophrenia affects just under 1% of the population and has a uniform ethnic and geographical distribution. Currently, it is a major cause of chronic disability, particularly in younger adults. The direct costs of hospitalisation, **antipsychotic drugs** and community health care in England and Wales were £711m in 1992/1993, or 6% of the nation's health budget (Knapp, 1997). The inclusion of indirect costs, such as loss of earnings, would increase that figure threefold. Schizophrenia can also be life-threatening, with 10% taking their own lives and between 18% to 55% attempting suicide (Siris, 2001).

Neuroimaging

Structural neuroimaging, or "brain scanning", techniques were first applied to schizophrenia in 1976 (Johnstone et al., 1976). Using computed tomography (CT) or computerised axial tomography (CAT) scans, in which the scattering of X-rays is proportional to brain tissue density, it was shown that in schizophrenia there was a small but statistically significant increase in ventricular brain ratio; this is due to an increase in the volume of the **cerebrospinal fluid** (CSF)-filled lateral ventricles and a decrease in cerebral cortical tissue. This initial finding has been confirmed by magnetic resonance imaging (MRI), which detects a radiofrequency (MHz) signal emitted by atomic nuclei with an odd mass number when placed in a strong magnetic field. The signals emitted from protons (as in ^1H_2O) in different physicochemical environments enable MRI to distinguish between grey matter (neuronal cell bodies and dendrites), white matter (axons) and CSF. MRI scans confirmed and extended the earlier CT findings (Mirsky and Duncan, 1986; Reveley and Trimble, 1987; Roberts and Crow, 1987). A meta-analysis of 40 studies with a total of 1,314 patients and 1,172 controls showed a 6% median decrease in the left temporal lobe and a 9.5% decrease in the right temporal lobe of the neocortex, with a 44% increase in the volume of the left lateral ventricle and 36% increase in the right lateral ventricle in schizophrenia (Lawre and Abukmeil, 1998).

These "soft" neurological signs, so-called to delineate them from the gross neuropathology seen in Alzheimer's and Parkinson's diseases, were associated with cognitive impairment and regarded as a distinguishing feature of type II schizophrenia (Crow, 1980). However, we now realise that this distinction is not so clear-cut as similar changes are observed in type I individuals and other psychotic disorders (Schweitzer et al., 2001). Other neuroimaging data have suggested decreased metabolic activity in the frontal part of the cerebral cortex, which may have symptomatic implications in schizophrenia (Mirsky and Duncan, 1986). Regional cerebral blood flow (rCBF) can be measured by inhalation of a radioactive inert gas (^{85}Kr or ^{133}Xe) or nowadays by using $H_2^{15}O$. Positron emission tomography (PET) uses atomic isotopes with a short half-life which emit positive electrons (e^+), which then collide with negative electrons (e^-) in the tissue and are annihilated. The resulting energy is dissipated as two γ-rays separated by 180°, and this is then detected by a rotating γ-camera (Feldman et al., 1997). These techniques show reduced central nervous system (CNS) regional blood flow and glucose utilisation, supporting the notion of reduced neuronal activity in schizophrenia (Mirsky and Duncan, 1986). In addition, PET and SPECT (single positron emission computerised tomography) scans with ^{123}I-labelled **dopamine** receptor antagonists have been used to quantify dopamine **receptor** occupancy by antipsychotic drugs and changes in dopamine receptor numbers in the **corpus striatum** (Kasper et al., 2002).

The recent application of functional MRI (fMRI) may reveal more findings about cerebral dysfunctions. Indeed, fMRI gives better spatial and temporal resolution than PET, thus allowing the measurement of brain changes in smaller areas over a shorter time period (Green, 2001). The principle of fMRI is based on the increase in the intensity of the radiofrequency signal emitted by oxyhaemoglobin compared with deoxyhaemoglobin in the blood (Morris, 1999). When there is increased activity in a localised brain region, rCBF increases, resulting in an increased concentration of oxygen in venous blood. Already, fMRI studies have provided support for the association between particular neurocognitive deficits and reduced neocortical activity in schizophrenia (Green, 2001). Magnetic resonance spectroscopy (MRS) is a related method that can be used to study the bio-energetic status of the brain by measuring the levels of endogenous, high-energy phosphate compounds, $AT^{31}P$ and creatine-^{31}P (phosphocreatine), or the metabolism of the energy substrate ^{13}C-glucose (Morris, 1999; Fukuzako, 2001).

In conclusion, neuroimaging techniques have shown structural changes and altered functional activity in many patients with schizophrenia. Together with the changes in nerve cell proliferation, migration and elimination, indicative of "faulty wiring" of neuronal networks observed in brain samples post-mortem (Murray et al., 1988), these findings support the idea that schizophrenia is a neurodevelopmental disorder. However, there remains the possibility that some of these changes may occur after the onset of the illness and, thus, might be indicative of a **neurodegenerative** disorder. Future neuroimaging studies should help to elucidate these issues, since physical measures are being used increasingly to study the complex mental phenomena of schizophrenia. APA ([1994] 2000, p. xxi) noted:

The term mental disorder unfortunately implies a distinction between "mental" disorders and "physical" disorders that is a reductionistic anachronism of mind/body dualism. . . . There is much "physical" in "mental" disorders and much "mental" in "physical" disorders.

Thus, these physical measures may provide useful insights not only about the nature of schizophrenia but also the comparative efficacy of single drugs and other multi-component therapeutic approaches (see later).

Genetic and environmental aspects.

If schizophrenia results from an abnormal development in the brain, then we need to briefly address the question of possible causes. It is now clear that there is a strong genetic component, although the mode of transmission is far from simple (Rose et al., 1984). The lifetime risk of developing schizophrenia in the general population is just under 1%, in first-degree relatives this increases to 10–17%, while for **monozygotic** twins it is 46–48% (Plomin et al., 2001). Schizophrenia has been described as an autosomal dominant trait with low-degree or incomplete penetrance; this means an individual may have the **genotype** for the disease but the **phenotype** is normal. The probability of expressing an abnormal phenotype and the nature of the behavioural dysfunction can be increased by a number of environmental factors giving rise to a spectrum of conditions from the milder or borderline **schizotypy** (schizotypical person-ality) through to chronic schizophrenia (Table 11.2). So, what are the possible environ-mental triggers for schizophrenia?

A number of insults *in utero* or at the time of birth may increase the risk of developing schizophrenia later in life; these include the exposure to the influenza virus, maternal malnutrition and the ingestion of **psychotropic** drugs. A disproportion-ate number of individuals who develop schizophrenia are born in the winter months, when viral infection is more prevalent. A meta-review of 13 studies revealed that 56–69% of schizophrenics were born in the three winter months (Bradbury and Miller, 1985). It has been suggested that reduced exposure to sunlight (UV light) leads to a decrease in vitamin D synthesis, which functions as a catalyst in the synthesis of nerve growth factor in **neuroglia** (Furlow, 2001). A higher incidence of complications due to anoxia and reduced weight at birth has been found by retro-spective analysis of the birth history of those with schizophrenia, as has increased anoxia in the twin with schizophrenia compared with his normal brother or sister (Parnas et al., 1981). Stress, trauma, poverty and social isolation can all increase the risk of schizophrenia; these factors are all more prevalent in lower socio-economic

Table 11.2. Percentage contribution of genetic and environmental factors to six phenotypes.

Disease	Genetic	Environment (shared)	Environment (non-shared)
Schizophrenia	0.63	0.29	0.08
Bipolar disorder	0.86	0.07	0.07
Unipolar depression	0.52	0.30	0.18
Reactive depression	0.08	0.54	0.38
Tuberculosis	0.06	0.62	0.32

These data show that for three psychotic disorders (schizophrenia, bipolar disorder and unipolar depression) the genetic contribution is over 50% but for reactive depression (in response to a traumatic "life event") and tuberculosis, an infectious disease caused by a species of *Mycobacterium*, environmental factors account for over 90% of the variance.
Adapted from McGuffin (1991).

groups and ethnic minorities. The disproportionate number of African Caribbeans diagnosed with schizophrenia may be due to transcultural misinterpretation of particular behaviours.

Early neurochemical models

Some of the early Victorian models of "insanity" proposed an alteration in the basic chemistry of the brain. One general hypothesis is that an error in basic metabolism, similar to phenylketonuria, might lead to the production of a specific psychotoxin. "Many forms of insanity are unquestionably the external manifestations of the effects upon the brain substance of poisons fermented within the body, just as mental aberration accompanying chronic alcohol intoxication are the accumulated effects of a relatively simple poison fermented out of the body," claimed JLW Thudicum (1829–1901), who is often referred to as the founder of brain biochemistry, quoted in Leonard (1975). In 1952, half a century after his death, Osmond and Smythies (Ridges, 1973) put forward the idea that this psychotoxin might be an abnormal metabolite of one of the catecholamines: **adrenaline**, **dopamine** or **noradrenaline**. However, after years of mixed research findings this hypothesis was eventually largely rejected (Ridges, 1973). Attention switched to looking for methylated metabolites of the indolylamines tryptamine and **serotonin**. However, as with the previous notion this was also not supported. These transmethylation hypotheses are now only of historical interest, although they did provide a solid groundwork for more recent theories.

One major flaw in the seemingly attractive hypothesis that schizophrenia results from the endogenous (over)production of a psychotoxin is that all the hallucinogenic or **psychotomimetic** drugs, such as **lysergic acid diethylamide** (LSD), are poor mimics of the disorder (Chapter 6). Thus, they induce powerful visual hallucinations, but in schizophrenia these are extremely rare. Auditory hallucinations are typical of schizophrenia, but are not produced by LSD or any of the other psychotomimetics. There are also fundamental differences in the insight and understanding retained by the drug taker compared with the individual suffering with the illness.

Dopamine model

The neurochemical model that has best stood the test of time is based on dopamine overactivity. The original model predicted an increase in dopamine activity in localised regions of the forebrain; this has been superseded by more complex models, based on relative changes in several neurotransmitters, most particularly dopamine, glutamate and serotonin (see below). However, the origins of the original model will now be described, as they are essential to understanding the most recent versions. The original hypothesis was derived from clinical observations with **amphetamine** and **chlorpromazine**. When high doses of amphetamine are taken regularly by recreational users, they can often result in psychotic breakdown; this is characterised by delusions of persecution and other archetypal symptoms, which Dr Philip Connell, a child psychiatrist working in London, described as being "indistinguishable from acute or chronic paranoid schizophrenia" (Angrist and van Kammen, 1984). Amphetamine has three actions that raise the concentration of dopamine in the synaptic cleft and, thus, increase its availability to the postsynaptic receptor; these are electrically independent stimulation of dopamine release, inhibition of presynaptic neuronal dopamine reuptake by the transporter and inhibition of catabolism by **MAO** (monoamine oxidase; Chapter 3).

The other key strand for the dopamine theory was the discovery of the first effective antipsychotic drug, chlorpromazine (see below for a summary of its discovery and development). Chlorpromazine and related antipsychotic drugs act as dopamine receptor antagonists; this was initially suspected by the use of a range of indirect methods and was confirmed by direct assessment of its receptor-binding **potency**, using [^{3}H]-haloperidol in the mid-1970s (Seeman, 1980). Further support for the hypothesis that certain brain-dopaminergic neuronal pathways are overactive in schizophrenia came from the observation that the administration of **L-dopa**, or levodopa (the dopamine precursor) in **Parkinson's disease** could induce severe **psychosis** in some patients. Furthermore, dopamine agonists, like **apomorphine**, could precipitate a psychotic state in healthy individuals and exacerbate the illness in those with schizophrenia. In contrast, **reserpine**, which produces a long-lasting depletion of the stores of dopamine in synaptic vesicles, has an antipsychotic effect, whereas the tyrosine-3-hydroxylase inhibitor, α-methyl-p-tyrosine (AMPT), which blocks dopamine biosynthesis, potentiates the antipsychotic effect of neuroleptics (Seeman, 1980).

One difficulty with neuropharmacological evidence is the assumption of receptor specificity. Do all the above examples only modify the actions of just a single neurotransmitter? The answer is no. Chlorpromazine was originally developed for its potent **histamine$_1$ (H$_1$)** receptor antagonist actions. It also blocks (noradrenergic) α_1-**adrenoceptors** to cause **hypotension**. The newer, atypical neuroleptics block the 5-HT$_2$ (hydroxytryptamine, or serotonin) receptor subtypes, while reserpine also inhibits the storage of 5-HT and noradrenaline. Amphetamine has similar effects on 5-HT, noradrenaline and dopamine. All the above evidence could therefore be used to construct serotonin and noradrenaline hypotheses for schizophrenia. In fact, a 5-HT model for schizophrenia, which was largely based on the antipsychotic actions of reserpine together with the psychotogenic actions of LSD, preceded the dopamine model by several years (Woolley and Shaw, 1954). Furthermore, a noradrenaline model for schizophrenia was outlined some years later (Hornykiewicz, 1982).

Another crucial problem for any neurochemical model is cause and effect. Neuroleptics have a high affinity for dopamine receptors, particularly the D$_2$-subtype. There is also a highly significant positive correlation ($r > +0.9$) between this receptor binding and their clinical potency (Seeman, 1980). But, this does not necessarily implicate elevated dopamine levels as the cause of schizophrenia. Moreover, blockade of dopamine receptors happens very rapidly, whereas clinical benefits are only seen after chronic treatment. Rose (1973) has criticised the reductionist statement that "an abnormal biochemistry causes schizophrenia" because it relates cause and effect at different organisational levels (namely, the molecular and behavioural). But, while it can be legitimate to discuss cause and effect at the same level that chlorpromazine blocks dopamine receptors (one molecule altering the response of another), it is not valid to infer that increased dopamine activity causes schizophrenia. Put another way:

At the molecular level, an explanation of the action of a drug is often possible; at the cellular level, an explanation is sometimes possible; but at the behavioural level, our ignorance is abysmal.

(COOPER et al., 1991, p. 4)

In order to test the dopamine hypothesis more directly, biochemical differences between normal controls and those with schizophrenia were sought. Up until the introduction of neuroimaging techniques the only way to assess brain biochemical function was post-mortem, which introduced a further variable of how temporal delay might affect the stability of the chemicals. The hypothesis as originally formulated did not specify the locus of the hyperactive dopamine neurons, but, from what we know of the physiological functions of the relevant brain regions, the mesolimbic and mesocortical dopaminergic tracts would be the most relevant to the pathogenesis of schizophrenia (Chapters 2 and 10). The neuronal cell bodies of these tracts are clustered together in the ventral tegmentum of the midbrain (mesencephalon) with the axons projecting to the limbic system and frontal cortex. The mesolimbic tract is involved in arousal, memory and motivation (reward), while the mesocortical tract is implicated in cognitive processes and social behaviours (Cooper et al., 1991). The other intermediate to long-length dopaminergic pathways are the **nigrostriatal**, running from the substantia nigra of the midbrain to the corpus striatum (caudate nucleus and putamen) of the forebrain and the **tuberohypophysial** (tuberoinfundibular) from the hypothalamus to the median eminence of the pituitary gland at the base of the brain. The nigrostriatal pathway is involved in the regulation of voluntary movement and is damaged in Parkinson's disease, while the tuberohypophysial provides an interface between the nervous and endocrine systems, with dopamine inhibiting the release of the hormone prolactin from the anterior pituitary.

   The results of numerous post-mortem studies remain equivocal, with no consistent changes in the concentrations of dopamine nor of its metabolites homo-vanillic acid (HVA) and 3,4-dihydroxyphenylacetic acid (DOPAC) (Deakin, 1988). There is no evidence of selective changes in activity in the mesolimbic and mesocortical pathways in schizophrenia, although reports of lateral asymmetry in dopamine concentrations in the **amygdala** are worthy of further investigation (Deakin, 1988). Similarly, inconsistent results have been found when assessing brain dopaminergic activity *ex vivo* by measuring dopamine turnover in CSF, and **prolactin** concentration in blood plasma or serum. However, neuroimaging techniques now allow us to measure dopaminergic synaptic function *in vivo*. Using SPECT with $[^{123}$I]-iodobenzamide to measure D_2-receptor occupancy following an acute D-amphetamine challenge, it was shown that the drug released significantly more dopamine from neurons in the corpus striatum of 34 patients with schizophrenia compared with 36 controls (Laruelle and Abi-Dargham, 1999). This apparent dopamine hyperactivity was seen in patients displaying acute psychotic symptoms, but not those in remission, and was independent of previous antipsychotic drug therapy.

   Just over 25 years ago, Lee and Seeman (1977) of the University of Toronto presented a conference paper entitled "Dopamine receptors in normal and schizophrenic human brains", which was reported in the *Los Angeles Times* under the headline "Scientists find sites of craziness" (Timnick, 1977). By using a radioligand-binding assay with the antipsychotic [^{3}H]-haloperidol they showed a significant and high (>50%) increase in receptor binding in the caudate nucleus, putamen and nucleus accumbens (limbic system) of schizophrenics (Seeman, 1980). Later studies using other radioligands and larger sample sizes confirmed and extended these findings; this led to the suggestion that dopamine hyperactivity arose through the development of super-sensitive postsynaptic D_2-receptors rather than an increase in presynaptic biochemical events (Seeman, 1980). However, the interpretation of this finding has been disputed, and an alternative explanation of it based on chronic neuroleptic treatment has been advanced. Despite the selectivity of the change (increasing D_2 but not D_1-receptors), its replicability and its occurrence in some patients who had not previously been treated with drugs, the debate over its cause by disease *or* drug has continued.

It seemed that this might be resolved with the publication of the first *in vivo* study in drug-naive patients 9 years later (Wong et al., 1986). Using PET and 3-N-[^{11}C]-methylspiperone, D_2-receptor binding was shown to be increased in the caudate nucleus of 10 patients who had never received a neuroleptic and 5 who had been drug-free for at least 2 weeks prior to the study compared with 11 controls; this increase was >250% and was independent of previous drug history (Wong et al., 1986). However, later studies using another D_2-receptor antagonist, [^{3}H]-raclopride, only showed very modest non-significant elevations, possibly explained by the difference in selectivity of the two radioligands (Seeman et al., 1993). To summarise, a simple monocausal model was never likely to explain this diverse and complex disorder. The most recent consensus is that dopamine hyperactivity may be related to positive symptoms, while dopamine hypoactivity is linked to negative symptoms. If this is the case, then it may explain why older neuroleptics, which are primarily dopamine receptor antagonists, are not very effective in treating negative symptoms.

Dopamine–glutamate imbalance theory

The excitatory amino acid neurotransmitter **glutamate** is widely distributed in the brain (Chapter 3), but the neocortical and hippocampal glutaminergic pathways are of most relevance for schizophrenia. Structural neuroimaging has indicated cortical atrophy in some patients with schizophrenia, together with an increase in the density of glutamate **NMDA** (N-methyl-D-aspartate) receptors in the corpus striatum and decreased concentration of glutamate in cerebrospinal fluid point; these findings suggest the probable loss of corticostriatal glutaminergic neurons in schizophrenia (Feldman et al., 1997). The NMDA receptor contains a number of different binding sites; these are for the glutamate neurotransmitter itself, for another amino acid glycine and further sites for the psychotomimetic drugs **phencyclidine** (PCP) and ketamine (Chapter 6). Glycine acts as an allosteric effector (positive modulator), meaning that both amino acids have to occupy their respective sites before the NMDA receptor is fully activated. In contrast, PCP and ketamine are non-competitive antagonists of glutamate binding which produce auditory hallucinations and cognitive impairment; this means that the PCP and ketamine may provide far better models for schizophrenia than any of the other hallucinogens and **psychostimulants** (Thaker and Carpenter, 2001; see Chapter 6). Low doses of **ketamine** administered to healthy volunteers produce neurocognitive profiles very similar to those seen in schizophrenia (Green, 2001).

These and other observations have led to some far more complex and realistic neurochemical models, where several transmitter systems are seen as contributing to dysfunctional behaviour. Dopamine, serotonin and glutamate remain the main foci of interest. However, within the neuron itself, reduced activity of a peptide co-transmitter, like **cholecystokinin** or **neurotensin**, could adversely affect dopamine activity. The increasing sophistication of these neurotransmitter models should not only improve our knowledge at the molecular level but also help to delineate a greater understanding of cognitive, behavioural and clinical aspects. As Zubin (1985) stated:

It does little good to continue to find a difference in overall response levels between normals and schizophrenics in our electrophysiological, positron emission, biochemical, and behavioural measures unless we use the knowledge to lead to new approaches to classification, treatment and etiology.

(QUOTED IN MIRSKY AND DUNCAN, 1986, p. 313)

Chlorpromazine: the first antipsychotic drug

Like many scientific endeavours the series of events that led to the discovery of chlor-promazine has more twists and turns than a fictional detective story. During World War II, large numbers of casualties died from surgical shock on the operating table. Pharmaceutical companies attempted to find a drug to reduce this shock, and the French military surgeon Laborit reported some success with **promethazine** (Spiegel, 1996). The search continued for more effective compounds, and one of these was chlorpromazine. Although not very effective against surgical shock, many patients seemed calm and unworried. They appeared drowsy, but did not fall asleep and were unbothered by environmental events. Laborit suggested to psychiatrist colleagues that chlorpromazine might be clinically useful, and the drug was informally assessed in a range of psychiatric disorders. Some initial success was evident in schizophrenic patients. By increasing the dosage levels, Delay and Deniker (1952) showed that symptoms of schizophrenia could be reduced quite dramatically. Other psychiatrists confirmed its effectiveness, and by 1955 psychiatric hospitals around the world were initiating chlorpromazine treatment programmes and discharging many schizophrenics back into the community (Spiegel, 1996).

Despite these positive reports, many remained cautious over whether the benefits were genuine or, instead, reflected a **placebo** response (Chapter 3); this had occurred previously, when "insulin shock" was introduced as a putative therapy for schizo-phrenia during the 1930s. The clinical response was often quite favourable, but later studies showed that these benefits were artefacts of various expectancy factors: selection of the best patients for the new treatment, being moved to well-equipped wards and more intensive nursing and medical interventions. Therefore, it was important to undertake double-blind, placebo-controlled studies. One of the largest was sponsored by the National Institute of Mental Health (1964) in the USA. In nine psychiatric hospitals every newly diagnosed schizophrenic patient was randomly assigned to one of four treatments: chlorpromazine, **thioridazine**, **fluphenazine** or placebo (Chapter 3).

The drugs were administered double-blind, with neither the patient nor the medical staff knowing which drug was being given. Patients were regularly monitored over successive weeks and rated on numerous standardised scales. Clinical ratings showed significant improvements with each antipsychotic drug compared with placebo, whereas there were no differences between the three drugs. On the psychoactive treatments, 75% of patients were either "much improved" or "very much improved", while 5% did not show any change. In contrast, under placebo most showed either minimal improvement, minimal worsening or no change, although a minority did show stronger improvements. Nearly every individual symptom's rating was significantly alleviated by the active drugs. All positive symptoms, such as ideas of persecution and auditory hallucinations, were considerably reduced. However, self-care and social participation in ward activities were also improved under active drug conditions. Thus, some relief of negative symptoms also occurred with these typical antipsychotics. In an extensive review, Kane (1996) confirmed that in over a hundred studies comparing typical antipsychotics every study except one found the different drugs to be indistinguishable in terms of clinical effectiveness. However, they often differed in terms of their side effects (see below).

Chlorpromazine is technically described as a **phenothiazine**, as are thioridazine and fluphenazine. Together with their structural analogues the **thioxanthenes** (e.g., clopenthixol) and the **butyrophenones** (e.g., haloperidol), the phenothiazines comprise the three major families of "typical" neuroleptics. They were developed in the late 1950s and early 1960s (Table 11.3). All these drugs block dopamine receptors, principally the D_2 subtypes, with an affinity that correlates highly ($r = +0.90$) with their clinical

Table 11.3. Typical and atypical neuroleptics.

Generic name	Family name	T or A
Chlorpromazine	Aliphatic phenothiazine	T
Thioridazine	Piperidine phenothiazine	T
Fluphenazine*	Piperazine phenothiazine	T
Trifluoperazine	Piperazine phenothiazine	T
Clopenthixol*	Thioxanthene	T
Haloperidol	Butyrophenone	T
Spiperone	Butyrophenone	T
Clozapine	Dibenzodiazepine (DBZ)	A
Olanzapine	DBZ derivative	A
Quetiapine	DBZ derivative	A
Zotepine	DBZ derivative	A
S-Sulpiride	Substituted benzamide	A
Raclopride	Substituted benzamide	A
Amisulpride	Substituted benzamide	A
Remoxipride	Substituted benzamide	A
Risperidone	Benzisoxazole	A
Sertindole	Indole derivative	A

T = typical.
* Available as a depot formulation.

potency. Their antipsychotic effects are thought to reflect the blockade of limbic and neocortical dopamine receptors, whereas the major side effects are related more to the blockade of striatal dopamine receptors (see below).

Side effects of typical antipsychotics

The **extrapyramidal side effects** of antipsychotic drugs comprise a range of postural and motor problems. These functions are controlled by a number of subcortical regions, including the substantia nigra, caudate nucleus and putamen, collectively known as the **basal ganglia**; these are distinct from those controlled by the cerebral cortex and spinal cord, which together comprise the pyramidal system. The acute extrapyramidal side effects include **akathisia** (motor restlessness), **dystonia** (abnormal body tone) and Parkinsonism ("cogwheel" rigidity, tremor and bradykinesia, or poverty of movement, stooped posture) in 20–40% of patients treated with antipsychotics (Carvey, 1998). These acute extrapyramidal side effects (EPSEs) are thought to be related to blockade of striatal D_2-receptors; this explains why drugs, such as **haloperidol**, which show a high degree of occupancy of striatal D_2-receptors generate the highest rates of severe extrapyramidal problems. Whereas some of the other typical (thioridazine) and atypical (**clozapine**) drugs generate far fewer of these particular side effects.

Even more worrying are chronic extrapyramidal side effects, such as **tardive dyskinesia**; these occur in 10–15% of patients and develop gradually after 3 months or more of continuous pharmacotherapy. They comprise an array of distressing involuntary movements. Technically, they may be choreiform (rapid, jerky, non-repetitive), athetoid (slow, sinuous, continual) or stereotyped (rhythmic, repetitive). Most commonly, they affect the orofacial muscles and, behaviourally, they result in repetitive lip smacking and sucking, side-to-side jaw movements and the in-and-out darting of the tongue, or "fly catching". These distressing and uncontrollable movements provide considerable embarrassment for people who are already suffering from a stigmatised disease (APA, 2000). Tardive dyskinesia is postulated to be due to the development of supersensitive D_2-receptors, so that the most potent typical neuro-leptics, fluphenazine and haloperidol, are most likely to cause these distressing effects. Other side effects are related to the blockade of D_2-receptors in the anterior pituitary and may result in abnormal lactation or breast enlargement. The potentially fatal neuroleptic malignant syndrome, a hypersensitivity reaction characterised by severe hyperthermia, muscle rigidity, tachycardia and hypertension, is also thought to be related to D_2-receptor blockade. Finally, neuroleptics are useful anti-emetics as they block D_2-receptors in the chemoreceptor trigger zone located in the **medulla oblongata**.

Dosage reduction and depot injections

While most schizophrenics maintain their medication for many years, it is often possible to gradually reduce the dosage. Kane and Marder (1993) noted that effective symptom control can often be achieved at low doses, which then reduces the incidence of side effects. The optimal dose varied considerably between individuals. When attempting to reduce the dosage, it was therefore necessary to monitor behaviour quite closely and return to a higher dose if thought disorder or other symptoms showed signs of returning. An extension of this procedure is the use of drug-free holidays, where medication is used intermittently rather than continuously. But again, the patients need to be closely monitored, since the probability of relapse is doubled during these drug-free periods (Kane, 1996). Another common problem is the failure to carry on taking the medication after discharge from hospital, a major cause of relapse. Long-term **depot injections** were designed to overcome this problem (e.g., fluphenazine decanoate; Table 11.3). Here, the patient sees their psychiatric nurse every 4 to 6 weeks and is given an intramuscular depot injection. The drug is slowly released into the circulation over successive weeks. Around 30–50% of schizophrenics may be administered their medication this way.

Atypical antipsychotic drugs

Atypical neuroleptics are defined as those antipsychotics that induce fewer extra-pyramidal side effects and display greater efficacy in the relief of negative symptoms (Möller, 2000). The first atypical neuroleptic was clozapine, which appeared in the late 1960s; but, it was not until 30 years later that this diverse group of drugs began to make their mark in the clinic (Table 11.3). The use of clozapine was initially short-lived, due to the occurrence of potentially fatal **agranulocytosis** (the depletion of granular leucocytes, or white blood cells) in 1–2% of patients. It was therefore withdrawn for a number of years. Following its re-introduction for a restricted number of patients, combined with regular monitoring of white blood cell counts, the incidence of this serious side effect has declined markedly.

The majority of atypical antipsychotics have a high affinity for 5-HT$_2$ in addition to D$_2$-receptors. They are thus often referred to as serotonin/dopamine receptor antagonists, or SDA antagonists. **Risperidone** is the first of this class. There are three 5-HT$_2$ receptor subtypes, of which 5-HT$_{2A}$ and 5-HT$_{2C}$ are principally involved. There is also a tendency for these atypical drugs to have a higher affinity for D$_4$ over D$_2$-receptor subtypes and to be more selective in blocking limbic than striatal dopamine receptors (compared with typical neuroleptics). A comparison of the D$_4$/D$_2$ and 5-HT$_{2A}$/D$_2$ potency ratios of clozapine and risperidone (atypical antipsychotics) with haloperidol (as a typical antipsychotic) is shown in Table 11.4. This table also summarises the occupancy of **D$_2$-like** and 5-HT$_2$-receptors *in vivo* by therapeutic doses of these three drugs.

Table 11.4 shows that clozapine has approximately 10 times higher affinity for the D$_4$ and 5-HT$_{2A}$-receptors than the D$_2$-receptor and shows a greater occupancy of the 5-HT$_2$ than the D$_2$-like receptors. The other atypical neuroleptic risperidone has a similar affinity for the two D$_2$-like receptors but an affinity for the 5-HT$_{2A}$-receptor that is just over 3 times lower than for the D$_2$-receptor. Receptor occupancy *in vivo* shows a similar profile to clozapine. In contrast, haloperidol's affinity for the D$_4$-receptor is just under 3 times lower and over 100 times lower for the 5-HT$_{2A}$-receptor, with no binding to the latter *in vivo*. The fractional occupancy of striatal

Table 11.4. Clozapine, haloperidol and risperidone: comparative values for *in vitro* receptor affinity ratio and *in vivo* receptor occupancy.

Drug	$D_4 : D_2$ affinity ratio	$5\text{-}HT_{2A} : D_2$ affinity ratio	D_2-like occupancy (%)	$5\text{-}HT_2$ occupancy (%)
Clozapine	0.102	0.095	20–68	84–100
Haloperidol	2.960	106.288	70–90	0
Risperidone	1.645	3.174	59–89	78–100

Affinity ratios represent the mean of three values, calculated from published K_i or K_D data (data from Seeman et al., 1997; Strange, 1998; Kerwin, 2000). Occupancy of D_2-like (basal ganglia) and $5\text{-}HT_2$ (neocortex) receptors was assessed using PET or SPECT (data from Waddington and Casey, 2000).

D_2-receptors correlates with the severity of EPSE. PET (using 3-N-^{11}C-methylspiper-one or ^{11}C-raclopride) and SPECT (^{123}I-iodobenzamide) studies show that an occupancy of 70–80% is likely to cause extrapyramidal side effects, while above 80% most patients will experience them (Kasper et al., 2002).

Treatment with clozapine and the related olanzapine leads to an increase in body weight of around 4.5 kg after 10 weeks, over 4 times the weight gain induced by haloperidol (Möller, 2000). However, apart from this and the rare haematological disturbances caused by clozapine, the main disadvantage of atypical drugs is their greater cost. A 28-day prescription for clozapine including the blood test is 104 times more expensive than haloperidol, while risperidone is 73 times more costly (Thomas and Lewis, 1998); this has led to formal guidelines for when atypicals, such as risperidone, should be used. Since they are far better tolerated than typical anti-psychotics, this improves patient compliance, with better long-term prognosis and reduced risk of relapse. For these reasons, atypical drugs like risperidone have been recommended for all first episodes of schizophrenia. They are also used with non-responders to typical drugs and with those "good" responders to typical antipsychotics who suffer from persistent extrapyramidal side effects. Clozapine is an exception to this rule and should only be prescribed for those patients who do not respond to *any* other antipsychotic (Campbell et al., 1999; McGrath and Emmerson, 1999).

Antipsychotic drug combined with behavioural psychotherapy

May (1968) reviewed the clinical efficacy of the different therapeutic approaches to schizophrenia and showed that drug therapy alone was consistently superior to psychotherapy alone. Furthermore, the addition of psychotherapy to drug therapy improved the clinical outcome only slightly. This review was followed by several further studies where drug treatment was combined with other forms of psychological therapy. Hogarty and Goldberg (1973) compared four treatment regimens in 374 schizophrenics, stabilized on chlorpromazine prior to discharge from hospital. The patients were randomly allocated to four treatment groups using the classic 2×2

factorial design: chlorpromazine or placebo, with or without regular therapy. The highest rate of hospital relapse within 1 year (73%) occurred with placebo without psychotherapy; this marginally improved when placebo was accompanied by regular psychotherapy (63%). Chlorpromazine alone led to a far better relapse rate (33%), whereas the best overall outcome was when chlorpromazine was combined with regular psychotherapy (26%). This study confirmed the importance of effective antipsychotic drug use, but showed that psychotherapy could add significantly to clinical improvement. Schooler and Hogarty (1987) reviewed the many other types of combined therapy: individual psychotherapy, group psychotherapy, social skills training, practical life skills, training in communication skills, etc. The main conclusion was that the best treatment outcomes always occurred with multi-component packages. It may be that the antipsychotic drug relieves cortical overarousal, which then allows the person to handle the new ideas and suggestions that arise during therapy sessions.

Future drug developments

The 5-HT_{1A} receptor has recently been proposed as a potential novel therapeutic target in schizophrenia (Bantick et al., 2001). This receptor subtype is located both presynaptically on the **soma** (cell body) and dendrites of 5-HT neurons in the brainstem **raphe nuclei** (somatodendritic autoreceptors), where it has an inhibitory effect on cell activity. It is also sited postsynaptically in the **hippocampus** and **neocortex**. A number of postmortem, radioligand-binding studies have shown an increased density of 5-HT_{1A} receptors in areas of the neocortex in schizophrenia. Furthermore in rats, 5-HT_{1A} agonists block haloperidol-induced **catalepsy**, a model for extrapyramidal side effects (Bantick et al., 2001). Two currently prescribed atypical neuroleptics, clozapine and quetiapine, have a high affinity for the 5-HT_{1A}-receptor. This property may underlie their favourable extrapyramidal side effect profile and efficacy in treating the negative symptoms of schizophrenia.

On the basis of evidence of neocortical glutamatergic neuronal hypoactivity, it might be predicted that drugs that enhance the activity of these neurons would also be of benefit. A limited number of trials using the amino acids **D-cycloserine** and D-serine, both agonists at the glycine site of the glutamate NMDA-receptor, in combination with a neuroleptic, have suggested an improvement in negative symptoms (Green, 2001). In view of the postulated role of the NMDA receptor in learning and memory, development of novel agonists would be particularly useful in treating neurocognitive defects.

Finally, an intriguing possible future therapy arises from a radical idea of Horrobin (2001): that schizophrenia is a nutritional disorder linked to a decreased intake of essential polyunsaturated fatty acids. Recent ^{31}P-MRS studies have shown changes in plasma membrane phospholipids in the neocortex of unmedicated schizophrenics, which would have deleterious consequences on synaptic neurotransmission (Fukuzako, 2001). A clinical trial with the ω6 fatty acid derivative ethyleicosapentaenoic acid (LAX-101) in patients who had been unresponsive to clozapine, reported that a daily dose of 2 g LAX-101 gave a 26% improvement in symptoms over 12 weeks compared with 6% with placebo (Peet and Horrobin, 2001). Maybe in schizophrenia, as with current ideas on the aetiology of many other clinical disorders, the importance of nutrition should not be too readily dismissed.

Questions

1   Describe the positive and negative symptoms of schizophrenia.

2   What can neuroimaging tell us about possible changes in the structure and function of the brain in schizophrenia?

3   Describe how the "dopamine hyperactivity" model for schizophrenia has changed and evolved over time.

4   Describe the historical origins of the first antipsychotic drug chlorpromazine, and evaluate the evidence for its efficacy.

5   List the principal side effects or adverse drug reactions of a typical neuroleptic.

6   What advantages and disadvantages do clozapine and/or risperidone display over haloperidol?

7   Name three potential novel targets and drugs for treating schizophrenia in the future.

Key references and reading

Buckland PR and McGuffin P (2000). Molecular genetics of schizophrenia. In: MA Reveley and JFW Deakin (eds), *The Psychopharmacology of Schizophrenia* (pp. 71–88). Edward Arnold, London.

Diamond RJ (2002). *Instant Psychopharmacology*. W.W. Norton, New York.

Green MF (2001). *Schizophrenia Revealed*. W.W. Norton, New York.

Kerwin R (2000). The neuropharmacology of schizophrenia: Past, present and future. In: M Reveley and JFW Deakin (eds), *The Psychopharmacology of Schizophrenia* (pp. 41–55). Edward Arnold, London.

Leonard BE (2003). *Fundamentals of Psychopharmacology* (3rd edn). John Wiley & Sons, Chichester, UK.

Möller H-J (2000). Definition, psychopharmacological basis and clinical evaluation of novel/ atypical neuroleptics: Methodological issues and clinical consequences. *World Journal of Biological Psychiatry*, **1**, 75–91.

Spiegel R (1996). *Psychopharmacology: An Introduction* (2nd edn). John Wiley & Sons, Chichester, UK.

Waddington J and Casey D (2000). Comparative pharmacology of classical and novel (second-generation) antipsychotics. In: PF Buckley and JL Waddington (eds), *Schizophrenia and Mood Disorders* (pp. 1–13). Butterworth-Heinemann, Oxford, UK.

Chapter 12

Antidepressants and mood stabilisers

Overview

The two main forms of affective disorder are depression and mania. Depression is where moods are very low, with feelings of worthlessness, negative beliefs and cognitions. Mania in contrast is a state of abnormally elevated moods, with energetic hyperactivity, flights of ever-changing ideas and impulsive behaviour. Manic depression or bipolar affective disorder is where these two extreme affective states alternate. The original catecholamine model proposed that depression was caused by a functional deficit in noradrenaline, while mania was characterised by a functional excess of this catecholamine. Later, this model was modified to include serotonin, since neuropharmacological data indicated its importance for depression. Antidepressants increase the synaptic concentrations of noradrenaline and/or serotonin, following acute administration; however, the clinical benefits are only seen after chronic treatment. These observations led to the proposal that depression occurred because of the development of supersensitive noradrenaline and/or serotonin receptor subtypes and that antidepressant drugs act by down-regulating or desensitising them, a process that takes several weeks. The typical monoamine oxidase inhibitors and tricyclic antidepressants prolong the synaptic actions of these neurotransmitters by inhibiting their enzymic and non-enzymic inactivation, respectively. The potentially serious side effects of these drugs led to the introduction of newer, safer drugs: hence, the selective serotonin reuptake inhibitors, typified by fluoxetine. Turning to the pharmacotherapy for mania, for decades lithium was the only effective drug treatment. More recently, a number of antiepileptic drugs including carbamazepine, lamotrigine and valproate have been shown to also act as mood stabilisers and are becoming established for the treatment and prophylaxis of both unipolar mania and bipolar manic depressive disorders.

Affective disorders

Until one has experienced a debilitating severe depression it is hard to understand the feelings of those who have it. Severe depression borders on being beyond description: it is not just feeling much lower than usual. It is a quite different state, a state that bears only a tangential resemblance to normal emotion. It deserves some new and special word of its own, a word that would somehow encapsulate both the pain and the conviction that no remedy will ever come. We could certainly do with a better word for this illness than one with the mere common connotation of being "down".

(WOLPERT, 1999, p. 1)

Depression as described here by one sufferer, Lewis Wolpert, a Professor of Biology at University College London, is one of the **affective disorders**. The depression he was suffering was far stronger than the normal mood changes experienced by most people. Thus, it is entirely normal to experience changes in feelings of happiness and sadness, ups and downs, over the day. The affective disorders are characterised by far more extreme mood states. Depression in particular is extremely disabling and distressing. In contrast, mania is far more of a problem for family and friends, as they try to cope with exhaustingly positive moods, frenetic periods of physical activity and excessive spending sprees. The symptoms of depression and mania are described more fully below.

In clinical psychiatric terms, the affective disorders can be subdivided into **unipolar** and **bipolar disorders**. Unipolar depression is also known as psychotic depression, endogenous depression, idiopathic depression and major depressive disorder. Bipolar disorder is now recognised as being heterogeneous: bipolar disorder I is equivalent to classical manic depressive **psychosis**, or manic depression, while bipolar disorder II is depression with hypomania (Dean, 2002). Unipolar mania is where periods of mania alternate with periods of more normal moods. Seasonal affective disorder (SAD) refers to depression with its onset most commonly in winter, followed by a gradual remission in spring. Some milder forms of severe depression, often those with an identifiable cause, may be referred to as reactive or neurotic depression. Secondary depression is associated with other illnesses, such as neurodegenerative or cardiovascular diseases, and is relatively common.

Symptoms

The classic symptoms of depression are listed in Table 12.1, which is based on *DSM-IV* criteria. For a diagnosis of major depressive disorder, most of these symptoms must be present, including the first two (APA, 2000). These symptoms should be of sufficient intensity and chronic duration (at least 2 weeks) to cause clinically significant distress and impairment in social or economic functioning. However, they should not be a result of another psychiatric or somatic illness, nor of **drug** misuse or bereavement. For a diagnosis of mania, the symptoms are a mirror image of those for depression (Table

Table 12.1. Symptoms of the affective disorders: major depression and mania.

Major depression	
Dysphoria	Depressed mood.
Anhedonia	Diminished interest or pleasure in activities.
Insomnia	Disturbed sleep, characterised by difficulty in falling asleep and early waking.
Psychomotor dysfunction	Agitation or retardation.
Fatigue	Loss of drive and energy; loss of sexual interest; reduced appetite.
Cognitive dysfunction	Decreased concentration ability; negative ruminations, feelings of worthlessness and guilt.
Suicidal thoughts	Recurrent thoughts of death; suicidal ideas; attempted and actual suicide.
Mania	
Euphoria	Elevated mood.
Hyperactivity	Bursting with energy; decreased need for sleep; inability to concentrate; initiating multiple tasks, but completing none.
Flights of fancy	Increased talkativeness, garrulousness and pressure of speech; flight of ideas; racing thoughts.
Grandiosity	Excessive confidence; inflated self-esteem; impulsive decisions leading to reckless behaviour, poor judgement, reduced inhibitions; disruptive social behaviours, such as financial extravagance, impulsive travel to exotic locations (by first-class travel, naturally); heightened sexual activity.

12.1). Bipolar disorder is characterised by a period of mania, then a period of comparatively normal behaviour (euthymia), before progressing to a period of depression. The rate at which these mood changes occur can vary, being prolonged in some individuals and shorter in others. This periodicity is often characteristic and unchanging for an individual. In some rare instances the mood cycle is not only predictable but also very rapid: for instance, 16 hours of mania, followed by 8 hours of euthymia, then 48 hours of depression.

In the 75–80% of patients who experience more than one episode of depression the average lifetime number of episodes of depression is four, with a typical duration of 20 weeks (Anderson et al., 2000). Estimates for annual prevalence rates vary from 3 to 10%, with the frequency two to three times higher in women (Anderson et al., 2000). However, because depression often goes unreported the real figure may be considerably higher. Twin study data show that there is a moderate **genetic** influence, particularly in earlier onset depression, with quoted concordance rates for **monozygotic** twins of 40–43%, about half that for bipolar depression (BPD; 62–72%) and over double that for **dizygotic** twins of 11–20% (Plomin et al., 2001).

Monoamine theories

Neurochemical theories for the affective disorders propose that there is a link between dysfunctional monoaminergic **synapses** within the central nervous system (CNS) and mood problems. The original focus was the neurotransmitter **noradrenaline**, or NA (note: noradrenaline is called norepinephrine, or NE, in American texts). Schildkraut (1965) suggested that depression was associated with an absolute or relative deficiency of NA, while mania was associated with a functional excess of NA. Subsequently, another monoamine neurotransmitter 5-hydroxytryptamine (5-HT), or **serotonin**, was put forward in a rival indoleamine theory (Chapter 2). However, it was soon recognised that both proposals could be reconciled with the available clinical biochemical and pharmacological evidence (Luchins, 1976; Green and Costain, 1979).

The monoamine theory proposes that depression is related to hypoactivity of forebrain NA and/or 5-HT-containing neurons, whereas mania is related to their hyperactivity (increased activity). Support for this model comes from two main sources: first, the behavioural and neurochemical effects of the drugs used to treat these disorders; and, second, the behavioural and neurochemical effects of **reserpine**. Reserpine is the pharmacologically active chemical extracted from the root of *Rauwolfia serpentina*, a plant found on the Indian subcontinent. Reserpine was first used to treat hypertension in the early 1950s. Subsequently, because of its observed calming effects in those patients, it was then used in the management of schizophrenia (Bein, 1982; see also Chapter 11). However, one untoward side effect with 15% of patients was severe depression that could sometimes result in suicide. Reserpine affects the stable storage of NA, 5-HT and dopamine in the vesicles located in the presynaptic neuronal terminal; it results in long-lasting depletion of these monoamines and a consequent reduction in neurotransmission.

The first two antidepressants, **iproniazid** and **imipramine**, were developed in the same decade. They were shown to reverse the behavioural and neurochemical effects of reserpine in laboratory rodents, by inhibiting the inactivation of these monoamine transmitters (Leonard, 1985). Iproniazid inhibits **MAO (monoamine oxidase)**, an **enzyme** located in the presynaptic neuronal terminal which breaks down NA, 5-HT and dopamine into physiologically inactive metabolites. Imipramine inhibits the reuptake of NA and 5-HT from the synaptic cleft by their transporters. Therefore, both of these drugs increase the availability of NA and 5-HT for binding to postsynaptic **receptors** and, therefore, result in enhanced synaptic transmission. Conversely, **lithium**, the oldest but still most frequently used mood stabiliser (see below), decreases synaptic NA (and possibly 5-HT) activity, by stimulating their reuptake and reducing the availability of precursor chemicals required in the biosynthesis of second messengers.

Although there has been a substantial body of pharmacological evidence in support of the monoamine theory of depression, clinical biochemical data have been less convincing (Luchins, 1976); this is where differences in the concentrations of NA and 5-HT and their metabolites or hormones, which are ultimately under the control of brain monoaminergic neurons (neuroendocrine markers), have been compared between depressed patients and normal controls. However, by the early 1970s a major difficulty with the theory was becoming apparent; this was the time lag between the *immediate* effects of the antidepressants in raising monoamine levels and the clinical benefits, which were only seen after 2 weeks or more of drug treatment. This temporal discrepancy between acute neurochemical changes and chronic behavioural changes led to the suggestion that: "Changes in adrenergic receptor sensitivity may be involved in the aetiology of affective disorders" (Eccleston, 1973).

In 1975, Vetulani and Sulser published their seminal experimental study suggesting that depression might result from the development of supersensitive postsynaptic β-**adrenoreceptors** and that antidepressants worked by desensitising or down-regulating these receptors; this would explain why repeated drug administration was necessary (Vetulani and Sulser, 1975). Subsequent animal studies have postulated supersensitivity of **postsynaptic** 5-HT$_2$ receptors and **presynaptic** α_2-NA, 5-HT$_{1A}$ and 5-HT$_{1B}$-receptors in depression. However, attempts to find corroborating evidence for these models in human patients have been disappointing (Leonard and Richelson, 2000).

Hypothalamic–pituitary–adrenal axis (HPA)

The contributions of stress and the increased responsiveness of the **Hypothalamic–Pituitary–Adrenal (HPA) axis** in depression have been well documented. A significant proportion of depressed patients show biochemical changes consistent with hyperactivity of the HPA axis; these include increased concentrations of the hypothalamic neuropeptide CRF (corticotrophin-releasing factor), the anterior pituitary hormone ACTH (adrenocorticotrophic hormone) and the adrenal cortical hormone **cortisol** (hydrocortisone; Hatzinger, 2000). Moreover, administration of the cortisol agonist dexamethasone to approximately half of depressed patients fails to reduce the concentration of cortisol in the blood. This failure of the **Dexamethasone Suppression Test** (DST) is generally interpreted as an impairment of the HPA axis negative feedback loop. Normally, this is activated by high levels of the glucocorticoids cortisol and/or dexamethasone, to reduce the further output of cortisol. As CRF release is inhibited by hypothalamic noradrenergic neurons, a possible hypoactivity of these neurons would be expected to result in increased CRF (also of ACTH and cortisol).

In animal studies, high levels of cortisol have been shown to induce (increase) the activity of the enzyme tryptophan 2,3-dioxygenase in the liver, thereby decreasing the bioavailability of tryptophan to the brain. It is interesting to note that low acute doses of a number of different antidepressants inhibit the activity of this enzyme and, as a result, increase brain tryptophan concentrations, thus stimulating 5-HT synthesis (Badawy and Evans, 1982). In this way a link between the two key monoamine neurotransmitters and the hormone may be seen: namely, reduced brain NA activity leads to decreased inhibition of the HPA axis, while increased levels of cortisol reduce 5-HT activity in the brain. Activation of the HPA axis has also been shown to result in tissue atrophy, in particular of the limbic system's hippocampus, and a reduction in the levels of **neurotrophic factors** responsible for the maintenance and optimal function of brain neurons (Manji et al., 2001). In conclusion, manipulation of the HPA axis (Nemeroff, 2002) and stimulation of neurotrophic factor activity (Manji et al., 2001) might open up new avenues for the treatment of affective disorders.

First antidepressant drugs

The year 1957 saw the beginning of a revolution in the psychopharmacotherapy of depression. Before that year there were no effective drugs, and **electroconvulsive therapy** (ECT) was the only effective physical therapy available. However, ECT was then given without the benefit of any neuromuscular blockers to relax the skeletal muscles. In 1951 isoniazid and iproniazid were first synthesised, and these two hydrazines showed potent antituberculosis effects *in vitro* (Sandler, 1990). The following year they were assessed on tubercular patients, and iproniazid, in particular, was found to produce feelings of euphoria as a side effect. However, it was another 5 years before its benefits in psychiatric patients were described by Kline, Loomer and Saunders (Sandler, 1990). Iproniazid was found to exert its antidepressant actions through MAO inhibition and was thus the first MAO inhibitor (see below). Hepatotoxicity and drug–diet interactions subsequently limited its clinical use, but its discovery was certainly of historical importance for psychopharmacology.

A second serendipitous discovery in 1957 was reported by Kuhn at the *Second International Congress of Psychiatry* held in Zurich. Imipramine was the first tricyclic antidepressant to be investigated; but, since it is a structural analogue (chemical relative) of chlorpromazine, it was initially assessed for its antipsychotic properties (Sandler, 1992; see Chapter 11). Imipramine displayed little benefits, except with those who displayed depressive feelings as a secondary feature of their illness. This observation led to an open trial on 100 patients with depression, and favourable findings were presented by Kuhn in September 1957 (Sandler, 1992). Imipramine is now considered as the prototype **tricyclic antidepressant** (TAD). Together with iproniazid, one of the first of the MAO inhibitors, they are referred to as first-generation **antidepressants**. Although their use has declined, following the introduction of second-generation antidepressants (see later), the tricyclics in particular are still widely used. Today, around 35 different antidepressants are used worldwide, giving beneficial responses in 50–75% of patients with major depression (Bauer et al., 2002), although a high **placebo** response can obscure any "benefits" of the antidepressant in some clinical trials. It is also generally noted that the newer antidepressants (see below), while causing fewer adverse side effects, do not demonstrate any significant clinical improvements in comparison with the original tricyclics.

Antidepressant drugs increase the levels of NA and/or 5-HT in the synaptic cleft by one of three principal mechanisms (Table 12.2): first, by selective or non-selective inhibition of MAO, which thus leads to increased neurotransmitter availability; second, non-selective or selective inhibition of NA and 5-HT reuptake, which again leads to an increase in functional neurotransmitter levels; and, third, blockade of the presynaptic inhibitory α_2-adrenoceptors, which results in increased release of NA from the presynaptic neuron. The increase in synaptic monoamine concentrations is then postulated to lead to down-regulation of both presynaptic and postsynaptic receptors after several weeks. It is this down-regulation that is thought to generate the remission of symptoms and general clinical improvement. ECT has been shown to increase the release of NA and 5-HT from neuronal terminals and down-regulate β-adrenoceptors as well. However, unlike antidepressant drugs it increases or up-regulates the sensitivity of postsynaptic 5-HT_2-receptors (Blier and De Montigny, 1994).

Table 12.2. Antidepressants and their neurochemical effects.

Drug family	Drug (generic) name	Neurochemical effect
Tricyclic antidepressants (TAD)	Imipramine	NA = 5-HT
	Desipramine	NA > 5-HT
	Clomipramine	5-HT > NA
	Amitriptyline	NA = 5-HT
	Nortriptyline	NA > 5-HT
	Lofepramine	NA > 5-HT
MAOI	Iproniazid	NA = 5-HT = DA
	Isocarboxazid	NA = 5-HT = DA
	Tranylcypromine	NA = 5-HT = DA
RIMA	Moclobemide	NA = 5-HT
Tetracyclic antidepressants (heterocyclics)	Mianserin	NA via α_2-antagonism
	Mirtazepine	NA via α_2-antagonism
SSRI	Citalopram	5-HT > NA
	Fluoxetine	5-HT > NA
	Fluvoxamine	5-HT > NA
	Paroxetine	5-HT > NA
	Sertraline	5-HT > NA
SNRI	Venlafaxine	NA = 5-HT
SNARI	Reboxetine	NA > 5-HT

MAOI: non-selective monoamine oxidase (A/B) inhibitors; RIMA: reversible inhibitor of monamine oxidase type A; SSRI: selective serotonin (5-HT) reuptake inhibitors; SNRI: serotonin/noradrenaline reuptake inhibitor; SNARI: selective noradrenaline (NA) reuptake inhibitor; NA = 5-HT = DA: potency of the drug is very similar in raising the level of both (or all three) monamines; NA > 5-HT: more selective for NA; 5-HT > NA: more selective for 5-HT; NA: increases the release of NA.

The amino acid precursor for 5-HT, L-tryptophan, increases the biosynthesis 5-HT and, therefore, has been investigated for potential antidepressant properties, but with mixed results (Green and Costain, 1979). It was withdrawn in 1990, following a number of fatal cases of eosinophilia myalgia (a disorder characterised by severe muscle pain and abnormally high levels of one type of white blood cell, the eosinophil) in individuals principally using it as a "natural" hypnotic.

Tricyclic antidepressants

Until the introduction of **selective serotonin reuptake inhibitors (SSRIs)** in the 1980s, tricyclic antidepressants were the most widely used drugs. The therapeutic effect of **amitriptyline** and imipramine are related to their ability to inhibit the presynaptic reuptake of both NA and 5-HT. They are referred to as non-selective reuptake inhibitors, whereas many of the other tricyclics are more selective: thus, **clomipramine** is a selective reuptake inhibitor for 5-HT and **desipramine** and **nortriptyline** are selective reuptake inhibitors for NA. The **potency** of these drugs in blocking the reuptake of dopamine is around 100 times less than for NA and/or 5-HT. This observation gave great support for a role for the latter two monoamines in depression. Desipramine and nortriptyline are the active hepatic metabolites of imipramine and amitriptyline, respectively, and tend to have weaker sedative effects, making them more appropriate for patients with psychomotor retardation.

Tricyclic antidepressants can give rise to numerous side effects, some of which can be fatal, a highly undesirable property when many patients have suicidal thoughts and/or intentions. For this reason the majority of patients are prescribed suboptimal doses that render the treatment less effective (Carvey, 1998). Many side effects arise through antagonism at the muscarinic **acetylcholine** or **cholinergic receptors** in the parasympathetic autonomic nervous system. This resultant reduction in salivary gland activity generates feelings of "dried mouth", impaired muscular control in the eye resulting in blurred vision and other parasympatholytic effects include tachycardia, urine retention and constipation. Many other side effects are caused by the blocking of cholinergic receptors in the CNS: cognitive impairments, dyskinesias and hypomania or mania (the so-called "switch" phenomenon). Blocking α_1-adrenoreceptors results in postural, or orthostatic, hypotension and sedation. Blockade of the **histamine$_1$** receptors can result in feelings of sedation. The most serious side effect is cardiotoxicity which may result in fatal dysrhythmias (arrhythmias) arising from a combination of the antimuscarinic effect (reduced vagal inhibition of the sinoatrial node) and inhibition of NA reuptake into the cardiac accelerator neuron (increased sympathetic drive). These effects are most problematic with amitriptyline, desipramine, imipramine and nortriptyline, less so with clomipramine and of little concern with the newest tricyclic antidepressant lofepramine (Anderson et al., 2000).

A general problem with antidepressant therapy is that only half of those treated fully respond to the drugs, a pattern that is similar among adolescent, adult and geriatric patients. Of the non-responders, 60% show a partial response with residual depressive symptoms that have a deleterious effect on their psychosocial and economic functioning and, therefore, quality of family, social and work life (Silva and Larach, 2000). Also, because depression is often a recurring condition the value of antidepressants for relapse prevention (prophylactic or continuation therapy) must be balanced against the adverse effects arising from chronic administration. In a review of 21 controlled studies with a total of 1,192 patients treated for between 0.5 to 3 years, 4.3% of the drug group discontinued their treatment because of side effects, almost five times higher than placebo, although the suicide rate was very similar (1.9% vs. 1.5%), with the non-selective tricyclic antidepressants imipramine and amitriptyline most frequently linked to suicide (Rouillon et al., 1992).

Monoamine oxidase inhibitors (MAOIs)

These drugs inhibit the activity of the principal enzyme involved in the catabolism of a number of physiological and pharmacological monoamines. MAO is bound to the outer membrane of mitochondria and, therefore, will be found in most cells throughout the body. First-generation drugs (Table 12.2) non-selectively inhibit both the A and B isoforms, but it is inhibition of MAO-A, which has a higher affinity for NA and 5-HT, that underlies the antidepressant effect. This classification into A and B originated some 30 years ago with the identification of the first selective MAO-A (**clorgyline**) and MAO-B (**selegiline**, or L-deprenyl) inhibitors. Both drugs were irreversible inhibitors, and, while clorgyline was too toxic for clinical use, selegiline, although of little benefit in depression, became established as both an adjunct to **L-dopa** and a monotherapy in **Parkinson's disease** (Carvey, 1998).

Today, the use of typical MAOIs is very much a second line of treatment, mainly reserved for patients who have not responded to other drugs. The reason for their unpopularity is their potential for precipitating a fatal hypertensive crisis, sometimes referred to as the cheese effect (Carvey, 1998). Tyramine is a sympathomimetic amine (indirect noradrenaline agonist) found particularly in mature cheeses, red wines like Chianti, pickled herring and proprietary yeast extracts like Marmite. It is normally broken down by MAO in the intestinal mucosa and liver, but in MAO-compromised patients dietary tyramine enters the systemic circulation and is taken up into sympathetic autonomic neuronal terminals from where it releases stored NA. NA increases cardiovascular activity through binding to α_1-adrenoreceptors on vascular smooth muscle, causing vasoconstriction (so, raising blood pressure), and binding to cardiac pacemaker β_1-adrenoreceptors to increase heart rate. A severe headache, accompanied by nausea, vomiting and palpitations, is the sign of a potential cardiovascular crisis that in susceptible individuals may result in a cerebrovascular accident (stroke) or fatal dysrhythmias.

In addition to this serious diet–drug interaction, irreversible MAOIs also potentiate the effects of sympathomimetic drugs like **ephedrine** found in over-the-counter cold remedies and recreational stimulants like **amphetamine**. The MAOIs also interact with drugs that increase synaptic concentrations of 5-HT, such as the tricyclic antidepressant clomipramine and the herbal SSRI antidepressant St John's wort (*Hypericum* spp.). The resulting "serotonin syndrome" is characterised by hyperthermia and muscle rigidity. While devoid of these side effects the reversible MAO-A inhibitor **moclobemide** has yet to establish itself as a first-line alternative to the SSRIs.

Despite public misconceptions, there is little firm evidence that the typical and atypical antidepressants produce **dependence** in clinical users. A review of 21 case reports of "antidepressant addiction" revealed that 12 were associated with tranylcypromine, although 8 of these 12 had a previous history of substance misuse (Haddad, 1999). **Tranylcypromine**'s structural similarity to amphetamine may account for the significant number of reports of its addictive potential, but even here the term (mild) "discontinuation reaction" rather than "withdrawal reaction" should be used to allay any concerns patients might have (Haddad, 1999).

Selective serotonin reuptake inhibitors (SSRIs)

With the long catalogue of adverse drug reactions produced by typical antidepressants, the search for safer and more efficacious drugs became a matter of priority by the late

1960s. After false hopes like **mianserin**, which was introduced and then withdrawn, the SSRIs have now become the most widely used:

The SSRIs represent an advance in the pharmacology of depression. Although they have higher individual costs, their favourable side-effect profile and reduced toxicity can add up to savings in overall health care costs. They increase the likelihood of better compliance at an adequate dose of antidepressant for a sufficient period of time, and appreciably improve the risk benefit ratio for antidepressant drug treatment. Benefits such as reduced toxicity in overdose, long-term safety and efficacy in the prevention of relapse and recurrence of depression, improved quality of life and decreased accident liability all have cost implications which must not be neglected when considering the relative cost of medication.

(LANE et al., 1995)

This certainly is a glowing endorsement of the SSRIs. Indeed, one of the original members of the group **fluoxetine** has even become a cultural icon, with some clinicians advocating its use for "cosmetic psychopharmacological" purposes: its use is advocated with non-clinical subgroups to make the individual feel "better than well" and/or to "enhance your personality" (Kramer, 1994). In contrast, another early SSRI **zimelidine** was withdrawn from the market after a short period of time because of the significant idiosyncratic responses (adverse hypersensitivity reactions). The side effects with SSRIs are generally mild, but include feelings of nausea and sexual dysfunction. Furthermore, in contrast to the typical tricyclic antidepressants and MAOIs, they usually decrease as treatment progresses. Fluoxetine has been associated with increased anxiety, agitation, hostility and insomnia in around 10% of patients (Goldstein and Goodnick, 1998). The implication that fluoxetine and, more recently, **paroxetine** are major contributing factors in a number of murders by patients taking these drugs is highly controversial and the subject of legal debate by representatives of the patients, their relatives and pharmaceutical companies. There is also some evidence that fluoxetine may be more likely to precipitate suicide in a small number of particularly vulnerable individuals; however, it is debatable whether this is attributable to the drug or the disease (Healy et al., 1999). Furthermore, typical antidepressants are far more strongly associated with depression-related suicides and fatalities. Thus, the death rates per million prescriptions are as follows: tranylcypromine (60 fatalities per million prescriptions), amitriptyline (48), imipramine (33) and clomipramine (8). The equivalent figures for the SSRIs are fluvoxamine (6), fluoxetine (1), paroxetine (1) sertraline (1) and citalopram (1), (Table 12.2; see also Grunze et al., 2002).

Fluoxetine and its active metabolite norfluoxetine have half-lives of 96 hours and 19 days, respectively. So, sudden cessation of treatment is unlikely to precipitate any withdrawal symptoms, although abrupt discontinuation may produce a noticeable reaction when using other SSRIs with far shorter half-lives. Potentially serious drug interactions may arise through competition for binding sites on the plasma protein albumin and inhibition of metabolism in the liver by **CYP2D6**. Fluoxetine is highly albumin-bound and as such may displace other drugs, most significantly warfarin, and, by inhibiting one of the principal enzymes responsible for metabolising drugs (CYP2D6), fluoxetine can potentiate the action of a wide variety of drugs. Caution must also be exercised in prescribing fluoxetine to the elderly, since its hepatic metabolism is reduced with age and lower doses are therefore needed (Vandel, 2003).

Serotonin–noradrenaline (SNRIs) and selective noradrenaline (SNARIs) reuptake inhibitors

These types of antidepressant were introduced around 10 years after the SSRIs. They include the serotonin–noradrenaline reuptake inhibitor **venlafaxine** and the selective noradrenaline reuptake inhibitor **reboxetine**. Although there are fewer data about these drugs, clinical experience has shown they are well tolerated and, unlike the SSRIs, they are only weak inhibitors of drug metabolism (Kent, 2000). Depression is a common psychiatric disorder seen in the elderly and often remains untreated or inadequately treated (Forsell and Fastbom, 2000). Venlafaxine was shown to improve the mood in a group of 36 older patients without any effect on cognitive function, an important consideration where there is the possibility of the coexistence of mild or undiagnosed dementia (Tsolaki et al., 2000).

Other therapies and future possibilities

Specifically used for SAD, phototherapy involves daily exposures to high-intensity fluorescent lighting and has been shown to generate clear clinical benefits (Bauer et al., 2002). Herbal remedies, or phytotherapy, is increasingly being tried in the treatment of depression. In Germany, St. John's wort is available on prescription, while in other countries it can be purchased from health food shops. As with any herbal medicine the precise nature and number of active ingredients is unknown, but one of them hyperforin is a non-selective reuptake inhibitor with a potency of just 10 times less than that of fluoxetine in inhibiting 5-HT reuptake (Nathan, 2001). Complementary, or alternative, medicine is gaining greater acceptance from "conventional" medical practitioners when supported by robust clinical data demonstrating its efficacy. A meta-analysis of a number of clinical trials showed the benefit of **hypericum** in 63.9% of depressed patients compared with 58.5% for conventional antidepressants and 22.3% for placebo (Nathan, 2001). Finally, it is important to note that a variety of psychological therapies including behavioural therapy, cognitive behavioural therapy (CBT) and interpersonal psychotherapy can be of benefit in treating particular depressed patients (Frank et al., 1992).

Future pharmacological treatments of depression may include drugs acting at novel targets including **neuropeptide** receptors and cellular neurotrophic (nerve growth) factors. The concentration of the neuropeptide **substance P** (SP) has been reported to be elevated in the blood serum and cerebrospinal fluid (CSF) of depressed patients, and a high density of the neurokinin NK_1-receptors for SP are located in the limbic system (Herpfer and Lieb, 2003). An antagonist at the NK_1-receptor has been reported to compare favourably with paroxetine in one clinical trial (Swain, 2002), while antagonists at the CRF_1-receptor have also been proposed as possible antidepressants (Manji et al., 2001; Nemeroff, 2002). Finally, it should be noted that many tricyclic antidepressants and SSRIs have been used in the treatment of generalised anxiety, panic disorder obsessive–compulsive disorder and post-traumatic stress disorder.

Mood-stabilising drugs

Mood stabilisers are used to regulate the cyclical change in mood characteristic of bipolar disorder, since they can attenuate both manic and depressive phases. Their main use is as a prophylactic for manic depression and unipolar mania. However, they can also be administered concomitantly with antidepressants for refractory (non-responsive) unipolar depression.

Lithium: the first mood stabiliser

The "calming" effect of lithium in agitated guinea pigs was first observed by Cade in 1949 (Rang et al., 2003), and this signalled the beginning of the modern era of evidence-based clinical psychopharmacology. Within 20 years they became widely established as effective treatments for both unipolar mania and bipolar manic depression. In clinical terms they attenuate the severe mood-state changes that characterise these disorders (Cookson and Sachs, 2000), but are probably slightly better at relieving the manic phase (Goodwin, 2003). Lithium salts are chemically the simplest of any psychotherapeutic drug. Yet, despite this simplicity of chemical structure, their mode of action is still rather unclear. The molecular target (synaptic receptor) for lithium and its relationship to the neurobiology of unipolar and bipolar disorder have been much debated (Dean, 2002; Post, 2000). Over the last 40 years, lithium (Li^+) has been shown to affect a number of neurochemical functions (Table 12.3), some of which it shares with newer mood stabilisers (Post, 2000; Manji et al., 2001).

Lithium toxicity can generate side effects even at therapeutic doses. Lithium

Table 12.3. Neurochemical effects of lithium.

Decrease in synaptic catecholamine activity.

Interference with the transmembrane flux of Na^+ and K^+ ions and, thus, the electrophysiological activity of the neuron.

Blocking the influx of Ca^{2+} ions controlled via the glutamate NMDA receptor.

Interference with signal transduction by reducing second-messenger synthesis *through*:

- uncompetitive inhibition of the monophosphatase enzymes involved in supplied inositol to synthesise the phosphatidylinositol used by G_q-protein-coupled receptors (e.g., α_1-NA and $5\text{-}HT_{2A}$); and
- inhibition of the activity of G_s-protein-coupled receptors (e.g., β_1-NA).

Increase in levels of the neuroprotective protein Bcl-2.

affects numerous physiological systems, but the gastrointestinal tract, cerebellum and cerebral cortex are the main sites for lithium-induced adverse drug reactions (Cookson and Sachs, 2000). The plasma concentration range over which lithium is clinically active $(0.5–1.5\,mmol\,L^{-1})$ is close to the minimum level for severe toxicity $(3.0\,mmol\,L^{-1})$, which means patients should have their levels of blood lithium checked regularly. Mild toxicity is indicated by nausea, diarrhoea, fine tremor and poor concentration. Severe toxicity is evident in the progression to choreiform and Parkinsonian motor symptoms, seizures, disorientation and coma. When the plasma lithium concentration exceeds $3.0\,mmol\,L^{-1}$, haemodialysis is required to increase the elimination of the drug and so reduce the likelihood of permanent neurological damage. At lower concentrations, stopping the drug coupled with the infusion of saline (NaCl) to decrease the reabsorption of lithium by the renal tubules should attenuate any potential toxicity. Medially unsupervised abrupt discontinuation of lithium can produce withdrawal symptoms of anxiety, irritability and mood swings. In overall terms, lithium demonstrates a very narrow therapeutic window (the ratio between an effective clinical dose and the dose at which toxicity commences). Indeed, the therapeutic window for lithium is probably the narrowest for any of the widely used psychotherapeutic agents. It can also produce unacceptable renal problems (polydipsia and polyuria) in a significant number of patients at "non-toxic" doses. These problems all lead to reduced drug-taking compliance, which obviously reduces clinical efficacy; this means there is an urgent need for safer mood-stabilising drugs.

Antiepileptic drugs as mood stabilisers

Carbamazepine, **valproate** and **lamotrigine** were originally introduced for the treatment of epilepsy, but they are increasingly being used to treat bipolar depressive disorder, while valproate is also effective in acute mania (Goodwin, 2003). The similarity between the abnormal neuronal excitability that characterises epilepsy and mania provides a rationale for using antiepileptic drugs in affective disorders. Carbamazepine is a structural relative of the tricyclic antidepressants. It reduces excitability in a number of ways, principally by blocking axonal voltage-operated Na^+ channels, thereby reducing the depolarisation phase of the **action potential**, and by blocking Ca^{2+} influx through the channel at the centre of the glutamate **N-methyl-D-aspartate (NMDA)** receptor protein. Valproate is chemically related to the amino acid neurotransmitter **GABA** (γ-aminobutyric acid). It causes a weak inhibition of the transaminase $GABA_T$ that inactivates GABA, thereby prolonging its inhibitory action. However, this relatively weak enzyme inhibition is unlikely to play anything other than a minor role in the clinical effects of this drug. The newest of the three antiepileptic drugs is lamotrigine. It has been shown to reduce presynaptic neuronal activity by blocking axonal Na^+ channels, thus reducing release of the excitatory amino acid neurotransmitter **glutamate** (Post, 2000).

The extensive clinical experience with these drugs in **epilepsy** shows they are better tolerated and less toxic than lithium (Bowden and Muller-Oerlinghausen, 2000; Rang et al., 2003). Since the dose regimens for epilepsy and affective disorders are similar, it would be expected that the levels of adverse drug reactions would also be similar. With both carbamazepine and lamotrigine, dizziness, ataxia and hypersensitivity reactions (such as skin rashes) may occur. For valproate there is an increased risk of liver failure; this is the reason it should not be given to patients with reduced hepatic function. Valproate and carbamazepine should be avoided in the first trimester of pregnancy as there is a slight risk of neural tube defects. Mood-stabilising drugs are often prescribed as monotherapy for bipolar manic depressive disorder and unipolar mania; however, they are also often combined with an SSRI as the first line of treatment for bipolar disorder (Grunze et al., 2002).

As with many forms of pharmacotherapy, improved clinical outcome is almost always found when the psychoactive drug is combined with psychological therapy. Even with disorders with such a strong biological component as mania and manic depression, this pattern still holds. Bipolar patients share many of the cognitive distortions shown by sufferers of unipolar depression; this means that they should also benefit from psychological interventions like CBT. Scott et al. (2001) showed that CBT with a group of bipolar subjects not only improved both the speed of recovery from the depressive phase but also prevented manic symptoms from developing into a more severe episode of mania. Various treatment packages have been developed, which include problem-solving skills and motivational programmes. Often, they include education about the effect of medicines and why they need be taken regularly; this leads to greater compliance and thus improves clinical outcome (Goodwin, 2003). Family-focused psychological and educational packages have also been developed. As in schizophrenia (Chapter 11), the greatest gains have been found to occur in those families with a high level of expressed emotion (Miklowitz et al., 2000).

Questions

1   Outline the main types of unipolar and bipolar affective disorder, and describe their clinical symptoms.

2   What is the evidence for the monoamine theory of depression, and which key observations led to its revision?

3   Explain how imipramine and iproniazid affect the synaptic concentrations of serotonin and noradrenaline.

4   List the side effects of imipramine that result from its blockade of muscarinic acetylcholine receptors.

5   What is the "cheese effect"?

6   Outline the neurochemical modes of action of two named antidepressant drugs from different classes (e.g., first-generation TAD, MAO inhibitor, SSRI).

7   Describe the advantages that fluoxetine and paroxetine offer over typical antidepressants.

8   Outline the clinical uses and side effects of "mood-stabilising" drugs.

Key references and reading

Anderson IM, Nutt DJ and Deakin JFW (2000). Evidence-based guidelines for treating depressive disorders: A revision of the 1993 British Association for Psychopharmacology guidelines. *Journal of Psychopharmacology*, **14**, 3–20.

Bauer M et al. (2002). World Federation of Societies of Biological Psychiatry (WFSBP) guidelines for biological treatment of unipolar depressive disorders. Part 1: Acute and continuation treatment of major depressive disorder. *World Journal of Biological Psychiatry*, **3**, 5–43.

Diamond RJ (2002). *Instant Psychopharmacology*. W.W. Norton, New York.

Kramer PD (1994). *Listening to Prozac*. Fourth Estate, London.

Montgomery S and Rouillon F (eds) (1992). *Long-Term Treatment of Depression*. John Wiley & Sons, Chichester, UK.

Nemeroff CB (2002). New directions in the development of antidepressants: The interface of neurobiology and psychiatry. *Human Psychopharmacology*, **17**(Suppl. 1), S13–S16.

Silva H and Larach V (2000). Treatment and recovery in depression: A critical analysis. *World Journal of Biological Psychiatry*, **2**, 119–123.

Chapter 13

Nootropics for Alzheimer's disease

Overview

Alzheimer's disease was first identified around a century ago, but its incidence has increased dramatically since then, due to the increasing number of older people within society. The disease has a profound impact on both sufferers and their carers. There is a progressive decline in cognitive and behavioural abilities, which makes all daily activities increasingly difficult. The impact and costs of the disease for society are enormous. The pathology of Alzheimer's disease is characterised by the presence of neural plaques containing high levels of the protein β-amyloid, neurofibrillary tangles and cholinergic nerve degeneration. These aspects of neural damage have all been implicated in development of the cortical atrophy and the progressive behavioural and cognitive deficits that characterise the disorder. There is also evidence for a genetic component to Alzheimer's disease, linked to the gene for apolipoprotein E4. In terms of pharmacotherapy, no effective remedies for Alzheimer's disease have been developed. However, there is good empirical evidence that cholinesterase inhibitors, such as tacrine, donepezil, rivastigmine and galantamine, can slow or temporarily halt the progression of the disease. Further work is being aimed at individually tailored therapeutic strategies that might prevent or retard the degenerative process. Several promising avenues are being followed, including the use of antioxidants, certain hormones, anti-inflammatory agents and vitamin supplements. Alzheimer's disease makes up two-thirds of all dementia cases, whereas senile dementia with Lewy bodies and vascular dementia account for 15–20% and 8–10% of dementias, respectively; the latter two types of dementia may require alternative forms of pharmacotherapy.

Alzheimer's disease

In 1901 a 51-year-old woman, Auguste D, was admitted to the state asylum in Frankfurt. She was suffering from cognitive and language deficits, auditory hallucinations, paranoia, delusions and exhibited aggressive behaviour. She was studied by Alois Alzheimer (1864–1915), a doctor who was working in the hospital. When Auguste died in April 1906 her brain was sent to Alzheimer for examination. He presented the case at a psychiatry meeting that November and published the talk in 1907 (Maurer et al., 1997). Three years later the term **Alzheimer's disease** was coined by Emil Kraepelin, one of the foremost psychiatrists of the era. In fact, the behavioural and pathological hallmarks of "senile dementia" were already recognised at the time and the name Alzheimer's disease (AD) caused something of a political stir in the highly competitive scientific community of the time (Alzheimer himself is viewed as an innocent in this argument).

AD, or senile dementia of the Alzheimer type (SDAT), is an ever-increasing problem, as it is so strongly associated with ageing. The number of individuals over 65 trebled during the 20th century, and the incidence of AD doubles for every 5 years of life in the over-60s. In comparative terms, average life expectancy during the Roman Empire was around 22 years, in 1900 it was approximately 50 and in 2000 it was around 75. Given this dramatic increase in life expectancy an increasing number of cases are encountered each year (Table 13.1). AD now affects nearly a million people in the UK, with around 10% of people aged over 65 and 20% of those aged over 75 displaying symptoms to a greater or lesser extent. It has been estimated that there are 18 million people worldwide with AD, and this figure is projected to rise to 34 million by the year 2025. It should also be noted that there are a number of other dementias largely associated with ageing including dementia with Lewy bodies and vascular dementia. They account for 15–20% and 8–10% of all dementias, respectively. This chapter will focus on AD, which represents around two-thirds of all dementias.

In the UK the annual cost of AD is estimated at £5.5bn (extrapolated from Alloul et al., 1998). As well as these economic costs there are enormous human costs, both for the individual who has the disease and for their family and/or carers who have to cope with the gradual and relentless disintegration of cognition and personality. Table 13.2 summarises the typical symptomatology and progression of the disorder. Typically, the disorder involves an initial blunting of emotional responses, which is sometimes described as a "coarsening of affect"; this is soon followed by decrements in

Table 13.1. Incidence of dementia and Alzheimer's disease by age and gender.

| Age | All dementia incidence | | Alzheimer's disease incidence | |
	Males	Females	Males	Females
75–79	700	1,700	300–500	750–1,250
80–84	2,400	4,100	1,050–1,750	1,800–3,000
85+	7,200	5,300	3,150–5,250	2,300–3,850
Overall	3,000	3,600	1,300–2,200	1,550–2,650

Table 13.2. Typical progression of Alzheimer's disease.

Typical course of AD	
Age of onset	45 years or over (usually 60s or older).
Premorbid history	Usually unremarkable for emotional/physical health.
Initial symptoms	*Emotional* – coarsening of affect.
	Psychiatric – depression; anxiety; agitation; withdrawal; halucination; paranoia; jealousy.
	Memory – forgetfulness (losing things, forgetting names, commitments, disorientation, getting lost).
Middle stage symptoms	*Language* – difficulty in finding words and naming objects.
	Social – familial withdrawal; purposeless overactivity.
	Other – poor judgement/insight; lack of concern for the future; inability in financial/professional matters; social indiscretion.
Late stage symptoms	*Language* – significant word-finding problems; poor verbal comprehension.
	Other – difficulty performing simple gestures; inability to use common/familiar objects or routines.
Very advanced symptoms	Gross disorientation in time and place; total dependence on carer for simple tasks (dressing, eating, toilet); inability to comprehend/communicate with anyone; no awareness of past or future.

cognitive functioning, with numerous memory lapses and many distressing inabilities in "functional", or everyday, aspects of cognition. Then, as the disease progresses, all aspects of behaviour become grossly disturbed.

The psychological impact of AD is sometimes divided into primary and secondary effects. The primary effects are those of the sufferer themselves (see Table 13.1 and below), whereas the secondary effects refer to the impact on family, nurses and other carers. It is not difficult to imagine the enormous physical/emotional demands on those who look after the person with AD. Typical descriptions of the carer's plight include "a living bereavement" and "the funeral that never ends". Self-report studies suggest high incidence of exhaustion, stress, depression, guilt, use of anxiolytic tranquillisers and antidepressants and greater use of alcohol (Chapters 9 and 10). There are also low self-ratings on quality of life, reduced feelings of self-esteem and even reductions in immune system functioning. People caring for an individual with AD are twice as likely to take prescription medicines and 50% more likely to have visited their general physician in the previous 12 months.

Neurobiological changes

At the visible level there is a marked atrophy or "withering" of the whole brain, although this is most evident during the later stages of the disease. Figure 13.1 shows

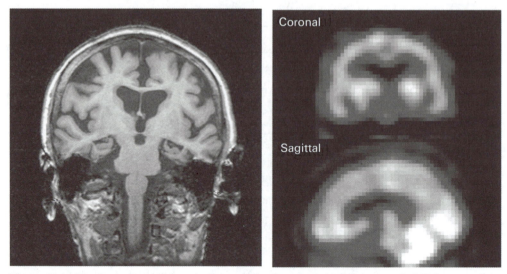

Figure 13.1. The brain in Alzheimer's disease. The figure on the left is a static MRI scan, where marked cortical atrophy is evident. The right-hand figure is a SPECT scan showing impoverished metabolism in the Alzheimer brain.

Reproduced by permission of Professor John O'Brien, Wolfson Research Centre, Newcastle-upon-Tyne, UK.

views of the brain of an Alzheimer's disease sufferer. The atrophy and lack of cortical activity in the cortex can be clearly observed in the living brain. However, more subtle damage precedes this large-scale cortical demolition. As has been emphasised throughout this book the optimal working of the brain requires a fully integrated neural network (Chapters 2, 3, 10 and 14). The disease process adversely affects neurons in a number of specific ways. The main features contributing to this degeneration include **cholinergic** nerve degeneration and the widespread presence of neurofibrillary plaques and tangles (see later). The next section will focus on **acetylcholine** nerves as the prime target for **drug** treatments. The role of plaques and tangles in Alzheimer's disease will be explored later.

Cholinergic degeneration in Alzheimer's disease

Neuronal loss in Alzheimer's disease is most evident in several regions, which are rich in cholinergic neurons (Isacson et al., 2002); these include the medial septal area which impinges on the **hippocampus**, a crucial area for learning and memory; the **anterior cingulate** which subserves attention and motivation; and the **hypothalamus** which controls appetitive behaviours (Perry et al., 1998) (Chapter 2). Marked degeneration is also observed in the **nucleus basalis of Meynert** (NBM) – an area containing around 1 million neurons. This relatively modest number of cells has a widespread influence on the cortex, innervating a cortical sheet that would measure around half a square metre if fully stretched out. The NBM represents the major cholinergic projection to the cortex (Mesulam, 1995) and, thus, influences many aspects of executive functioning,

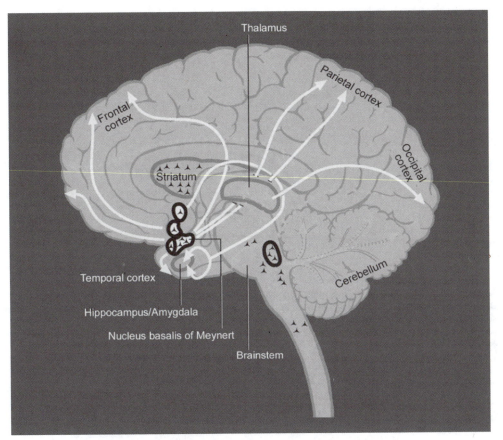

Figure 13.2. The major cholinergic pathways of the human brain.
Reproduced from Perry et al. (eds) (2002). With kind permission by John Benjamins Publishing Company,
Amsterdam/Philadelphia. www.benjamins.com

language, perceptuo-motor functions and emotional processing (Blokland, 1996). Some
studies have suggested that the loss of cholinergic neurons may be as high as 75% in
this area, leading to the proposal that AD might result from the depletion of this
neurotransmitter system.

The major cholinergic systems of the human brain are shown in Figure 13.2. The
functioning of a cholinergic **synapse** and some of the agents that mediate these functions
are shown in Figure 13.3. The important role of acetylcholine is also indicated by
investigations into the effects of scopolamine and atropine in young healthy individuals.
These two drugs acutely inhibit the cholinergic system and generate Alzheimer-like
cognitive impairments for a number of hours. Indeed, this fact can be exploited to
test the effects of potential drugs for the treatment of AD. For example, a number of
studies from Wesnes and colleagues have examined the potential for certain drugs to
reverse scopolamine-induced cognitive deficits (e.g., Ebert et al., 1998; Wesnes et al.,
1991). These have revealed that drugs like **physostigmine**, a cholinesterase inhibitor (see
later), reverse deficits caused by blocking cholinergic activity. They are also reasonably
effective in treating some of the behavioural symptoms of AD. While some of the more

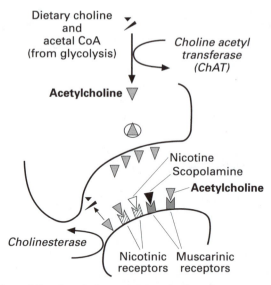

Figure 13.3. An overview of the chemical events at a cholinergic synapse and agents commonly used to alter cholinergic transmission: acetyl CoA, acetyl coenzyme A; Ch, choline. Nicotine and scopolamine bind to nicotinic and muscarinic receptors, respectively (nicotine is an agonist while scopolamine is an antagonist). Most anti-Alzheimer drugs inhibit the action of the enzyme cholinesterase.

effective treatments for the symptoms of AD target the cholinergic system, there are large individual differences in the effectiveness of such treatments and they generally provide only temporary relief. We will return to this issue later in the chapter.

Psychological approaches to treatment

Until recently the only "treatment" available for AD and other forms of senile dementia was clinical management. The disease was progressive and the best that could be offered was some sort of support for the carers at home or maintenance in the protective environment of a nursing home. Attempts to place such strategies into a psycho-biological framework generally have little empirical or theoretical worth. However, there have been various attempts at more psychological and/or cognitive therapies (Brodaty, 1999; Zanetti et al., 1995; Woods, 1996).

Additionally, in the early stages of AD there may be value in the use of techniques to supplement residual capabilities; these may just involve the use of external memory aids, such as notebooks, tape recorders or memory stickers, but they can be very useful. Similarly, the use of visual imagery and/or mnemonics may be effective to some degree in enhancing retention (Zanetti et al., 1995).

Probably, the most common type of cognitive treatment used in dementia and ageing is reality orientation. The individual is encouraged to be oriented in time, place and person by the use of repetition, signs, labels and (sometimes) mnemonics, often within an institution (Zanetti et al., 1995; Woods, 1996). The evidence for its usefulness is equivocal, mainly because systematic research involving the prolonged follow-up of patients has been rare. It has been suggested that this technique may activate underused neural pathways, but there is little empirical evidence to support this idea. The treatment may provide a temporary slowing of dementing processes, but most of the improvement may be explained by the increased enthusiasm/expectancy of the carers, although this itself may be an important factor in the progression of the disorder (Brodaty, 1992; Mittelman et al., 1996; Knight et al., 1993). The technique of selective (or guided) reminiscence involves the use of records of past events to make use of residual memory for remote events. The main impact is on improved self-esteem, an outcome whose value should not be underestimated.

Pharmacotherapy

The search for an effective drug treatment for AD is a major focus for research. Hundreds of potential new treatments are patented each year, but so far none has proved a clinically effective treatment. Progress has been delayed by several factors. Unfortunately, there is no good animal model of AD (McDonald and Overmier, 1998), although some drugs that slow age-related mnemonic decline in animals have been developed. The testing of putative therapeutic agents thus depends heavily on human drug trials; these are far more time-consuming and expensive and need to be designed with care and sophistication if they are going to detect potential benefits. There is also the crucial problem that AD brains are no longer capable of responding to pharmaco-therapy. Additionally, despite the fact that AD reflects dysfunctions in multiple systems (Cutler and Sramek, 2001), most therapies have targeted just a single neurotransmitter, most usually acetylcholine but more recently **glutamate** as well.

Figure 13.4 illustrates some of the factors known to be involved in the develop-ment of AD; many of the known and putative links between factors are also shown. It should also be noted that the patterns of inter-factor modulation may be either positive or negative. However, it is clear that no single factor or combination of factors can explain all AD cases. It is best to conceptually model AD as a broad "end point" that can be reached in numerous ways. Similar multi-factorial models have been proposed for **schizophrenia** and depression (Chapters 11 and 12) and almost certainly underlie every other complex psychobiological concept.

Cholinergic drugs

Nearly every drug currently used for the treatment of AD is an **anticholinesterase**, or, to use its more recent label, a **cholinesterase inhibitor** (ChEI). This type of drug inhibits the action of cholinesterase, the **enzyme** that metabolises acetylcholine in the synaptic cleft. Cholinesterase inhibitors thus boost activity at cholinergic synapses, by increasing the probability of an acetylcholine molecule binding to a **receptor**. The rationale is that by reversing the cholinergic deficits in synaptic transmission the drug may help to restore cholinergic functioning or at least slow its decline (Figure 13.5).

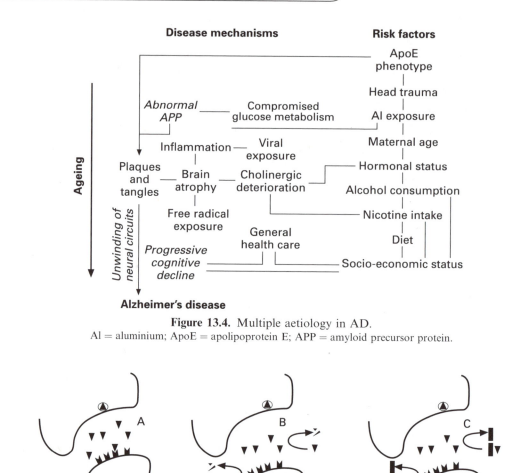

Figure 13.4. Multiple aetiology in AD.
Al = aluminium; ApoE = apolipoprotein E; APP = amyloid precursor protein.

Figure 13.5. The action of cholinesterase inhibitors. Acetylcholine is released (A) and then broken down by cholinesterase (B). Cholinesterase inhibitors (ChEIs) prevent this breakdown, thereby increasing transmission at these synapses.

Tacrine (tetrahydroaminoacridine, or THA) was one of the earliest cholinesterase inhibitors to be developed. Tacrine needs to be administered at high doses (80–160 mg/day) since only 17% of the orally administered drug is available to the nervous system. It also needs to be given regularly as it has a rapid half-life ($t_{1/2}$) of around 3 hours. Early trials were fairly promising and included some reports of actual improvement, as distinct from slowing the rate of AD deterioration. Unfortunately, a large proportion of individuals on tacrine showed unpleasant side effects, most commonly liver toxicity, which obviously limited its practical utility. Thus, although tacrine was reasonably effective as a short-term treatment for some patients with mild to moderate AD, its value lay more as a "gateway" in the development of more effective cholinesterase inhibitors. These have included donepezil, rivastigmine and galantamine.

Donepezil, or Aricept, received UK approval for use in mild to moderate AD in

1997. Unlike tacrine it does not cause liver toxicity, although 20% of patients show some side effects. Most usually, these are gastrointestinal reactions, although less common side effects include nightmares and confusion. Another benefit of donepezil is that it is administered as single daily doses. Clinical trials have been fairly positive, although the relative psychological and cognitive benefits on donepezil are only in relation to the **placebo** group – which inevitably shows some decline over the trial period. One of the most widely used measures to assess dementia is the Mini-Mental State Examination (MMSE). Rogers et al. (1998) found an improvement in MMSE scores in those given donepezil, compared with the pre-drug baseline at 12 and 18-week assessments. Scores for the active treatment groups returned baseline at week 24, but were still higher than for the placebo group, since the latter's MMSE scores had declined over the trial period. Winblad et al. (2001) similarly examined the effects of donepezil in individuals with mild to moderate AD. In their large multi-centre trial, 286 patients received either daily donepezil or daily placebo for a year. The active drug group's MMSE scores remained relatively stable over time and became significantly higher than the placebo group at the 12, 24, 36 and 52-week assessments. A standardised measure of global functioning declined in both groups, but the decline was significantly less under donepezil at the three final sessions.

Another influential study looked at the effects of switching on and off donepezil over the course of a clinical trial (Doody et al., 2001). One arm of the trial involved 390 patients who received 5 or 10 mg/day of donepezil or placebo. In the first 15 weeks there was a dose-dependent improvement in a more comprehensive scale – the ADAS-cog. At this point all patients were switched to daily donepezil. Initially, the groups who had received placebo or 5 mg/day donepezil improved while the 10-mg group's scores were maintained at a higher level. Over the subsequent 84 weeks of the trial all the group's ADAS-cog scores deteriorated with the 10-mg group having higher scores in all but the latest assessments (when all groups had declined to a similar clinical level). In a separate arm of the study, 365 patients initially received one of the same three treatments, and again those in the active conditions exhibited a clinical improvement. After 24 weeks the drug was withdrawn for a period of 6 weeks. At the end of this "washout" period the group's score had declined to a similar level. They were all switched to donepezil and the group's ADAS-cog scores improved for 6 weeks, then deteriorating over the rest of the 102-week trial. The above studies demonstrated that donepezil can transiently improve the clinical symptoms of AD and stabilise the condition for 6–12 months. Other studies have focused more on functional aspects of the disease, using scales that measure activities of daily living (ADL). In a large-scale multi-centre study by Mohs et al. (2001), it was found that donezepil can delay the median time to functional decline by around 6 months.

Another reasonably effective anticholinesterase drug is **rivastigmine**. As well as acting as a cholinesterase inhibitor, it inhibits the action of another brain enzyme, butyryl cholinesterase. As a consequence it may offer broader therapeutic effects than donepezil. Rivastigmine requires careful patient-tailored dosing, and clinical efficacy is rarely seen below 6 to 12 mg/day. Such doses are usually achieved by gradually increasing the amount of the drug administered from two daily doses of 1.5 mg. In a comparison of rivastigmine with donepezil, both produced similar benefits as measured by the ADAS-cog at weeks 4 and 12, but rivastigmine was associated with more adverse side effects, particularly nausea, vomiting and headache (Wilkinson et al., 2002).

Galantamine is a cholinesterase inhibitor derived from extracts of snowdrop and daffodil bulbs which targets other neurotransmitter systems in addition to the cholinergic. It has the advantage of binding to nicotinic cholinergic receptors and, thus, has a two-pronged positive effect at cholinergic synapses. In a direct comparison of galantamine with donepezil in AD, there were no differences in primary outcomes (including the ADAS-cog), although there was a slight advantage for galantamine on some of the other measures. Another recent drug is **memantine**, a glutamate NMDA (N-methyl-D-aspartate) receptor antagonist. It works because these receptors are usually blocked by magnesium (Mg^{2+}) and binding them with glutamate results in the removal of the Mg^{2+} blockade causing an influx of calcium (this is important for several processes relevant to learning and memory). In untreated AD, background levels of magnesium are often abnormally high, so that the relatively small changes in calcium influx into the cell are ineffective in producing a signal-to-noise ratio high enough to cause the usual modulation of physiological processes. Memantine effectively replaces the Mg^{2+} blockade, although the blockade is removed by the relatively high levels of glutamate associated with some learning-relevant events. Thus, the drug restores the signal-to-noise ratio of cellular calcium influx. As a second mode of action, memantine appears to slow the accelerated cell death associated with abnormally high intracellular calcium. Finally, several putative AD drugs act as specific muscarinic or nicotinic agonists. However, at present even the most promising of these cholinergic drugs offer no more than temporary relief from AD.

Plaques and tangles

Alzheimer himself described the neuropathology of the disease and referred to "military foci", which are now termed neuritic, or amyloid, plaques, and "peculiar changes of the neurofibrils", which are now referred to as neurofibrillary tangles. Plaques and tangles are found throughout the brain in AD, particularly in areas of high cellular loss, and have therefore become the distinguishing markers of the disease. In fact, a definitive diagnosis of AD can only be made post-mortem – confirmed by the presence of plaques and tangles. In living individuals it should more properly be called senile dementia of the Alzheimer type (SDAT), although we will continue to use the term Alzheimer's disease (AD) here.

Neuritic plaques are diffuse spherical structures (5–100 μm in diameter), with an extracellular (outside the neuron) mass of thin filaments and dying neurons. At the centre the plaque contains a substance called β-**amyloid**, which is also sometimes called amyloid b protein, or A4. Neurofibrillary tangles are abnormal intracellular (inside the neuron) structures, consisting of pairs of threadlike filaments that form helices, which are termed paired helical filaments (PFAs). Using the analogy of a broken electrical circuit, plaque formation is similar to the melting and meshing together of components of a circuit, whereas tangles are like abnormalities in the copper within the wire.

The relationship between brain biology and psychology can be demonstrated by considering where these cellular abnormalities are found, since they are responsible for "unwiring" the brain. Plaques are found in: the **frontal cortex**, an area responsible for

Table 13.3. A guide to genes and proteins. All life forms are made up of material that includes proteins, which are involved in nearly every aspect of structure and function. In humans there are around 40,000 different *types* of proteins (there may be thousands or millions of each type). The same protein can differ slightly between individuals although it does the same job.

Name	What is it?
Genome	The "recipe book" for all the proteins in a given species; distinct from the genotype, which is the recipe for an individual and gives rise to the phenotype – the structural, functional and (sometimes) behavioural characteristics of an individual; each cell of the body contains a copy of the entire genome.
Chromosome	Individual chapter of the recipe book; in humans there are 23 pairs of chromosomes (which are made of DNA); we can recognise which pair an individual chromosome belongs to by its characteristic size and shape.
Gene	The recipe itself; a gene can be thought of as an instruction for making a protein; the gene for a specific protein is always found on the same place of the same chromosome between individuals.
Allele	Variations in the recipe between individuals; just as there are slightly different recipes for the same dish, there are slightly different genes for the same protein; since humans have pairs of each chromosome (one from each parent), for each gene a given individual can have two alleles that are the same or different.
Protein	This is the "dish" itself; just as there are different forms of the same meal, so there are different forms of the same protein; the forms the 40,000 proteins in a human take depend on the particular alleles which that individual carries.

executive functioning and aspects of personality; the parietal cortex, which controls spatial processing and aspects of somatosensory information; the temporal lobe, responsible for hearing, some visual information processing and aspects of memory; and the underlying hippocampus and **amygdala**, which are crucial for memory and emotional processing. Perhaps crucially, the highest levels of plaques and tangles are often found in those areas that show a marked reduction in the neurotransmitter acetylcholine (considered later); however, the functional relationship between these processes is not clear.

The core of each plaque contains high levels of the protein β-amyloid, which is a small portion of a much larger protein called amyloid precursor protein (APP), whose **gene** is on **chromosome** 21 (see Table 13.3 for a guide to genes and proteins). Interestingly, people with **Down's syndrome** have three copies of chromosome 21, hence the alternative name "Trisomy 21". Very often, they show the plaque neuropathology characteristic of AD in their 30s and 40s (Isacson et al., 2002). Additionally, the appearance of such pathology seems to correlate with a marked cognitive decline at this time. Could it be that an overproduction of amyloid (because of the extra chromosome producing it) is a common mechanism underlying the similar pathology of Down's syndrome and AD? Down's patients dying at a younger age show abnormally large numbers of diffuse "presenile" plaques, suggesting that these accumulate as a precursor to AD. There is similar evidence in very elderly individuals who do not have full-blown AD.

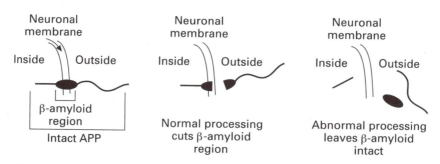

Figure 13.6. *From left to right*: location of the β-amyloid region of amyloid precursor protein (APP) in relation to the neuronal membrane; normal processing of APP inactivates β-amyloid; abnormal processing of APP in Alzheimer's disease liberates intact β-amyloid.

APP and β-amyloid are found on the surface of all cells, but large amounts are found in neurons. β-amyloid is continually being "cut off" from the larger APP as part of normal processing, by biochemical "scissors" called secretases. Once liberated, β-amyloid is either cleared from the body or its components are recycled to build new proteins. However, it appears that a form of β-amyloid is liberated in AD which cannot be recycled in this way (Figure 13.6). In fact, this pathological form of β-amyloid appears to be insoluble and, therefore, forms deposits in the brain. As the β-amyloid deposits accumulate, plaques are formed, producing the type of damage described above.

Hereditary cerebral haemorrhage with amyloidosis of the Dutch type (HCHWA-Dutch) is a rare genetic disorder in two villages in Holland. Patients die in midlife from cerebral haemorrhage following massive deposits of amyloid caused by a mutation in the gene for APP. However, the brains of HCHWA-Dutch sufferers are not typical of AD in that they contain no tangles and the plaques are unusual. Moreover, there is no evidence of dementia in the disease, although the time of death is early. In any case, research has shown that mutation in APP can cause amyloid deposits. Another possibility is that individuals with AD overproduce APP and that different enzymes are called on to process APP, thus causing the abnormal form of amyloid that leads to plaque formation. While this is an attractive hypothesis for Down's syndrome, there is little direct evidence for it in AD. Whatever its role in AD it is extremely unlikely that deposition of β-amyloid is solely responsible for the disorder. There are many other possible causative factors including excessive aluminium exposure, maternal age, head trauma and genetic disposition (Brodaty, 1999; Alloul et al., 1998; Smith and Perry, 1998).

In 1993/1994 a series of publications caused a stir in the AD research community, since for the first time they linked a specific neuropathological process in late-onset AD to a genetic marker. Researchers looking at the composition of plaques found that the protein **apolipoprotein E (ApoE)** was associated with β-amyloid in the cerebrospinal fluid (CSF) of AD patients (Strittmatter et al., 1993). The gene for ApoE is on the same human chromosome (number 19) which was a risk factor in some AD pedigrees. The gene for ApoE comes in three versions (alleles): Apo ε2, Apo ε3 and, most importantly, Apo ε4; these result in three slightly different variants of the protein. Humans carry two versions of the allele and so can have none, one or two of any of the versions of the Apo ε4 genes. Most people have the Apo ε3 allele, but in AD most patients have at least one copy of the Apo ε4 allele. In 500 patients who had "sporadic" (or "non-genetic") AD, 64% had at least one copy of the ε4 allele. Even more interesting is that as the mean age of AD onset goes down so the gene dose of Apo ε4 increases from zero to two (Corder et al., 1993). Numerous studies over the last decade have subsequently confirmed the link between AD and Apo E4. Procedures such as this will allow future drug trails to genotypically target the most at-risk individuals. Indeed, as the techniques of psychopharmacology and neuroscience become more sophisticated, this targeted approach will be used far more frequently. It should benefit our understanding of not only AD but also of schizophrenia, depression and, indeed, every other clinical disorder (Chapters 11–14).

Psychopharmacological prospects for Alzheimer's disease

There are a number of promising prospects for reducing the incidence of AD or delaying its progression; these include antioxidants, certain hormones, anti-inflammatory agents and even vitamin supplements. The following sections outline some of the disease processes being targeted by these types of intervention (see also Cutler and Sramek, 2001; Post, 1999).

APP is probably involved in normal cellular repair, and these metabolic processes are glucose-dependent. There is a 50–70% decline in glucose metabolism in AD, and it has been postulated that this may result in abnormal APP processing, consequent amyloid deposition and neuronal death. Thus, any drug that enhances glucose utilisation might delay disease progression (Hoyer, 2000). In the body some oxygen molecules become so highly chemically reactive that they disrupt certain physiological processes. These molecules are called "free radicals", and the damage they inflict is termed oxidative damage, or oxidative stress; this has been implicated in many diseases, such as cancer and heart disease. Furthermore, a high-fat diet and cigarette smoking (Chapter 5) also greatly increase the number of **free radicals** in the blood. Free radicals also contribute to the development of AD. Two copies of the Apo E4 allele results in higher concentrations of low-density lipoprotein, the so-called "bad" form of cholesterol. High levels of low-density lipoprotein have also been linked to risk of AD. In addition, high levels of low-density lipoprotein seem to promote the deposition of β-amyloid. A closely related finding is that β-amyloid causes an increase in the number of free radicals, although this can be neutralised by **antioxidant** therapy. β-amyloid appears to react with the cells that line blood vessels in the brain to produce excessive quantities of free radicals; these damage brain tissue even more – possibly by starving the cellular tissues of oxygen. Brain tissue is highly susceptible to free radical damage because, unlike many other tissues, it does not contain significant amounts of protective antioxidant compounds (Rottcamp et al., 2000). A few studies have investigated the effects of antioxidants (vitamin A, vitamin C, vitamin E, selenium, the carotenoids) on AD (see Rottkamp et al., 2000). In one study people with mild to moderate AD were given the antioxidant drug **selegiline** (L-deprenyl). At 6 months' follow-up, their memory improved significantly. Other studies have shown that selegiline may enhance the effects of tacrine (see Birks and Flicker, 2003).

There is some evidence that low levels of the hormone estrogen may be involved in the aetiology of AD. Females have a higher incidence of AD than men (Table 13.1), and women with AD have lower estrogen levels than controls. Several studies show that women who take estrogen as hormone replacement therapy after the menopause have an unexpectedly low incidence of AD. Furthermore, among women with AD, those taking estrogen may suffer less severe symptoms and a slower rate of cognitive decline. Various studies have shown that estrogen replacement therapy is protective against AD (Diesner, 1998). One study examined the risk of developing AD among over 1,000 older women. During the follow-up period the disease developed in about 15% of the overall sample. However, among those women who had never used estrogen, the figure was nearly 3 times higher than in the estrogen users. It may be that estrogen therapy enhances the protective effects of cholinesterase inhibitors.

Another prospect for the prevention of AD is anti-inflammatory agents. Populations who take **anti-inflammatory** agents for disorders like rheumatoid arthritis have been found to display unusually low levels of AD (McGeer and McGeer, 1998). Leprosy patients taking anti-inflammatory drugs also had less than half the incidence of AD compared with controls. The treatment of both leprosy and arthritis involves large doses of non-steroidal anti-inflammatory drugs (NSAIDs). These drugs include over-the-counter medications, such as aspirin and ibuprofen. Inflammation of brain tissue may play a key role in the development of plaques and tangles. These observations suggest that NSAIDs might delay the progression of AD. In one study, patients with mild to moderate AD took daily doses of placebo or between 100 and 150 mg of **indomethacin**. After 6 months the placebo group showed a decline in cognitive functioning, whereas those on NSAIDs actually improved slightly. Studies based on retrospective medical record data have also reported that as NSAID use increased, so the rate of mental deterioration in AD decreased.

Vitamin supplements may also offer some protection against AD. Some studies have suggested that low levels of **folate** may be involved in AD aetiology; this appears to be due to problems in absorption/utilisation of vitamins rather than poor diet. A study by Fioravanti et al. (1997) used subjects with abnormal age-related cognitive decline and low folate levels (<3 ng/ml). Following just 60 days of folic acid treatment, participants showed significant improvements in memory and attention. The widely taken herbal extract *Ginkgo biloba* may also offer some protection against AD and vascular dementia (Chapter 14). In 1994 the German equivalent of the Food and Drug Administration endorsed ginkgo for early-stage dementias.

As nerve cells die, they lose the ability to regulate the flow of calcium across the cell membrane. Some researchers have speculated that calcium channel blockers, which affect this mineral flow in and out of cells, may prolong neuronal life. Nerve growth factor is a hormone that stimulates the growth of the nerve cells that release acetylcholine, the neurotransmitter that declines in people with AD. Some researchers believe that by introducing nerve growth factor (or a similar compound) into the brains of people with early AD, they may be able to slow or reverse cognitive deterioration. Unfortunately, nerve growth factor does not cross the **blood–brain barrier**, so the hormone cannot be given orally or by systemic injection (Table 13.4).

To summarise, it must be emphasised that many of the therapeutic approaches

Table 13.4. The current state of development of selected anti-Alzheimer drugs.

Principle of action	Status
Anticholinesterases	On the market: donepezil, rivastigmine, galantamine
Glutamate receptor antagonists	On the market: memantine
Cholinomimetics	In late clinical development
Nerve growth factors	Pilot clinical trials
Inhibition of amyloid secretases	In late preclinical development
Inhibition of amyloid fibril formation	Early experimental studies
Inhibition of tangle formation	Early experimental studies
Neuroprotective	Experimental studies
Antioxidant	Clinical trials (vitamin E. selegeline)
Anti-inflammatory	Pilot clinical trials

described above are in the early stages of development. Furthermore, even if successful, they are only likely to be effective in a proportion of those suffering from the disorder. AD is a etiologically complex and diverse, and as an area for clinical research it abounds with confounding factors. There is dementia with Lewy bodies and vascular dementia; these are likely to involve somewhat different approaches. Future studies will probably identify the most at-risk individuals through genotyping, but this is likely to add yet more potential confounds, especially in the early stages. However, future trials will benefit from the more sophisticated techniques for brain imaging and cognitive assessment that are currently being developed. In practical terms the prospects for those diagnosed with AD has improved in recent years, but the gains have only been very slight. Pharmaceutical companies are still attempting to develop more effective medications for the disorder. As a final point and as mentioned earlier, the incidence of AD doubles in ageing populations for every 5 years of life; this means that delaying its onset by a similar period could effectively halve the number of cases. But this equation does assume that the average duration of life will not increase any further.

Questions

1   Describe the key features of Alzheimer's disease and its progression.

2   Explain the changes in the brain in Alzheimer's disease at both the structural and microscopic level.

3   Describe how changes in the cholinergic system relate to the neurocognitive and behavioural aspects of Alzheimer's disease.

4   Summarise the actions of cholinesterase inhibitors, and describe their efficacy for Alzheimer's disease in clinical trials.

5   Describe your understanding of the role of β-amyloid in the disease process of Alzheimer s disease.

6   Outline some future prospects for pharmacotherapy in Alzheimer's disease.

Key references and reading

Alloul K, Sauriol L, Kennedy W, Laurier C , Tessier G, Novosel S and Contandriopoulos A. (1998). Alzheimer's disease: A review of the disease, its epidemiology and economic impact. *Archives of Gerontology and Geriatrics*, **27**, 189–221.

Grossberg GT (2003). Cholinesterase inhibitors for the treatment of Alzheimer's disease: Getting on and staying on. *Current Therapeutic Research*, **64**, 216–235.

Brodaty H (1999). Realistic expectations for the management of Alzheimer's disease. *European Neuropsychopharmacology*, **9**, S43–S52.

Cutler NR and Sramek JJ (2001). Review of the next generation of Alzheimer's disease therapeutics: Challenges for drug development. *Progress in Neuro-Psychopharmacology and Biological Psychiatry*, **25**, 27–57.

Maier-Lorentz MM (2000) Neurobiological bases for Alzheimer's disease. *Journal of Neuroscience Nursing*, **32**, 117–125.

Maurer K, Yolk S and Gerbalso H (1997). Auguste D and Alzheimer's disease. *Lancet*, **349**, 1546–1549.

Smith MA and Perry G (1998). What are the facts and artifacts of the pathogenensis and etiology of Alzheimer disease? *Journal of Chemical Neuroanatomy*, **16**, 35–41.

Villareal DT and Morris JC (1998). The diagnosis of Alzheimer's disease *Alzheimer's Disease Review*, **3**, 142–152.

Chapter 14

Cognitive enhancers

Overview

Improving the speed, capacity and overall performance of the human brain has been an enduring topic of interest, not only for psychopharmacologists but also members of the general public. Any new putative method for improving mental performance always receives considerable media attention. The traditional psychophysiological viewpoint is that the brain has evolved to function optimally in the atmosphere in which we live. The suggestion that cognitive performance might be improved via natural or artificial interventions has been largely dismissed. Nonetheless, there is increasing evidence that enhancement of central nervous system metabolic activity may help to augment cognitive performance. Often, this does not involve any drugs: for instance, physical exercise can aid cognitive performance, probably by providing extra fuel or energy for the brain. Several psychoactive compounds have been assessed as potential cognitive enhancers including piracetam, hydergine and vinpocetine. A number of promising findings have emerged, although expectancy effects may have confounded some of the earlier studies. These putative cognitive enhancers, or nootropics, are often used by the elderly as self-medications to retard cognitive decline. When used in young, healthy populations they are generally labelled as "smart drugs". Several plant products have been recognised for centuries as therapeutic, or arousing, and they have been scientifically evaluated in recent years. Oriental herb extracts from *Ginkgo biloba* and *Panax ginseng* (ginseng) have been confirmed to display a range of subtle cognitive effects. Traditional, European garden herbs can also display psychoactive properties. *Melissa officinalis*, or lemon balm, has been found to improve calmness, while *Salvia officinalis*, or sage, may improve memory recall.

Brain metabolism and cognition

The brain is disproportionately metabolically active for its size. Although it comprises only 2–3% of the body mass, it accounts for up to 30% of its basal energy expenditure. Energy is required for the maintenance and regulation of all physiological functions within the body. In the central nervous system (CNS) and peripheral nervous system (PNS), energy is needed for all aspects of information processing (Chapter 2). We use energy for all sensory awareness, cognitive decisions, psychomotor or behavioural actions; energy is expended whenever we perceive, think and move. It is also used during rest and sleep, because the body and nervous system remains metabolically active all the time. However, relative changes in energy production in the brain can be detected directly and indirectly using neuroimaging: positron emission tomography (PET) detects blood flow, oxygen consumption and glucose utilisation associated with localised neuronal activity; functional magnetic resonance imaging (fMRI) detects such activity as a function of blood oxygen levels; and magnetic resonance spectroscopy (MRS) identifies the spatio-temporal patterns of glucose or lactate levels (see Chapter 11 for more detailed descriptions). These techniques have demonstrated the differential uptake and utilisation of neural substrates, relative to the type of cognitive task undertaken.

The brain is remarkable in its dependence on an uninterrupted blood supply for its immediate energy needs. It needs a constant supply of the essential energy substrates glucose and oxygen. Any interruption to their delivery will lead within seconds to unconsciousness, and within minutes it will cause irreversible changes resulting in cell death. Compared with the other body organs the brain is very vulnerable, being highly sensitive to small and transient fluctuations in its energy supply. Hence, the dangers of **hypoglycaemia** in diabetics controlled by insulin, when low blood sugar leads to mental confusion; this needs to be reversed by immediate administration of sweets or a sugary drink, when the restoration of normal cognition should be rapid. There are low levels of essential metabolic resources stored within the brain. Glycogen storage levels in liver, muscles and brain are in the ratio of 100/10/1, with brain levels being in the region of 2–4 μmol/g of tissue, an amount capable of sustaining function for up to 10 minutes. By comparison there is no storage capacity for oxygen, with a disruption of supply having an almost instantaneous effect; this means that oxygen delivery must be adjusted within seconds in response to changes in metabolic rate, such as under cognitive demand. Under normal conditions, metabolic activity is limited by the rate of glucose and oxygen delivery.

Influencing cognition by manipulating blood glucose and oxygen levels

Since mild hypoglycaemia reduces memorial performance (see above), there has been great interest in investigating the possible cognitive benefits of increased glucose availability. Glucose can be injected directly into the brain or ingested via food and delivered by means of the cerebral arteries. Animal studies have shown that raised blood glucose levels are associated with improved memory performance (Gold, 1986, 1991, 1992). These results have been mirrored by those from human studies on the healthy elderly (Hall et al., 1989) and patients with **Alzheimer's disease** (Manning et al., 1993; see also Chapter 13). The influence of increased blood glucose levels on cognition in healthy young adults has also been extensively investigated. A clear glucose facilitation of declarative memory performance has been reported in various studies (Craft et al., 1994; Foster et al., 1998; Messier et al., 1998, 1999), and this has been most strongly recorded in memory tasks requiring intentional recollection of previous experiences (e.g., word recall). More specifically, glucose has been shown to significantly improve delayed paragraph recall performance. The general finding is that cognitive perform-ance over a number of tasks correlates with blood glucose levels, irrespective of resting basal level. Furthermore, Kennedy and Scholey (2003) and Scholey (2001) demon-strated that demanding tasks were more susceptible to enhancement by glucose and resulted in significantly accelerated reduction of blood glucose levels, compared with semantically matched easy tasks. This finding supports the proposition that harder tasks impose greater metabolic demands (Figure 14.2; see later). On the other hand, some tasks that do not appear particularly demanding may also be susceptible to glucose enhancement. One example is kinaesthetic memory where individuals rely on a memory for a sequence of movements. Scholey and Fowles (2002) demonstrated that post-learning administration of glucose improved performance on this task, although crucially in this study glucose was administered after learning. It is possible that such retrograde enhancement may affect different memory mechanisms.

The effects of ischaemic oxygen deprivation on cognitive function have been widely documented, and mnemonic deficits in humans and animals have been compre-hensively researched and described (Volpe and Hirst, 1983). In addition, there is indirect evidence that even fleeting fluctuations in cerebral oxygen delivery within normal physiological limits can impact on cognitive performance (Sandman et al., 1982). Disturbances of psychological functioning after exposure to altitude have also been recognised for many years. It is generally accepted that altitudes above 10,000 feet lead to profound effects on human cognitive performance and that these effects result from **hypoxia** induced by the low levels of available oxygen (Fowler et al., 1985). Altitude-induced transient impairments of aspects of memory, grammatical reasoning and the Stroop test recorded at an altitude of 15,000 feet have been shown to be reversed instantly through oxygen administration (Crowley et al., 1992). Similarly, the adverse cognitive effects of both ischaemia and carbon monoxide poisoning are successfully reversed by early treatment with oxygen. However, the impairment effects may be permanent if treatment is not instigated in time. Some conditions with pronounced cognitive consequences are not open to successful oxygen therapy. Elderly patients with significant cognitive impairment have been treated with either normobaric (atmospheric pressure) or hyperbaric (greater than atmospheric pressure) oxygen. The treatment did not improve cognitive functioning or reduce symptoms, in comparison with the controls (Raskin et al., 1978); this confirms that the marked deficits and gross physiological atrophy concomitant with senile disorders are indeed very difficult to overcome (Chapter 13).

The effects of oxygen breathing on cognition in healthy people has only received limited attention. In the 1970s, Edwards and Hart examined the effects of hyperbaric oxygen administration on healthy elderly outpatients and found substantial improvements in performance on tests of short-term memory and visual organisation, but their conclusions are only tentative due to the lack of a comparative control group. More recent studies have demonstrated that transient oxygen inhalation may enhance long-term memory and reaction times when compared with air-breathing controls (Moss and Scholey, 1996; Scholey et al., 1998). Comparison of performance on the cognitively "demanding" serial subtractions clearly indicated that oxygen breathing produced significantly fewer errors with numerically more responses, a finding that demonstrates improvements in quality of mental operations – not just speed. Significant improvements have also been reported for everyday tasks, such as memory for shopping lists and putting names to faces (Winder and Borrill, 1998), although not all studies have found beneficial effects for oxygen inhalation (Andersson et al., 2002). The available "therapeutic window" for the impact of oxygen on cognition is limited to the period when arterial haemoglobin saturation levels are significantly increased above baseline and, therefore, available for increasing neural metabolism. Furthermore, the dose response of oxygen on cognitive performance has been shown to follow the classic Yerkes–Dodson inverted U shape. Shorter doses (30 seconds to 3 minutes depending on the type of task) prior to task performance produce the greatest beneficial effects, and continuous oxygen breathing (longer than 10 minutes) lead to an overall decline in performance compared with air-breathing controls.

Cholinergic or global influence?

One possible explanation for the enhancing effects of glucose or oxygen administration on cognition is that they lead to increased levels of **acetylcholine** (ACh) synthesis (Figure 14.1), a neurotransmitter that has long been associated with attention and memory. However, it may be the case that the increase in fuel supplies leads to an upgrade in **adenosine triphosphate** (ATP) production at times of high demand. ATP is the cellular energy currency and increased production may facilitate information

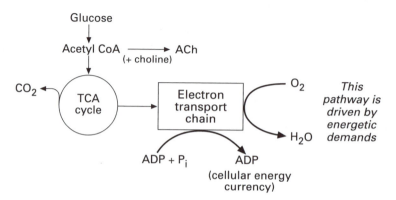

Figure 14.1. Outline of the relationship between glucose metabolism, acetylcholine synthesis and energy production. TCA = tricarboxylic acid; ADP = adenosine diphosphate; P_i = inorganic phosphate.

processing during cognitive task performance. Such improvements would be manifest as cognitive enhancement.

The modes of influence for oxygen and glucose on cognition may be educed through the use of tasks that are believed to tap into differing neural subsystems. Impaired performance on memory and attentional tasks is consistently found after **scopolamine** administration, with the degree of decrement being significantly dose-related (Parrott, 1986). Scopolamine is a cholinergic antagonist, and it has been proposed that scopolamine primarily disrupts the storage of new information into long-term memory. Similar amnesic effects are evident with another cholinergic antagonist **atropine**, the psychoactive ingredient of *Atropa belladonna*, or deadly nightshade. These findings have led to the conclusion that acetylcholine is instrumental in memory formation. However, Nissen et al. (1987) demonstrated that the effect of scopolamine is specific to declarative memory, causing significant impairment in recall, recognition and cued recall tests. However, results from an implicit serial reaction time task indicated that the learning and retention of procedural knowledge is not affected by central cholinergic blockade. In addition, focused and broadened attention tasks have been shown to be differentially sensitive to the influence of scopolamine and nicotine. Being a cholinergic antagonist scopolamine impairs sustained attention ability, whereas nicotine is a cholinergic agonist that (acutely at least, see Chapter 5) improves sustained attention (Wesnes and Revell, 1984). Such tasks along with tests of implicit and declarative memory have further demonstrated that oxygen and glucose administration are not impacting on the cholinergic system alone. Rather, it appears that all aspects of information processing may be available for enhancement.

Nootropics, or "smart drugs"

In order to understand the mechanisms underlying cognition, to discover ways of enhancing mental performance and to treat clinical dysfunctions, researchers have studied numerous neuroactive compounds. A number of compounds have shown a degree of promise. Together they have been labelled the "nootropics", but really they comprise a most heterogeneous grouping of compounds. The common property they share is that they are believed to facilitate learning and memory and/or to overcome cognitive impairments (Gouliaev and Senning, 1994). Numerous studies have reported the positive effects of **nootropics** on learning and memory. The general trend has been to evaluate cognitive and behavioural performance changes in elderly participants suffering some impairment and/or in healthy young volunteers. Gains have been demonstrated using a number of paradigms, although they differ in the degree of methodological sophistication and experimental control. The available findings on the mode of action of such compounds can be grouped into four main categories: (1) effects on energy metabolism; (2) effects on cholinergic mechanisms; (3) effects on excitatory amino acid **receptor**-mediated functions; and (4) steroid sensitivity. Many nootropics display minimal effects on traditional (transmitter-sensitive) psychopharmacological tests, and the search for underlying mechanisms has shifted more toward their effects on energy metabolism (Mondadori, 1993). The main nootropics and their probable underlying mechanisms of action are summarised in Table 14.1 (see p. 210).

Piracetam (2-oxo-pyrrolidone) was first developed in the mid-1960s as a possible treatment for travel sickness (Gouliaev and Senning, 1994). However, between 1968 and 1972 a considerable amount of research revealed its ability to facilitate learning, prevent amnesia induced by hypoxia and accelerate the return to normal of electro-encephalograms (EEGs) in hypoxic animals. An early study of the effect of piracetam on human memory by Dimond and Brouwers (1976) indicated improvements in healthy adults. Verbal memory improvements were found at daily doses of 400 mg piracetam, although they took 14 days to appear. Similarly, Mindus et al. (1976) reported improvements in performance on a series of perceptual motor tasks in healthy elderly volunteers following 4 weeks of treatment with piracetam. In a real world setting, Reidel et al. (1998) investigated the effects of 4 weeks of treatment with piracetam on the motoring performance of healthy elderly volunteers; the results were described as disappointing, although there was a non-significant trend toward improvement. Other associated compounds, such as aniracetam, etiracetam and oxiracetam, have also been found to exert direct effects on the acquisition and retention performance of rats and mice on a number of tasks (Gouliaev and Senning, 1994).

Pramiracetam is another chemical relative of piracetam and has similar effects including an influence on the neurotransmitter acetylcholine. Pramiracetam appears to be more potent than piracetam, although it is less commonly used, as it has not been so thoroughly investigated and is less readily available. DeVreese et al. (1996) assessed the influence of pramiracetam and memory training on the performance of a group of healthy, aged participants. Their results indicated significantly better memory performance for the **drug** alone, and drug combined with training groups, compared with training alone and a control group. An assessment of young males with cognitive problems following head injuries or anoxia also reported performance improvements especially for memory, compared with **placebo** (McLean et al., 1991). These improvements were maintained over an 18-month treatment period and remained at the 1-month follow-up, after treatment had been discontinued. It has been suggested that pramiracetam may have a possible role in the treatment of Alzheimer's disease (Chapter 13), where effects on memory due to damage to the cholinergic system are considerable.

Hydergine was discovered in the 1940s when it was extracted from mould growing on rye grain. It has putative cognition-enhancing properties and was widely used as an anti-dementia treatment in the USA until the 1980s, when its clinical efficacy was widely questioned. A more recent study of more than 200 dementia patients has produced results indicating only marginal improvements compared with placebo (Cucinotta et al., 1996). In an open prospective study involving both young, normal volunteers and geriatric patients some cognitive changes were apparent, especially on critical flicker fusion, which is widely used as an index of cortical arousal; however, the absence of a placebo group severely limits the findings (Parrott and Hindmarch, 1975; Hindmarch et al., 1979). In a review of previous studies on dementia patients, Olin et al. (2003) conclude that improvements in global measures have been reliably found, but that uncertainty still remains regarding the efficacy of hydergine treatment because many of the double-blind assessments were made prior to the development of consensus-based diagnostic criteria for dementia in the 1980s.

L-acetylcarnitine is produced naturally in the CNS and indirectly stimulates acetylcholine production, as well as purportedly modulating cerebral metabolism. A study of nearly 500 geriatric patients in Italy provided evidence that L-acetylcarnitine may be able to improve cognition and reduce depression and stress, in the absence of any adverse drug reactions (Salvioli and Neri, 1994). Animal studies have suggested that the improvements in mood and stress may be a result of increased dopamine and serotonin release, particularly in the **nucleus accumbens** (Tolu et al., 2002). Furthermore, this compound is reported to produce beneficial effects in both major depressive disorders and for Alzheimer's patients (Pettigrew et al., 2000).

Vinpocetine has been shown to increase cerebral blood flow (Solti et al., 1976). It increases energy production by enhancing oxygen release in the brain in patients with dementia and those with cerebrovascular disorders (Tohgi et al., 1990). These physiological and metabolic changes may be responsible for improvements in memory performance recorded for healthy volunteers (Subhan and Hindmarch, 1987; Coleston and Hindmarch, 1988), as well as the successful treatment of sensorineural disorders of the auditory (Zelen et al., 1976) and visual systems (Kahan and Olah, 1976). Hindmarch et al. (1991) studied the efficacy and tolerability of orally administered vinpocetine in patients with mild to moderate dementia. In a placebo-controlled, double-blind trial, 203 patients received daily doses of 30 mg vinpocetine, 60 mg vinpocetine or placebo for 16 weeks. Improvements were found for the vinpocetine treatments when compared with placebo for both the clinical global impression scale and cognitive performance measures. Furthermore, no serious side effects related to vinpocetine treatment have been found (Balestreri et al., 1987; Kiss, 1990; Feigin et al., 2001).

Xanthinol nicotinate is a form of the B vitamin niacin that passes easily through cell membranes and is thus easily absorbed by the brain. Xanthinol nicotinate has been shown to increase brain glucose metabolism, improve brain ATP levels and improve brain blood flow, since it acts as a vasodilator. As a consequence it has been used to treat short-term memory disorders, vigilance and attentional deficits, as well as circulatory disorders in the extremities. In one study xanthinol nicotinate improved the reaction speed of the elderly (Loriaux et al., 1985). At high doses xanthinol nicotinate can cause blood pressure changes and must therefore be avoided by persons suffering from peptic ulcers, liver problems, severe hypotension, myocardial infarction or other congenital heart problems. Minor side effects, such as flushing, nausea, heartburn, itchy skin and/or vomiting, may occur, although they normally dissipate with continued use or a dosage reduction.

Phosphatidylserine is a phospholipid, a major building block for all membranes including the neural membranes. It is believed that its membrane actions facilitate the production and action of many **neurotransmitters** including dopamine and acetylcholine. The underlying mode of action is possibly by increasing the number of neurotransmitter receptor sites, as well as increasing their release (see Toffano, 1987 for a review). In addition, phosphatidylserine may increase brain energy production and, possibly, prevent age-related decline to some degree (Heiss et al., 1993). Improvements in cognitive performance have been recorded in a number of double-blind trials employing elderly participants suffering from cognitive decline (Delwaide et al., 1986; Crook et al., 1992; Cenacchi et al., 1993), as well as improvements in mood and other behavioural measures (Maggioni et al., 1990). Beneficial effects on mood have also been reported for healthy young volunteers (Benton et al., 2001), but reliable evidence to support retailers' claims for improvements in mental ability is harder to find.

Nimodipine is a racemic mixture (i.e., it is a compound in two mirror image forms, one of which is more active than the other). Veng et al. (2003) reported the reversal of

Table 14.1. Nootropics: the proposed modes of actions for several putative cognitive enhancers.

Nootropic substance	Claimed mode of influence
Piracetam	Improved cerebral microcirculation; increased ATP production.
Hydergine	Increased cerebral metabolism; increased cerebral oxygen delivery.
Vinpocetine	Improved cerebral microcirculation; increased ATP synthesis; increased utilisation of oxygen and glucose.
Xanthinol nicotinate	Increased glucose metabolism; increased ATP production.
Gingko	Promotion of vasodilation and increased blood flow.
Phosphatidylserine	Increased glucose metabolism.
Nimodipine	Increased cerebral blood flow.

age-related decrements in working memory following chronic nimodipine treatment, and Deyo et al. (1989) provided evidence for the facilitation of associative learning in aged rabbits. The usefulness of nimodipine in patients with Alzheimer's disease and other forms of dementia is still somewhat controversial (Lopez-Arrieta and Birks, 2002). In spite of the uncertainties about its efficacy, nimodipine is currently frequently prescribed for cognitive impairment and dementia in several continental European countries. Recent investigations have also indicated that the calcium channel-blocking properties of nimodipine may make it useful in the **detoxification** treatment of **opiate** addiction (Jimenez-Lerma et al., 2002; see also Chapter 10).

The evidence cited here is only a very small sample of the vast quantity of research into putative cognitive enhancers. However, many of these compounds that have demonstrated positive effects are believed to influence cerebral metabolism, whether through increased blood flow, glucose metabolism or other indirect routes, as outlined above. Furthermore, these metabolic effects are hypothesised to be at least partly responsible for the cognitive improvements documented. Indeed, many of the putative **cognitive enhancers** currently available claim modes of influence (Table 14.1) that would fall in line with a metabolic model of cognitive enhancement.

Metabolic resource model of cognitive enhancement

As cognitive demand increases, so do the requirements for metabolic resources, such as glucose and oxygen. These energy changes are reflected in physiological alterations, such as increased heart rate (Carroll et al., 1986a) and increased regional cerebral blood flow (Roland, 1993). It has been suggested that increasing the supply of these reactants above normal levels will allow for increased metabolism, with the resultant increment in available energy (in the form of ATP) being utilised for cognitive performance; this would raise the ceiling for cognitive performance levels, effectively producing an enhancement. A schematic representation of this model is presented in Figure 14.2. It

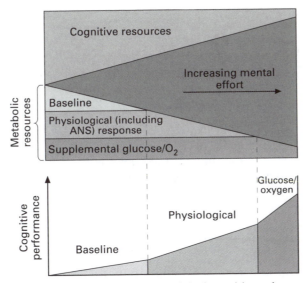

Figure 14.2. A metabolic resource model of cognitive enhancement.
ANS = autonomic nervous system.

can be seen that, up to a point, baseline levels of metabolism allow cognitive operations to be undertaken without significant physiological adjustments. Increasing mental effort is then associated with declining cognitive resources, and physiological responses are required to enable the processing to be fuelled effectively. An additional supply of resources, such as glucose and oxygen, might then enable even more efficient processing above and beyond normal limits; this would then be manifest as enhanced performance.

Figure 14.2 also helps to explain the sources of "error" variance in human psychopharmacology research. Increasing mental effort may mask any putative drug effects, as when a drink-driver sees a police vehicle in the wing mirror and reduces vehicle sway by focusing more on road-tracking accuracy (Chapter 9). Differences in baseline ability and innate/learned cognitive resources are also important factors. They can help explain individual variation in response to recreational stimulants (Chapters 4–6), recreational depressants (Chapters 7–9) and therapeutic medications (Chapters 11–13).

Traditional and more novel approaches to cognitive enhancement

In recent years, various means for achieving cognitive enhancement have been investigated. Although these approaches have been entitled "novel" due to the contemporary nature of the research, they often represent activities that have been employed for thousands of years. In other words, although comprehensive scientific investigation is only very recent, their practice and belief has formed part of collective human wisdom for considerably longer.

Aromatherapy has been used as a therapeutic treatment for many physical and affective disorders and is described in the historical literature of many different cultures. The essential oils used in aromatherapy are highly concentrated essences extracted from plants, and each oil is believed to produce reliable and predictable effects on psychological states when inhaled. The sedative nature of lavender (*Lavandula* spp.) has consistently been demonstrated through the relief of anxiety, tension and other improvements in mood (Buchbauer et al., 1991). Similar subjective relaxing effects have been found for spiced apple (Schwartz et al., 1986) and sandalwood (*Santalum* spp.) (Steiner, 1994). Changes in subjective state brought about by aroma inhalation and, in particular, changes in arousal and alertness may impact on cognitive performance. Diego et al. (1998) found both lavender (sedating) and rosemary (arousing) improved the speed of maths computations, but only lavender increased accuracy. Similarly, both arousing (peppermint) and relaxing (muguet) aromas have been found to produce significant increases in sensitivity on a visual sustained attention task compared with no odour controls. Moss et al. (2003) reported a significant improvement in long-term memory performance following the breathing of rosemary (*Rosmarinus officinalis*) aroma. In contrast, lavender was found to impair both memory accuracy and general speed of performance. Subsequent study has indicated that peppermint (*Mentha × piperita*) aroma may also improve memory performance and overall quality of memory (a factor that comprises both long-term and working memory components). Interestingly, studies have also investigated situations where the expectation of an ambient odour is produced in participants, but when none is actually presented (Gilbert et al., 1997). Furthermore, the participants were misled into believing that the feigned odour would affect cognitive performance. However, the objective test data demonstrated no differences to exist between the conditions, indicating that expectancies may be secondary to the pharmacological effect of any actual odour presented.

Although it is not clear how aromas impinge on cognition, two possibilities have been put forward. Compounds within the odour may directly interact with the **olfactory nerve** and modulate arousal levels through the nerve's connections to the **limbic system**, consequently impinging on cognition. Alternatively, volatile compounds may be absorbed into the bloodstream through the nose and lungs, and these compounds may possess direct pharmacological activity that is expressed in the brain.

Chewing gum is often reported by its aficionados to subjectively "aid concentration" and "help thinking". However, until recently no scientific evidence was available to support such claims. Experimental findings provided by Wilkinson et al. (2002) indicate that chewing sugar-free gum can indeed improve mental performance, specifically aspects of long-term and working memory. It has been suggested that these effects may be mediated by the concomitant increases in heart rate or regional cerebral blood flow that have been recorded during mastication (Farella et al., 1999; Sesay et al., 2000). Such changes could increase delivery of neural substrates and consequently increase neural metabolism as outlined for glucose and oxygen above.

Physical exercise has been investigated in a number of studies. The relationship between exercise and cognitive performance has been studied in both older adults (Kramer et al., 2000; Wood et al., 1999; Laurin et al., 2001) and young, healthy volunteers. The general consensus is of beneficial effects. In a classic cross-sectional study Spirduso and Clifford (1978) demonstrated that reaction time among older adults who were physically active resembled reaction time for active younger adults and surpassed that of non-active younger adults. With regard to healthy young adults, Hogervorst et al. (1996) found that strenuous exercise had a positive effect on performance speed in simple tasks (i.e., simple reaction time) and more complex tasks (i.e., Stroop test). The physiological arousal that results from exercise appears to have an impact on cognitive functioning in both young and elderly adults, and this may be related to the increase in heart rate during exercise providing greater levels of "fuel" for the brain as well as the muscles. Sparrow and Wright (1993) reported no evidence that physical exercise facilitated cognitive performance. However, it should be noted that the exercise regime was of short duration, resulting in low levels of cardiovascular reactivity; this was clearly reflected by only slight increases in heart rate during and after exercise and may explain the negative findings.

Herbal extracts

Over the past decade or so there has been increasing evidence of the possible psychopharmacological effects of herbal products, or phytomedicines. Investigation into the potential efficacy of these agents has been hampered by a resistance of mainstream psychopharmacology to accept herbal products as worthy of serious research; this is despite the fact that numerous psychoactive agents were originally derived from plants. Many of the psychoactive substances discussed in the other chapters are plant products including caffeine, alcohol, cannabis, nicotine, cocaine, hypericum, atropine and opiates (Chapters 1–14). **Caffeine** is traditionally classed as a CNS stimulant and was therefore covered in Chapter 4. However, caffeine displays few similarities to amphetamine and cocaine and might well be considered more appropriate for this section. The antidepressant efficacy of St John's wort, or **hypericum**, was also covered earlier in Chapter 12. It should also be noted that animal products like cod liver oil, which is rich in omega-3, may also facilitate learning and memory.

Herbal medicine has always been the predominant form of medical therapy in Asia, Africa and South America. In recent years, herbal compounds have become increasingly popular throughout Europe, North America and Australasia. The British House of Lords Select Committee on Science and Technology (*Complementary and Alternative Medicine*, 2000) noted that herbal products comprised a significant proportion of all health products used in the UK. The Committee heard that just a handful of products – ginkgo, St John's wort, ginseng, garlic, echinacea, saw palmetto and kava – constituted the majority of herbal medicines. The total retail value of all herbal products in the UK is around £240m/year, while in Germany the phytopharmaceutical market has been estimated to be worth $3bn/year. Worldwide herbal retail sales approximate $16.5bn, with Europe accounting for 45% of total sales (Scimone and Scimone, 1998). The following two subsections will focus on two of the most widely used phytomedicines, ginkgo and ginseng.

Ginkgo

The *Ginkgo biloba* tree is one of the oldest surviving tree species on earth (Major, 1967) and has probably existed in its current form for up to 200 million years, leading to its description by Darwin as a "living fossil". The ginkgo tree can live for more than a thousand years. Extracts and infusions made from ginkgo leaves have been used in traditional Chinese medicine for at least 5,000 years. It is sold either as an "over the counter" (OTC) food supplement or as a prescription medicine throughout the world, and is the market leader among herbal medication in Western marketplaces. Unlike many other OTC preparations, ginkgo has benefited from the development in the mid-1960s of high-quality standardised extracts. These extracts, derived by a complex drying process, are concentrated in a ratio of approximately 1 part extract to 50 parts dried leaves and are generally standardised to a content of 24–25% flavonoids and 6% terpenoids. The most important active substances in ginkgo are thought to be these flavonoids and the terpenoids (Kleijnen and Knipschild, 1992). They have been attributed to a number of physiological effects, with potential relevance for cognitive enhancement; these include antagonism of platelet-activating factor, which has the effect of reducing blood viscosity and improving blood flow (Stromgaard et al., 2002). They are also capable of **free radical** scavenging (Siddique et al., 2000) and can modulate various neurotransmitter systems (e.g., Kristoikova and Klaschka, 1997). The net result of such actions includes beneficial effects on blood circulation and **neuroprotection** in the face of a number of challenges to the brain.

There is strong evidence that ginkgo may protect against cognitive decline. A recent Cochrane review (Birks et al., 2003) examined 33 well-controlled studies involving groups suffering from age-related cognitive impairment or dementia. The review concludes that ginkgo improves cognitive performance at various doses (usually approximately 200 mg/day) when taken for up to a year. The authors concluded that, "there is promising evidence of improvement in cognition and function associated with ginkgo." The evidence in healthy older individuals is less clear. Mix and Crews (2000) reported improved speed of performance on a number of tasks following 6 weeks' administration of 180 mg/day of the ginkgo preparation "Egb 761" vs. placebo. Likewise, Mix and Crews (2002) assessed the effects of 6 weeks' administration of 180 mg/day Egb 761 or placebo to 249 healthy older individuals; they demonstrated better memory performance both subjectively and objectively. In contrast, Solomon et al. (2002) found no effect of 120 mg/day ginkgo on the cognitive performance of elderly participants.

A number of studies have examined the effects of single doses of ginkgo in healthy adults using double-blind, counterbalanced, crossover designs. The first of these reported shortened reaction times on a working memory task following the highest (600 mg) of three single doses of ginkgo taken by a small cohort of eight healthy females (Hindmarch, 1986). Warot et al. (1991) failed to replicate this effect on the Sternberg task, but did find an improvement in free recall scores again for the 600-mg dose. In a more robust study, Rigney et al. (1999) examined the effects of 1 and 2 days' administration regimens of four doses (120–300 mg) of ginkgo in 31 participants. Performance was only significantly improved on reaction times for the Sternberg numeric working memory task. A series of studies into the acute cognitive effects of herbal extracts was performed by Kennedy and colleagues. The Kennedy series shared the same randomised, double-blind, placebo-controlled, balanced, crossover design, with 20 participants receiving three different single doses of the relevant extract and an identical placebo on separate occasions 7 days apart. Cognitive performance was tested over the following 6 hours. Kennedy et al. (2000) found dose-dependent improvements in speed across three attention tasks in 20 young participants administered single doses of 120, 240 and 360 mg ginkgo extract. There was also evidence of improved secondary memory performance following the lowest dose. In a partial replication of this study (Kennedy et al., 2002a) a different cohort of 20 young participants ingested single doses of ginkgo, ginseng and a ginkgo–ginseng combination. In this case the speed of performing attention tasks was unaffected; however, the 360-mg ginkgo dose improved secondary memory performance.

Ginseng

Ginseng is generally taken to refer to the dried root of several species in the plant genus *Panax* (Araliaceae family). The most widely used family member is *Panax ginseng* which was first cultivated around 11 BC and has a medical history stretching back more than 5,000 years (Yun, 2001). Ginseng is possibly the most widely taken herbal product in the world, being used as a tonic and general health prophylactic and to treat memory loss and reverse "absentmindedness" (see Kennedy and Scholey, 2003). The major active constituents of the *Panax* genus are thought to be the 30 or so ginsenosides (Tachikawa et al., 1999). The ginsenoside content of ginseng extracts can vary depending on a number of factors including the species, the age and part of the plant used and even the time of year of harvest. Unlike ginkgo there is only one standardised extract that has attracted widespread research attention, G115, which contains an invariable 4% of ginsenosides.

Ginseng has a number of properties that are potentially relevant to the modulation of cognitive performance (Kennedy and Scholey, 2003); these include effects on blood flow, shifting the balance of the **Hypothalamic–Pituitary–Adrenal** axis and modulation of a number of neurotransmitter systems and blood glucose levels in both diabetic and non-diabetic humans (Kennedy and Scholey, 2003). However, unlike ginkgo, the behavioural pharmacology of ginseng has not been investigated thoroughly. There is some evidence that improvements in some aspects of cognition are evident following an 8–12 week dosing period. Additionally, there is accumulating evidence that single doses of the standardised *Panax ginseng* extract (G115) can modulate cognitive performance (Kennedy et al., 2001a, b, 2002a; Scholey and Kennedy, 2002). In studies from the Kennedy series described earlier, all three doses of ginseng (200, 400 and 600 mg) were associated with improvements on a secondary memory measure. These improvements were most pronounced for the 400-mg dose, while the higher and lower doses impaired attentional performance. The improved secondary memory performance following 400-mg G115 was replicated in a second study (Kennedy et al., 2002a). A further experiment also assessed the effects of the same doses of G115 on serial subtraction mental arithmetic tasks. On the most demanding (Serial 7s) task the 400-mg dose proved beneficial, with increased accuracy, but once again the 200-mg dose led to decrements, this time in terms of the number of responses made (Scholey and Kennedy, 2002).

The CNS effects of *Panax ginseng* have also been assessed using EEG experiments that compare the effects of both 360 mg of ginkgo and 200 mg of ginseng G115. The results suggested that there were similarities in the topographic EEG effects elicited by both extracts, which were in keeping with those of cognition enhancers – specifically, reductions in the power of frontal theta and beta wavebands (Kennedy et al., 2003a).

However, the effects were more marked for ginseng and were accompanied by reductions in frontal alpha waveband activity and decreased latency of the P300 component of the auditory evoked potential, a result that suggests more efficient stimulus assessment.

Salvia and melissa

There is strong historical and *in vitro* evidence to suggest two types of sage, *Salvia officinalis* and *Salvia lavandulaefolia*, and *Melissa officinalis*, or lemon balm, may be effective cognition enhancers. Both are capable of modulating cholinergic activity, in the case of the *Salvia* species by acetylcholinesterase inhibition (Perry et al., 2000, 2002). *Melissa*, on the other hand, binds to both nicotinic and muscarinic receptors (Wake et al., 2000). Recent empirical studies have confirmed that these members of the Labiatae family may enhance cognitive performance. In healthy adults, single doses of *Salvia lavandulaefolia* improved word recall in 20 healthy, young participants (Tildesley et al., 2003). More recently, it has been demonstrated that single doses of *Salvia officinalis* could improve the secondary memory and attention in a cohort of elderly participants (Tildesley et al., submitted). As for *Melissa officinalis* the most consistent findings pertain to mood changes. *Melissa* can modulate cognitive performance in positive and negative ways depending on the dose and extract used. However, it appears to have a fairly consistent effect in improving calmness (Kennedy et al., 2002b, 2003b).

Questions

1   Describe how the nervous system depends on nutrients for efficient cognitive functioning.

2   Outline the conditions that may compromise the delivery of important nutrients to the brain.

3   Describe how the administration of glucose and oxygen might enhance cognition.

4   Outline the mechanisms by which three named "smart drugs" could alter human cognition.

5   How compelling is the empirical evidence for "smart drugs" improving cognition?

6   Describe how smells can affect mood and cognition.

7   Is the brain normally functioning at an optimal peak?

8   Summarise the use of herbal extracts to improve cognition and mood.

Key references and reading

Craft S, Murphy C and Wernstrom J (1994). Glucose effects on complex memory and non-memory tasks: The influence of age, sex and glucoregulatory response. *Psychobiology*, **2**, 95–105.

Diego MA, Jones N, Field F, Hernandez-Reif M, Schanberg S, Kuhn C, McAdam V, Galamaga R and Galamaga M (1998). Aromatherapy positively affects mood: EEG patterns of alertness and math computations. *International Journal of Neuroscience*, **96**, 217–224.

Foster JK, Lidder PG and Sünram SI (1998). Glucose and memory: Fractionation of enhancement effects? *Psychopharmacology*, **13**, 259–270.

Hogervorst E, Riedel W, Jeukendrup A and Jolles J (1996). Cognitive performance after strenuous physical exercise. *Perceptual and Motor Skills*, **8**, 479–488.

Moss MC, Scholey AB and Wesnes K (1998). Oxygen administration selectively enhances cognitive performance in healthy young adults: a placebo-controlled, double blind crossover study. *Psychopharmacology*, **138**, 27–33.

Moss MC, Cook J, Wesnes KA and Duckett P (2003). Aroma of rosemary and lavender essential oils differentially affect cognition and mood in healthy adults. *International Journal of Neuroscience*, **113**, 1507–1530.

Scholey AB (2001). Fuel for thought. *The Psychologist*, **14**, 196–201.

Scholey AB, Moss MC, Neave N and Wesnes KA (1999). Cognitive performance, hyperoxia and heart rate following oxygen administration in healthy young adults. *Physiology and Behavior*, **67**, 783–789.

PART IV

Final Overview

Chapter 15

Current knowledge and future possibilities

Drug use and misuse – an overview of some core issues

We hope that this book has increased your knowledge about drugs and behaviour and stimulated your interest in undertaking further reading. Our aim was to describe the fundamental mechanisms of drug action and show how different chemicals can induce such contrasting behavioural effects. Thus, while some drugs induce sleep, others induce feelings of euphoria, many impair memory, some enhance cognition, a few intensify sensory perceptions and many are crucial for the pharmacotherapy of clinical disorders. Thus, the clinical outlook for people suffering from depression or schizophrenia has dramatically improved in the last 50 years; this is largely due to the development of some highly effective therapeutic drugs.

The aim of this final chapter is to review the main findings from every chapter and offer some theoretical and practical links between them. Various topics will be debated. How problematic is recreational **drug** use? In order to address this question the notion of cost–benefit ratios will be introduced. Numerous factors may affect this ratio and a few of them will be debated: for instance, it will be proposed that the cost–benefit ratio deteriorates with repeated drug usage as drug-related gains decrease and socio-psychobiological problems increase. A related issue is whether recreational drug use should be dealt with in a legal context or whether it is best conceptualised as a health and well-being issue. Next, we will briefly consider the nature of addiction. The traditional Western approach is to treat addiction as a medical disease and offer medicinal treatments, such as methadone for opiate addiction. A more Eastern approach is to see addiction as a state of mind, and this more psychological model has a number of important implications for any interventions.

Turning to the section on drugs for clinical disorders, we will examine some general principles about best clinical practice. In many chapters it was concluded that the best therapy comprises an effective drug combined with psychological therapy; this has emerged in studies of schizo-phrenia, depression, anxiety and even mania (Chapters 11 and 12). So, why has this pattern emerged in so many areas? Some general explanatory principles will be offered. Next, we will consider the prospects for future drug development. Finally, we would like to emphasise that one of the core aims of this section is to be thought-provoking and challenging. We hope to stimulate a few ideas for future investigation.

Psychoactive drugs: modes of action

The first chapter presented a broad overview of **psychoactive** drugs. We learned that, far from being a 20th or 21st century phenomenon, recreational and medicinal drug use can be traced back to the historical origins of humanity, although the speed of drug development has increased dramatically in the past 50 years. Since 1955 many new psychotherapeutic compounds have been introduced, the product of years of careful development using sophisticated methods for synthesis, screening, testing and final assessment. Novel scientific techniques have been used to develop new compounds targeted for particular psychopathological disorders, although similar procedures have also been used to develop illicit recreational compounds. It is clear from the material in Chapter 1 and, indeed, all subsequent chapters that the "benefits" associated with any psychoactive drug need to be weighed against its neuropsycho-logical "costs". The most obvious of these is drug dependency or addiction, but there are many other adverse effects on psychological health that need to be considered (see below). Chapter 1 also presented a classification system for psychoactive drugs; this was based on drug groups that share similar underlying mechanisms and, thus, display broadly equivalent behavioural effects (Table 1.1). However, it was also noted that most drugs do not fall neatly into an unambiguous category; this is because most drugs are neurochemically "messy", affecting multiple neurotransmitter systems, and, so, their behavioural effects are similarly complex (Figure 15.1).

The second chapter introduced many of the factors that affect a drug's behav-ioural profile. Numerous routes of drug administration were described, and the ways in which these contribute to the drug "hit" and time course of action were explained. Other factors that contribute to the psychopharmacological profiles were also considered, including dosing, metabolism and elimination. However, it is clear that drug effects cannot be attributed solely to physiological factors. An individual's history of drug use, as well as their age and gender, can all affect the response to a drug, as can less easily identifiable factors, such as current mood state, drug setting and expectancy. This topic was revisited again in Chapter 14. An overview of the basic information processing units of the brain, the neuron and **synapse**, was then given in the third chapter. It was shown that the rules of neuronal and synaptic processing are basically quite simple, involving electrical and chemical signals, respectively. The over-whelming complexity and unpredictability of human behaviour arises from the multitude of interactions that the neural network allows. There are seemingly countless possible links between multiple pathways involving dozens of different neuro-transmitters, with each neurotransmitter influencing a range of **receptor** subtypes, both **presynaptic** and **postsynaptic**, some inhibitory and others excitatory. In the face of this

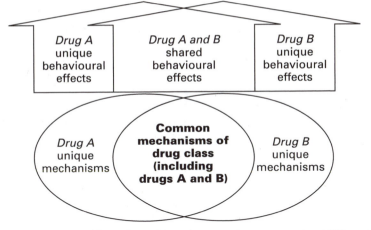

Figure 15.1. An illustration of how drugs from the same class can produce different behavioural effects. Drugs A and B are of the same classification, as defined by their shared mechanisms and behavioural effects. However, each also has its own unique mechanisms and behavioural effects; hence, it could be argued that the subjective effects of drugs of the same class are "the same but different".

enormous complexity it is not surprising that drug effects can be complex too, since they can affect each of these stages! Chapter 3 also introduced the concepts of withdrawal and tolerance and their relationship with **dependence** and addiction. These same topics were revisited in more depth in Chapter 10, where it was emphasised that addiction and drug misuse cannot be simply reduced to physiological changes. Psychological factors are of crucial importance, with differences in expectancy, learning and motivation playing key roles in the development of drug-related problems.

Recreational drugs

The second part of the book was concerned with drugs used for social and recreational purposes, although their clinical uses were also described (Chapters 4–10). The first type of drug to be considered was the CNS stimulant (Chapter 4). **Amphetamine** and **cocaine** act as sympathomimetics, since they enhance alertness and arousal and boost subjective mood states. However, these drug-induced gains are short-lived, so that their recreational use causes increased health risks, both in the short term and longer term. The cost–benefit ratio decreases rapidly over time, with tolerance and dependence being important problems (see below). Hence, the more heavily they are used the greater the psychobiological distress they cause; these drug-induced health problems increase dramatically when users graduate to injecting. **Caffeine** is a milder stimulant that is widely consumed in many everyday drinks, foods and over-the-counter medicines. However, it is still unclear whether its apparent mood effects and anti-fatigue properties are genuine gains or whether they reflect a combination of expectancy effects, together with the relief of caffeine-withdrawal symptoms.

Nicotine and cigarette smoking were considered in Chapter 4. Here, we learned that the addictive power of a drug can be quite subtle, often making it very difficult to disentangle the complex psychophysiological and neurocognitive changes that underlie its usage. Indeed, the behavioural effects of nicotine are surprisingly ephemeral, such that smokers are often hard-pressed to describe the reasons for their tobacco cravings. Nevertheless, nicotine is extremely addictive, with most regular cigarette smokers needing to maintain a steady intake of nicotine over the day. But, unlike the drive for many other drugs, the sole purpose of smoking seems to be the alleviation of withdrawal symptoms. The paradox of cigarettes is that smokers only need them to try and remain feeling "normal"! Furthermore, the repeated daily experience of these negative withdrawal symptoms means that nicotine dependency actually causes increased stress and depression. Adolescents who take up cigarette smoking become more stressed, although those adults who quit gradually become less stressed. The adverse health effects of tar and carbon monoxide on the health of smokers are well known, with tobacco smoke directly killing the majority of smokers. The adverse psychological effects of nicotine dependency are less well known and need to be far more widely recognised.

Chapter 6 dealt with the prototypical psychedelic drug **lysergic acid diethylamide (LSD)** and the artificial amphetamine derivative **MDMA** (methylenedioxymethamphetamine), or **Ecstasy**. LSD intensifies sensory input so that colours become more intense, movements and motions alter in unpredictable ways and thoughts and cognitions take deeper apparent meanings. The neurochemical mechanisms for these profound perceptual and cognitive distortions are not well understood, but probably stem from serotonergic and noradrenergic changes. As with all other psychoactive chemicals the drug can only modulate the normal functioning of the brain. Hence, whether LSD induces a good or bad trip will depend on factors, such as prior experience, psychosocial setting, prevailing moods and cognitive expectancies. In some cases LSD causes a profound personality disintegration, which is probably best explained by the diathesis stress model: this states that psychologically vulnerable individuals are most at risk from an adverse drug reaction. However, it is never easy to predict who these individuals might be.

The other drug covered in Chapter 6 was Ecstasy, or MDMA. This drug has been used by many adolescents and young adults, with its popularity in modern Westernised culture ironically stemming from its criminalisation in the 1980s. In terms of its behavioural pharmacology, MDMA leads to an acute boost in serotonin, dopamine and other neurotransmitter activity. Thus, it enhances numerous mood states and facilitates many aspects of social interaction. Afterwards, neurotransmitter activity levels are reduced, so that subsequent days are predominated by feelings of lethargy and anhedonia – the so-called "midweek blues". The Ecstasy chapter debated many of the problems of establishing causal links between psychoactive drug use and psychosocial consequences. People who take an illicit drug are most often polydrug users, and the effects of mixing drugs like cannabis, alcohol, nicotine, ketamine, amphetamine and Ecstasy/MDMA itself are hard to disentangle. Additionally, the effects of overheating, dehydration and challenges to circadian rhythms may also contribute to any long-term psychobiological consequences. However, animal research can be very useful here, since it allows specific drug effects to be isolated under **placebo**-controlled laboratory conditions. The emerging consensus is that repeated recreational Ecstasy use leads to selective impairments in some cognitive functions (memory), as well as a number of longer term psychobiological problems (depression). These conditions appear to stem from damage to the fragile serotonergic projections that subserve higher brain regions. It remains to be seen how profound the impact of the drug will prove for a generation of Ecstasy users.

Chapter 7 described the psychopharmacology of **cannabis**, which is also widely used as a recreational drug. Like nicotine, cannabis users can self-titrate their required cannabinoid intake by modulating the depth and frequency of their smoke inhalation. But, unlike nicotine, cannabis leads to a clear state of intoxication. Thus, users typically report feelings of well-being and relaxation, although excessive doses can induce paranoia, followed by feelings of hunger – the so-called "munchies". The mode of action is unclear, but is almost certainly related to the brain's natural **anandamides**, which normally bind to **cannabinoid** synaptic receptors and act as neurotransmitters or neuromodulators. The health risks of cannabis smoking are similar to those of cigarette smoking. Just as nicotine is delivered to the body on the tar droplets of tobacco smoke, so psychoactive cannabinols, such as **THCs (tetrahydrocannabinols)**, are delivered on the misty smoke of burning cannabis – the tar needing to settle on the inside of the lungs to release hundreds of chemicals into the blood circulation. Thus, the adverse health consequences of cannabis and tobacco smoking are not easy to distinguish. Current regular cannabis users display a number of selective cognitive deficits, particularly on everyday memory tasks. Some heavy users also display the so-called "amotivational syndrome", where cannabis predominates over other daily activities. The long-term consequences of cannabis intake are less clear-cut, although some studies report enduring neurocognitive deficits in former users. The addictive potential of cannabis also appears to be less than with other recreational drugs, and there are no reported cases of overdose. Several potential medicinal uses for cannabinoids have been identified for **multiple sclerosis**, **glaucoma** and as an anti-emetic relaxant during chemotherapy. Some large-scale prospective medicinal studies are currently under way.

In contrast, the medical use of opiates as analgesics can be traced back to ancient Greece. They remain the drug of choice in the clinical management of many forms of chronic pain (Chapter 8). However, opiates display a very high addiction potential. Indeed, studies on this class of drugs have provided the substrate for our classic models of addiction, based on the concept of tolerance and withdrawal (see also Chapter 10). As with cannabis, the **opiates** act on their "own" chemical system of natural **endorphins** in the brain. But, whereas their acute effects are strongly euphoric, recreational users find that the "hit" associated with earlier episodes of **heroin** use is gradually replaced by tolerance and dependence. In order to obtain the increasingly elusive hit, dosage escalation followed by progression to injection as the mode of administration is commonplace. Deaths due to heroin overdose are not uncommon, especially in comparison with other drugs of abuse. Like cigarette smokers, chronic users of heroin do not appear to gain any absolute benefit from the drug: daily drug use just returns them to a state of relative "normality".

In Chapter 9 we were introduced to another class of drugs – central nervous system (CNS) depressants. This class of drugs includes many that are used for their anxiety-reducing properties. Alcohol is the most widely used of our recreational depressants, and its use has immense health costs for society. Furthermore, alcohol, unlike most of the other recreational drugs we have encountered, is legal in most countries. It produces a clear pattern of intoxication, with equally clear dose-related deficits. Intoxication depends on a number of factors including personality and other dispositional factors and on the psychosocial environment and cognitive expectancy. Drunkenness can best be described in terms of "alcohol myopia", where immediate sensory needs and gratifications predominate over more reflective considerations. However, this qualitative model may be underpinned by a specific pattern of cognitive changes. In particular, there is shift in the speed–accuracy trade-off, with alcohol uniquely impairing error processing, while leaving speed processing relatively intact. This pattern is the opposite of most CNS depressants: for instance, when intoxicated by cannabis, both speed and accuracy are impaired, so that motorists tend be rather inaccurate, slow and cautious. Alcohol intoxication is uniquely dangerous in that motorists are not only more error-prone but also typically fast and reckless.

Cost–benefit ratios

One undercurrent implicit throughout this whole part has been the relative costs of recreational drug use vs. their perceived benefits. Hence, we would like to introduce the hypothetical notion of a cost–benefit ratio. All recreational drugs have some positive effects – which is why they are taken. But every drug also displays detrimental effects – which is why their use is problematic. However, this cost–benefit ratio is never easy to calculate. It differs for each drug, varies between individuals and generally deteriorates with repeated drug usage. This latter factor can be illustrated with reference to MDMA, or Ecstasy: the first time MDMA is taken the cost–benefit ratio is extremely positive for most people. They describe a strong positive experience and the come-down effects afterwards are seen as relatively minor (Chapter 6). This positive cost–benefit ratio typically leads to further use, given the desire to regain the euphoric feelings. To do this, regular users need to take more tablets, but ultimately describe the experience as familiar and less intense and the come-down effects as worse over time (Chapter 6). As the cost–benefit ratio deteriorates, regular users take it less frequently and the majority stop using it altogether. It should also be noted that long-term neurotoxicity has not been entered into the above equation. Had it been, this hypothesised cost–benefit ratio would probably deteriorate even more rapidly over time (Chapter 6). Similar deteriorating ratios are apparent with other CNS stimulants, such as amphetamine and **cocaine**. Here, the cost–benefit ratio rapidly deteriorates as tolerance develops, usage escalates, cravings intensify and drug-induced socio-psychological problems increase. As the hippie poet Allen Ginsburg stated in 1960s San Francisco, "the hyper-alert paranoid stimulant abuser is not a pretty sight" (Chapter 5).

Recreational CNS depressants, such as alcohol and cannabis, show different cost–benefit ratios. Many light users of these relaxant drugs manage to maintain a fairly healthy ratio. Thus, the occasional light use of alcohol and/or cannabis is associated with comparatively minor deficits, such as acute cognitive impairment and impaired psychomotor performance. As far as their prosocial and relaxant effects are concerned, the overall cost–benefit ratios *of low doses* of these two drugs remain fairly neutral. (Note: this may be compared with the strongly positive cost–benefit ratio for non-drug users. Those who drink non-alcoholic beverages gain the positive advantages of social relaxation with their friends, but without untoward experiences, such as drowsiness and headache.) If alcohol and cannabis users always followed light and intermittent consumption patterns, then these two drugs would not be particularly problematic. But, unfortunately, the overall trend with all psychoactive drugs is for usage to intensify over time (Chapters 4–10; see below). Certainly, as the usage of these CNS depressants increases so their cost–benefit ratio also deteriorates.

One of the core factors underlying the increase in alcohol use over time is chronic tolerance (Chapter 10). As regular drinkers increase their intake, so the subjective effects become weaker, bingeing commences and intake increases yet further. Heavy drinkers continually recalculate their own personal cost–benefit ratios. They intend to "go on the wagon", but go out again on another binge, resulting in consequences that are as predictable as night following day. Heavy drinkers have miserable lives. The adverse effects of their drinking on other people's lives are so extensive that they are difficult to list. The deleterious effects on family, friends, work colleagues, driving-related deaths and injuries, the health service and criminal justice system are almost impossible to quantify (Chapters 9 and 10). Worldwide, hundreds of millions of lives are horribly blighted by alcohol, yet the alcohol industry increases its sales and the age of first drinking continues to fall. The number of people who will suffer from alcohol will increase further in the future. Government tax revenues may increase, but they will need to spend the money raised, on health, social services and the criminal justice system. In global terms, alcohol is one of the most damaging drugs known to humankind.

In comparison with alcohol the cost–benefit ratio for cannabis is somewhat better: that is the good news for regular cannabis users. The bad news is that the ratio is also very negative. Although tolerance is not an issue (as it is with alcohol), the on-drug effects become rather familiar as with all repetitive habitual behaviours. Furthermore, as drug usage increases over time, the negative cognitive and other psychobiological consequences increase (Chapter 7). The regular use of cannabis is also associated with an impoverished and monothematic lifestyle, its aficionados limited to enthusing over the comparative qualities of different supplies of cannabis. The reduction in meaningful daily activities can adversely impinge on family, social and occupational relationships. In comparison with excessive alcohol users, most cannabis users are not a great social problem, although some heavy users do experience increased rates of psychiatric distress, such as **paranoia** and other clinical disorders. This leads us nicely to the next topic of dosage.

Dosage

The cannabis smoked by President Clinton probably had a THC content of around 1–2% – presuming that he had obtained it from a reputable supplier. He stated that he did not inhale, but it would not have made too much difference if he had, since the psychoactive effects of this level of THC are not very strong. Research papers from the 1960s and early 1970s describe cannabis as a fairly innocuous drug. There are few descriptions of drug-induced paranoia, despite the millions of social users during that period. The reason was its psychoactive weakness. This situation changed in the 1970s when the sensemilla strain of cannabis was developed, with a THC content of around

7%. Further "improvements" in plant breeding and hydroponic culture techniques led to cannabis products with THC contents of 13% and over. Thus, the modern cannabis product can be extremely powerful, with just a few puffs inducing feelings of paranoia and/or subjective overdose in some users. The trend toward increasing dosage is a similar problem with alcohol. Beer and cider have traditionally been low-alcohol products, particularly the cheapest and most widely sold preparations. In Victorian times, weak beer with a low alcohol content was widely drunk by adults and children alike, since it was a far purer beverage than water from polluted sources. In modern times, the alcohol industry has moved more toward high-alcohol beverages, with fruit juices laced with vodka to attract even younger drinkers – the so-called "alco-pops". Dosage and increased purity has been a similar problem with the opiates. Raw **opium** is weaker than the morphine isolate, while heroin is three times stronger than **morphine** (Chapter 8).

A crucial element of the positive response to a recreational drug is learned or conditioned behaviour; this helps to explain why low-dosage preparations can often approach the efficacy of high-dose products in inducing the desired positive outcome. Hence, the efficacy of low-dose cannabis and low-alcohol products in fostering pleasant states of sociability. In Chapter 8 we also looked at "needle freaks" – opiate addicts who can become "high" just by going through the usual injection routine with an empty syringe. One positive trend might be a return to more low-dosage products. The subjective effects would not be markedly diminished, whereas the adverse after-effects would be considerably reduced. In overall terms it might be suggested that low-dose products probably display a far better cost–benefit ratio than equivalent high-dosage products. However, as with all the above notions of cost–benefit ratios, currently it is very much a hypothetical descriptive construct.

Addictive drugs and their legal status

Chapter 10 debated the numerous factors that influence the development of occasional drug use into the pathological spiral of addiction. The crucial role of the midbrain dopamine system was described, since it underlies the reinforcing effects of drugs. Biologically, the system subserves naturally motivated behaviours, such as eating, drinking and sex. But, it also provides the ideal substrate for secondarily learned appetitive behaviours, such as gambling, overeating, excessive jogging and sex addiction. Maladaptive eating patterns are characterised by excessive food intake, coupled with low feelings of pleasure or satisfaction. Similar unfulfilling patterns of repetitive behaviour typify sex addiction and gambling. Drug dependence is also characterised as a situation where a person likes the drug less and less, while craving it more and more. Aldous Huxley described this scenario in *The Doors of Perception* (1954): "Lung cancer, traffic accidents and the millions of miserable and misery-creating alcoholics are facts even more certain than was in Dante's day, the fact of the inferno. But all such facts are unsubstantial when compared with the near, felt act of craving, here and now, for release or sedation, for a drink or a smoke." Addiction results in health risks that have a huge economic burden, and the human costs are even greater. However, we learned in Chapter 10 that given the appropriate treatment and support it is possible to break the crippling behavioural cycle of addiction.

Another important topic is the legal status of recreational drugs, both addictive and non-addictive. It has been suggested that were alcohol newly discovered its adverse effects would be so clearly apparent that it would not be allowed to be marketed. However, this is a rather naive belief, since when drugs are first introduced the main focus is always on their immediate effects – which are invariably positive. It takes far longer for their adverse effects to be fully revealed. When cocaine was first introduced it was seen as a socially acceptable pick-me-up or tonic. The Pope even gave a gold medal to the originator of a particular cocaine cocktail that he liked, citing them as a benefactor for humanity (Chapter 4). Freud originally extolled the virtues of cocaine and introduced it to his friends, changing his mind when one of them died of cocaine addiction (Chapter 4). When amphetamine was first introduced it was seen as non-problematic, and it took years for its addictive properties to be scientifically acknowledged (Chapter 4). Benzodiazepines were first introduced in the early 1960s and were seen as non-addictive improvements over the barbiturates; it took two decades for their high addictive potential to be scientifically recognised (Chapter 9). So, if alcohol was introduced now, the focus would be on its short-term relaxant properties and would probably gain a licence. Only after 15 or 20 years would its problems become widely recognised. Even today, nicotine is still regarded by some as harmless and its adverse consequences are still not universally recognised (Chapter 5).

The rationale behind some recreational drugs being legal and others illegal is based on a series of historical accidents. Given current knowledge about their adverse health effects, nobody today would legally sanction alcohol or nicotine (except the alcohol and tobacco industry). However, this raises the question of whether psychoactive drug use should be considered within a legal context. Can it be demonstrated that an a priori criminal activity is being perpetuated, when someone smokes cannabis or self-injects opiates? It may be medically and/or psychobiologically inadvisable, but it is difficult to identify any inherent criminal aspects to these activites. Thus, a core issue is that there is no clear underlying rationale for identifying the personal use of any psychoactive drug as a "criminal" behaviour. Furthermore, there are few benefits to society by incarcerating a cannabis smoker or opiate injector in jail. Teenagers regard the selective targeting of particular drugs as an unjustifiable attack on their youth culture by elderly government health ministers smoking cigars and drinking whisky. Another issue is that, by considering recreational drug use primarily within the criminal agenda, the main focus is on social order. European governments are mainly concerned with two types of drug – opiates and crack cocaine – because of their strong link to crime; this deflects them from the need to focus on nicotine and alcohol. Finally, the above arguments do not apply to supplying illicit drugs, which should remain a criminal activity.

Addiction as a health issue

It may be better to conceptualise recreational drug use as an issue of personal well-being, given that their use impairs both physical and psychological health. That regular psychoactive drug use is medically and psychologically inadvisable has been very apparent in every chapter (Chapters 4–10). It is also the most disadvantaged individuals who are most at risk from developing drug-related problems. Furthermore, if drug use was seen primarily as a health issue by young people, it might make drug taking appear less attractive. Suppose nicotine and tobacco products like cigarettes were only available at pharmacies, how would it affect their attractiveness for 12 to 13-year-olds – the modal ages for commencement of smoking? The alcohol industry should also be far more aware of its health responsibilities. It should actively promote low and alcohol-free products, so that drinkers can benefit from the prosocial atmosphere without suffering the massive alcohol-related problems, as at present.

Marlatt has questioned whether the medical model is the most appropriate for addiction (Chapter 10). He proposes instead a far more psychological model. In some writings, the state of feeling addicted has been contrasted with the meditation and mindfulness of Eastern states. Marlatt asks dependent persons exactly what their "craving" means and what will happen if they do not give in to it. Addicts come to recognise that nothing much will happen, except that the craving will subside. Coming from West Coast America, Marlatt talks of riding the urge like surfers riding waves on their surfboards. He describes this process as learning to "urge-surf". The core emphasis is on dependency as a psychological concept, rather than as an inescapable biological state. Smokers and drinkers who are attempting to quit can thus learn to cope with their urges. They need to see them as temporary and transitory states that will soon pass. Furthermore, the longer the period of abstention the weaker the urges become, until eventually they no longer appear. This process generally takes only a few weeks or months (Chapter 5). But what happens if one does relapse? The medical model states that a relapse confirms the person as an addict, doomed to the wheel of addiction for ever. In contrast, Marlatt notes that a relapse is just a brief and transitory phenomenon and that one can learn from it to reduce the probability of relapsing again.

Most approaches to addiction offered by health services are based firmly within the medical tradition. They typically take the approach that addiction is too difficult to cure and that the only realistic option is to offer harm reduction (e.g., needle exchange schemes for opiate users). However, if addiction is seen as a psychological state, then a far more positive outcome should be possible. Clinical and health psychologists should offer a far more ambitious and proactive approach to addictive behaviours. They have all the skills necessary for genuine treatment of drug dependency. Although this may be difficult the potential successes would certainly make the approach worthwhile. Finally, it should be noted that the recreational use of illicit drugs is very much a minority activity. While a number of young people try illicit drugs at parties and other social occasions the overwhelming majority do not graduate to regular usage. Comparatively few people are regular cannabis smokers (Chapter 7). In the UK there is a sea of difference between those who have tried MDMA on a few occasions and heavy or regular users (Chapter 6).

Pharmacotherapy: drugs with clinical and medical uses

The 1950s represented a golden age for pharmacotherapy. The first antipsychotic drug, **chlorpromazine**, was developed in the first few years of that decade (Chapter 11), the first effective **antidepressants** were developed around 1957 (Chapter 12) and the first **benzodiazepine** anxiolytics were introduced in 1960 (Chapter 9). Cade reported the anti-manic properties of lithium in Australia in 1949, although it took several years for its clinical efficacy to be demonstrated and accepted (Chapter 12). Until this period, every city had one or more long-stay mental hospitals on its outskirts. The majority of occupants were long-stay schizophrenics, who had been diagnosed in early adulthood and were still incarcerated 30 or 40 years later. Many of the others suffered from unipolar or bipolar depression. The clinical outcome was poor for the patients, while the staff who spent their lives caring for the inmates saw few rewards for their years of dedication.

This situation changed dramatically with the advent of chlorpromazine. Many patients experienced a dramatic reduction in their symptoms of **schizophrenia**. Back in the community, they held down steady positions of employment and lived full and active lives. Others were less fortunate, since although the antipsychotic drug provided some relief of many symptoms, they remained socially impaired. Only a small minority experienced no symptomatic improvements. Since the mid-1950s most of these long-stay hospitals have closed and the clinical outlook for people diagnosed as "schizophrenic" has improved dramatically; this is particularly the case in those countries with a well-funded health service, such as Finland, where teams of psychiatrists, psychologists, outreach workers and psychiatric nurses work with schizophrenic patients and their carers/families to provide a fully integrated support service. The situation is similar for the treatment of affective disorders. Since the late 1950s a range of effective medications have been developed, so that now the clinician has a range of pharmacotherapeutic options. Furthermore, second and third-generation anti-depressants have proved significant advances, due to fewer side effects and higher rates of compliance (Chapter 12). Similar advances have been made in antipsychotics, although the degree of improvement is possibly less dramatic.

Drug plus psychological therapy: the optimal therapeutic package

As noted in Chapters 11 and 12 the use of drugs alone is not the optimal treatment. The best clinical outcome is generally observed when an effective medication is combined with a good psychological therapy. Social skills training, cognitive behavioural therapies and various other psychotherapeutic programmes have all been used as part of an overall package. There is a clear theoretical rationale for this general pattern: first, the drug relieves the underlying biological problem; and, second, this then allows the psychological therapy to be handled appropriately. Thus, psychological intervention can now help to foster the development of better cognitive beliefs, attitudes and expectancies. It also allows the (re)learning of crucially important psychosocial skills. Drugs alone generally only relieve the core symptoms, while therapy alone can be highly stressful and may be counterproductive, especially in those who are susceptible to stress (Chapter 11). This model helps to explain why therapeutic drug and psychological intervention are both needed in order to achieve the optimal outcome of complete social integration.

This same pattern will probably occur with **Alzheimer's disease** (Chapter 13); this is a very disabling disorder, characterised by the degeneration of the cholinergic system and many other psychoneurological deficits. Despite the fact that most clinicians accept that Alzheimer's disease has a multiple aetiology, most drug treatments target the cholinergic system alone. However, many newer types of drug with broader neurochemical targets are also being developed. Some of these cognition enhancers are from rather esoteric sources. Currently, the clinical outcome is very poor. However, the development of more effective anti-dementia agents is seen as a key topic for pharmaceutical company research. Although, once effective drugs have been developed, they will need to be supplemented by additional social and psychological support in order to achieve the optimal clinical outcome.

Optimal brain functioning

The final chapter developed the theme of **cognitive enhancement**, by examining the intriguing possibility that enhancement may be possible even in healthy young adults. Many of these studies have been performed on university undergraduates, who might be considered to represent the peak of human intellectual functioning. The finding that cognitive performance can sometimes be boosted is very interesting, since it challenges received wisdom that the human brain has evolved to function optimally. It should also be noted that many of these advances are produced by products that target energy supply mechanisms. Thus, a core conclusion of Chapter 14 was the importance of maximising basic cell metabolism processes in order to optimise neuronal activity, a good supply of food/energy and oxygen being of crucial importance. Several herbal products were also identified as having potential neurocognitive benefits. There is also confirmation of the old wives tale that "eating fish makes you brainy", with recent indications that omega-3 (present in cod liver oil) may help to enhance neurocognitive functioning. There was a recurring suggestion in Chapter 14 that activities traditionally identified as healthy may indeed have cognitive enhancing effects. So, perhaps the optimal psychobiological state can be achieved without any psychoactive drugs. Fresh air, regular physical exercise and some nicely grilled fish with freshly chopped parsley and sage may well help to maintain brain functioning at its peak.

Questions.

You may benefit from additional reading and research, in order to answer these questions:

1   Develop a cost–benefit ratio for two named recreational drugs.

2   Compare the cost–benefit ratios for regular drinkers of medium-strength beer, high-alcohol spirits and low-alcohol beverages.

3   Describe how individual difference factors might affect a hypothetical cost–benefit ratio for cannabis, nicotine or Ecstasy/MDMA.

4   Debate whether recreational drug use should be considered as a legal issue or as a health and well-being issue.

5   Compare the use of pharmacotherapy alone, psychological therapy alone, and both therapies together, in the treatment of either schizophrenia or major depression.

6   Describe how you might optimise CNS activity.

Glossary

Abuse   The use of a drug outside sociocultural and medical/clinical norms. The term misuse is tending to replace abuse because it is considered less judgemental.

Acamprosate   A drug that reduces the craving for alcohol after withdrawal and, therefore, of potential benefit in relapse prevention.

Acetylcholine (ACh)   The first neurotransmitter to be discovered. It is located at numerous synapses and neuroeffector junctions, in both the central and peripheral nervous systems.

Acetylcholinesterase   The catabolic enzyme that rapidly terminates the physiological action of acetylcholine at synapses and neuroeffector junctions.

Acquired Immunodeficiency Syndrome (AIDS)   A clinical syndrome due to infection with the RNA human immunodeficiency (retro)virus (HIV) which produces severe immunosuppression (depletion of natural killer T cells), thereby exposing the individual to a variety of opportunistic infections and cancers.

Action potential, or nerve impulse   The wave of electrical activity that passes from the dendrites of the neuronal cell body, down the axon to the synaptic bouton.

Adenosine triphosphate (ATP)   The principal chemical energy source for cellular processes. It is largely produced during aerobic metabolism. In the neuron most ATP is used in the maintenance of the electrochemical gradient required to generate an action potential.

Adenyl cyclase   The enzyme (also known as adenylate, or adenylyl cyclase) that catalyses the formation of the second messenger cyclic adenosine-3′,5′-monophosphate (cAMP) from ATP following the activation of a G_s protein-coupled receptor.

Adipose tissue   Fat tissue making up about 10% of the adult body weight but with a different distribution between males and females; it consists of clusters of adipocytes which synthesise and store lipids (fats).

Adrenal gland   A triangle-shaped organ positioned at the top of the kidney which functions as a "double endocrine gland". The larger outer adrenal cortex secretes three classes of steroid hormones: glucocorticoids (e.g., cortisol), minerlocorticoids (aldosterone) and small amounts of sex steroids (e.g., testosterone). The inner adrenal medulla secretes catecholamines (e.g., adrenaline and noradrenaline).

Adrenaline   A catecholamine hormone and neurotransmitter (also known as epinephrine).

Adrenoreceptors   Receptors (also called adrenergic) for noradrenaline and adrenaline classified into two broad categories: α and β, each comprising a number of subtypes including α_1, α_2, β_1 and β_2.

Affective disorders   A group of psychoses characterised by a pathological and long-lasting disturbance of mood or affect. They include the unipolar disorders (e.g., depression and mania), and bipolar disorders (e.g., manic depression).

Agonist   A drug that binds to a receptor and pharmacologically mimics the physiological effects of the endogenous neurotransmitter.

Agranulocytosis   A severe form of neutropenia where the number of neutrophils (the major type of leucocyte or white blood cell) is very low, so reducing an individual's ability to fight infection. It is a potentially serious side effect of the atypical antipsychotic clozapine.

Akathisia   The motor restlessness often noted as a side effect of long-term administration of typical antipsychotic drugs.

Albumin   The most abundant of the plasma proteins to which a number of different drugs bind.

Alcohol   The family name of a group of structurally related organic chemicals. It is also applied specifically to one member of that family – ethanol, or ethyl alcohol – the psychoactive ingredient of alcoholic drinks.

Alzheimer's disease   A progressive neurodegenerative disorder and the most common type of senile dementia. It is characterised by a marked decline in cognitive functioning and severe behavioural disturbances.

Amine   Molecules containing the atom nitrogen (N) and classified according to the nature of their functional group into: monoamines ($-NH_2$, e.g., dopamine); secondary amines ($-NHR$, e.g., adrenaline); tertiary amines ($-NR_2$, e.g., imipramine); and quaternary amines ($-N^+R_3$, e.g., acetylcholine) (where R is a methyl group).

Amino acid   There are 20 different amino acids that provide the building blocks of proteins. Three of them – aspartate, glutamate and glycine (together with GABA, or γ-aminobutyric acid) – also function as neurotransmitters.

Amitriptyline   A non-selective tricyclic antidepressant.

Amphetamine   The family name for a group of CNS stimulants, which is also applied specifically to one of them. Amphetamine exists in two forms or isomers, with d-amphetamine (dexamphetamine) being the more potent.

Amygdala   A structure of the limbic system.

Amyloid protein A 42-amino acid protein found in the core of the microscopic senile plaques in the brains of individuals with Alzheimer's disease. β-amyloid protein is synthesised from the much larger amyloid precursor protein (APP).

Anabolism The biosynthesis of complex molecules (chemicals) from simpler ones (e.g., glycogen from glucose in the liver).

Analgesic A drug that relieves pain by raising the pain threshold. In the case of the opiates or narcotic analgesics, it also produced a feeling of well-being and tranquillity.

Analogues Chemicals with similar molecular structures (e.g., adrenaline differs from noradrenaline by the addition of one methyl group to the N atom).

Anandamide One of the endogenous ligands, or endocannabinoids, which is active at cannabinoid receptors.

Anorectic A drug that reduces appetite and, thus, is sometimes used in the treatment of obesity. Many are amphetamines or amphetamine-like drugs (e.g., fenfluramine).

Anoxia Deficiency of oxygen.

Antagonist A drug that binds to the receptor to block the access of the neurotransmitter. The pharmacological action of the antagonist, will be the opposite to that of the neurotransmitter or agonist.

Anterior cingulate An area of the forebrain rich in cholinergic neurons.

Anti-inflammatory Drugs that reduce inflammation, including the non-steroidal anti-inflammatory drugs (NSAIDs) aspirin, ibuprofen and indomethacin and the glucocorticoids (e.g., dexamethasone and cortisol).

Anticholinergic Drugs that block acetylcholine receptors, although the term is used specifically for antagonists at muscarinic acetylcholine receptors (antimuscarinics), like atropine and scopolamine.

Anticholinesterase A drug that inhibits the enzyme acetylcholinesterase, which normally inactivates acetylcholine at the synapse. The effect of an anticholinesterase (or cholinesterase inhibitor) is thus to prolong the duration of action of the neurotransmitter. An example is rivastigmine, used in the treatment of Alzheimer's disease.

Anticonvulsant A drug used in the treatment of epilepsy, and to reduce the risk of seizures during detoxification from sedative-hypnotics. More recently these drugs have been used in the clinical management of bipolar disorders.

Antidepressant A drug used principally to treat major depressive disorder (unipolar depression).

Antioxidants Reducing agents, such as vitamins C (ascorbic acid) and E (α-tocopherol), which "scavenge" toxic free radicals generated by oxidative reactions in the cell.

Antipsychotic, or neuroleptic drug Used in the treatment of schizophrenia. They are also used in the management of psychotic episodes associated with psychotropic drug toxicity and some neurodegenerative disorders.

Anxiolytic The most commonly prescribed type of psychotropic drug, used chiefly to treat generalised anxiety disorders.

Apolipoprotein E (ApoE) A protein involved in cholesterol transport that has three major isoforms, one of which, $ApoE_4$, significantly increases the risk of developing Alzheimer's disease.

Apomorphine A D_2-like receptor agonist.

2-Arachidonylglycerol (2-AG) An endocannabinoid, like anandamide.

Ascending Reticular Activating System (ARAS) A network of neurons running up (ascending) through the core of the brainstem to the diencephalon and descending to the spinal cord. Also known as the reticular formation.

Aspartate An excitatory amino acid neurotransmitter.

Astrocyte A large multifunctional glial cell.

Atropine *See* **Anticholinergic**.

Attention Deficit Hyperactivity Disorder (ADHD) A learning and behavioural disorder characterised by reduced attention span and hyperactivity. ADHD is a diagnosis applied to young children and is typically treated with the amphetamine derivative methylphenidate (Ritalin).

Axon A single slender extension of the neuron's cell body that ranges in length from <1 mm in the brain to 1 m in the voluntary nervous system.

Barbiturate The family name for a group of drugs with anticonvulsant, anaesthetic and sedative–hypnotic properties. Examples include amylobarbitone and phenobarbitone. The problem of dependence and the introduction of safer benzodiazepine alternatives has resulted in a marked reduction in their clinical use.

Basal ganglia A group of networked structures in the brain which control voluntary movement. Two basal ganglia disorders are Huntington's disease and Parkinson's disease.

Benzodiazepine The family name for a group of drugs with anticonvulsant, muscle relaxant and sedative–hypnotic properties. Examples include chlorodiazepoxide (Librium), diazepam (Valium), flunitrazepam and temazepam. These drugs have largely superseded the barbiturates.

Bioavailability The proportion of the administered drug that enters the systemic circulation and, therefore, is distributed to its target. A drug given by the intravenous route has a maximum bioavailability of 1 (or 100%).

Biosynthesis *See also* **Anabolism** Biosynthesis is also used to describe the conversion of inactive (precursor) molecules into physiologically active ones as in the biosynthesis of a neurotransmitter.

Bipolar disorder A group of affective disorders characterised by alternating periods of pathologically elevated moods, followed by severely reduced moods. Previously known as manic depression, or manic depressive psychosis.

Blood–brain barrier A physicochemical barrier formed by astrocytes and capillary endothelial cells. It prevents toxic chemicals from entering CNS neurons from the systemic blood circulation.

Bupropion A drug that inhibits the presynaptic neuronal reuptake of both dopamine and noradrenaline which is used as an antidepressant and to prevent relapse following smoking cessation.

Butyrophenones A family of typical antipsychotic drugs (neuroleptics), the most commonly used being haloperidol.

Caffeine The psychostimulant found in coffee, tea and a wide variety of carbonated soft drinks. Chemically related to the purine neurotransmitter adenosine, the drug blocks adenosine receptors in the nervous system.

Caffeinism A dependence on caffeine characterised by an abstinence syndrome on withdrawal.

Cannabinoids Chemicals synthesised from precursor terpenes in *Cannabis sativa* including cannabidiol, cannibinol and THC.

Cannabis The name for the genus of plant (e.g., *Cannabis sativa*), from which the drug of that name is extracted.

Carbamazepine A mood-stabilising and antiepileptic drug.

Carbidopa An inhibitor of aromatic L-amino acid decarboxylase used with L-dopa in the treatment of Parkinson's disease.

Carbon monoxide A poisonous gas found in tobacco smoke and a causative factor in the cardiovascular damage arising through smoking. Carbon monoxide has also been found to function as a gaseous neuromodulator in the brain.

Catabolism The breakdown of complex molecules to simpler ones to yield energy (e.g., triacylglycerols to fatty acids) and the inactivation of physiologically active molecules (e.g., acetylcholine to choline and acetic acid).

Catalepsy A severe difficulty in initiating voluntary movement (rigidity).

Catechol-O-methyltransferase (COMT) An enzyme that inactivates dopamine and noradrenaline.

Cathinone An amphetamine derivative found in khat extracted from *Catha edulis* growing in the Horn of Africa, where it is widely used as a recreational stimulant.

Caudate nucleus One of the forebrain basal ganglia.

Cerebellum A large structure in the hindbrain that co-ordinates smooth voluntary movement, posture and balance.

Cerebral cortex Together with the two underlying cerebral hemispheres is the largest part of the brain.

Cerebrospinal fluid (CSF) A plasma ultrafiltrate (volume = 125 mL) that circulates through the central nervous system.

Chemoreceptor A sensory receptor responding to a chemical stimulus (e.g., smell or taste) or change in the concentration of a chemical (e.g., H^+ ions in the blood or pH).

Chloral hydrate A sedative–hypnotic drug.

Chlorpromazine The first successful antipsychotic drug, chemically a phenothiazine.

Cholecystokinin A gut–brain neuropeptide.

Cholinergic receptors Receptors for acetylcholine are classified into muscarinic (muscarine is a selective agonist) and nicotinic (nicotine is a selective agonist). There are five muscarinic (m_1 to m_5) and two nicotinic (neuronal, or ganglionic, and skeletal muscular) subtypes.

Cholinesterase inhibitor   *See* **Anticholinesterase**.

Chromosome   A subnuclear structure comprising DNA and associated proteins. Apart from the sex cells, each human cell has 23 pairs of chromosomes comprising 22 autosomes and a pair of sex chromosomes (XX in females, XY in males).

Cirrhosis   A liver disease commonly associated with chronic alcohol misuse and characterised by the replacement of once-healthy hepatocytes with abnormal connective tissue.

Clomipramine   A tricyclic antidepressant that selectively inhibits serotonin reuptake into the presynaptic neuron.

Clorgyline   An irreversible MAO-A inhibitor.

Clozapine   The first atypical antipsychotic drug.

Cocaine   A potent psychostimulant with local anaesthetic properties extracted from the South American plant *Erythroxylon coca*.

Codeine   An opiate analgesic.

Cognitive enhancer   *See* **Nootropic**.

Corpus callosum   A bridge of nerve fibres between the two cerebral hemispheres.

Corpus striatum   A forebrain basal ganglion comprising the caudate nucleus and putamen.

Cortisol   The major glucocorticoid of the adrenal cortex.

Cot death   *See* **SIDS**

Cotinine   The main metabolite of nicotine.

Crack cocaine   A concentrated form of the drug (free base) formed by heating cocaine hydrochloride (the salt) with sodium bicarbonate: Cocaine $HCl + NaHCO_3 \rightarrow$ Cocaine $+ NaCl + H_2O + CO_2$.

Cross-tolerance   A condition where an individual who is tolerant to the pharmacological effects of one member of a drug family also shows tolerance to other members of that family. Cross-dependence allows drug substitution during detoxification (e.g., methadone for heroin or clomethiazole for ethanol), so reducing the severity and potential danger of withdrawal symptoms.

CYP2D6   The principal isoenzyme (isoform) of cytochrome P-450 involved in the metabolism of psychotropic drugs.

Cyclic AMP   Stimulation or inhibition of the biosynthesis of the second messenger cyclic adenosine-3',5'-monophosphate occurs through the activation of G_s or G_i protein-coupled neurotransmitter receptors, respectively.

Cytochrome P-450   A superfamily of isoenzymes principally involved in hepatic drug metabolism.

D-amphetamine   The more potent of the two enantiomers of the psychostimulant amphetamine.

D-cycloserine   An amino acid analogue of D-serine that has been reported to show benefits in treating the negative symptoms of schizophrenia.

D-glucose   The major energy source for the neuron.

Delirium tremens   The most severe sign of alcohol withdrawal characterised by hallucinations and paranoia ("delirium"), marked tremor and convulsions ("tremens").

Dendrite   Abundant, short, thread-like extensions of the neuronal cell body.

Deoxyribose nucleic acid (DNA)   Comprises a backbone with four nucleotide bases, adenine, cytosine, guanine and thymine, bound to it. The genetic information in all cells is encoded in this genome of double-stranded DNA, comprising 3 billion base pairs located in the chromosomes.

Dependence   A state of mind or body where the individual cannot function normally without the presence of a particular drug. Although perpetuating mind–body dualism, the terms "psychological" and "physical" dependence are still widely used.

Depot injection   A long-acting formulation of an antipsychotic drug given by occasional (often monthly) intramuscular injection.

Desipramine   An active metabolite of imipramine that is more selective for inhibiting noradrenaline reuptake into the presynaptic neuron.

Detoxification   Medically supervised withdrawal from a drug to which an individual has become dependent.

Dexamethasone Suppression Test   A neuroendocrine assessment of hypothalamic noradrenergic neuronal activity used in depression.

Diacetylmorphine   *See* **Heroin.**

Diamorphine   *See* **Heroin.**

Diathesis stress model   A multifactorial model of pathogenesis suggesting that schizophrenia is due to the complex interaction between a number of internal and external factors.

Diencephalon   The "between" brain connecting the midbrain and forebrain which comprises the thalamus and hypothalamus.

Dimethoxymethylamphetamine (DOM)   A hallucinogenic catecholamine derivative.

Dimethyltryptamine (DMT)   A hallucinogenic indolylamine (indoleamine) structurally related to serotonin.

Disulfiram   An inhibitor of hepatic aldehyde dehydrogenase that converts acetaldehyde (a metabolite of alcohol) into acetic acid. It is used to prevent relapse following alcohol detoxification.

Dizygotic   A non-identical or fraternal twin.

Donepezil   An anticholinesterase used in Alzheimer's disease.

Dopamine   A catecholamine neurotransmitter, involved in mesolimbic reward and other important neural pathways.

Down's syndrome   A congenital learning disorder arising from a chromosomal abnormality (trisomy 21 – an extra chromosome 21).

Drug   Any biologically active chemical that does not occur naturally in the human body. Drugs can be used to prevent and treat disease, alter mood and cognition or otherwise change behaviour. Drugs are classified into families according to their chemical structure and/or pharmacological effect. They are most commonly referred to by their generic name (e.g., fluoxetine, amphetamine), pharmaceutical company brand name (e.g., Prozac) or recreational street name (e.g., speed).

DSM-IV   The fourth edition of the American Psychiatric Association's *Diagnostic and Statistical Manual of Mental Disorders* which along with the tenth edition of the World Health Organisation's *International Classification of Diseases* (ICD-10) are widely used for psychiatric evaluation, especially in clinical pharmacology.

Dysphoria   A depressed mood.

Dystonia   Abnormal body tone.

D_2-like receptor   Dopamine receptors are classified into the D_1-like G_s (D_1 and D_5 subtypes) and D_2-like G_i (D_2, D_3 and D_4 subtypes) coupled protein receptors.

Ecstasy (MDMA)   The common street name for the amphetamine derivative 3,4-methylenenedioxymethamphetamine.

Electroconvulsive therapy   A physical therapy used in the treatment of a major depressive disorder that does not respond to pharmacotherapy.

Enantiomer   A molecule with a chiral centre (asymmetric carbon atom) existing as two isomers designated D and L that may have different physiological or pharmacological activities.

Endorphin   An endogenous opiate neuropeptide (**end**ogenous **morphin**e).

Enzyme   A protein that catalyses or accelerates the conversion of one chemical (the substrate) to another (the product).

Ephedrine   An amphetamine-like drug used as a nasal decongestant.

Epilepsy   A group of neurological disorders characterised by abnormal electrical activity of brain neurons (seizures).

Euphoria   An elevated mood.

Extrapyramidal side effects   These are caused by antipsychotic drugs. They are characterised by motor and postural disturbances, of which the most serious is late-onset tardive dyskinesia.

Fenfluramine   An amphetamine-like drug that stimulates the release of serotonin from neurons.

Fetal alcohol syndrome   A congenital disorder arising from excessive (>50 g per day) alcohol intake during pregnancy.

First-pass effect (metabolism)   The metabolism of a drug when it first passes through the liver. This is one of the major determinants of bioavailability for orally administered drugs.

Fluoxetine   The first clinically available selective serotonin reuptake inhibitor (SSRI).

Fluphenazine   A phenothiazine neuroleptic that is often formulated as a long-acting decanoate.

Folate   A member of the B vitamin group, a deficiency of which may be related to the development of Alzheimer's disease.

Free radical   Highly reactive species (atoms or molecules with an unpaired electron) which can damage cells in a variety of ways. Oxygen containing hydroxyl and superoxide free radicals (ROS) is implicated in a number of neurodegenerative disorders.

G-protein   A protein coupled to a metabotropic receptor; for example, when noradrenaline binds to a β receptor it activates a G_s protein which then activates adenyl cyclase.

GABA (γ-aminobutyric acid)   The major inhibitory amino acid neurotransmitter of the CNS.

$GABA_A$ receptor   An ion channel (ionotropic) receptor for GABA. The $GABA_B$ receptor is a G_i protein-coupled receptor.

Galantamine   An anticholinesterase used in Alzheimer's disease.

Gene   A length of DNA coding for a protein. Nuclear DNA is now thought to comprise some 32,000 genes.

Genotype   The genetic make-up or composition of an individual.

Glaucoma   A major cause of blindness in people over 40 years of age for which cannabinoids may be of benefit.

Globus pallidus   A forebrain basal ganglion.

Glutamate   An excitatory amino acid neurotransmitter.

Glycine   An inhibitory amino acid neurotransmitter.

Hallucinogen   A drug that disturbs sensory perception. Visual hallucinations are the most common effect of the psychedelic drug LSD. In contrast, auditory hallucinations predominate in schizophrenia.

Haloperidol   *See* **Butyrophenones**.

Heroin, or diamorphine   A commonly misused opiate.

Hippocampus   A structure of the limbic system.

Histamine   A monoamine neurotransmitter.

Hydergine$^{\circledR}$ A mixture of the three dihydro-derivatives of the alkaloids in ergotoxine. It is used as a cerebral vasodilator and reported to have nootropic effects.

Hydrocortisone   *See* **Cortisol**.

Hypericum   An extract of *Hypericum perforatum* (St John's wort) used in the phytotherapy of depression.

Hypertension   A blood pressure above the systolic value of 120 mm (of mercury) and diastolic value of 80 mm.

Hyperthermia   An increase in body core temperature, as caused by MDMA, for instance.

Hypoglycaemia   A lower-than-normal blood glucose concentration.

Hyponatraemia   A lower-than-normal blood Na^+ concentration.

Hypothalamic–Pituitary–Adrenal (HPA) axis   An integrated neuroendocrine system linking the hypothalamus (noradrenaline and corticotropin-releasing factor CRF) with the anterior pituitary (corticotropin or ACTH) and the adrenal cortex (cortisol).

Hypothalamus   *See* **Diencephalon**.

Hypoxia   Decreased oxygen levels.

ICD-10   *See* **DSM-IV**.

Imipramine   A non-selective tricyclic antidepressant drug.

Indomethacin   A non-steroidal anti-inflammatory drug.

Interneuron   A neuron positioned between two neurons in the CNS or one localised to a particular brain region.

Ion   A charged particle formed when an atom gains (chloride Cl^-) or loses (sodium Na^+) one or more electrons. Ions carry the electrical current of the action potential.

Ion channel   A pore located in the centre of a voltage-operated or receptor-operated ion channel protein which, when opened by a change in membrane potential or the binding of a neurotransmitter, allows ions to enter or leave the cell.

Iproniazid   *See* **MAO inhibitor**.

Ischaemia   Reduced blood flow to a tissue.

Isoenzymes   Structurally related enzyme proteins that catalyse very similar or identical reactions (e.g., monoamine oxidase A and B, cytochrome P-450).

Isoreceptors   Different receptor proteins that recognise and bind the same neurotransmitter (e.g., muscarinic and nicotinic cholinergic receptors).

Ketamine   A dissociative anaesthetic related to phencyclidine.

Khat (Qat)   The Horn of Africa plant *Catha edulis* containing the amphetamine-like drugs, cathine and cathinone (norpseudoephedrine).

Korsakoff's syndrome   A dementia commonly associated with chronic alcohol misuse.

L-acetylcarnitine   A potential nootropic drug.

L-dopa   An amino acid precursor of dopamine used in the treatment of Parkinson's disease.

L-tryptophan   An amino acid precursor of serotonin, once used as an antidepressant.

Lamotrigine   A mood-stabilising and antiepileptic drug.

Laudanum   The alcoholic tincture of opium.

Lignocaine (lidocaine)   A local anaesthetic and voltage-operated Na^+ channel blocker.

Limbic system   A network of brain structures involved in the regulation of a number of behavioural functions.

Lithium   The first drug to be used in the treatment of unipolar mania and bipolar disorder.

Locus coeruleus   A collection of noradrenergic neuronal cell bodies located in the pons, from which the axons project to a number of forebrain structures.

Lofexidine   An α_2-adrenoceptor agonist used during drug detoxification.

Lysergic acid diethylamide (LSD)   A potent indolylamine with psychedelic, or hallucinogenic, properties.

MAO (monoamine oxidase) inhibitor   Non-selective inhibitors of the enzyme monoamine oxidase. An example is iproniazid, one of the first-generation antidepressants. Moclobemide, a selective MAO-A inhibitor, is less toxic and thus more clinically useful.

MDMA   *See* **Ecstasy**.

Mechanoreceptor   A sensory receptor responding to mechanical stimuli, such as touch and air pressure.

Median forebrain bundle   A bundle of monoaminergic neuronal axons travelling from the brainstem through the diencephalon to various limbic structures.

Medulla oblongata   Part of the brainstem.

Memantine   A new drug for Alzheimer's disease, acting at the glutamate NMDA receptor.

Meninges   Three layers of protective membranes surrounding the brain.

Mescaline   A catecholamine hallucinogen, obtained from the peyote cactus (*Lophophora williamsii*).

Mesencephalon   The midbrain.

Metabolism   The sum of anabolism and catabolism, although also used to describe the biotransformation of drugs in the liver.

Metabotropic receptor   A G protein-coupled neurotransmitter receptor.

Metencenphalon   Part of the hindbrain.

Methadone   A synthetic opiate used in the maintenance therapy of former heroin and morphine dependents.

Methylenedioxyamphetamine (MDA)   A hallucinogenic catecholamine derivative.

Methylphenidate   An amphetamine-like psychostimulant used to treat ADHD.

Mianserin   An α_2-adrenoceptor antagonist used as an antidepressant.

Mirtazepine   An α_2-adrenoceptor antagonist used as an antidepressant.

Moclobemide   *See* **MAO inhibitor**.

Monosynaptic reflex   A reflex arc (pathway) with a single synapse.

Monozygotic   An identical twin.

Morphine   A naturally occurring opiate, found in the dried sap or opium of *Papaver somniferum*.

Multiple sclerosis   A disease characterised by the progressive demyelination of CNS neurons and the loss of oligodendrocytes. Cannabinoids may be of benefit in treating MS.

Muscle-relaxant   A drug that relaxes skeletal (voluntary) muscle either directly by blocking nicotinic cholinergic receptors or indirectly through the activation of inhibitory spinal cord interneurons.

Myelin   A segmented laminated lipoprotein sheath formed by glial cells (oligodendrocytes and Schwann cells). It is wrapped round the axon and acts as a biological insulating material.

Myelencephalon   Part of the hindbrain.

N-methyl-D-aspartate (NMDA) An amino acid agonist at the glutamate NMDA receptor.

Naloxone An opiate or narcotic antagonist.

Narcolepsy A rare disorder of unknown aetiology, characterised by suddenly and uncontrollably falling asleep.

Neocortex The cerebral cortex overlying the cerebral hemispheres.

Neostigmine An anticholinesterase used to treat peripheral cholinergic disorders like glaucoma.

Neurodegeneration Localised or widespread death of neurons, a feature of a number of brain disorders, such as Alzheimer's disease, Parkinson's disease and cerebro-vascular stroke. It can also be caused by neurotoxic drugs like MDMA/Ecstasy, although there is debate over whether this occurs in humans as well as laboratory animals.

Neuroglia Non-neuronal "support" cells in the nervous system, such as astrocytes and oligodendrocytes.

Neuromodulator A neuropeptide that co-exists with an amine neurotransmitter in the synaptic bouton and has a modulatory (regulatory) effect on the release of the amine.

Neuron The electrically excitable cell of the nervous system.

Neuropeptide A family of neurotransmitters and neuromodulators comprised of unique sequences of amino acids.

Neuroprotection A prophylactic treatment designed to stop potential or further neurodegeneration.

Neurotensin A gut–brain neuropeptide.

Neurotransmitter A chemical stored in the synaptic bouton of the neuron that is involved in cell-to-cell signalling.

Neurotrophic factor A protein involved in the maintenance of neuronal viability.

Nicotine The psychoactive drug found in *Nicotiana tabacum* that underlies cigarette smoking and tobacco dependence.

Nigrostriatal tract The major dopaminergic neuronal pathway linking midbrain and forebrain basal ganglia.

Nimodipine A voltage-operated Ca^{2+} channel blocker with potential benefits in treating cognitive deficits and managing opiate and alcohol detoxification.

Nitric oxide (NO) A poisonous "greenhouse gas" that also serves as a neuromodulator in the central and peripheral nervous systems.

Nociceptor A pain receptor.

Node of Ranvier The small gap between adjacent segments (internodes) of the myelin sheath.

Nootropic A drug that enhances memory.

Noradrenaline A catecholamine neurotransmitter also known as norepinephrine.

Norepinephrine *See* **Noradrenaline**.

Nortriptyline   An active metabolite of amitriptyline.

Nucleus accumbens   A forebrain structure innervated by a branch of the mesolimbic dopaminergic tract, implicated in reward and motivation.

Nucleus basalis of Meynert   One of the forebrain structures where neurodegeneration occurs in Alzheimer's disease.

Occipital lobe   One of four, together with the frontal, parietal and temporal, lobes of the cerebral hemispheres.

Ondansetron   A 5-HT$_3$ receptor antagonist that may have a nootropic effect.

Opiate   A drug related to morphine, derived from opium.

Opioid peptide   A neuropeptide (e.g., β-endorphin), whose actions are mimicked by opiate drugs.

Opium   The extract from *Papaver somniferum* containing morphine and codeine.

Paranoia   A delusion of persecution or grandeur, one of the positive clinical symptoms of schizophrenia.

Parkinson's disease   A basal ganglia disorder characterised by neurodegeneration of the nigrostriatal dopaminergic nerve tract.

Paroxetine   A selective serotonin reuptake inhibitor.

Peripheral neuritis   Inflammation of peripheral nerves.

Pharmacodynamics   The study of drug–receptor interactions.

Pharmacogenetics   The study of the genetic determinants of drug metabolism.

Pharmacokinetics   The study of physiological and pathophysiological effects on drug handling in the body.

Phencyclidine   A dissociative anaesthetic that causes auditory hallucinations.

Phenmetrazine   A psychostimulant and anorectic drug.

Phenobarbitone   A barbiturate sedative–hypnotic used to treat epilepsy. It is a potent inducer (stimulator) of cytochrome P-450 activity.

Phenothiazines   A family of neuroleptics which includes chlorpromazine and fluphenazine.

Phenotype   The observable characteristics of an individual determined by the genotype.

Photoreceptor   A sensory receptor located in the retina of the eye.

Physostigmine   An anticholinesterase also known as eserine.

Phytotherapy   A branch of complementary medicine also known as herbal medicine.

Piracetam   A nootropic drug.

Placebo   A "dummy" pill identical in appearance to the "active" pill, except for the exclusion of the drug under investigation. The placebo helps to control for non-pharmacological effects that might influence the outcome of an investigation.

Pons   Part of the brainstem.

Postsynaptic receptor   A receptor located on the postsynaptic neuronal membrane mediating the physiological effects of the neurotransmitter.

Potency   A quantitative measure of the binding of a drug to its receptor, and therefore of its pharmacological effect.

Presynaptic receptor   A receptor, either an autoreceptor or heteroreceptor, located on the presynaptic neuronal membrane which regulates the release of the neurotransmitter.

Prolactin   A hormone released from the anterior pituitary.

Promethazine   A phenotheiazine antihistamine (H_1 receptor antagonist).

Protein kinase   An enzyme activated by second messengers like cyclic AMP (protein kinase A) and 1,2-diacylgycerol (protein kinase C).

Psilocybin   An indolylamine hallucinogen found in a number of mushrooms of the globally distributed genus *Psilocybe*.

Psychoactive   A drug that alters mood, cognition, and/or other aspects of behaviour.

Psychosis, or psychotic disorder   A major psychiatric illness including schizophrenia and the affective disorders.

Psychostimulant   A drug that causes increased alertness, excitement and decreased fatigue.

Psychotomimetic   *See* **Hallucinogen**.

Psychotropic   A drug that is administered to modify behaviour, *literally* mind-turning.

Putamen   A forebrain basal ganglion and part of the corpus striatum.

Raphe nuclei   Clusters of serotonin neurons in the midbrain and pons with a diffuse projection to the forebrain and spinal cord.

Reboxetine   An antidepressant that is a selective noradrenaline reuptake inhibitor.

Receptor   Broadly applied to the molecular site of drug action. More specifically, this term describes the plasma membrane proteins to which neurotransmitters, agonists and antagonists bind.

Relapse   This occurs when an individual returns to misusing a drug following a period of abstinence. Relapse prevention, or breaking this cycle of on–off drug misuse, is one the most problematic stages in rehabilitation.

Reserpine   A drug extracted from *Rauwolfia serpentina* which was once clinically used in the treatment of essential hypertension and schizophrenia.

Reticular formation   A dense neuronal network running through the core of the brainstem into the thalamus and involved in sleep and wakefulness (arousal).

Risperidone   An atypical antipsychotic drug.

Rivastigmine   An anticholinesterase used to treat Alzheimer's disease.

Schizophrenia   A term applied to one or more psychotic disorders characterised by a major disruption of thought processes.

Schizotypy   A generally milder variant of schizophrenia.

Scopolamine   A muscarinic cholinergic receptor antagonist that has amnesic side effects.

Sedative–hypnotic   A CNS depressant used to reduce anxiety (sedation) and promote sleep (hypnotic).

Selective serotonin reuptake inhibitor (SSRI) Currently, the most widely used antidepressants (e.g., fluoxetine and paroxetine).

Selegiline A selective MAO-B inhibitor, also called L-deprenyl, used in the treatment of Parkinson's disease.

Serotonin, or 5-hydroxytryptamine (5-HT) An indolylamine neurotransmitter.

Sertraline A selective serotonin reuptake inhibitor.

SIDS (sudden infant death syndrome) Commonly known as cot death.

Soma The cell body, or perikaryon, of the neuron.

Stroke A transient ischaemic attack or cerebrovascular accident due to occlusion (blockage) of blood vessels supplying an area of the brain. The subsequent nerve cell death may result in major disability.

Strychnine A potent CNS stimulant and convulsant.

Substance P A gut–brain peptide.

Substantia nigra A basal ganglion located in the midbrain.

Suprachiasmatic nucleus A hypothalamic nucleus involved in the maintenance of circadian (diurnal) rhythms.

Synaesthesia A mixing together of sensory modalities that is occasionally experienced during a hallucinogenic LSD "trip" (e.g., tasting colours).

Synapse The area where two neurons meet. It includes the presynaptic neuronal terminal plasma membrane of one neuron and the postsynaptic membrane of another neuron. More specifically, it refers to the space or gap between them, often called the synaptic cleft.

Tachycardia A heart rate over the typical resting value of $70\,min^{-1}$ (70 bpm).

Tacrine An anticholinesterase used in the treatment of Alzheimer's disease.

Tardive dyskinesia A collection of involuntary movements that are a side effect of long-term administration of typical antipsychotic drugs.

Telencephalon The forebrain.

Thalamus Part of the diencephalon.

THC (Δ^9-tetrahydrocannibinol) The major psychoactive drug from cannabis or marijuana.

Thermoreceptor A sensory receptor responding to changes in temperature.

Thiamine Vitamin B_1, a deficiency of which in alcoholics can lead to Wernicke–Korsakoff's syndrome.

Thioridazine A typical neuroleptic but with fewer side effects.

Thioxanthenes A family of typical neuroleptics including clopenthixol.

Tolerance Tolerance to a drug arises when increasingly higher doses of the drug have to be given to achieve the same pharmacological effect.

Transporter A protein molecule that actively moves neurotransmitters (e.g., dopamine) from the synaptic cleft into the cytoplasm of the presynaptic bouton.

Tranylcypromine An irreversible non-selective MAO inhibitor.

Tricyclic antidepressant A family of first-generation (typical) antidepressants with a three-ringed structure that inhibit the action of monoamine transporters.

Tuberohypophysial tract A dopaminergic nerve tract running from the hypothalamus to the anterior pituitary.

Unipolar disorder An affective disorder characterised by chronic dysphoria. The two contrasting forms of unipolar disorder are major depression and mania.

Valproate A mood stabiliser and antiepileptic drug.

Venlafaxine An atypical antidepressant that inhibits the reuptake of both serotonin and noradrenaline.

Ventral tegmental area (VTA) The location of the dopaminergic cells projecting to the nucleus accumbens.

Vinpocetine A potential nootropic durg.

Wernicke's encephalopathy A neurological condition characterised by visual disturbances, motor dysfunction and confusion which, like Korsakoff's syndrome, is commonly associated with long-term alcohol misuse.

Xanthinol nicotinate A nootropic drug.

Zimelidine A now-withdrawn selective serotonin reuptake inhibitor.

Key psychopharmacology and addiction journals

Addiction
Addictive Behaviors
Alcohol and Alcoholism
Alcoholism: Clinical and Experimental Research
American Journal of Drug and Alcohol Abuse
Drug and Alcohol Dependence
Drug and Alcohol Review
Experimental and Clinical Psychopharmacology
Human Psychopharmacology
International Clinical Psychopharmacology
International Journal of Geriatric Psychopharmacology
International Pharmacopsychiatry
Journal of Clinical Psychopharmacology
Journal of Psychoactive Drugs
Journal of Psychopharmacology
Journal of Studies on Alcohol
Journal of Substance Abuse Treatment
Neuropsychobiology
Neuropsychopharmacology
Nicotine and Tobacco Research
Pharmacological Reviews
Pharmacology, Biochemistry and Behavior
Psychology of Addictive Behaviours
Psychopharmacology
Trends in Pharmacological Science
World Journal of Biological Psychiatry

Internet sources of information about psychoactive drugs

General drugs information, cognitive neuroscience, and biological psychology

Neurosciences on the internet
www.neuroguide.com

The Whole Brain Atlas from Harvard Medical School
www.med.harvard.edu/AANLIB/home.html

The famous neuroscience education page of Dr Eric Chudler
http://faculty.washington.edu/chudler/ehceduc.html

The Dana site for brain information
www.dana.org

Information from the United Nations about drugs and crime
www.undcp.org

Recreational drug use sites

Recreation Drugs Information Site
www.a1b2c3.com/drugs/

The Drugs Forum
www.drugs-forum.com/

The Vaults of Erowid
www.erowid.com

UK national statistics on smoking, drinking and drug use
www.doh.gov.uk/public/statspntables.htm

News about drug use

The Daily Dose of Drug and Alcohol News
www.dailydose.net

A similar site aimed at professionals and the public
www.substancemisuse.net

Alcohol and alcoholism

The US National Institute for Alcoholism and Alcohol Abuse information pages
www.etoh.niaaa.nih.gov/
www.niaaa.nih.gov/

Alcohol Concern
www.alcoholconcern.org.uk/

A good general health resource site
www.omni.ac.uk/

Tobacco smoking

Smoking from All Sides
www.smokingsides.com/

Cannabis smoking

The International Association for Cannabis as Medicine
www.acmed.org

Opiates

Information pages
www.termisoc.org/~harl/heroin.html

US National Institute on Drug Abuse information
www.nida.nih.gov/ResearchReports/Heroin/heroin.html

Animation showing the effects of opiates on dopamine
www.wnet.org/closetohome/animation/opi-anim-main.html

Schizophrenia and antipsychotic drugs

Information pages
www.schizophrenia.com/
www.mentalhealth.com/dis/p20-ps01.html

Depression and antidepressants

Information pages
www.psycom.net/depression.central.html
www.nimh.nih.gov/publicat/depressionmenu.cfm

Alzheimer's disease

National Institute of Neurological Disorders and Stroke
www.ninds.nih.gov/health_and_medical/disorders/alzheimersdisease_doc.htm

Alzheimer's Disease Forum
www.alzforum.org/

Internet resources
www.ohioalzcenter.org/links.html

News updates on dementia
www.pslgroup.com/ALZHEIMER.HTM

The Alzheimer's Disease Society (England and Wales)
http://www.alzheimers.org.uk/

The Alzheimer's Association (USA)
http://www.alz.org/

Parkinson's disease

Parkinson's Disease Foundation (USA)
www.pdf.org/

Parkinson's Disease Society (UK)
www.parkinsons.org.uk/

Information from the US National Institute of Neurological Disorders and Stroke
www.ninds.nih.gov/health_and_medical/disorders/parkinsons_disease.htm

Nootropics

Information from mind-brain.com
www.mind-brain.com/nootropic.php

References

Abel EL (1980). *Marihuana: The First Twelve Thousand Years*. Plenum Press, New York.

Abraham HD and Aldridge AM (1993). Adverse consequences of lysergic acid diethylamide. *Addiction*, **88**, 1327–1334.

Abraham HD, Aldridge AM and Gogia P (1996). The psychopharmacology of hallucinogens. *Neuropsychopharmacology*, **14**, 285–298.

Adams KM, Gilman S, Koeppe R, Kluin K, Brunberg J, Dede D, Berent S and Kroll PD (1993). Neuropsychological deficits are correlated with frontal hypometabolism in positron emission tomography studies of older alcoholic patients. *Alcoholism: Clinical and Experimental Research*, **17**, 205–210.

Alloul K, Sauriol L, Kennedy W, Laurier C, Tessier G, Novosel S and Contandriopoulos A (1998). Alzheimer's disease: A review of the disease, its epidemiology and economic impact. *Archives of Gerontology and Geriatrics*, **27**, 189–221.

Almkvist O (2000). Functional brain imaging as a looking-glass into the degraded brain: Reviewing evidence from Alzheimer disease in relation to normal aging. *Acta Psychologica*, **105**, 255–277.

Altman J, Everitt BJ, Glautier S, Markou A, Nutt D, Oretti R, Phillips G and Robbins TW (1996). The biological, social and clinical bases of drug addiction: Commentary and debate. *Psychopharmacology*, **125**, 285–345.

Anda RF, Croft JB, Felitti VJ, Nordenberg D, Giles WH, Williamson DF and Giovino GA (1999). Adverse childhood experiences and smoking during adolescence and adulthood. *Journal of the American Medical Association*, **282**, 1652–1658.

Andersen SN and Skullerud K (1999). Hypoxic/ischaemic brain damage, especially pallidal lesions, in heroin addicts. *Forensic Science International*, **102**, 51–59.

Anderson IM, Nutt DJ and Deakin JFW (2000). Evidence-based guidelines for treating depressive disorders: A revision of the 1993 British Association for Psychopharmacology guidelines. *Journal of Psychopharmacology*, **14**, 3–20.

Andersson J, Berggren P, Gronkvist M, Magnusson S and Svenson E (2002). Oxygen saturation and cognitive performance. *Psychopharmacology*, **162**, 119–128.

Andreasson S, Allebeck P, Engstrom A and Rydberg U (1987). Cannabis and schizophrenia: A longitudinal study of Swedish conscripts. *Lancet*, **2**, 1483–1486.

Angrist B (1987). Clinical effects of central nervous system stimulants: A selective update. In: J Engel and L Oreland (eds), *Brain Reward Systems and Abuse*. Raven Press, New York.

Angrist B and van Kammen DP (1984). CNS stimulants as tools in the study of schizophrenia. *Trends in Neurosciences*, **7**, 388–390.

APA ([1994] 2000). *Diagnostic Statistical Manual* (Vol. IV). American Psychiatric Association, Washington, DC.

Argyropoulous SV, Sandford JJ and Nutt DJ (2000). The psychobiology of anxiolytic drugs. Part 2: Pharmacological treatments of anxiety. *Pharmacology and Therapeutics*, **88**, 213–227.

Ashton CH (1999). Adverse effects of cannabis and cannabinoids. *British Journal of Anaesthesia*, **83**, 637–649.

Ashton H, Savage RD, Telford R, Thompson JW and Watson DW (1972). The effects of cigarette smoking on the response to stress in a driving simulator. *British Journal of Pharmacology*, **45**, 546–556.

Badawy AA-B and Evans M (1982). Inhibition of rat liver tryptophan pyrrolase and elevation of brain tryptophan concentrations by acute administration of small doses of antidepressants. *British Journal of Pharmacology*, **77**, 59–67.

Baker D, Pryce G, Croxford J, Brown P, Pertwee RG, Huffman JW and Layward L (2000). Cannabinoids control spasticity and tremor in a multiple sclerosis model. *Nature*, **404**.

Balestreri R, Fontana L and Astengo F (1987). A double-blind placebo controlled evaluation of the safety and efficacy of vinpocetine in the treatment of patients with chronic vascular senile cerebral dysfunction. *Journal of the American Geriatrics Society*, **35**, 425–430.

Bantick RA, Deakin JFW and Grasby PM (2001). The 5-HT$_{1A}$ receptor in schizophrenia: Promising target for novel atypical neuroleptics. *Journal of Psychopharmacology*, **15**, 37–46.

Barker RA, Barsai S and Neal MJ (1999). *Neuroscience at a Glance*. Blackwell, Oxford, UK.

Barnet G, Licko V and Thompson T (1985). Behavioural pharmacokinetics of marijuana. *Psychopharmacology*, **85**, 51–56.

Bauer M, Whybrow PC, Angst J, Versiani M and Möller H-J (2002). World Federation of Societies of Biological Psychiatry (WFSBP) guidelines for biological treatment of unipolar depressive disorders. Part 1: Acute and continuation treatment of major depressive disorder. *World Journal of Biological Psychiatry*, **3**, 5–43.

Baum-Baicker C (1985). The psychological benefits of moderate alcohol consumption: A review of the literature. *Drug and Alcohol Dependence*, **15**, 305–322.

Beal JE, Olson R, Laubenstein L, Morales JO, Bellman P, Yangco B, Lefkowitz L, Plasse TF and Shepard KV (1995). Dronabinol as a treatment for anorexia associated with weight loss in patients with AIDS. *Journal of Pain and Symptom Management*, **10**, 89–97.

Bein HJ (1982). *Rauwolfia* and biological psychiatry. *Trends in Neurosciences*, **5**, 37–39.

Benton D, Donohoe RT, Sillance B and Nabb S (2001). The influence of phosphatidylserine supplementation on mood and heart rate when faced with an acute stressor. *Nutritional Neuroscience*, **4**, 169–178.

Berridge KC and Robinson TE (1998). What is the role of dopamine in reward: Hedonic impact, reward learning, or incentive salience? *Brain Research Review*, **28**(3), 309–369.

Berridge V (1997). Two tales of addiction: Opium and nicotine. *Human Psychopharmacology*, **12**, s45–s52.

Birks J and Flicker L (2003). *Selegiline for Alzheimer's disease* (The Cochrane Library No. 4). John Wiley & Sons, Chichester, UK.

Birks J, Grimley Evans J and Van Dongen M (2003). *Ginkgo Biloba for Cognitive Impairment and Dementia* (The Cochrane Library No. 1). Update Software, Oxford, UK.

Bishop KI and Curran HV (1995). Psychopharmacological analysis of implicit and explicit memory: A study with lorazepam and the benzodiazepine antagonist flumazenil. *Psychopharmacology*, **121**, 267–278.

Blier P and De Montigny C (1994). Current advances and trends in the treatment of depression. *Trends in Pharmacological Sciences*, **15**, 220–226.

Blinick G, Wallach RC and Jerez E (1969). Pregnancy in narcotic addicts treated by medical withdrawal. *American Journal of Obstetrics and Gynecology*, **105**, 997.

Bloch E (1983). Effects of marijuana and cannabinoids on reproduction, endocrine function, development and chromosomes. In: KO Fehr and H Kalant (eds), *Cannabis and Health Hazards*. Addiction Research Foundation, Toronto.

Block RI and Wittenborn JR (1986). Marijuana effects on the speed of memory retrieval in the letter-matching task. *International Journal of Addictions*, **21**, 281–285.

Blokland A (1996). Acetylcholine: A neurotransmitter for learning and memory? *Brain Research Reviews*, **21**, 285–300.

Bloom FE, Nelson CA and Lazerson A (2001). *Brain, Mind and Behavior*. Worth, New York.

Bloomquist ER (1971). *Marijuana: The Second Trip*. Glencoe Press, Beverly Hills, CA.

Bolla KJ, McCann UD and Ricaurte GA (1998). Memory impairment in abstinent MDMA (Ecstasy) users. *Neurology*, **51**, 1532–1537.

Bondy B and Zill P (2001). Psychopharmacogenetics – A challenge for pharmacotherapy in psychiatry. *World Journal of Biological Psychiatry*, **2**, 178–183.

Botvin GJ, Griffin KW, Diaz T, Scheier LM, Williams C and Epstein JA (2000). Preventing illicit drug use in adolescents: Long-term follow-up data from a randomized control trial of a school population. *Addictive Behaviors*, **25**(5), 769–774.

Boutros NN and Bowers MB (1996). Chronic substance-induced psychotic disorders: State of the literature. *Journal of Neuropsychiatry and Clinical Neurosciences*, **8**, 262–269.

Bovasso GB (2001). Cannabis use as a risk factor for depressive symptoms. *American Journal of Psychiatry*, **158**, 2033–2037.

Bowden C and Muller-Oerlinghausen B (2000). Carbamazepine and valproate: Use in mood disorders. In: PF Buckley and JL Waddington (eds), *Schizophrenia and Mood Disorders* (pp. 179–189). Butterworth-Heinemann, Oxford, UK.

Bradbury TN and Miller GA (1985). Season of birth in schizophrenia: A review of evidence, methodology, and etiology. *Psychological Bulletin*, **98**, 569–594.

Brady KT, Grice DE, Dustan L and Randall C (1993). Gender differences in substance use disorders. *American Journal of Psychiatry*, **150**, 1707–1711.

Breslau N, Peterson EL, Schultz LR, Chilcoat HD and Andreski P (1998). Major depression and stages of smoking: A longitudinal investigation. *Archives of General Psychiatry*, **55**, 161–166.

Brice C and Smith A (2001). The effects of caffeine on simulated driving, subjective alertness and sustained attention. *Human Psychopharmacology*, **16**, 523–531.

Brick J and Erickson CK (1999). *Drugs, the Brain and Behaviour: The Pharmacology of Abuse and Dependence*. The Haworth Medical Press, New York.

Brodaty H (1992). Carers: Training informal carers. In: T Arie (ed.), *Recent Advances in Psychogeriatrics*. Churchill-Livingstone, Edinburgh.

Brodaty H (1999). Realistic expectations for the management of Alzheimer's disease. *European Neuropsychopharmacology*, **9**, S43–S52.

Brooner RK, King VL, Kidorf M, Schmidt CW Jr and Bigelow GE (1997). Psychiatric and substance use comorbidity among treatment-seeking opioid abusers. *Archives of General Psychiatry*, **54**(1), 71–80.

Brown B (1973). Additional characteristic EEG differences between heavy smokers and non-smoker subjects. In: WL Dunn (ed.), *Smoking Behaviour: Motives and Incentives*. Winston & Sons, Washington, DC.

Brown CS and Cooke SC (1994). Attention deficit hyperactivity disorder, clinical features and treatment options. *CNS Drugs*, **1**, 95–106.

Brunning J, Mumford JP and Keaney FP (1986). Lofexidine in alcohol withdrawal states. *Alcohol and Alcoholism*, **21**, 167–170.

Buchbauer G, Jirovetz L, Jäger W, Dietrich H, Plank C and Karamat E (1991). Aromatherapy: Evidence for the sedative effect of the essential oil of lavender after inhalation. *Zeitschrift für Naturforschung (Tübingen, Germany)*, **46c**, 1067–1072.

Buck KJ and Harris RA (1991). Neuroadaptive responses to chronic alcohol. *Alcoholism: Clininical and Experimental Research*, **15**, 460–470.

Buckland PR and McGuffin P (2000). Molecular genetics of schizophrenia. In: MA Reveley and JFW Deakin (eds), *The Psychopharmacology of Schizophrenia* (pp. 71–88). Edward Arnold, London.

Burroughs WS (1985). *Junky*. Viking Press, New York.

Cabral GA and Pettit DAD (1998). Drugs and immunity: Cannabinoids and their role in decreased resistance to infectious disease. *Journal of Neuroimmunology*, **83**, 116–123.

Caldwell AE (1978). History of psychopharmacology. In: WG Clark and J DelGuidice (eds), *Principles of Psychopharmacology*. Academic Press, New York.

Campbell M, Young PI, Bateman DN, Smith JM and Thomas SHL (1999). The use of atypical antipsychotics in the management of schizophrenia. *British Journal of Clinical Pharmacology*, **47**, 13–22.

Carlini EA and Cunha JM (1981). Hypnotic and antiepileptic effects of cannabidiol. *Journal of Clinical Pharmacology*, **21**(Suppl. 8–9), 417s–427s.

Carlson NR (1999). *Foundations of Physiological Psychology*. Allyn & Bacon, Needham Heights, MA.

Carroll D, Turner JR and Prasad R (1986) The effects of level of difficulty of mental arithmetic challenge on heart rate and oxygen consumption. *International Journal of Psychophysiology*, **4**(3), 167–173.

Carroll KM (1998). *A Cognitive-Behavioral Approach: Treating Cocaine Addiction* (NIH Publication No. 98-4308). National Institute on Drug Abuse, Rockville, MD.

Carvey PM (1998). *Drug Action in the Central Nervous System* (pp. 279–309). Oxford University Press, New York.

Cenacchi B, Bertoldin T, Farina C, Fiori MG and Crepaldi G (1993). Cognitive decline in the elderly: A double blind, placebo-controlled multicenter study on efficacy of phosphatidylserine administration. *Aging, Clinical and Experimental Research*, **5**, 123–133.

Chait LD and Pierri J (1992). Effect of smoked marijuana on human performance: A critical review. In: A Murphy and J Bartke (eds), *Marijuana/Cannabinoids: Neurobiology and Neurophysiology*. CRC Press, New York.

Chait LD and Zacny JP (1992). Reinforcing and subjective effects of oral D9-THC and smoked marijuana in humans. *Psychopharmacology*, **107**, 255–262.

Chen J, Paredes W, Li J, Lowinson J and Gardner EL (1990a). Δ^9-tetrahydrocannabinol produces naloxone-blockade enhancement of presynaptic basal dopamine efflux in nucleus accumbens of conscious, freely-moving rats as measured by intracerebral microdialysis. *Psychopharmacology*, **102**, 156–162.

Chen J, Paredes W, Li J, Lowinson J and Gardner EL (1990b). Δ^9-tetrahydrocannabinol enhances presynaptic dopamine efflux in medial prefrontal cortex. *European Journal of Pharmacology*, **190**, 259–262.

Chesher GB and Jackson DM (1985). The quasi-morphine withdrawal syndrome: Effect of cannabinol, cannabidiol and THC. *Pharmacology, Biochemistry and Behaviour*, **23**, 13–15.

Chiang CN and Hawks RL (eds) (1990). *Research Findings on Smoking of Abused Substances* (p. 72). National Institute on Drug Abuse, Bethesda, MD

Chopra GS and Smith JW (1974). Psychotic reactions following cannabis use in East Indians. *Archives of General Psychiatry*, **30**, 24–27.

Chung T, Martin CS, Armstrong TD and Labouvie EW (2002). Prevalence of DSM-IV alcohol diagnoses and symptoms in adolescent community and clinical samples. *Journal of American Acadamy of Child and Adolescent Psychiatry*, **41**(5), 546–554.

Co BT, Goodwin DW, Gado M, Mikhael M and Hill SY (1977). Absence of cerebral atrophy in chronic cannabis users. *Journal of the American Medical Association*, **237**, 1229–1230.

Cohen MJ and Rickles WH Jr (1974). Performance on a verbal learning task by subjects of heavy past marijuana usage. *Psychopharmacologia*, **37**, 323–330.

Cohen RS (1998). *The Love Drug: Marching to the Beat of Ecstasy*. Haworth Medical Press, New York.

Cohen S and Lichtenstein E (1990). Perceived stress, quitting smoking, and smoking relapse. *Health Psychology*, **9**, 466–478.

Coleston DM and Hindmarch I (1988). Possible memory-enhancing properties of vinpocetine. *Drug Development and Research*, **14**, 191–193.

Comer SD, Collins ED, Kleber HJD, Nuwayser ES, Kerrigan JH and Fischman MW (2002). Depot naltrexone: Long-lasting antagonism of the effects of heroin in humans. *Psychopharmacology*, **159**, 351–360.

Comitas L (1975). Ganja use in Jamaica: A socio-cultural investigation. *Annals of the New York Academy of Sciences*, **24**.

Connaughton JF, Reeser D and Finnegan LP (1977) Pregnancy complicated by drug addiction. In: R Bolognese and R Schwartz (eds), *Perinatal Medicine*. Williams & Wilkins, Baltimore.

Consroe PF, Wood GC and Buchsbaum H (1975). Anticonvulsant nature of marijuana smoking. *Journal of the American Medical Association*, **234**, 306–307.

Consroe P, Musty R, Tillery W and Pertwee RG (1996). The perceived effects of cannabis smoking in patients with multiple sclerosis. *Proceedings of the International Cannabinoid Research Society*, **7**.

Cook CC and Gurling HM (1990). Candidate genes and favoured loci for alcoholism. In: CR Cloninger and H Begleiter (eds), *Genetics and Biology of Alcoholism* (Banbury Report No. 33, pp. 227–236). Cold Spring Harbor Press, New York.

Cookson J and Sachs G (2000). Lithium: Clinical use in mania and prophylaxis of affective disorders. In: PF Buckley and JL Waddington (eds), *Schizophrenia and Mood Disorders* (pp. 155–178). Butterworth-Heinemann, Oxford, UK.

Cooper JR, Bloom FE and Roth RH (1991). *The Biochemical Basis of Neuropharmacology*. Oxford University Press, New York.

Corder EH, Saunders AM, Strittmatter WJ, Schmechel DE, Gaskell PC, Small GW, Roses AD, Haines JL and Pericak-Vance MA (1993). Gene dose of apolipoprotein E type 4 allele and the risk of Alzheimer's disease in late onset families. *Science*, **261**, 921–923.

Corder EH, Saunders AM, Risch NJ, Strittmatter WJ, Schmechel DE, Gaskell PC, Rimmler JB, Locke PA, Conneally PM and Schmader KE (1994). Protective effect of apolipoprotein E type 2 allele for late onset Alzheimer disease. *Nature Genetics*, **7**, 180–184.

Cotton NS (1979). The familial incidence of alcoholism: A review. *Journal of Studies on Alcohol*, **40**, 89–116.

Court JA, Martin-Ruiz C, Graham A and Perry E (2000). Nicotinic receptors in human brain: Topography and pathology. *Journal of Chemical Neuroanatomy*, **20**, 281–298.

Craft S, Murphy C and Wernstrom J (1994). Glucose effects on complex memory and non-memory tasks: The influence of age, sex and glucoregulatory response. *Psychobiology*, **2**, 95–105.

Cravatt BF, Demarest K, Patricelli MP, Bracey MH, Giang DK, Martin BR and Lichtman AH (2001). Supersensitivity to anandamide and enhanced endogenous cannabinoid signaling in mice lacking fatty acid amide hydrolase. *Proceedings of the National Academy of Science*, **98**, 9371–9376.

Crombag HS and Shaham Y (2002). Renewal of drug seeking by contextual cues after prolonged extinction in rats. *Behavioural Neuroscience*, **116**, 169–173.

Crook TH, Petrie W, Wells C and Massari DC (1992). Effects of phosphatidylserine in Alzheimer's disease. *Psychopharmacology Bulletin*, **28**, 61–66.

Crow TJ (1980). Molecular pathology of schizophrenia: More than one disease process? *British Medical Journal*, **280**, 66–68.

Crowley JS, Wesensten N, Kamimori G, Devine J, Iwanyk E and Balkin T (1992). Effect of high terrestrial altitude and supplemental oxygen on human performance and mood. *Aviation, Space and Environmental Medicine*, **63**, 696–701.

Cucinotta D, De Leo D, Frattola L, Trabucchi M and Parnetti L (1996). Dihydroergokryptine vs. placebo in dementia of Alzheimer type: Interim results of a randomized multicentre study after a 1 year follow up. *Archives of Gerontology and Geriatrics*, **22**, 169–180.

Cunha JM, Carlini EA, Pereira AE, Ramos OL, Pimentel C, di Gagliardi R, Sanvito WL, Lander N and Mechoulam R (1980). Chronic administration of cannabidiol to healthy volunteers and epileptic patients. *Pharmacology*, **21**, 175–185.

Cunningham CL and Dworkin SI (1999). Alcoholism and drug addiction: What determines vulnerability? *Molecular Medicine Today*, **6**, 101–103.

Curran HV and Hildebrandt M (1999). Dissociative effects of alcohol on recollective experience. *Consciousness and Cognition*, **8**, 497–509.

Curran HV and Travill RA (1997). Mood and cognitive effects of 3,4-methylenedioxymethamphetamine (MDMA, "ecstasy"): Weekend "high" followed by midweek "low". *Addiction*, **92**, 821–831.

Cushing H (1925). *The Life of Sir William Osler* (Vol. 1, Chapter 14). Oxford University Press, New York.

Cutler NR and Sramek JJ (2001). Review of the next generation of Alzheimer's disease therapeutics: Challenges for drug development. *Progress in Neuro-Psychopharmacology and Biological Psychiatry*, **25**, 27–57.

Dafters RI (1994). Effects of ambient temperature on hyperthermia and hyperkinesis induced by 3,4-methylenedioxymethamphetamine (MDMA or "ecstasy") in rats. *Psychopharmacology*, **114**, 505–508.

Davison RM and Neale RM (1998). *Abnormal Psychology*. John Wiley & Sons, Chichester, UK.

Deakin JFW (1988). The neurochemistry of schizophrenia. In: P Bebbington and P McGuffin (eds), *Schizophrenia: The Major Issues* (pp. 56–72). Heinemann, Oxford, UK.

Dean B (2002). Molecular structure of the brain in bipolar disorder: Findings using human postmortem brain tissue. *World Journal of Biological Psychiatry*, **3**, 125–132.

Deas D, Riggs P, Langenbucher J, Goldman M and Brown S (2000). Adolescents are not adults: Developmental considerations in alcohol users. *Alcohol Clinical Experimental Results*, **24**, 232–237.

Delay J and Deniker P (1952). Trente-huit cas de psychoses traitées par la cure prolongée et continué de 4560RP. *Compte Rendu du Congrès Alien Neurologique*, **50**, 497–502.

De Lima MS, de Oliveira Soares BG, Reisser AA and Farrell M (2002). Pharmacological treatment of cocaine dependence: A systematic review. *Addiction*, **97**, 931–949.

Delwaide PJ, Gyselynck-Mambourg AM, Hurlet A and Ylieff M (1986). Double-blind randomized controlled study of phosphatidylserine in senile demented patients. *Acta Neurologica Scandinavica*, **73**, 136–140.

Denning P (2002). Harm reduction psychotherapy: An innovative alternative to classical addictions theory. *American Clinical Laboratory*, **21**, 16–18.

De Quincey (1822). *Confessions of an English Opium Eater*. Penguin English Library/Viking Press, New York.

Devane WA, Hanus L, Breuer A, Pertwee RG, Stevenson LA, Griffin G, Gibson D, Mandelbaum A, Mechoulam R and Etinger A (1992). Isolation and structure of a brain constituent that binds to the cannabinoid receptor (arachidonylethanolamide, "anandamide"). *Science*, **258**, 1946–1949.

DeVreese LP, Neri M, Boiardi R, Ferrari P, Belloi L and Salvioli G (1996). Memory training and drug therapy act differently on memory and metamemory functioning: Evidence from a pilot study. *Archives of Gerontology and Geriatrics*, **S5**, 9–22.

Deyo RA, Straube KT and Disterhoft JF (1989). Nimodipine facilitates associative learning in aging rabbits. *Science*, **243**, 809–811.

Diamond RJ (2002). *Instant Psychopharmacology*. W.W. Norton, New York.

Di Chiara G (1995). The role of dopamine in drug abuse viewed from the perspective of its role in motivation. *Drug and Alcohol Dependence*, **38**, 95–137.

Di Chiara G and North RA (1992). Neurobiology of opiate abuse. *Trends in Pharmacological Sciences*, **13**, 185–193.

Diego MA, Jones N, Field F, Hernandez-Reif M, Schanberg S, Kuhn C, McAdam V, Galamaga R and Galamaga M (1998). Aromatherapy positively affects mood: EEG patterns of alertness and math computations. *International Journal of Neuroscience*, **96**, 217–224.

Diesner JW (1998). A review of estrogen replacement therapy use in the prevention and treatment of Alzheimer disease. *Primary Care Update for OB/GYNS*, **5**, 50–53.

Dimond SJ and Brouwers EM (1976). Increase in the power of human memory in normal man through the use of drugs. *Psychopharmacology*, **49**, 307–309.

DoH (2001). *Smoking, Drinking and Drug Use among Young People in England in 2000*. Department of Health/HMSO, London. Also available at www.doh.gov.uk/public/statspntables.htm

Dole VP, Nyswander ME and Kreek MJ (1966). Narcotic blockade. *Archives of International Medicine*, **118**, 304–309.

Doll R and Peto R (1976). Mortality in relation to smoking: 20 years' observations on male British doctors. *British Medical Journal*, **ii**, 1525–1536.

Doody RS, Geldmacher DS, Gordon B, Perdomo CA and Pratt RD (2001). Open-label, multicenter, phase 3 extension study of the safety and efficacy of donepezil in patients with Alzheimer disease. *Archives of Neurology*, **58**, 427–433.

Duffy A and Millin R (1996). Case study: Withdrawal syndrome in adolescent chronic cannabis users. *Journal of the American Academy of Child and Adolescent Psychiatry*, **35**, 1618–1621.

Dufour MC, Archer L and Gordis E (1992). Alcohol and the elderly. *Clinics in Geriatric Medicine*, **8**, 127–141.

Duka T, Weissenborn R and Dienes Z (2000). State-dependent effects of alcohol on recollective experience, familiarity and awareness of memories. *Psychopharmacology*, **153**, 295–306.

Duncan DF (1987). Lifetime prevalence of "amotivational syndrome", among users and non-users of hashish. *Psychology of Addictive Behaviours*, **1**, 114–119.

Dunn M and Davies R (1974). The perceived effect of marijuana on spinal cord injured males. *Paraplegia*, **12**, 175.

Dunnett SB (1991). Cholinergic grafts, memory and ageing. *Trends in Neuroscience*, **14**, 371–376.

Ebert U, Oertel R, Wesnes K and Kirch W (1998). Effects of physostigmine on scopolamine-induced changes in quantitative electroencephalogram and cognitive performance. *Human Psychopharmacology – Clinical and Experimental*, **13**, 199–210.

Eccleston D (1973). Adenosine 3 : 5'-cyclic monophosphate and affective disorders: Animal models. In: LL Iversen and SPR Rose (eds), *Biochemistry and Mental Illness* (pp. 121–126). Biochemical Society, London.

Edwards AE and Hart GM (1974). Hyperbaric oxygenation and the cognitive function of the aged. *Journal of the American Geriatrics Society*, **22**, 376–379.

Elliott VS (2000). Lab test offers new way to spot alcoholism. Viewed at: http://www.ama-assn.org/sci-pubs/amnews/pick_00/hlsc0828.htm

Epstein DH, Hawkins WE, Covi L, Umbricht A and Preston KL (2003). Cognitive behavioural therapy plus contingency management for cocaine use: Findings during treatment and across 12-month follow-up. *Psychology of Addictive Behavior*, **17**, 73–82.

Esteban J, Gimeno C, Barril J, Aragones A, Climent JM and de la Cruz-Pellin M (2003). Survival study of opioid addicts in relation to its adherence to methadone maintenance treatment. *Drug and Alcohol Dependence*, **70**, 193–200.

Eysenck HJ (1983). Psychophysiology and personality: Extraversion, neuroticism and psychoticism. In: A. Gale and JA Edwards (eds), *Physiological Correlates of Human Behavior* (Vol. 3). Academic Press, London.

Fant RV, Schuh KJ and Stizer ML (1995). Response to smoking as a function of prior smoking amounts. *Psychopharmacology*, **119**, 385–390.

Farella M, Bakke M, Michelotti A, Marotta G and Martina R (1999). Cardiovascular responses in human to experimental chewing of gums of different consistencies. *Archives of Oral Biology*, **44**, 835–842.

Feigin VL, Doronin BM, Popova TF, Gribatcheva EV and Tchervov DV (2001). Vinpocetine treatment in acute ischaemic stroke: A pilot single-blind randomized clinical trial. *European Journal of Neurology*, **8**, 81.

Feldmann J and Rouse BA (eds) (1999). *National Household Survey on Drug Abuse*. US Department of Health and Human Services, Rockville, MD.

Feldman RS, Meyer JS and Quenzer LF (1997). The opiates. *Principles of Neuropsychopharmacology*. Sinnauer Associates, Sunderland, MA.

Ferguson DM and Horwood LJ (2001). Cannabis use and traffic accidents in a birth cohort of young adults. *Accident Analysis and Prevention*, **33**, 703–711.

Fergusson DM, Lynskey MT and Horwood JL (1995). The role of peer affiliations, social, family and individual factors in continuities in cigarette smoking between childhood and adolescence. *Addiction*, **90**, 647–659.

Fillmore MT and Vogel-Sprott M (1998). Behavioural impairment under alcohol: Cognitive and pharmacokinetic factors. *Alcoholism: Clinical and Experimental Research*, **22**, 1476–1482.

Finnegan LP (1979). Pathophysiological and behavioural effects of the transplacental transfer of narcotic drugs to the foetuses and neonates of narcotic-dependent mothers. United Nations Office on Drugs and Crime. Available at http://www.unodc.org/unodc/en/bulletin/bulletin_1979-01-01_3_page002.html#n05

Fioravanti M, Ferrario F, Massaio M, Cappab G, Rivoltac G, Grossic E and Buckleyd AE (1997). Low folate levels in the cognitive decline of elderly patients and the efficacy of folate as a treatment for improving memory deficit. *Archives of Gerontology and Geriatrics*, **26**, 1–13.

Fiorino DF, Coury A, Fibiger HC and Phillips AG (1993). Electrical stimulation of reward sites in the ventral tegmental area increases dopamine release in the nucleus accumbens of the rat. *Behavioral Brain Research*, **55**, 131–141.

Forsell Y and Fastbom J (2000). Psychotropic drug use in relation to psychiatric syndromes in a very elderly population. *International Journal of Geriatric Psychopharmacology*, **2**, 86–89.

Forster RE and Eastabrook RW (1993). Is oxygen an essential nutrient? *Annual Review of Nutrition*, **13**, 383–403.

Foster JK, Lidder PG and Sünram SI (1998). Glucose and memory: Fractionation of enhancement effects? *Psychopharmacology*, **13**, 259–270.

Fowler B, Paul M, Porlier G, Elcombe DD and Taylor M (1985). A re-evaluation of the minimum altitude at which hypoxic performance decrements can be detected. *Ergonomics*, **28**, 781–791.

Fox H, Parrott AC and Turner JJD (2001). Ecstasy/MDMA related cognitive deficits: A function of dosage rather than awareness of problems. *Journal of Psychopharmacology*, **15**, 273–281.

Fox HC, McLean A, Turner JJD, Parrott AC, Rogers R and Sahakian BJ (2002). Neuropsychological evidence of a relatively selective profile of temporal dysfunction in drug-free MDMA (Ecstasy) polydrug users. *Psychopharmacology*, **162**, 203–214.

Frank E, Johnson S and Kupfer DJ (1992). Psychological treatments in prevention of relapse. In: S Montgomery and F Rouillon (eds), *Long-Term Treatment of Depression* (pp. 197–228). John Wiley & Sons, Chichester, UK.

Fride E and Mechoulam R (1993). Pharmacological activity of the cannabinoid receptor agonist, anandamide, a brain constituent. *European Journal of Pharmacology*, **231**, 313–314.

Fried PA (1993). Perinatal exposure to tobacco and marijuana: Effects during pregnancy, infancy and early childhood. *Clinical Obstetrics and Gynaecology*, **36**, 319–336.

Friedmann PD, Lemon SC, Anderson BJ and Stein MD (2003). Predictors to follow-up health status in the drug treatment outcome study (DATOS). *Drug and Alcohol Dependence*, **69**, 243–251.

Frischer M, Hickman H, Kraus L, Mariani F and Wiessing L (2001). A comparison of different methods for estimating the prevalence of problematic drug misuse in Great Britain. *Addiction*, **96**, 1465–1476.

Fukuzako H (2001). Neurochemical investigation of the schizophrenic brain by *in vivo* phosphorus magnetic resonance spectroscopy. *World Journal of Biological Psychiatry*, **2**, 70–82.

Furlow B (2001). The making of mind. *New Scientist*, **171**, 38–41 (21st July).

Gansler DA, Harris GJ, Oscar-Berman M, Streeter C, Lewis RF, Ahmed I and Achong D (2000). Hypoperfusion of inferior frontal brain regions in abstinent alcoholics: A pilot SPECT study. *Journal of Studies on Alcohol*, **61**, 32–37.

Gawin FH (1991). Cocaine addiction: Psychology and neuropsychology. *Science*, **251**, 1580–1586.

Gentil V, Tavares S, Gorenstein C, Bello C, Mathias L, Gronich G and Singer J (1990). Acute reversal of flunitrazepam effects by Ro 15-1788 and Ro 15-3505: Inverse agonism, tolerance and rebound. *Psychopharmacology*, **100**, 54–59.

Gilbert AN, Knasko SC and Sabini J (1997). Sex differences in task performance associated with attention to ambient odour. *Archives of Environmental Health*, **52**, 195–199.

Girdler NM, Lyne JP, Fairbrother K, Neave N, Scholey A, Hargaden N, Wesnes KA, Engler J and Rotherham NA (2002). A Study of post-operative cognitive and psychomotor recovery from benzodiazepine sedation: Effects of reversal with flumazenil over a prolonged recovery period. *British Dental Journal*, **192**, 335–339.

Glantz M and Pickens R (1992). *Vulnerability to Drug Abuse*. American Psychological Association, Washington, DC.

Glennon RA (1996). Classic hallucinogens. In: CR Schuster and MJ Kuhar (eds), *Pharmacological Aspects of Drug Dependence: Towards an Integrated Neurobehavioral Approach*. Springer-Verlag, Berlin.

Gold MS (1992). Marihuana and hashish. In: G Winger, FG Hoffmann and JH Woods (eds), *A Handbook of Drug and Alcohol Abuse. The Biological Aspects* (pp. 117–131). Oxford University Press, Oxford, UK.

Gold PE (1986). Glucose modulation of memory storage processing. *Behavioural and Neural Biology*, **45**, 342–349.

Gold PE (1991). An integrated memory regulation system: From blood to brain. In: RCA Fredrickson, JL McGaugh and DL Felton (eds), *Peripheral Signalling of the Brain: Role in Neural-immune Interactions, Learning and Memory*. Hogrefe and Huber, Toronto.

Gold PE (1992). Modulation of memory processing: Enhancement of memory in rodents and humans. In: LR Squire and N Buttes (eds), *Neuropsychology of Memory* (pp. 402–414). Guilford Press, New York.

Golding JF (1992). Cannabis. In: A Smith and D Jones (eds), *Handbook of Human Performance: Health and Performance* (Vol. 2, p. 175). Academic Press, New York.

Goldman D (1988). Molecular markers for linkage of genetic loci contributing to alcoholism. In: M. Galenter (ed.), *Recent Developments in Alcoholism* (Vol. 6, pp. 333–349). Plenum Press, New York.

Goldstein A (1991). Heroin addiction: Neurology, pharmacology, and policy. *Journal of Psychoactive Drugs*, **23**, 123–133.

Goldstein A (1994). *Addiction from Biology to Drug Policy*. W.H. Freeman, New York.

Goldstein BJ and Goodnick PJ (1998). Selective serotonin reuptake inhibitors in the treatment of affective disorders. III: Tolerability, safety and pharmacoeconomics. *Journal of Psychopharmacology*, **12**(Suppl. B), S55–S87.

Goodman E and Capitman J. (2000). Depressive symptoms and cigarette smoking among teens. *Pediatrics*, **196**, 748–755.

Goodwin GM (2003). Evidence-based guidelines for treating bipolar disorder: Recommendations from the British Association for Psychopharmacology. *Journal of Psychopharmacology*, **17**, 149–173.

Gossop M, Green L, Phillips G and Bradley BP (1989). Lapse, relapse and survival among opiate addicts after treatment: A prospective follow-up study. *British Journal of Psychiatry*, **154**, 348–353.

Goudie AJ and Emmett-Oglesby MW (eds) (1989). *Psychoactive Drugs: Tolerance and Sensitization*. Humana Press, Clifton, NJ.

Gouliaev AII and Senning A (1994). Piracetam and other structurally related nootropics. *Brain Research Review*, **19**, 180–222.

Gouzoulis-Meyfrank E, Daumann J and Tuchtenbergen F (2000). Impaired cognitive performance in drug-free users of recreational Ecstasy/MDMA. *Journal of Neurology, Neurosurgery and Psychiatry*, **68**, 719–725.

Grahame-Smith DG and Aronson JK (1992). *Oxford Textbook of Clinical Pharmacology and Drug Therapy*. Oxford University Press, Oxford, UK.

Grant I, Reed R and Adams KM (1987). Diagnosis of intermediate duration and subacute organic mental disorders in abstinent alcoholics. *Journal of Clinical Psychiatry*, **48**, 319–323.

Green AR and Costain DW (1979). The biochemistry of depression. In: ES Paykel and A Coppen (eds), *Psychopharmacology of Affective Disorders* (pp. 14–40). Oxford University Press, Oxford, UK.

Green AR, Mechan AO, Elliott JM, O'Shea E and Colado MI (2004). The pharmacology and clinical pharmacology of 3,4-methylenedioxymethamphetamine (MDMA, "ecstasy"). *Pharmacological Reviews*, **55**, 463–508.

Green MF (2001). *Schizophrenia Revealed*. W.W. Norton, New York.

Greenfield S (1998). *The Human Brain: A Guided Tour*. Phoenix, London.

Greer G and Tolbert R (1986). Subjective reports of the effects of MDMA in a clinical setting. *Journal of Psychoactive Drugs*, **18**, 319–327.

Grilly DM (2001) *Drugs and Human Behavior*. Allyn & Bacon, Boston.

Grinspoon L and Bakalar JB (1993). *Marihuana, the Forbidden Medicine*. Yale University Press, New Haven, CT.

Grossberg GT (2003). Cholinesterase inhibitors for the treatment of Alzheimer's disease: Getting on and staying on. *Current Therapeutic Research*, **64**, 216–235.

Grunze H, Kasper S, Goodwin G, Bowden C, Baldwin D, Licht R, Vieta E and Möller H-J (2002). World Federation of Societies of Biological Psychiatry (WFSBP) guidelines for biological treatment of bipolar disorders. Part 1: Treatment of bipolar depression. *World Journal of Biological Psychiatry*, **3**, 115–124.

Guardian, The (6 February 1998). Viewed online January 2002 at: http://www.ukcia.org/lib/stats/ukcan.htm

Gupta BS and Gupta U (1999). *Caffeine and Behaviour: Current Views and Research Trends*. CRC Press, London.

Gurley RJ, Aranow R and Katz M (1998). Medicinal marijuana: A comprehensive review. *Journal of Psychoactive Drugs*, **30**, 137–147.

Haddad P (1999). Do antidepressants have potential to cause addiction? *Journal of Psychopharmacology*, **13**, 300–307.

Haefely WE (1977). Synaptic pharmacology of barbiturates and benzodiazepines. *Agents Actions*, **7**(3), 353–359.

Haley JE (1998). Gases as neurotransmitters. In: SJ Higgins (ed.), *Molecular Biology of the Brain* (Essays in Biochemistry No. 33, pp. 79–91). Portland Press, London.

Hall JL, Gonder-Fredrick LA, Chewing WW, Silvera J and Gold PE (1989). Glucose enhancement of performance on memory tests in young and aged humans. *Neuropsychologica*, **27**, 1129–1138.

Hall W and Solowij N (1998). Adverse effects of cannabis. *Lancet*, **352**, 1611–1616.

Hall W, Solowij N and Lemon J (1994). *The Health and Psychological Consequences of Cannabis Use* (National Drug Strategy Monograph Series No. 25). Australian Government Publishing Service, Canberra.

Halpern JH, Pope HG, Sherwood AR, Barry S, Hudson JI and Yurgelun-Todd D (2004). Residual neuropsychological effects of illicit 3,4-methylenedioxymethamphetamine (MDMA) in individuals with minimal exposure to other drugs. *Drug and Alcohol Dependence* (in press).

Hammarström A (1994). Health consequences of youth unemployment: Review from a gender perspective. *Social Science Medicine*, **38**, 699–709.

Harrison LD (1992) The drug–crime nexus in the USA. *Contemporary Drug Problems*, **19**, 181–202.

Hart CL, van Gorp W, Haney M, Foltin RW and Fischman MW (2001). Effects of acute smoked marijuana on complex cognitive performance. *Neuropsychopharmacology*, **25**, 757–765.

Harvey SC (1985). Hypnotics and sedatives. In: A Gilman, LS Goodman, TW Rall and F Murad (eds), *The Pharmacological Basis of Therapeutics* (pp. 13–31). Macmillan, New York.

Hatzinger M (2000). Neuropeptides and the hypothalamic–pituitary–adrenocortical (HPA) system: Review of recent research strategies in depression. *World Journal of Biological Psychiatry*, **1**, 105–111.

HEA (1998). Perceptions of alcohol related attendances in A&E departments in England: A national survey. *Alcohol and Alcoholism*, **33**, 354–361 (Health Education Authority).

Healy D, Langmark C and Savage M (1999). Suicide in the course of the treatment of depression. *Journal of Psychopharmacology*, **13**, 94–99.

Heishman SJ, Taylor RC and Henningfield JE (1994). Nicotine and smoking: A review of effects on human performance. *Experimental and Clinical Psychopharmacology*, **2**, 345–395.

Heishman SJ, Arasteh K and Stitzer ML (1997). Comparative effects of alcohol and marijuana on mood, memory, and performance. *Pharmacology, Biochemistry and Behaviour*, **58**, 93–101.

Heiss WD, Kessler J, Slansky I, Mielke R, Szelies B and Herholz K (1993). Activation PET as an instrument to determine therapeutic efficacy in Alzheimer's disease. *Annals of the New York Academy of Science*, **695**, 327–331.

Herbert M, Foulds J, Fife-Schaw C (2001). No effect of cigarette smoking on attention or mood in non-deprived smokers. *Addiction*, **96**, 1349–1356.

Herkenham M, Lynn AB, Johnson MR, Melvi LS, de Costa BR and Rice KC (1991). Characterisation and localisation of cannabinoid receptors in rat brain: A quantitative *in vitro* autoradiographic study. *Journal of Neuroscience*, **11**, 563–583.

Herpfer I and Lieb K (2003). Substance P and substance P receptor antagonists in the pathogenesis and treatment of affective disorders. *World Journal of Biological Psychiatry*, **4**, 56–63.

Herzog CD, Stackman RW and Walsh TJ (1996). Intraseptal flumazenil enhances, while diazepam binding inhibitor impairs, performance in a working memory task. *Neurobiology of Learning and Memory*, **66**, 341–352.

Hill SY, Shen S, Lowers L and Locke J (2000). Factors predicting the onset of adolescent drinking in families at high risk for developing alcoholism. *Biological Psychiatry*, **48**, 265–275.

Hindmarch I (1986). Activity of *Ginkgo biloba* extract on short-term memory. *Presse Medicale*, **15**, 1592–1594.

Hindmarch I, Parrott AC and Lanza M (1979). The effects of ergot alkaloid derivative (Hydergine) on aspects of psychomotor performance, arousal, and cognitive processing ability. *Journal of Clinical Pharmacology*, **19**, 726–732.

Hindmarch I, Aufdembrinke A and Ott H (1988). *Psychopharmacology and Reaction Time*. John Wiley & Sons, Chichester, UK.

Hindmarch I, Fuchs HH and Erzigkeit H (1991). Efficacy and tolerance of vinpocetine in ambulant patients suffering from mild to moderate organic psychosyndromes. *International Clinical Psychopharmacology*, **6**, 31–43.

Hirayama T (1981). Non-smoking wives of heavy smokers have a higher risk of lung cancer. *British Medical Journal*, **282**, 183–185.

Hirst RA, Lambert DG and Notcutt WG (1998). Pharmacology and potential therapeutic uses of cannabis. *British Journal of Anaesthesia*, **81**, 77–84.

Hoffman BB, Lefkowitz RJ and Taylor P (1996). Neurotransmission: The autonomic and somatic motor nervous systems. In: JG Hardman, LE Limbird, PB Molinoff, RW Ruddon and AG Gilman (eds), *Goodman and Gilman's Pharmacological Basis of Therapeutics* (9th edn, pp. 105–139). McGraw-Hill, New York.

Hofmann A (1980). *LSD: My Problem Child*. McGraw-Hill, New York.

Hogarty GE and Goldberg S (1973). Drug and sociotherapy in the aftercare of schizophrenic patients: One year relapse rates. *Archives of General Psychiatry*, **28**, 54–64.

Hogervorst E, Riedel W, Jeukendrup A and Jolles J (1996). Cognitive performance after strenuous physical exercise. *Perceptual and Motor Skills*, **8**, 479–488.

Hollister LE (1986). Health aspects of cannabis. *Pharmacology Review*, **38**, 1–20.

Home Office Report (1998). UK Government Home Office. Available at http://www.home office.gov.uk/tacklingdrugs/index.html

Hornykiewicz O (1982). Brain catecholamines in schizophrenia: A good case for noradrenaline. *Nature*, **299**, 484–486.

Horrobin D (2001). *The Madness of Adam and Eve*. Bantam Press, London.

Houde RW (1989). Misinformation: Side effects and drug interactions. In: CS Hill Jr and WS Fields (eds), *Advances in Pain Research and Therapy* (Vol. 11, pp. 145–162). Raven Press, New York.

Hoyer S (2000). Brain glucose and energy metabolism abnormalities in sporadic Alzheimer disease. Causes and consequences: An update. *Experimental Gerontology*, **351**, 1363–1372.

Hughes J (1991). *An Outline of Modern Psychiatry*. John Wiley & Sons, Chichester, UK.

Hughes JR (1992). Tobacco withdrawal in self-quitters. *Journal of Consulting and Clinical Psychology*, **60**, 689–697.

Hughes JR, Higgins ST and Hatsukami D (1990). Effects of abstinence from tobacco. In: LT Kowzlowski (ed.), *Recent Advances in Alcohol and Drug Problems* (Vol. 10). Plenum Press, New York.

Hughes PH and Rieche O (1995). Heroin epidemics revisited. *Epidemiology Review*, **17**, 63–73.

Hunt WA, Barnett LW & Branch LG (1971). Relapse rates in addiction programs. *Journal of Clinical Psychology*, **27**, 455–456.

Huxley A (1954). *Doors of Perception*. Penguin, London.

Ilaria RL, Thornby JI and Fann WE (1981). Nabilone, a cannabinoid derivative, in the treatment of anxiety neuroses. *Current Therapeutic Research*, **29**, 943–949.

Illes P (1989). Modulation of transmitter and hormone release by multiple neuronal opioid receptors. *Review of Physiological and Biochemical Pharmacology*, **112**, 139–233.

Indian Hemp Commission (1898). Report to the British House of Commons.

Isacson O, Seo H, Lin L, Albeck D and Granholm A-C (2002). Alzheimer's disease and Down's syndrome: Roles of APP, trophic factors and ACh. *Trends in Neurosciences*, **25**, 79–84.

Jacobs MR and Fehr K (1987). Cannabis. In: *Drugs and Drug Abuse: A Reference Text* (2nd edn, pp. 225–239). Addiction Research Foundation, Toronto.

Jain AK, Ryan JR, McMahon FG and Smith G (1981). Evaluation of intramuscular levonantradol and placebo in acute post-operative pain. *Journal of Clinical Pharmacology*, **21** (Suppl. 8–9), 320s–326s.

James JE (1994). Does caffeine enhance or merely restore degraded psychomotor performance? *Neuropsychobiology*, **30**, 124–125.

Jimenez-Lerma JM, Landabaso M, Iraurgi I, Calle R, Sanz J and Gutierrez-Fraile M (2002). Nimopidine in opiate detoxification: A controlled trial. *Addiction*, **97**, 819–824.

Johnson BA, Roache JD and Javors MA (2000). Ondansetron for reduction of drinking among biologically predisposed alcoholic patients: A randomized controlled trial. *Journal of American Medical Association*, **284**(8), 963–971.

Johnson DAW (1988). Drug treatment of schizophrenia. In: P Bebbington and P McGuffin (eds), *Schizophrenia: The Major Issues* (pp. 158–171). Heinemann, Oxford, UK.

Johnson IR (1982). The role of alcohol in road crashes. *Ergonomics*, **25**, 941–946.

Johnson JG, Cohen P, Pine DS, Klein DF, Kasen S and Brook JS. (2000). Association between cigarette smoking and anxiety disorders during adolescence and early childhood. *Journal of the American Medical Association*, **284**, 2348–2351.

Johnstone EC, Crow TJ, Frith CD, Stevens J and Kreel L (1976). Cerebral ventricular size and cognitive impairment in chronic schizophrenia. *Lancet*, **1**, 924–926.

Julien RM (2001). *A Primer of Drug Action* (10th edn). Freeman, New York.

Kahan A and Olah M (1976). Use of ethyl vinpocetine in ophthalmological therapy. *Arznei-mittelforschung*, **26**, 1969–1972.

Kaltenbach K and Finnegan L (1997). Children of maternal substance misusers. *Current Opinions in Psychiatry*, **10**, 220–224.

Kane JM (1996). Schizophrenia: Drug treatment. *New England Journal of Medicine*, **334**, 34–41.

Kane JM and Marder SR (1993). Psychopharmacologic treatment of schizophrenia. *Schizophrenia Bulletin*, **19**, 287–302.

Kantak KM (2003). Vaccines against drugs of abuse: A viable treatment option? *Drugs*, **63**(4), 342–352.

Kaplan HJ and Sadock BJ (1996). *Pocket Handbook of Psychiatric Drug Treatment*. Williams and Wilkins, Baltimore.

Karlin A (1993). Structure of nicotine acetylcholine receptors. *Current Opinion in Neurobiology*, **3**, 299–309.

Karp RW (1992). D2 or not D2? *Alcoholism: Clinical and Experimental Research*, **16**, 786–787.

Kasper S, Tauscher J, Willeit M, Stamenkovic M, Neumeister A, Kufferle B, Barnas C, Stastny J, Praschak-Rieder N, Pezawas L et al. (2002). Receptor and transport imaging studies in schizophrenia, depression, bulimia and Tourette's disorder: Implications for psychopharmacology. *World Journal of Biological Psychiatry*, **3**, 133–146.

Keeler MH and Reifler CB (1967). Grand mal convulsions subsequent to marijuana use. *Diseases of the Nervous System*, **18**, 474–475.

Keen J, Oliver P, Rowse G and Mathers N (2000). Keeping families of heroin addicts together: Results of a thirteen months' intake for community detoxification and rehabilitation at a Family Centre for drug users. *Family Practice*, **17**, 484–489.

Kennedy DO and Scholey AB (2000). Glucose administration, heart rate and cognitive performance: Effects of increasing mental effort. *Psychopharmacology*, **149**, 63–71.

Kennedy DO and Scholey AB (2003). Ginseng: Potential in the enhancement of cognitive performance and mood. *Pharmacology, Biochemistry and Behavior*, **75**, 687–700.

Kennedy DO, Scholey AB and Wesnes KA (2000). The dose dependent cognitive effects of acute administration of *Ginkgo biloba* to healthy young volunteers. *Psychopharmacology*, **151**, 416–423.

Kennedy DO, Scholey AB and Wesnes KA (2001a). Differential, dose dependent changes in cognitive performance following acute administration of a *Ginkgo biloba/Panax ginseng* combination to healthy young volunteers. *Nutritional Neuroscience*, **4**, 399–412.

Kennedy DO, Scholey AB and Wesnes KA (2001b). Differential, dose-dependent changes in cognitive performance and mood following acute administration of ginseng to healthy young volunteers. *Nutritional Neuroscience*, **4**, 295–310.

Kennedy DO, Scholey AB and Wesnes KA (2002a). Modulation of cognition and mood following administration of single doses of *Ginkgo biloba*, ginseng and a ginkgo/ginseng combination to healthy young adults. *Physiology and Behavior*, **75**, 739–751.

Kennedy DO, Scholey AB, Tildesley NTJ, Perry EK and Wesnes KA (2002b) Modulation of mood and cognitive performance following acute administration of single doses of *Melissa officinalis* (lemon balm). *Pharmacology, Biochemistry and Behavior*, **72**, 953–964.

Kennedy DO, Scholey AB, Drewery L, Marsh R, Moore B and Ashton H (2003a). Electroencephalograph (EEG) effects of single doses of *Ginkgo biloba* and *Panax ginseng* in healthy young volunteers. *Pharmacology, Biochemistry and Behavior*, **75**, 701–709.

Kennedy DO, Wake G, Savealev S, Tildesley NTJ, Perry EK, Wake G, Wesnes KA and Scholey AB (2003b). Modulation of mood and cognitive performance following administration of single doses of *Melissa officinalis* (lemon balm) with human CNS nicotinic and muscarinic receptor binding properties. *Neuropsychopharmacology*, **28**, 1871–1881.

Kent JM (2000). SNaRIs, NaSSAs and NARIs: New agents for the treatment of depression. *Lancet*, **355**, 911–918.

Kerwin R (2000). The neuropharmacology of schizophrenia: Past, present and future. In: M Reveley and JFW Deakin (eds), *The Psychopharmacology of Schizophrenia* (pp. 41–55). Edward Arnold, London.

Kety SS (1956). Human cerebral blood flow and oxygen consumption as related to aging. *Journal of Chronic Disease*, **3**, 478–486.

Khantzian EJ and Treece C (1985). DSM-III psychiatric diagnosis of narcotic addicts. Recent findings. *Archives of General Psychiatry*, **42**(11), 1067–1071.

Kim HS, Iyengar S and Wood P (1986). Opiate actions on mesocortical dopamine metabolism in the rat. *Life Sciences*, **39**, 2033–2036.

King GR and Ellinwood EH (1992) Amphetamines and other stimulants. In: JH Lowinson and P Ruiz (eds), *Substance Abuse: A Comprehensive Textbook* (pp. 247–266). Williams & Wilkins, Baltimore.

Kinsey R (ed.) (2000). *Turning Point Annual Report*. Turning Point Alcohol and Drug Centre, Sydney.

Kiss E (1990). Adjuvant effect of cavinton in the treatment of climacteric symptoms. *Therapia Hungarica (Budapest)*, **38**, 170–173.

Kleijnen J and Knipschild P (1992). *Ginkgo biloba*. *Lancet*, **12**, 1474.

Klonoff H (1974). Marijuana and driving in real-life situations. *Science*, **186**, 317–324.

Knapp M (1997). Costs of schizophrenia. *British Journal of Psychiatry*, **171**, 509–518.

Knight BG, Lutzky SM and Macofsky-Urban F (1993). A meta-analytic review of interventions for caregiver distress: Recommendations for future research. *Gerontologist*, **33**, 240–248.

Koelega HS (1995). Alcohol and vigilance performance: A review. *Psychopharmacology*, **118**, 233–249.

Kokavec A and Crowe SF (1999). A comparison of cognitive performance in binge versus regular chronic alcohol misusers. *Alcohol and Alcoholism*, **34**, 601–608.

Kolansky H and Moore WT (1972). Toxic effects of marijuana use. *Journal of the American Medical Association*, **222**, 35–41.

Kolb B and Wishaw IQ (2001). *An Introduction to Brain and Behavior*. Worth, New York.

Koob GF (1992). Neural mechanisms of drug reinforcement. *Annals of the New York Academy of Sciences*, **654**, 171–191.

Koob GF and Bloom FE (1988). Cellular and molecular mechanisms of drug dependence. *Science*, **242**, 715–723.

Kramer AF, Hahn S and McAuley E (2000). Influence of aerobic fitness on the neurocognitive function of older adults. *Journal of Aging and Physical Activity*, **8**, 379–385.

Kramer PD (1994). *Listening to Prozac*. Fourth Estate, London.

Kranzler HR, Modesto-Lowe V and Van Kirk J (2000). Naltrexone vs. nefazodone for treatment of alcohol dependence: A placebo controlled trial. *Neuropsychopharmacology*, **22**(5), 493–503.

Kristoikova Z and Klaschka J (1997). In vitro effect of *Ginkgo biloba* extract (EGb 761) on the activity of presynaptic cholinergic nerve terminals in rat hippocampus. *Dementia & Geriatric Cognitive Disorders*, **8**, 43–48.

Krystal JH, Price LH, Opsahl C, Ricaurte GA and Heninger GR (1992). Chronic 3,4-methylenedioxymethamphetamine (MDMA) use: Effects on mood and neuropsychological function? *American Journal of Drug & Alcohol Abuse*, **18**, 331–341.

Kuehnle J, Mendelson JH, Davis KR and New PFJ (1977). Computed tomographic examination of heavy marijuana smokers. *Journal of the American Medical Association*, **237**, 1231–1232.

Kumar RN, Chambers WA and Pertwee RG (2001). Pharmacological actions and therapeutic uses of cannabis and cannabinoids. *Anaesthesia*, **56**, 1059–1068.

Kupfer D, Levin E and Burstein SH (1973). Studies on the effects of tetrahydrocannabinol and ddt on the hepatic microsomal metabolism of thc and other compounds in the rat. *Chemical–Biological Interactions*, **6**, 59–66.

Laing RD (1965). *The Divided Self*. Penguin Books, London.

Lands WEM (1998). A review of alcohol clearance in humans. *Alcohol*, **15**, 147–160.

Lane R, Baldwin D and Preskorn S (1995) The SSRIs: Advantages, disadvantages and differences. *Journal of Psychopharmacology*, **9**(Suppl. 2), 163–178.

Langenbucher J, Martin CS, Labouvie E, Sanjuan PM, Bavly L and Pollock NK (2000). Toward the DSM-V: The withdrawal-gate model versus the DSM-IV in the diagnosis of alcohol abuse and dependence. *Journal of Consulting and Clinical Psychology*, **68**, 799–809.

Langer SZ (1997). 25 years since the discovery of presynaptic receptors: Present knowledge and future perspectives. *Trends in Pharmacological Sciences*, **18**, 95–99.

Laruelle M and Abi-Dargham A (1999). Dopamine as the wind of psychotic fire: New evidence from brain imaging studies. *Journal of Psychopharmacology,* **13**, 358–371.

Lassen NA and Ingvar DH (1980). Blood flow studies in the aging normal brain and in senile dementia. Aging of the brain and dementia. *Aging*, **13**, 91–98.

Laurin D, Verreault R, Lindsay J, MacPherson K and Rockwood K (2001). Physical activity and risk of cognitive impairment and dementia in elderly persons. *Archives of Neurology*, **58**, 498–504.

Lawre SM and Abukmeil SS (1998). Brain abnormality in schizophrenia. *British Journal of Psychiatry*, **172**, 110–120.

Lee T and Seeman P (1977). Dopamine receptors in normal and schizophrenic human brains. Paper presented at *Society for Neuroscience Conference, Anaheim, CA*.

Legradi GA, Rand WM, Hitz S, Nillni EA, Jackson IMD and Lechan RM (1996). Opiate withdrawal increases ProTRH gene expression in the ventrolateral column of the midbrain periaqueductal gray. *Brain Research*, **729**, 10–19.

Lemberger L, Tamarkin NR, Axelrod J and Kopin IJ (1971). Delta-9-tetrahydrocannabinol: Metabolism and disposition in long-term marihuana smokers. *Science*, **2**, 72–74.

Leonard BE (1975). Neurochemical and neuropharmacological aspects of depression. *International Review of Neurobiology*, **18**, 357–387.

Leonard BE (1985). Animal models of depression and the detection of antidepressants. In: SD Iversen (ed.), *Psychopharmacology: Recent Advances and Future Prospects* (pp. 33–43). Oxford University Press, Oxford, UK.

Leonard BE (1997). *Fundamentals of Psychopharmacology*. John Wiley & Sons, Chichester, UK.

Leonard BE (2003). *Fundamentals of Psychopharmacology* (3rd edn). John Wiley & Sons, Chichester, UK.

Leonard BE and Richelson E (2000). Synaptic effects of antidepressants: Relationships to their therapeutic and adverse effects. In: PF Buckley and JL Waddington (eds), *Schizophrenia and Mood Disorders* (pp. 67–84). Butterworth-Heinemann, Oxford, UK.

Lewis DFV (1996). *Cytochromes P-450: Structure, Function and Mechanism*. Taylor & Francis, London.

Licata A, Taylor S, Berman M and Cranston J (1993). Effects of cocaine on human aggression. *Pharmacology, Biochemistry and Behaviour*, **45**, 549–552.

Lieberman HR, Wurtman RJ, Emde GC, Roberts C and Coviella LG (1987). The effects of low doses of caffeine on human performance and mood. *Psychopharmacology*, **92**, 308–312.

Lindstrom P, Lindblom U and Boreus L (1987). Lack of effect of cannabidiol in sustained neuropathia. Paper presented at *Marijuana: International Conference on Cannabis, Melbourne, June*.

Linford Rees WL (1976). *A Short Textbook of Psychiatry*. Hodder & Stoughton, London.

Liska K (2000). *Drugs and the Human Body: With Implications for Society*. Prentice Hall, Englewood Cliffs, NJ.

Loeber RT and Yurgelun-Todd DA (1999). Human neuroimaging of acute and chronic marijuana use: Implications for frontocerebellar dysfunction. *Human Psychopharmacology: Clinical and Experimental*, **14**, 291–304.

Lopez-Arrieta JM and Birks J (2002). Nimodipine for primary degenerative, mixed and vascular dementia. *Cochrane Database of Systematic Reviews*, **3**, CD000147.

Loriaux SM, Deijen JB, Orlebeke JF and DeSwart JH (1985). The effect of niacin and xanthinol nicotinate on human memory in different age categories. *Psychopharmacology*, **87**, 390–395.

Luchins D (1976). Biogenic amines and affective disorders. A critical analysis. *International Pharmacopsychiatry*, **11**, 135–149.

Lyketsos CG, Garrett E, Liang KY and Anthony M (1999). Cannabis use and cognitive decline in persons under 65 years of age. *American Journal of Epidemiology*, **149**, 794–800.

MacAndrew C and Edgerton RB (1969). *Drunken Comportment: A Social Explanation*. Aldine, Chicago.

MacGregor S (2000) The drugs–crime nexus. *Drugs: Education, Prevention and Policy*, **7**, 311–316.

Maggioni M, Picotti GB, Bondiolotti GP, Panerai A, Cenacchi T, Nobil P and Brambilla F (1990). Effects of phosphatidylserine therapy in geriatric subjects with depressive disorders. *Acta Psychiatra Scandinavica*, **81**, 265–270.

Maier-Lorentz MM (2000) Neurobiological bases for Alzheimer's disease. *Journal of Neuroscience Nursing*, **32**, 117–125.

Maisto SA, Galizio M and Connors GJ (1998). *Drug Use and Abuse* (3rd edn). Harcourt Brace Jovanovich, Fort Worth, TX.

Major RT (1967) The ginkgo, the most ancient living tree. *Science*, **15**, 1270–1273.

Malberg JE and Seiden LS (1998). Small changes in ambient temperature cause large changes in 3,4-methylenedioxymethamphetamine (MDMA)-induced serotonin neurotoxicity and core body temperature in the rat. *Journal of Neuroscience*, **18**, 5086–5094.

Mangan GL and Golding JF (1984). *The Psychopharmacology of Smoking*. Cambridge University Press, Cambridge, UK.

Manji HK, Drevets WC and Charney DS (2001). The cellular neurobiology of depression. *Nature Medicine*, **7**, 541–547.

Manning CA, Ragozzino ME and Gold PE (1993). Glucose enhancement of memory in patients with senile dementia of the Alzheimer type. *Neurobiology of Ageing*, **14**, 523–528.

Marlatt GA (1996). Taxonomy of high-risk situations for alcohol relapse: Evolution and development of a cognitive–behavioral model. *Addiction*, **91**, S37–49.

Marshall A (1997). Laying the foundations for personalised medicines. *Nature Biotechnology*, **15**, 954–957.

Martyn CN, Illis LS and Thom J (1995). Nabilone in the treatment of multiple sclerosis. *Lancet*, **345**, 579.

Masterman DL and Cummings JL (1997). Frontal-subcortical circuits: The anatomic basis of executive, social and motivated behaviours. *Journal of Psychopharmacology*, **11**, 99–106.

Matthews GG (2001) *Neurobiology: Molecules, Cells and Systems*. Blackwell, Malden, MA.

Maurer K, Yolk S and Gerbalso H (1997). Auguste D and Alzheimer's disease. *Lancet*, **349**, 1546–1549.

Maurer M, Henn V, Dittrich A and Hofmann A (1990). Delta-9-THC shows antispastic and analgesic effects in a single-case double-blind trial. *European Archives of Psychiatry and Clinical Neuroscience*, **240**, 1–4.

May PRA (1968). *Treatment of Schizophrenia*. Science House, New York.

McCann UD, Eligulashvili V and Ricaurte GA (2000). (+-)3,4-methylenedioxymethamphetamine ("Ecstasy")-induced serotonin neurotoxicity: Clinical studies. *Neuropsychobiology*, **42**, 11–16.

McCann UD, Mertl M, Eligulasvili V and Ricaurte GA (1999). Cognitive performance in (+-)3,4-methylenedioxymethamphetamine (MDMA, "Ecstasy") uses: A controlled study. *Psychopharmacology*, **143**, 417–425.

McDonald MP and Overmier JB (1998). Present imperfect: A critical review of animal models of the mnemonic impairments in Alzheimer's disease. *Neuroscience and Biobehavioral Reviews*, **22**, 99–120.

McGeer EG and McGeer PL (1998). The importance of inflammatory mechanisms in Alzheimer disease. *Experimental Gerontology*, **33**, 371–378.

McGehee DS and Role LW (1995). Physical diversity of nicotinic acetylcholine receptor. *Annual Review of Physiology*, **57**, 512–546.

McGhee R, Williams S, Poulton R and Moffitt T. (2000). A longitudinal study of cannabis use and mental health from adolescence to early adulthood. *Addiction*, **95**, 491–504.

McGlothlin WH and West LJ (1968). The marijuana problem: An overview. *American Journal of Psychiatry*, **125**, 1126–1134.

McGrath J and Emmerson WB (1999). Treatment of schizophrenia. *British Medical Journal*, **319**, 1045–1048.

McGuffin P (1991). Genetic models of madness. In: P McGuffin and RM Murray (eds), *The New Genetics of Mental Health* (pp. 27–43). Butterworth-Heinemann, Oxford, UK.

McKenzie E (1965). Amphetamine and barbiturate use in aircrew. *Aerospace Medicine*, **36**, 774.

McKim WA (2003). *Drugs and Behaviour: An Introduction to Behavioural Pharmacology* (pp. 284–304). Prentice Hall, Englewood Cliffs, NJ.

McLaughlin PJ, Delevan CE, Carnicom S, Robinson JK and Brener J (2000). Fine motor control in rats is disrupted by delta-9-tetrahydrocannabinol. *Pharmacology, Biochemistry and Behaviour*, **66**, 803–809.

McLean A Jr, Cardenas DD, Burgess D and Gamzu E (1991). Placebo-controlled study of pramiracetam in young males with memory and cognitive problems resulting from head injury and anoxia. *Brain Injury*, **5**, 375–380.

McNeill AD, Jarvis M and West R (1987). Subjective effects of cigarette smoking in adolescents. *Psychopharmacology*, **92**, 115–117.

McQuay H (2001). Opioids in pain management. *Lancet*, **357**, S1.

Mechoulam R (2000). Looking back at cannabis research. *Current Pharmaceutical Design*, **6**(13), 1313–1322.

Mechoulam R, Fride E and Di Marzo V (1998). Endocannabinoids. *European Journal of Pharmacology*, **359**, 1–18.

Merritt JC, Crawford WJ and Alexander PC (1980). Effect of marihuana on intraocular and blood pressure in glaucoma. *Opthalmology*, **87**, 222–228.

Messier C, Pierre J, Desrochers A and Gravel M (1998). Dose-dependent action of glucose on memory processes in women: Effect on serial position and recall priority. *Brain Research: Cognition*, **7**, 221–233.

Messier C, Desrochers A and Gagnon M (1999). Effect of glucose, glucose regulation, and word imagery value on human memory. *Behavioral Neuroscience*, **113**, 431–438.

Mesulam HM (1995) The cholinergic contribution to neuromodulation in the cerebral cortex. *The Neurosciences*, **7**, 297–307.

Metz L and Page S (2003). Oral cannabinoid for spasticity in multiple sclerosis: Will attitude continue to limit use? *Lancet*, **362**, 1513.

Miklowitz DJ, Simoneau TL, George EL, Richards JA, Kalbag A, Sachs-Ericsson N and Suddath R (2000). Family focused treatment of bipolar disorder: 1 year effects of a psychoeducational programme in conjunction with pharmacotherapy. *Biological Psychiatry*, **48**, 582–592.

Miller LL and Branconnier RJ (1983). Cannabis: Effects on memory and the cholinergic limbic system. *Psychological Bulletin*, **93**, 441–456.

Miller NS and Gold MS (1989). The diagnosis of marijuana (cannabis) dependence. *Journal of Substance Abuse and Treatment*, **6**, 183–192.

Miller NS and Gold MS (1993). A hypothesis for a common neurochemical basis for alcohol and drug disorders. *Psychiatric Clinics of North America*, **16**, 105–117.

Miller P and Plant M (2002). Heavy cannabis use among UK teenagers: An exploration. *Drug and Alcohol Dependence*, **65**(3), 235–242.

Mindus P, Cronholm B, Levander SE and Schalling D (1976). Piracetam-induced improvement of mental performance: A controlled study on normally aging individuals. *Acta Psychiatrica Scandinavica*, **54**, 150–160.

Mirsky AF and Duncan CC (1986). Etiology and expression of schizophrenia: Neurobiological and psychosocial factors. *Annual Review of Psychology*, **37**, 291–319.

Mittelman MS, Ferris SH, Shulman E, Steinberg G and Levin B (1996). A family intervention to delay nursing home placement of patients with Alzheimer disease: A randomised controlled trial. *Journal of the American Medical Association*, **276**, 1725–1731.

Mix JA and Crews WD (2000). An examination of the efficacy of *Ginkgo biloba* extract EGb761 on the neuropsychologic functioning of cognitively intact older adults. *Journal of Alternative and Complementary Medicine*, **6**, 219–229.

Mix JA and Crews WD (2002). A double-blind, placebo-controlled, randomized trial of *Ginkgo biloba* extract EGb 761® in a sample of cognitively intact older adults: Neuropsychological findings. *Human Psychopharmacology – Clinical and Experimental*, **17**, 267–277.

Mohs RC, Doody RS, Morris JC, Ieni JR, Rogers SL, Perdomo CA and Pratt RD (2001). A 1-year, placebo-controlled preservation of function survival study of donepezil in AD patients. *Neurology*, **57**, 481–488.

Möller H-J (2000). Definition, psychopharmacological basis and clinical evaluation of novel/atypical neuroleptics: Methodological issues and clinical consequences. *World Journal of Biological Psychiatry*, **1**, 75–91.

Mondadori C (1993). The pharmacology of the nootropics: New insights and new questions. *Behavioural Brain Research*, **59**, 1–9.

Montgomery S and Rouillon F (eds) (1992). *Long-Term Treatment of Depression*. John Wiley & Sons, Chichester, UK.

Morgan MJ (1999). Memory deficits associated with recrational use of "Ecstasy" (MDMA). *Psychopharmacology*, **141**, 30–36.

Morgan MJ, McFie L, Fleetwood LH and Robinson JA (2002). Ecstasy (MDMA): Are the psychological problems associated with its use reversed by prolonged abstinence? *Psychopharmacology*, **159**, 294–303.

Morgenstern J and Longabaugh R (2000). Cognitive behavioural treatment for alcohol dependence: A review of evidence for its hypothesized mechanisms of action. *Addiction*, **95**, 1475–1490.

Morris PG (1999). Magnetic resonance imaging and magnetic resonance spectroscopy assessment of brain function in experimental animals and man. *Journal of Psychopharmacology*, **13**, 330–336.

Moss MC and Scholey AB (1996). Oxygen administration enhances memory formation in healthy young adults. *Psychopharmacology*, **124**, 255–260.

Moss MC, Scholey AB and Wesnes K (1998). Oxygen administration selectively enhances cognitive performance in healthy young adults: a placebo-controlled, double blind crossover study. *Psychopharmacology*, **138**, 27–33.

Moss MC, Cook J, Wesnes KA and Duckett P (2003). Aroma of rosemary and lavender essential oils differentially affect cognition and mood in healthy adults. *International Journal of Neuroscience*, **113**, 1507–1530.

Moulin DE, Iezzi A, Amireh R, Sharpe WK, Boyd D and Merskey H. (1996). Randomised trial of oral morphine for chronic non-cancer pain. *Lancet*, **347**, 143–147.

Mulder AH and Schoffelmeer ANM (1993). Multiple opioid receptors and presynaptic modulation of neurotransmitter release in the brain. In: A Herz (ed.), *Opioids. I: Handbook of Experimental Pharmacology* (Vol. 104, pp. 125–144). Springer-Verlag, New York.

Murgraff V, Parrott AC and Bennett P (1998). Risky single occasion drinking amongst young people: A broad overview of research findings. *Alcohol and Alcoholism*, 33, 1–12.

Murray RM, Lewis SW, Owen MJ and Foerster A (1988). The neurodevelopmental origins of dementia praecox. In: P Bebbington and P McGuffin (eds), *Schizophrenia: The Major Issues* (pp. 90–106). Heinemann, Oxford, UK.

Musto DF (1973). *The American Disease: Origins of Narcotic Control*. Yale University Press, New Haven, CT.

Narahashi T, Aistrup GL, Marszalec W and Nagata K (1999). Neuronal nicotinic acetylcholine receptors: A new target site for ethanol. *Neurochemistry International*, 35, 131–141.

Nathan PJ (2001). *Hypericum perforatum* (St. John's Wort): A non-selective reuptake inhibitor? *Journal of Psychopharmacology*, 15, 47–54.

National Household Survey on Drug Abuse (1999). *National Institute on Drug Abuse*. National Institute of Health, Bethesda, MD.

National Institute of Mental Health Collaborative Study Group (1964). Phenothiazine treatment in acute schizophrenia. *Archives of General Psychiatry*, 246–261.

National Institute on Drug Abuse (1990). Problems of drug depencence. *Proceedings of the 52nd Annual Scientific Meeting* (Research Monograph No. 105). Committee on Problems of Drug Dependence, National Institute of Health, Bethesda, MD.

Neave N, Reid C, Scholey AB, Thompson JM, Ayre G and Wesnes K (2000). Dose-dependent effects of flumazenil on cognition, mood and cardio-respiratory physiology in healthy volunteers. *British Dental Journal*, 189, 668–674.

Nemeroff CB (2002). New directions in the development of antidepressants: The interface of neurobiology and psychiatry. *Human Psychopharmacology*, 17(Suppl. 1), S13–S16.

Netrakom P, Krasuski JS, Miller NS and O'Tauma NA (1999). Structural and functional neuroimaging findings in substance-related disorders. *Psychiatric Clinics of North America*, 22, 313–329.

Nicholls JG, Martin AR, Wallace BG and Fuchs PA (2001) *From Neuron to Brain*. Sinauer Associates, Sunderland, MA.

NIH (1993). *Respiratory Effects of Passive Smoking*. National Institute of Health, Bethesda, MD.

Nissen MJ, Knopman DS and Schacter DL (1987). Neurochemical dissociation of memory systems. *Neurology*, 37, 789–794.

Noël X, Paternot J, Van der Linden M, Sferrazza R, Verhas M, Hanak C, Kornreich C, Martin P, De Mol J, Pelc I and Verbanck P (2001). Correlation between inhibition, working memory, and delimited frontal area blood flow measured by the ^{99M}Tc-Bicisate SPECT in alcohol-dependent patients. *Alcohol and Alcoholism*, 36, 556–563.

Novick DM, Richman BL, Friedman JM, Friedman JE, Fried C, Wilson JP, Townley A and Kreek MJ (1993). The medical status of methadone maintained patients in treatment for 11–18 years. *Drug and Alcohol Dependence*, 33, 235–245.

Noyes R, Brunk SF, Baram DA and Canter AC (1975a). Analgesic effect of delta-9-tetrahydrocannabinol. *Journal of Clinical Pharmacology*, 15, 139–143.

Noyes R, Brunk SF, Avery DAH and Canter AC (1975b). The analgesic properties of delta-9-tetrahydrocannabinol and codeine. *Clinical Pharmacology and Therapeutics*, 18, 84–89.

Nunes EV, Weissman MM, Goldstein RB, McAvay G, Seracini AM, Verdeli H and Wickramaratne PJ (1998). Psychopathology in children of parents with opiate dependence and/ or major depression. *Journal of the American Academy of Child and Adolescent Psychiatry*, 37(11), 1142–1151.

Olin J, Schneider L, Novit A and Luczak S (2003). *Hydergine for Dementia* (The Cochrane Library No. 1). John Wiley & Sons, Chichester, UK.

Oliver P, Keen J and Mathers N (2002). Deaths from drugs of abuse in Sheffield 1997–1999: What are the implications for GPs prescribing to heroin addicts? *Family Practice*, **19**(1), 93–94.

O'Malley SS, Jaffe AJ and Chang G (1992). Naltrexone and coping skills therapy for alcohol dependence: A controlled study. *Archives of General Psychiatry*, **49**, 881–887.

ONS (2000). *Living in Great Britain: Results from the 1998 General Household Survey* (Office of National Statistics). HMSO, London.

ONS (2001a). National statistics online (Office of National Statistics). Available at http://www.statistics.gov.uk/census2001/default.asp

ONS (2001b). Psychiatric morbidity among adults, 2000 (Office of National Statistics). Available at: www.statistics.gov.uk

Ornstein TJ, Iddon JL, Baldacchino AM, Sahakian BJ, London M, Everitt BJ and Robbins TW (2000). Profiles of cognitive dysfunction in chronic amphetamine and heroin abusers. *Neuropsychopharmacology*, **23**, 113–126.

Ouimette PC, Finney JW and Moos RH (1997). Twelve-step and cognitive behavioural therapy for substance abuse: A comparison of treatment effectiveness. *J. Consult. Clin. Psychology*, **65**, 230–240.

Palfai T and Jankiewicz H (1997). *Drugs and Human Behavior*. Wm. C. Brown, USA.

Pardridge WM (ed.) (1998). Introduction to the blood–brain barrier. *Methodology, Biology and Pathology*. Cambridge University Press, Cambridge, UK.

Parnas J, Mednick SA and Moffett TE (1981). Perinatal complications and adult schizophrenia. *Trends in Neurosciences*, **4**, 262–264.

Parrott AC (1986). The effects of transdermal scopolamine and four dose levels of oral scopolamine (0.15, 0.3, 0.6, and 1.2 mg) upon psychological performance. *Psychopharmacology*, **89**(3), 347–354.

Parrott AC (1987). Assessment of psychological performance in applied situations. In: I Hindmarch and PD Stonier (eds), *Human Psychopharmacology: Measures and Methods* (Vol. 1). John Wiley & Sons, Chichester, UK.

Parrott AC (1989). Transdermal scopolamine: A review of its effects upon motion sickness, psychological performance, and physiological functioning. *Aviation, Space and Environmental Medicine*, **60**, 1–9.

Parrott AC (1994). Individual differences in stress and arousal during cigarette smoking. *Psychopharmacology*, **115**, 389–396.

Parrott AC (1995). Smoking cessation leads to reduced stress, but why? *International Journal of the Addictions*, **30**, 1509–1516.

Parrott AC (1998a). Social drugs: Effects upon health. In: M. Pitts and K Phillips (eds), *The Psychology of Health*. Routledge, London.

Parrott AC (1998b). Nesbitt's Paradox resolved? Stress and arousal modulation during cigarette smoking. *Addiction*, **93**, 27–39.

Parrott AC (1999). Does cigarette smoking cause stress? *American Psychologist*, **54**, 817–820.

Parrott AC (2000a). Human research on MDMA (3,4-methylenedioxymethamphetamine) neurotoxicity: Cognitive and behavioral indices of change. *Neuropsychobiology*, **42**, 17–24.

Parrott AC (2000b). Smoking and adverse childhood experiences. *Journal of the American Medical Association*, **283**, 1959.

Parrott AC (2001). Human psychopharmacology of Ecstasy/MDMA: A review of fifteen years of empirical research. *Human Psychopharmacology: Clinical and Experimental*, **16**, 557–577.

Parrott AC (2002). Recreational Ecstasy/MDMA, the serotonin syndrome, and serotonergic neurotoxicity. *Pharmacology Biochemistry & Behaviour*, **71**, 837–844.

Parrott AC (2003). Cigarette derived nicotine is not a medicine. *World Journal of Biological Psychiatry*, **4**, 49–55.

Parrott AC (2004). Is Ecstasy MDMA? A review of the proportion of ecstasy tablets containing MDMA, and the changing perceptions of their purity. *Psychopharmacology* (in press).

Parrott AC and Garnham NJ (1998). Comparative mood states and cognitive skills of cigarette smokers, deprived smokers, and non-smokers. *Human Psychopharmacology*, **13**, 367–376.

Parrott AC and Hindmarch I (1975). Arousal and performance – the ubiquitous inverted U relationship. Comparison of changes in response latency and arousal level in normal subjects induced by CNS stimulants, sedatives and tranquillizers. *IRCS Medical Science, Clinical Pharmacology and Therapeutics, Psychiatry and Clinical Psychology*, **3**, 176.

Parrott AC and Kaye FJ (1999). Daily uplifts, hassles, stresses and cognitive failures: In cigarette smokers, abstaining smokers, and non-smokers. *Behavioural Pharmacology*, **10**, 639–646.

Parrott AC and Kentridge R (1982). Personal constructs of anxiety under the 1.5-benzodiazepine derivative clobazam, related to trait-anxiety levels of the personality. *Psychopharmacology*, **78**, 353–357.

Parrott AC and Lasky J (1998). Ecstasy (MDMA) effects upon mood and cognition before, during, and after a Saturday night dance. *Psychopharmacology*, **139**, 261–268.

Parrott AC and Winder G (1989). Nicotine chewing gum (2 mg, 4 mg) and cigarette smoking: Comparative effects upon vigilance and heart rate. *Psychopharmacology*, **97**, 257–261.

Parrott AC, Garnham NJ, Wesnes K and Pincock C (1996). Cigarette smoking and abstinence: Comparative effects upon cognitive task performance and mood state over 24 hours. *Human Psychopharmacology*, **11**, 391–400.

Parrott AC, Lees A, Garnham NJ, Jones M and Wesnes K (1998). Cognitive performance in recreational users of MDMA or "Ecstasy": Evidence for memory deficits. *Journal of Psychopharmacology*, **12**, 79–83.

Parrott AC, Thurkle J and Ward M (2000). Nicotine abstinence: Time course of mood and cognitive performance changes over 3 hours. *International Journal of Neuropsychopharmacology*, **3**, s325.

Parrott AC, Milani R, Parmar R and Turner JJD (2001). Ecstasy polydrug users and other recreational drug users in Britain and Italy: Psychiatric symptoms and psychobiological problems. *Psychopharmacology*, **159**, 77–82.

Parrott AC, Buchanan T, Scholey AB, Heffernan T, Ling J and Rodgers J (2002). Ecstasy/MDMA attributed problems reported by novice, moderate, and heavy users. *Human Psychopharmacology*, **17**, 309–312.

Peet M and Horrobin DF (2000). Eicosapentaenoic acid in the management of treatment-unresponsive schizophrenia. *Journal of Psychopharmacology*, **14**(Suppl. 3), A63.

Pencer A and Addington J (2003). Substance use and cognition in early psychosis. *Journal of Psychiatry and Neuroscience*, **28**, 48–54.

Perry E, Ballard C, Spurden D, Cheng A, Johnson M, McKeith I, Piggott M and Perry R (1998). Cholinergic systems in the human brain: Psychopharmacology and psychosis. *Alzheimer's Disease Review*, **3**, 117–124.

Perry EK, Ashton H and Young AH (eds) (2002). *Neurochemistry of Consciousness*. Benjamins, Amsterdam.

Perry NSL, Houghton P, Theobald A, Jenner P and Perry EK (2000). In-vitro inhibition of human erythrocyte acetylcholinesterase by *Salvia lavandulaefolia* essential oil and constituent terpenes. *Journal of Pharmacy and Pharmacology*, **52**, 895–902.

Perry NSL, Houghton PJ, Jenner P, Keith A and Perry EK (2002). *Salvia lavandulaefolia* essential oil inhibits cholinesterase in vivo. *Phytomedicine*, **9**, 48–51.

Pertwee RG (1990). The central neuropharmacology of psychotropic cannabinoids. In: DJK Balfour (ed.), *Psychotropic Drugs of Abuse* (pp. 355–429). Pergamon Press, Elmsford, New York.

Pertwee RG (1995). Pharmacological, physiological and clinical implications of the discovery of cannabinoid receptors: An overview. In: R Pertwee (ed.), *Cannabinoid Receptors* (pp. 829–832). Raven Press, New York.

Pertwee RG (1997). Pharmacology of CB1 and CB2 receptors. *Pharmacology and Therapeutics*, **74**, 129–180.

Pertwee RG (1997). Cannabis and cannabinoids: Pharmacology and rationale for clinical use. *Pharmacology and Science*, **3**, 539–545.

Pertwee RG (1998). Advances in cannabinoid receptor pharmacology. In: D Brown (ed.), *Cannabis* (pp. 125–174). Harwood Academic Publishers, Amsterdam.

Pertwee RG (1999). Pharmacology of cannabinoid receptor ligands. *Current Medical Chemistry*, **6**, 635–664.

Petro DJ (1980). Marihuana as a therapeutic agent for muscle spasm or spasticity. *Psychosomatics*, **21**, 81–85.

Pettigrew JW, Levine J and McClure RJ (2000). Acetyl-L-carnitine physical-chemical, metabolic, and therapeutic properties: Relevance for its mode of action in Alzheimer's disease and geriatric depression. *Molecular Psychiatry*, **5**, 626–632.

Pettinati HM, Volpicelli JR and Kranzler HR (2000). Sertraline treatment for alcohol dependence: Interactive effects of medication and alcohol subtype. *Alcohol Clinical and Experimental Research*, **24**, 1041–1049.

Pickens RW, Svikis DS, McGue M., Lykken DT, Heston LL and Clayton PJ (1991). Heterogeneity in the inheritance of alcoholism. *Archives of General Psychiatry*, **48**, 19–28.

Pinel JP (1998). *Biopsychology*. Allyn & Bacon, Boston.

Pingitore D and Sansone RA (1998). Using DSM-IV primary care version: A guide to psychiatric diagnosis in primary care. *American Family Physician*, October.

Plant M and Miller P (2000) Drug use has declined among teenagers in United Kingdom. *British Medical Journal*, **320**, 1536a.

Plomin R, DeFries JC, McClearn GE and McGuffin P (2001). *Behavioral Genetics*. Worth, New York.

Pope HG (2002). Cannabis, cognition and residual confounding. *Journal of the American Medical Association*, **287**, 1172–1175.

Pope HG and Yurgelun-Todd D (1996). The residual cognitive effects of heavy marijuana use in college students. *Journal of the American Medical Association*, **275**, 521–527.

Pope HG, Gruber AJ and Yurgelun-Todd D (1995). The residual neuropsychological effects of cannabis: The current status of research. *Drug and Alcohol Dependence*, **38**, 25–34.

Pope HG, Gruber AJ, Hudson JI, Huestis MA and Yurgelun-Todd D (2001a). Neuropsychological performance in long-term cannabis users. *Archives of General Psychiatry*, **58**, 909–915.

Pope HG, Ionescu-Pioggia M and Pope KW (2001b). Drug use and lifestyle among college undergraduates: A 30-year longitudinal study. *American Journal of Psychiatry*, **158**, 1519–1521.

Porter J and Jick H (1980). Addiction rare in patients treated with narcotics. *New England Journal of Medicine*, **302**(2), 123.

Post R (2000). Psychopharmacology of mood stabilizers. In: PF Buckley and JL Waddington (eds), *Schizophrenia and Mood Disorders* (pp. 127–154). Butterworth-Heinemann, Oxford, UK.

Post SG (1999). Future scenarios for the prevention and delay of Alzheimer Disease onset in high-risk groups: An ethical perspective. *American Journal of Preventative Medicine*, **16**, 105–110.

Purves D, Augustine GJ, Fitzpatrick D, Katz LC, LaMantia A-S, McNamara JO and Williams SM (2001). *Neuroscience*. Sinauer Associates, Sunderland MA.

Raft D, Gregg J and Ghiaj Harris L (1977). Effects of intravenous tetrahydrocannabinol on experimental and surgical pain: Psychological correlates of the analgesic response. *Clinical Pharmacology and Therapeutics*, **21**, 26–33.

Ramsay M, Baker P, Goulden C, Sharp C and Sondhi A (2001). *Drug Misuse Declared in 2000: Results from the British Crime Survey* (Home Office Research Study No. 224). HMSO, London.

Rang HP, Dale MM, Ritter JM and Moore PK (2003). *Pharmacology*. Churchill-Livingstone, Edinburgh.

Raine CS (1976) Neurocellular anatomy. In: GJ Siegel, RW Albers, R Katzman and BW Agranoff (eds), *Basic Neurochemistry* (pp. 5–32). Little & Brown, Boston.

Rao R (2001). Cannabis: Some psychiatric aspects. *Primary Care Psychiatry*, **7**, 101–105.

Raskin A, Gershon S, Crook TH, Sathananthan G and Ferris S (1978). The effects of hyperbaric and normobaric oxygen on cognitive impairment in the elderly. *Archives of General Psychiatry*, **35**, 50–56.

Reason JT and Brand JJ (1975). *Motion Sickness*. Academic Press, London.

Regelson W, Butler JR, Schulz J, Kirk T, Peek L, Green ML and Zalis MO (1976). Delta-9-THC as an effective antidepressant: An appetite stimulating agent in advanced cancer patients. In: MC Braude and S Szara (eds), *The Pharmacology of Marihuana* (pp. 763–775). Raven Press, New York.

Reidel WJ, Peters ML, VanBoxtel MPJ and Ohanlon JF (1998). The influence of piracetam on actual driving behaviour in elderly subjects. *Human Psychopharmacology – Clinical and Experimental*, **13**, S108–S114.

Reinherz HZ, Giaconia RM, Lefkowitz ES, Pakiz B and Frost AK (1993). Prevalence of psychiatric disorders in a community population of older adolescents. *Journal of American Academy of Child and Adolescent Psychiatry*, **32**, 369–377.

Reneman L, Booij J, Schmand B, Brink W, Gunning B (2000). Memory disturbances in "Ecstasy" users are correlated with an altered brain serotonin neurotransmission. *Psychopharmacology*, **148**, 322–324.

Reneman L, Booij J, Majoie CBL, van den Brink W and den Heeten GJ (2001). Investigating the potential neurotoxicity of Ecstasy (MDMA): An imaging approach. *Human Psychopharmacology*, **16**, 579–588.

Reveley MA and Trimble MR (1987). Imaging techniques. *British Medical Bulletin*, **43**, 616–633.

Revell A (1988). Smoking and performance: A puff-by-puff analysis. *Psychopharmacology*, **96**, 563–565.

Rey JM, Sawyer MG, Raphael B, Patton GC and Lynskey MT (2002). The mental health of teenagers who use marijuana. *British Journal of Psychiatry*, **180**, 222–226.

Ricaurte GA, Yuan J and McCann UD (2000). (+−)3,4-methylenedioxymethamphetamine (MDMA, "Ecstasy")-induced serotonin neurotoxicity: Studies in animals. *Neuropsychobiology*, **42**, 5–10.

Ricaurte GA, Yuan J, Hadzidimitriou G, Cord BJ and McCann UD (2002). Severe dopaminergic neurotoxicity in primates after a common recreational dose regimen of MDMA ("Ecstasy"). *Science*, **297**: 2260–2263.

Rice AS (2001). Cannabinoids and pain. *Current Opinion in Investigational Drugs*, **2**(3), 399–414.

Ridges AP (1973). Abnormal metabolites in schizophrenia. In: LL Iversen and SPR Rose (eds), *Biochemistry and Mental Illness* (pp. 175–188). Biochemical Society, London.

Rigney U, Kimber S and Hindmarch I (1999). The effects of acute doses of standardised *Ginkgo biloba* extract on memory and psychomotor performance in volunteers. *Phytotherapy Research*, **13**, 408–415.

Robb HWJ and O'Hanlon JF (1993). Marijuana's effect on actual driving: Summary of a 3-year experimental program. In: HD Utzelmann, G Berghaus and G Kroj (eds), *Alcohol, Drugs and Traffic Safety* (No. T92, pp. 603–611). Verlag TUV, Cologne.

Roberts GW and Crow TJ (1987). Neuropathology of schizophrenia. *British Medical Bulletin*, **43**, 599–615.

Robson P (2001). Therapeutic aspects of cannabis and cannabinoids. *British Journal of Psychiatry*, **178**, 107–115.

Rodgers J (2000). Cognitive performance amongst recreational users of "Ecstasy". *Psychopharmacology*, **151**, 19–24.

Rodgers J, Buchanan T, Scholey AB, Heffernan TM, Ling J and Parrott A (2001). Differential effects of ecstasy and cannabis on self reports of memory ability: A web-based study. *Human Psychopharmacology*, **16**, 619–626.

Rodin EA, Domino EF and Porzak JP (1970). The marijuana induced "social high". *Journal of the American Medical Association*, **213**, 1300–1302.

Rogers PJ, Richardson NJ and Dernoncourt C (1995) Caffeine use: Is there a net benefit for mood and psychomotor performance? *Neuropsychobiology*, **301**, 194–199.

Rogers SL, Farlow MR, Doody RS, Mohs R and Friedhoff LT (1998). A 24-week, double-blind, placebo-controlled trial of donepezil in patients with Alzheimer's disease. *Neurology*, **50**, 136–145.

Roland PE (1993). *Brain Activation* (pp. 9–83). Wiley-Liss, Chichester, UK.

Rose SPR (1973). What do you mean: The cause of schizophrenia? In: LL Iversen and SPR Rose (eds), *Biochemistry and Mental Illness* (pp. 219–220). Biochemical Society, London.

Rose S (1976). *The Conscious Brain*. Penguin, London.

Rose S, Lewontin R and Kamin L (1984). *Not in Our Genes*. Penguin Books, London.

Rottkamp CA, Nunomura A, Hirai K, Sayre LM, Perry G and Smith MA (2000). Will antioxidants fulfill their expectations for the treatment of Alzheimer disease? *Mechanisms of Ageing and Development*, **116**, 169–179.

Rouillon F, Lejoyeux M and Filteau MJ (1992). Unwanted effects of long-term treatment. In: S. Montgomery and F Rouillon (eds), *Long-Term Treatment of Depression* (pp. 81–111). John Wiley & Sons, Chichester, UK.

Ruijter J, De Ruiter MB, Snel J, Lorist MM (2000). The influence of caffeine on spatial attention: An event potential study. *Clinical Neurophysiology*, **111**, 2223–2233.

Russell MAH, Peto J and Pavel VA (1974). The classification of smoking by a factorial structure of motives. *Journal of the Royal Statistical Society*, **137**, 313–346.

Salvioli G and Neri M (1994). L-acetylcarnitine treatment of mental decline in the elderly. *Drugs, Experimental and Clinical Research*, **20**, 169–176.

Samson HH and Harris RA (1992). Neurobiology of alcohol abuse. *Trends in Pharmacological Science*, **13**, 206–211.

Sandford, JJ, Argyropoulos SV and Nutt DJ (2000). The psychobiology of anxiolytic drugs. Part 1: Basic neurobiology. *Pharmacology and Therapeutics*, **88**, 197–212.

Sandler M (1990). Monoamine oxidase inhibitors in depression: History and mythology. *Journal of Psychopharmacology*, **4**, 136–139.

Sandler M (1992). Development of anxiolytic and antidepressant drugs: A historical perspective. In: JM Elliot, DJ Heal and CA Marsden (eds), *Experimental Approaches to Anxiety and Depression* (pp. 1–8). John Wiley & Sons, Chichester, UK.

Sandman CA, McCanne TR, Kaiser DN and Diamond B (1982). Heartrate and cardiac phase influences on visual perception. *Journal of Comparative Physiological Research*, **91**, 189–202.

Saric J, Sakoman S and Zdunic D (2002). Drug abuse and involvement in criminal behaviour. *Drustvena Istrazivanja*, **11**, 353–377.

Saunders AM, Strittmatter WJ, Schmechel D, George-Hyslop PH, Pericak-Vance MA, Joo SH, Rosi BL, Gusella JF, Crapper-MacLachlan DR, Alberts MJ et al. (1993). Association of apolipoprotein E allele epsilon 4 with late-onset familial and sporadic Alzheimer's disease. *Neurology*, **43**, 1467–1472.

Saunders N (1995). *Ecstasy and the Dance Culture*. Neal's Yard Desktop Publishing, London.

Schifano F (2000). Potential human neurotoxicity of MDMA ("Ecstasy"): Subjective self-reports, evidence from an Italian drug addiction centre and clinical case studies. *Neuropsychobiology*, **42**, 25–33.

Schifano F, Di Furia L, Forza G, Minicuci N and Bricolo R (1998). MDMA ("ecstasy") consumption in the context of polydrug abuse: A report on 150 patients. *Drug and Alcohol Dependence*, **52**, 85–90.

Schildkraut JJ (1965). The catecholamine hypothesis of affective disorders: A review of supporting evidence. *American Journal of Psychiatry*, **122**, 509–522.

Scholey AB (2001). Fuel for thought. *The Psychologist*, **14**, 196–201.

Scholey AB and Fowles K (2002). Retrograde enhancement of kinesthetic memory by low dose alcohol and by glucose. *Neurobiology of Learning and Memory*, **78**, 477–483.

Scholey AB and Kennedy DO (2002). Acute, dose-dependent cognitive effects of *Ginkgo biloba*, *Panax Ginseng* and their combination in healthy young volunteers: Differential interactions with cognitive demand. *Human Psychopharmacology – Clinical and Experimental*, **17**, 35–44.

Scholey AB, Moss MC and Wesnes KA (1998). Oxygen and cognitive performance: The temporal relationship between hyperoxia and enhanced memory. *Psychopharmacology*, **140**, 123–126.

Scholey AB, Moss MC, Neave N and Wesnes KA (1999). Cognitive performance, hyperoxia and heart rate following oxygen administration in healthy young adults. *Physiology and Behavior*, **67**, 783–789.

Scholey AB, Harper S and Kennedy DO (2001). Cognitive demand and blood glucose. *Physiology and Behavior*, **73**, 585–592.

Schooler NR and Hogarty GE (1987). Medication and psychological strategies in the treatment of schizophrenia. In: MA Lipton, A DiMascio and KF Killam (eds), *Psychopharmacology: A Generation of Progress*. Raven, New York.

Schulteis G and Koob G (1994). Neuropharmacology: Dark side of drug dependence. *Nature*, **371**, 108–109.

Schultz W, Dayan P and Montague RR (1997). A neural substrate of prediction and reward. *Science*, **275**, 1593–1599.

Schwartz GE, Whitehorn D, Hernon JC and Jones M (1986). Subjective and respiratory differences of fragrances: Interaction with hedonics. *Psychophysiology*, **23**, 460.

Schweitzer I, Tuckwell V, Ames D and O'Brien J (2001). Structural neuroimaging techniques in late-life depression. *World Journal of Biological Psychiatry*, **2**, 83–88.

Scimone A and Scimone A (1998). US sees the green in herbal supplements. *Chemical Market Reports*, 13 July, fr3–fr4.

Scott J, Garland and Moorhead S (2001). A pilot study of cognitive therapy in bipolar disorders. *Psychological Medicine*, **31**, 459–467.

Searles JS (1988). The role of genetics in the pathogenesis of alcoholism. *Journal of Abnormal Psychology*, **97**, 153–167.

Seashore RH and Ivy AC (1953) The relief of fatigue by analeptic drugs. *Psychological Monographs*, **67**(865).

Seeman P (1980). Brain dopamine receptors. *Pharmacological Reviews*, **32**, 229–313.

Seeman P, Guan H-C and van Tol HHM (1993). Dopamine D4 receptors elevated in schizophrenia. *Nature*, **365**, 441–445.

Seeman P, Tallerico T, Corbett R, van Tol HHM and Kamboj RK (2000). Role of dopamine D$_2$, D$_4$ and serotonin$_{2A}$ receptors in antipsychotic and anticataleptic action. *Journal of Psychopharmacology*, **11**, 15–17.

Segal M (1986). Cannabinoids and analgesia. In: R Mechoulam (ed.), *Cannabinoids as Therapeutic Agents* (pp. 105–120). CRC Press, Boca Raton, FL.

Self DW (1998). Neural substrates of drug craving and relapse in drug addiction. *Annals of Medicine*, **30**(4), 379–389.

Self DW and Stein L (1992). Receptor subtypes in opioid and stimulant reward. *Pharmacology and Toxicology*, **70**, 87–94.

Selkoe DJ (1998). The cell biology of APP and presenelin in Alzheimer's disease. *Neuron*, **16**, 921–932.

Sell LA, Morris J, Bearn J, Frackowiak RSJ, Friston KJ and Dolan RJ (1999). Activation of the reward circuitry in opiate addicts. *European Journal of Neuroscience*, **11**, 1042–1048.

Selzer ML (1971). The Michigan Alcoholism Screening Test: The quest for a new diagnostic instrument. *American Journal of Psychiatry*, **127**, 1653–1658.

Sesay M, Tanaka A, Ueno Y, Lecaroz P and De Beaufort DG (2000). Assessment of regional cerebral blood flow by xenon-enhanced computed tomography during mastication in humans. *Keio Journal of Medicine*, **49**, A125–A128.

Sexton BF, Tunbridge RJ, Brook-Carter N, Jackson PG, Wright K, Stark MM and Englehart K (2000). *The Influence of Cannabis on Driving* (No. 477). Transport Research Laboratory, Crowthorne, UK.

Shiffman S (1989). Tobacco "chippers": Individual differences in tobacco dependence. *Psychopharmacology*, **97**, 539–547.

Shors TJ, Miesegaes G, Beylin A, Zhao M, Rydel T and Gould E (2001). Neurogenesis in the adult is involved in the formation of trace memories. *Nature*, **410**, 372–376.

Shulgin AT (1986) The background and chemistry of MDMA. *Journal of Psychoactive Drugs*, **18**, 291–304.

Siddique MS, Eddeb F, Mantle D and Mendelow AD (2000). Extracts of *Ginkgo biloba* and *Panax ginseng* protect brain proteins from free radical induced oxidative damage in vitro. *Acta Neurochirurgica*, **76**, 87–90.

Silva H and Larach V (2000). Treatment and recovery in depression: A critical analysis. *World Journal of Biological Psychiatry*, **2**, 119–123.

Siris SG (2001). Suicide and schizophrenia. *Journal of Psychopharmacology*, **15**, 127–135.

Smith AP (1992). Time of day and performance. In: AP Smith and DM Jones (eds), *Handbook of Human Performance* (Vol. 3). Academic Press, London.

Smith GM and Beecher HK (1959). Amphetamine sulfate and athletic performance: 1. Objective effects. *Journal of the American Medical Association*, **30**, 542–557.

Smith MA and Perry G (1998). What are the facts and artifacts of the pathogenensis and etiology of Alzheimer disease? *Journal of Chemical Neuroanatomy*, **16**, 35–41.

Smith PB, Compton DR, Welch SP, Razdan RK, Mechoulam R and Martin B (1994). The pharmacological activity of anandamide, a putative endogenous cannabinoid, in mice. *Journal of Pharmacology and Experimental Therapeutics*, **270**, 219–227.

Snyder SH (1996). Stimulants. *Drugs and the Brain*. WH Freeman, New York.

Soar K, Turner JJD and Parrott AC (2001). Psychiatric disorders in recreational Ecstasy (MDMA) users: A literature review focusing upon personal predisposition factors and drug histories. *Human Psychopharmacology*, **16**, 641–645.

Soldatos CR, Kales A and Cadieux R (1979). Narcolepsy: Evaluation and treatment. In: DE Smith, ME Wessen et al. (eds), *Amphetamine Use, Misuse and Abuse*. Prentice Hall, Boston.

Solomon PR, Adams F, Silver A, Zimmer J and DeVeaux R (2002). Ginkgo for memory enhancement: A randomized controlled trial. *Journal of the American Medical Association*, **288**, 835–840.

Solowij N (1995). Do cognitive impairments recover following cessation of cannabis use? *Life Sciences*, **56**, 2119–2126.

Solowij N (1998). *Cannabis and Cognitive Functioning*. Cambridge University Press, Cambridge, UK.

Solowij N, Stephens RS, Roffman RA, Babor T, Kadden R, Miller M, Christiansen K, McRee B and Vendetti J (2002). Cognitive functioning of long-term heavy cannabis users seeking treatment. *Journal of the American Medical Association*, **287**, 1123–1132.

Solti F, Iskum M and Czako E (1976). Effect of ethyl apovincaminate on the cerebral circulation: Studies in patients with obliterative cerebral arterial disease. *Arzneimittelforschung*, **26**, 1945–1947.

Sparrow WA and Wright BJ (1993). Effects of physical exercise on the performance of cognitive tasks. *Perceptual and Motor Skills*, **77**, 675–679.

Spiegel R (1996). *Psychopharmacology: An Introduction* (3rd edn). John Wiley & Sons, Chichester, UK.

Spirduso WW and Clifford P (1978). Replication of age and physical activity effects on reaction and movement time. *Journal of Gerontology*, **33**, 26–30.

Stapleton JA, Russell MAH, Feyerabend C, Wiseman SM, Gustavsson G, Sawe U and Wiseman D (1995). Dose effects and predictors of outcome in a randomised trial of transdermal nicotine patches in general practice. *Addiction*, **90**, 31–42.

Steele CM and Josephs RA (1990). Alcohol myopia: Its prized and dangerous effects. *American Psychologist*, **45**, 921–933.

Steele TD, McCann UD and Ricaurte GA (1994). 3,4-Methylenedioxymethamphetamine (MDMA; "Ecstasy"): Pharmacology and toxicology in animals and humans. *Addiction*, **89**, 539–551.

Stefanis C, Dornbush R and Fink M (eds) (1977). *Hashish: Studies of Long-Term Use*. Raven Press, New York.

Steffen T, Christen S, Blättler R and Gutzwiller F (2001). Infectious diseases and public health: Risk taking behaviour during participation in the Swiss Programme for a Medical Prescription of Narcotics (PROVE). *Journal of Substance Use and Misuse*, **36**, 71–89.

Steiner W (1994). The effect of odours on human experience and behaviour. In: P Jellinek (ed.), *The Psychological Basis of Perfumery* (4th edn, pp. 200–217). London: Blackie Academic and Professional.

Steinweg DL and Worth H (1993). Alcoholism: The keys to the CAGE. *American Journal of Medicine*, **94**, 520–523.

Stevenson R (1998). Gold standards for drugs. *Chemistry in Britain*, **34**, 31–35.

Strange P (1998). Pathology and drug action in schizophrenia. In: SJ Higgins (ed.), *Molecular Biology of the Brain* (Essays in Biochemistry No. 33, pp. 105–116). Portland Press, London.

Strittmatter WJ, Saunders AM, Schmechel D, Pericak-Vance M, Enghild J, Salvesen GS and Roses AD (1993). Apolipoprotein E: High-avidity binding to beta-amyloid and increased frequency of type 4 allele in late-onset familial Alzheimer disease. *Proceedings of the National Academy of Science USA*, **90**, 1977–1981.

Stromgaard K, Saito DR, Shindou H, Ishii S, Shimizu T and Nakanishi K (2002). Ginkgolide derivatives for photolabeling studies: Preparation and pharmacological evaluation. *Journal of Medicinal Chemistry*, **45**, 4038-4046.

Struve FA, Straumanis JJ, Patrick G, Leavitt J, Manno JF and Manno BR (1999). Topographic quantitative EEG sequelae of chronic marihuana use: A replication using medically and psychiatrically screened normal subjects. *Drug and Alcohol Dependence*, **56**, 167–179.

Subhan Z and Hindmarch I (1987). Psychopharmacological effects of vinpocetine in normal healthy volunteers. *European Journal of Clinical Pharmacology*, **28**, 567–571.

Supreme Court of the United States (1962). Robinson v. California, 370 U.S. 660. Appeal from the appellate department, Superior Court of California, Los Angeles County, No. 554.

Surgeon General (1988). *Nicotine Addiction*. US Government Printing Office, Washington, DC.

Surgeon General (1990). *The Health Benefits of Smoking Cessation*. US Government Printing Office, Washington, DC.

Swain CP (2002). NK$_1$ receptor antagonists. In: FD King (ed.), *Medicinal Chemistry: Principles and Practice* (pp. 415–427). Royal Society of Chemistry, Cambridge, UK.

Swift RM (1999). Drug therapy for alcohol dependence. *New England Journal of Medicine*, **340**, 1482–1490.

Szasz T (1974). *The Myth of Mental Illness*. Harper & Row, New York.

Szeto HH, Inturrisi CE, Houde R, Saal S, Cheigh J and Reidenberg M (1977). Accumulation of norperidine, an active metabolite of meperidine [pethidine], in patients with renal failure or cancer. *Annals of Internal Medicine*, **86**, 738–741.

Tachikawa E, Kudo K, Harada K, Kashimoto T, Miyate Y, Kakizaki A and Takahashi E (1999). Effects of ginseng saponins on responses induced by various receptor stimuli. *European Journal of Pharmacology*, **369**, 23–32.

Taracha E, Habrat BS, Wozniak P, Walkowiak J and Szukalski B (2001). The activity of β-hexosaminidase (uHex) and γ-glutamyltransferase (uGGT) in urine as non invasive markers of alcohol abuse: I. Alcohol-dependent subjects. *World Journal of Biological Psychiatry*, **2**, 184–189.

Tarter RE (1995). Cognition, aging and alcohol. In: T. Beresford and E Gomberg (eds), *Alcohol and Aging*, Oxford University Press, New York.

Tashkin DP, Shapiro BJ and Frank IM (1976). Acute effects of marihuana on airway dynamics in spontaneously and experimentally produced bronchial asthma. In: MC Braude and S Szara (eds), *The Pharmacology of Marihuana* (pp. 84–92). Raven Press, New York.

Thaker G.K and Carpenter WT, Jr (2001). Advances in schizophrenia. *Nature Medicine*, **7**, 667–671.

Thomas CS and Lewis S (1998). Which atypical antipsychotic? *British Journal of Psychiatry*, **172**, 106–109.

Thompson JM, Neave N, Moss MC, Scholey AB, Wesnes K and Girdler NM (1999). Cognitive properties of sedation agents: Comparison of the effects of nitrous oxide and midazolam on memory and mood. *British Dental Journal*, **187**, 557–562.

Tildesley NTJ, Kennedy DO, Perry EK, Ballard CG, Savalev S, Wesnes KA, Hylands P and Scholey AB (2003). *Salvia lavandulaefolia* (Spanish sage) enhances on memory in healthy young volunteers. *Pharmacology, Biochemistry and Behavior*, **75**, 669–674.

Timnick L (1977). Scientists find "sites of craziness". *Los Angeles Times*.

Tiplady B, Drummond GB, Cameron E, Gray E, Hendry J, Sinclair W and Wright P (2001). Ethanol, errors, and the speed–accuracy trade-off. *Pharmacology, Biochemistry and Behavior*, **69**, 635–641.

Toffano G (1987). The therapeutic value of phosphatidylserine effect in the aging brain. In: I Hanin and GB Ansell (eds), *Lecithin: Technological, Biological, and Therapeutic Aspects* (pp. 137–146). Plenum Press, New York.

Tohgi H, Sasaki K, Chiba K and Nozaki Y (1990). Effect of vinpocetine on oxygen release of hemoglobin and erythrocyte organic polyphosphate concentrations in patients with vascular dementia of the Binswanger type. *Arzneimittelforschung*, **40**, 640–643.

Tolu P, Masi F, Leggio B, Scheggi S, Tagliamonte A, De Montis MG and Gambarana C (2002). Effects of long-term acetyl-L-carnitine administration in rats: (I) Increased dopamine output in mesocorticolimbic areas and protection toward acute stress exposure. *Neuropsychopharmacology*, **27**, 410–420.

Topp L, Hando J, Dillon P, Roche A and Solowij N (1999). Ecstasy use in Australia: Patterns of use and associated harm. *Drug and Alcohol Dependence*, **55**, 105–115.

Tortorice P and O'Connell M (1990). Management of chemotherapy-induced nausea and vomiting. *Pharmacotherapy*, **10**, 129–145.

Town T, Schinka J, Tan J and Mullen M (2000). The opioid receptor system and alcoholism: A genetic perspective. *European Journal of Pharmacology*, **410**, 243–248.

Tsolaki M, Fountoulakis KN, Nakopoulou E and Kazis A (2000). The effect of antidepressant pharmacotherapy with venlafaxine in geriatric depression. *International Journal of Geriatric Psychopharmacology*, **2**, 83–85.

Turner WM and Tsuang MT (1990). Impact of substance abuse on the course and outcome of schizophrenia. *Schizophrenia Bulletin*, **16**, 87–95.

Tyler A (1995). *Street Drugs: The Facts Explained, the Myths Exploded*. Hodder & Stoughton, London.

Tyrer P, Seivewright N, Ferguson B and Tyrer J (1992). The general neurotic syndrome: A coaxial diagnosis of anxiety, depression and personality disorder. *Acta Psychiatra Scandinavica*, **85**, 201–206.

United Nations Office for Drug Control and Crime Prevention (1991). Viewed online January 2002 at: http://www.undcp.org/bulletin/bulletin_1997-01-01_1_page004.html

US Department of Health (1994). *Preventing Tobacco Use among Young People* (A report). Surgeon General, Atlanta, GA.

US Department of Justice Drug Enforcement Administration (2002). Available at http://www.usdoj.gov/dea/index.htm

Vandel P (2003). Antidepressant drugs in the elderly: Role of the cytochrome P4502D6. *World Journal of Biological Psychiatry*, **4**, 74–80.

Velleman R, Bennett G, Miller T, Orford J, Rigby K and Tod J (1993). The families of problem drug users: A study of 50 close relatives. *Addiction*, **88**, 1281–1289.

Veng LM, Mesches MH and Browning MD (2003). Age-related working memory impairment is correlated with increases in the L-type calcium channel protein a1D (Cav1.3) in area CA1 of the hippocampus and both are ameliorated by chronic nimodipine treatment. *Molecular Brain Research*, **110**, 193–202.

Verheul R, van den Brink W and Hartgers C (1995). Prevalence of personality disorders among alcoholics and drug addicts: An overview. *European Addiction Research*, **1**, 166–177.

Verkes RJ, Gigsman HJ, Pieters MSM, Schoemaker RC, de Visser S and Kuijpers M (2001). Cognitive performance and serotonergic function in users of Ecstasy. *Psychopharmacology*, **153**, 196–202.

Vetulani J and Sulser F (1975). Action of various antidepressant treatments reduces reactivity of noradrenergic cyclic AMP-generating system in limbic forebrain. *Nature*, **257**, 495–496.

Villareal DT and Morris JC (1998). The diagnosis of Alzheimer's disease. *Alzheimer's Disease Review*, **3**, 142–152.

Viswesvaran C and Schmidt FL (1992). A meta-analytic comparison of the effectiveness of smoking cessation methods. *Journal of Applied Psychology*, **77**, 554–561.

Volpe BT and Hirst W (1983). The characterisation of an amnesic syndrome following hypoxic ischemic injury. *Archives of Neurology*, **40**, 436–440.

Volpicelli JR, Alterman AI, Hayashida M and O'Brien CP (1992). Naltrexone in the treatment of alcohol dependence. *Archives of General Psychiatry*, **49**, 876–880.

Vormefelde SV and Poser W (2000). How to count methadone-related deaths. *Drug and Alcohol Review*, **19**(4), 469–470.

Vuksan V, Sievenpiper JL, Koo VYY, Francis T, Beljan-Zdravkovic U, Xu Z and Vidgen E (2000). American ginseng (*Panax quinquefolius* L.) reduces postprandial glycemia in nondiabetic subjects and subjects with type 2 diabetes mellitus. *Archives of Internal Medicine*, **160**, 1009–1013.

Waddington J and Casey D (2000). Comparative pharmacology of classical and novel (second-generation) antipsychotics. In: PF Buckley and JL Waddington (eds), *Schizophrenia and Mood Disorders* (pp. 1–13). Butterworth-Heinemann, Oxford, UK.

Wake G, Court J, Pickering A, Lewis R, Wilkins R and Perry E (2000). CNS acetylcholine receptor activity in European medicinal plants traditionally used to improve failing memory. *Journal of Ethnopharmacology*, **69**, 105–114.

Walsh DC, Hingson RW and Merrigan DM (1991). A randomised trial of treatment options for alcohol-abusing workers. *New England Journal of Medicine*, **325**, 775–782.

Ward NJ and Dye L (1999). *Cannabis and Driving: A Review of the Literature and Commentary* (A report). Department of Environment Transport and Regions, London.

Wareing M, Fisk JE and Murphy PN (2000). Working memory deficits in current and previous users of MDMA ("Ecstasy"). *British Journal of Psychology*, **91**, 181–188.

Warot D, Lacomblez L, Danjou P, Weiller E, Payan C and Puech AJ (1991). Comparative effects of *Ginkgo biloba* extracts on psychomotor performances and memory in healthy subjects. *Therapie*, **46**, 33–36.

Webb E, Ashton CH, Kelly P and Kamali F (1996). Alcohol and drug use in UK university students. *Lancet*, **348**, 922–925.

Webb E, Ashton CH, Kelly P and Kamali F (1998). An update on British medical students' lifestyles. *Medical Education*, **32**, 325–331.

Weinberg NZ and Glanz MD (1999). Child psychopathology risk factors for drug abuse: Overview. *Journal of Clinical Child Psychology*, **28**, 290–297.

Wesnes K and Parrott AC (1992). Smoking, nicotine and human performance. In: A Smith and D Jones (eds), *Factors Affecting Human Performance* (Vol. 2). Academic Press, London.

Wesnes K and Revell A. (1984). The separate and combined effects of scopolamine and nicotine on human information processing. *Psychopharmacology*, **84**, 5–11.

Wesnes K and Warburton DM (1983). Smoking, nicotine and human performance. *Pharmacology and Therapeutics*, **21**, 189–208.

Wesnes K, Simpson PM, White L, Pinker S, Jertz G, Murphy M and Siegfried K (1991). Cholinesterase inhibition in the scopolamine model of dementia. *Annals of the New York Academy of Sciences*, **640**, 268–271.

West R and Gossop M (1994). Overview: A comparison of withdrawal symptoms from different drug classes. *Addiction*, **89**, 1483–1489.

White AM, Matthews DB and Best PJ (2000). Ethanol, memory, and hippocampal function: a review of recent findings. *Hippocampus*, **10**, 88–93.

Wikler A (1973). Dynamics of drug dependence: Implications of a conditioning theory of research and treatment. *Archives of General Psychiatry*, **28**, 611–616.

Wilkinson D, Passmore P, Bullock R, Hopker SW, Smith R, Potocnik FCV, Maud CM, Engelbrecht I, Ieni JR and Bahra RS (2002). A multinational, randomized, 12-week comparative study of donepezil and rivastigmine in patients with mild to moderate Alzheimer's disease. *International Journal of Clinical Practice*, **56**, 441–446.

Wilkinson F (2001). *Time to Tackle Heroin Crisis*. Centre for Reform Think Tank, London.

Wilkinson L, Scholey AB and Wesnes K (2002). Chewing gum selectively improves aspects of memory in healthy volunteers. *Appetite*, **38**, 235–236.

Williamson EM and Evans FJ (2000). Cannabinoids in clinical practice. *Drugs*, **60**, 1303–1314.

Wilson MA (1996). GABA physiology: Modulation by benzodiazepines and hormones. *Critical Reviews in Neurobiology*, **10**, 1–13.

Winblad B, Engedal K, Soininen H, Verhey F, Waldemar G, Wimo A, Wetterholm A-L, Zhang R, Haglund A and Subbiah P (2001). A 1-year, randomized, placebo-controlled study of donepezil in patients with mild to moderate AD. *Neurology*, **57**, 489–495.

Winder R and Borrill J (1998). Fuels for memory: The role of oxygen and glucose in memory enhancement. *Psychopharmacology*, **136**, 349–356.

Wise RA (1988). The neurobiology of craving: Implications for the understanding and treatment of addiction. *Journal of Abnormal Psychology*, **97**, 118–132.

Wise RA (1996). Neurobiology of addiction. *Current Opinions in Neurobiology*, **6**, 243–251.

Wise RA and Bozarth MA (1987). A psychomotor stimulant theory of addiction. *Psychological Review*, **94**, 469–492.

Wolpert L (1999). *Malignant Sadness*. Faber & Faber, London.

Wong DF, Wagner HN, Tune LF et al. (1986). Positron emission tomography reveals elevated D_2 dopamine receptors in drug-naïve schizophrenics. *Science*, **234**, 1558–1563.

Wood RH, Reyes-Alvarez R, Maral B, Metoyer KL and Welsch MA (1999). Physical fitness, cognitive function, and health-related quality of life in older adults. *Journal of Aging and Physical Activity*, **7**, 217–230.

Woods RT (1996). Psychological "therapies" in dementia. In: RT Woods, M Grundman, P Woodbury, J Growdon, CW Cotman and E Pfeiffer (eds), *Handbook of the Clinical Psychology of Ageing*. John Wiley & Sons, Chichester, UK.

Woody GE, McLellan AT, Alterman AA and O'Brien CP (1991). Encouraging collaboration between research and clinical practice in alcohol and other drug abuse treatment. *Alcohol Health Research of the World*, **15**, 221–227.

Woolley DW and Shaw E (1954). A biochemical and pharmacological suggestion about certain mental disorders. *Science*, **119**, 587–588.

Woolverton WL and Johnson KM (1992). Neurobiology of cocaine abuse. *Trends in Pharmaceutical Science*, **13**, 193–200.

Wu LT and Anthony JC (1999). Tobacco smoking and depressed mood in late childhood and early adolescence. *American Journal of Public Health*, **89**, 1837–1840.

Yun TK (2001). *Panax ginseng*: A non-organ-specific cancer preventive? *Lancet Oncology*, **2**, 49–55.

Zajicek J, Fox P, Sanders H, Wright D, Vickery J, Nunn A and Thompson A (2003). Cannabinoids for the treatment of spasticity and other symptoms related to multiple sclerosis (CAMS study): Multicentre randomised placebo-controlled trial. *Lancet*, **362**, 1517–1526.

Zakzanis KK and Young DA (2001). Memory impairment in abstinent MDMA ("Ecstasy") users: A longitudinal investigation. *Neurology*, **56**, 966–969.

Zammit S, Allebeck P, Andreasson S, Lundberg I and Lewis G (2002). Self reported cannabis use as a risk factor for schizophrenia in Swedish conscripts of 1969: Historical cohort study. *British Medical Journal*, **325**, 1199–1201.

Zanetti O, Frisoni GB, De Leo D, Dello Buono M, Bianchetti A and Trabucchi M (1995). Reality orientation therapy in Alzheimer disease: useful or not? A controlled study. *Alzheimer Disease and Associated Disorders*, **9**, 132–138.

Zelen O, Kollar B and Ribari B (1976). Vinpocetine in the treatment of sensorineural impairment of hearing. *Arzneimittelforschung*, **26**, 1977–1980.

Zevin S, Gourlay SG and Benowitz NL (1998). Clinical pharmacology of nicotine. *Clinics in Dermatology*, **16**, 557–564.

Ziedonis DM and Kosten TR (1991). Pharmacotherapy improves treatment outcome in depressed cocaine addicts. *Journal of Psychoactive Drugs*, **23**, 417–425.

Zubin J, Steinhauser SR, Day R and van Kammen DP (1985). Schizophrenia at the crossroads. *Comprehensive Psychiatry*, **26**, 217–240.

Zuckerman M (1994). *Behavioral Expressions and Biosocial Bases of Sensation Seeking*. Cambridge University Press, New York.

Index